# Southern Capitalism

# Southern Capitalism

The Political Economy of North Carolina,

1880–1980

Phillip J. Wood

Duke University Press

DURHAM, NORTH CAROLINA 1986

Library of Congress Cataloging-in-Publication Data

Wood, Phillip J., 1951–
  Southern capitalism.

  Bibliography: p.
  Includes index.
  1. North Carolina—Economic conditions. 2. Capital-
ism—North Carolina—History. 3. North Carolina—
Industries—History. 4. North Carolina—Economic policy.
I. Title.
HC107.N8W66   1986        338.9756         86-11469
ISBN 0-8223-0673-5
ISBN 0-8223-0746-4 (pbk.)

*For Gail and Lindsey*

# Contents

# Tables and Figures

*Figure*

# Acknowledgments

Books are usually the result of collective rather than individual efforts, and this book is no exception. I am grateful to a number of friends and colleagues for advice, criticism, and encouragement: Bruce Berman, Phil Goldman, Dennison Moore, Alan Stern, David Price, Frank Harrison, and particularly Colin Leys, Richard Simeon, and Ian Parker. I would also like to thank Guy B. and Guion G. Johnson for giving me access to an early draft of their book on the Institute for Research in Social Science at the University of North Carolina at Chapel Hill; Richard Sylla, for his thoughtful review of the manuscript and for allowing me to draw on his as yet unpublished work on state and local government finance in North Carolina; and one other, anonymous, referee. I'm also pleased to acknowledge the support of the St. Francis Xavier University Council for Research, the help given me by the staff of the North Carolina Collection at the Louis Round Wilson Library, University of North Carolina at Chapel Hill, and the patience, good humor, and skills of Frances Gammon and Enid Wood, who typed the drafts. Last, but by no means least, I would like to thank Elizabeth Gratch of Duke University Press, who provided encouragement and assistance above and beyond the call of duty. Naturally, none of the above bears any responsibility for the errors of fact or interpretation which may remain in this work.

I

# Introduction

This book has its origins in two different but related problems, one empirical and one theoretical. Its empirical concern is the widespread persistence in the southern states of the United States of below-average wage levels and material conditions generally in a context of rapid economic growth. In 1978, despite several decades of rapid capital accumulation associated with the "rise of the sunbelt," the average hourly wage of production workers in southern manufacturing was $5.27, 82.7 percent of the U.S. average of $6.37.[1] In the following year, with less than 27 percent of the U.S. population, the South accounted for 35 percent of all American families living below the poverty line.[2] Similar differentials can be found in a host of other indicators of social well-being.

The theoretical concern of the book is to find a framework that allows the connection between capital accumulation and general social and material conditions to be investigated in a coherent and rigorous yet historically sensitive manner. Crucially, such an approach should not only permit the analysis of situations in which capital accumulation has been accompanied by high wages, mass consumption, and a liberal welfare system (the regime of accumulation that a number of French economists, following Gramsci, have termed "Fordism"[3]), but also those, for instance in the South, where the historical pattern seems to be different.

The orthodox neoclassical competitive model of regional development cannot provide such an analysis. The reason for this is the limited range of explanatory variables that the theory has at its disposal. Most important in this respect is the radical and artificial separation this theory makes between the market and its sociopolitical context.[4] The market economy, as the object of study, is defined simply in terms of final market transactions, that is, in terms of the purchase price of the "factors of production" (land, labor, and capital) in a context in which the formal-legal equality of the factor owners is assumed to permit free and rational individual decision-making.

This model therefore provides no analysis of the origins or historical development of capital and labor, either as factors of production or, more important, as social classes. Nor does it deal with the political and other nontechnical factors, originating in the unequal ownership of productive property, that shape the content of market transactions and open up the possibility that different patterns of capitalist development may occur in different historical contexts, even where levels of capitalization have converged.

According to the competitive model in its most abstract form, in situations characterized by competitive market relations (that is, in an economy without "frictions"), systematic differences between regions in terms of wages, prices, and profit rates will gradually disappear as a result of rational economic decisions by individual owners of capital and labor.[5] As these factor owners invest their resources in areas in which rates of return are highest, capital will flow into formerly capital-short regions, raising productivity, wage levels, and profit rates. Over time a "competitive equilibrium" will be created, within which capital/labor ratios, wage levels, and profit rates converge. In this model the engine of change is capital. Wages and profits are seen as being determined in a technical fashion by the level of capitalization of the production process and the level of productivity that this capital confers upon labor.

To some extent the process of convergence predicted by the neoclassical competitive model cannot be denied. As a result of rapid capital accumulation during the twentieth century, for instance, per capita personal income in the South has risen from 51 percent of the national average in 1880 to 90.8 percent in 1982.[6] Growth has been very unevenly distributed within the South, however, with seven of the eleven states significantly below this level (ranging from 70 percent to 86.3 percent). In addition, as we have seen, progress in terms of manufacturing wage rates has not been as substantial. It is in situations such as these, where convergence is limited and where regional differences persist in the long term despite large-scale capital accumulation, that the limitations of the competitive model show up most clearly. Usually, explanations of such situations that use the competitive model suggest that the persistence of regional differences is the result of "barriers," "frictions," or "rigidities" that impede the market's operation.[7] These factors can be political, demographic, cultural, racial, or historical in nature. What is most important about them is that they enter the analysis only to the extent that they affect supply and demand, and they do so as "exogenous" variables, without theoretical status. Despite their obvious historical and causal importance, they remain outside the competitive market theory. The theory's assumptions are consequently insulated from historical analysis, and discussion of the complex interactions of social and economic factors that are essential to an adequate understanding of southern capitalist development is precluded.

Unlike the competitive market approach to regional change, the "new social history"[8] of the South attempts to develop an explanation of southern development that incorporates its historical peculiarities. This school of southern history rejects the free market hypothesis that incorporation into a wider capitalist market inevitably dissolves regionally specific social relations and suggests rather that the latter can persist in the long term. From this point of view the characteristics of southern development in the twentieth century—widespread black and white poverty, low-wage, labor-intensive production, and retarded social and infrastructural development—are results of the continued domination of an essentially precapitalist planter ruling class. This ruling class pursued a strategy of exploitation that retained a number of components used in pre–Civil War slave-based plantation production. The chief characteristic of this strategy of exploitation was its coercive nature, which was exhibited in a variety of nonmarket constraints on economic activity—agreements to limit labor market competition; anti-enticement and vagrancy laws; the cultivation of racial fears; paternalistic control of religion, education, housing, and credit; the creation of systematic indebtedness among sharecroppers, tenant farmers, and factory workers by means of the lien system and the company store; and the frequent use of violence and state power.[9]

In attempting to move beyond the narrowly economic approach of competitive market theory and to deal with society as a whole, the new social historians make a significant contribution to the study of southern regional development. Yet this approach also has a major limitation. The crux of the problem lies precisely in the focus on the South's peculiarities. In order to stress the regionally specific, coercive production relations that occurred in the South, these authors choose to define the southern pattern of development as noncapitalist. Jonathan M. Wiener and Dwight B. Billings, Jr., follow Barrington Moore's theory of a "Prussian Road" to modernity, characterized by a "revolution from above."[10] Mandle sees the southern economy as a "plantation mode of production."[11] In all three cases the "squeezing" of workers by coercive means is a noncapitalist alternative to "genuinely capitalist" development based on free competitive contractual relations between capital and labor and the use of labor-saving machinery to increase productivity. Whereas the latter results in growth and prosperity, the former, according to these authors, creates stagnation and regional marginalization. They concede that industrialization did occur in the Carolina Piedmont and northern Alabama, for instance, but emphasize that it remained minimal and subordinate to the planters' other interests, duplicating the coercive, noncapitalist production relations of plantation agriculture. It therefore did nothing to disrupt the system the planters had created. Consequently, this noncapitalist, specifically southern mode of production was able to resist internal and external challenges until well into the twentieth century.[12]

This rigid and unwarranted distinction between "genuinely capitalist" development and the coercive, stagnant nondevelopment that is said to have occurred in the South seriously undercuts the value of these authors' contributions to the study of the southern labor process, strategies of social and political control, and the continuities in the ownership of the means of production. On the one hand, it obscures the extent to which a variety of forms of "coercion" and state intervention are present at all levels of capitalist development and exaggerates the theoretical importance of planter values. On the other, it seriously underestimates the impact of the abolition of slavery, the extent of capital accumulation in the South after the Civil War, and the impact of the tendencies thus introduced into the region.

With this distinction the new social history can no more explain the pattern of development in the South than can the competitive market model. In order to direct attention to the peculiarities of southern development, these authors use a theoretical framework that prevents them from developing an adequate explanation of the South's distinctive combination of high rates of capital accumulation and low levels of social and material development. Whereas the competitive market model asserts that capital accumulation eliminates regional social and economic variations (and loses its theoretical coherence when dealing with situations in which these variations persist), the new social history explains their persistence in terms of the absence of capital accumulation in a noncapitalist economy. Ultimately, these interpretations may reinforce rather than undermine each other.

Since neither of these approaches permits an adequate understanding of the pattern of southern development, this book attempts to use the framework of Marxian political economy to develop such an account. To be sure, regional variations in the process of capitalist development were not a central concern of Marx, despite his interest in "regional" issues such as the American Civil War. Nevertheless, it will be argued that Marxian political economy provides a more fruitful framework for understanding the development of the American South than the two approaches discussed above. The chief advantage that this framework enjoys over its challengers, as scholars from a variety of political perspectives have stressed, is that it is an integrated social theory of class conflict and exploitation under capitalism.[13] It is a theory of tendencies subject to historical confirmation, that is, in which real social outcomes are created not as the result of inexorable economic laws, but as the result of the concrete historical struggle between social classes over the power to control production and the values that result from it. Since the struggle is not simply an economic one, but is also political, ideological, and social in the broadest sense, the Marxian framework avoids the positivism of the other approaches, which are forced to abstract economic or social "facts" from their context and wider historical meaning. Consequently, this framework provides the conceptual tools needed to account for the pattern of capitalist development that has emerged in the South. It does not demand that *either* capital accumulation *or* retarded social and material conditions be selected as the most significant theoretical or historical factor in southern development. Rather, it is able to integrate both of these characteristics into a pattern of capitalist development that is both theoretically and historically meaningful, and not paradoxical. And it can provide an explanation, in terms of the historical development of productive relations in the South, of why such a pattern has emerged. In so doing, it assimilates the most useful findings of the other approaches, while overcoming their explanatory weaknesses.

## The Marxian framework

At the most abstract level the key to Marx's analysis of the capitalist mode of production[14] and to an explanation of the development of the American South is the category of "free" labor. Under capitalism, labor is free in two respects. First, workers are free in the sense that they are able to sell their capacity to work for limited periods of time in exchange for money payments, without legal or other social constraints. In other words, workers are free in a way in which slaves, serfs, and indentured laborers under other modes of production are not.

Second, workers are free in the related sense that they have no commodity to sell other than their capacity to work in order to guarantee their own subsistence. For the vast majority of workers in a capitalist setting, any direct links with an alternative means of subsistence, such as land, are severed. When workers are "free" in both of these senses, the sale of the capacity to work (which Marx called "labor power") becomes an economic necessity.[15] Workers are free to sell their labor power to any capitalist. Otherwise they are free to starve. Thereafter, labor power becomes the necessary foundation for the two main features of capitalist production—the generalized production of commodities for sale on the market, and the production and capitalization of surplus value.[16]

Under capitalism, labor power is a commodity like any other in the sense that it is bought and sold in a market. Yet in another, more important sense, labor power is not a typical commodity. This is because it has the special capacity to produce other commodities, the value of which (defined by Marx as the labor time socially necessary to produce them) is greater than the value of the wages paid to workers. Whereas "constant capital" ($c$) such as machinery or raw materials simply transfers its value to the final commodities, the value workers give to these commodities is equal to the value of their labor power ($v$) plus a "surplus value" ($s$) for which they are unpaid. The capitalist therefore begins production with commodities whose value is ($c + v$) and ends it with commodities whose value is ($c + v + s$). If the capitalist is able to sell these commodities, he realizes this surplus value, i.e., he transforms it into money, which can be used to invest in new commodities and to begin a new, expanded round of production. The exploitation of labor power is therefore also the key to capital's potential for expansion.

When he referred to labor power and workers themselves as "variable capital," Marx wished to emphasize that once the worker has sold his labor power to capital, it becomes the property of capital, just as are machines. But he also wished to stress that, in contrast to the situation with constant capital, the contribution of labor power to the value of production is variable. When labor power is sold to capital, it is not necessarily completely alienated. How much value workers create therefore depends upon how effectively their labor power can be controlled and consumed by capital and how well workers can limit or resist its consumption during the production process. The degree of exploitation will therefore depend in part on the technical composition of the production process, as the free market economists suggest. But both the level and means of exploitation will depend in a more fundamental sense on broader historical and political considerations. This point can best be appreciated by considering Marx's theory of wages.

Since labor power is a commodity in the capitalist mode of production, its value and also, within certain limits, its market price (wages) can be determined in the same way as the value of other commodities is determined. According to the labor theory of value, the value of any commodity is the value of the labor time necessary for the production of that commodity. Since labor power exists only in living human beings, its value is based on the labor time necessary for the production of the means of human subsistence—food, clothing, fuel, and other necessities that sustain the worker and his offspring.[17] This total varies in a technical way according to the type of work done, its physical and skill requirements, climatic conditions, and so on. In addition,

> the number and extent of his so-called necessary requirements[,] as also the manner in which they are satisfied, are themselves products of history and depend therefore to a great extent on the level of civilization attained by a country; in particular they depend on the conditions in which, and consequently on the habits and expectations

with which, the class of free workers has been formed. In contrast, therefore, with the case of other commodities, the determination of the value of labor power contains a historical and moral element.[18]

Wage levels therefore reflect the broader political, social, and historical dimensions of the relationship between capital and labor as social classes, over and above the technical makeup of the production process and necessary subsistence levels. Generally, it is the relationship between the speed and extent of capitalist development and the number of available jobs on the one hand, and the supply of available labor power on the other that will determine the relative strengths of capital and labor, rates of exploitation, and wage levels.[19] The ability of a strong working class to organize in order to control the influx of labor into a particular industry may increase wage levels significantly above the value of labor power. On the other hand, a large excess of labor power will allow capital to reduce wages toward or even below their value, transforming the workers' fund for necessary consumption into a fund for the accumulation of capital.[20]

In capitalist production the working day may therefore be divided as follows:

|  A  |  B  |
|-----|-----|
| Necessary labor | Surplus labor |
| Wages | Surplus value |

The struggle between capital and labor over the relative magnitudes of these distinct portions of the working day, that is, over the rate of surplus value $(s/v)$ is not only the basis of class conflict in capitalist society but also the major determinant of the amount of profit, the rate of capital accumulation, and general living standards.

In contrast with the competitive market model, therefore, Marxist theory sees the relationship between capital and labor not as an equal exchange between owners of the factors of production in which wages and profits reflect the contribution of each to the value of the final commodity. Rather, Marxist theory sees it as a social relationship that is subject to the ongoing struggle over the production and distribution of surplus value. For present purposes what is important about this view is that it introduces the possibility that under varying historical conditions productive relations (and therefore the rate of surplus value) may vary, even though the narrowly technical or economic aspects of production, such as capital/labor ratios, do not. It therefore opens up the possibility of explaining the pattern of development in the American South more easily than competitive market theory can.

It is also possible to see at this point that Marxian political economy can also overcome the central weakness of the new social history school's interpretation of southern development. As we saw earlier, this school's contribution has been its explicit focus on a mode of southern exploitation that is in some senses "extraordinary" in comparison with that in modern American capitalism. In contrast, the major drawback of this theory is that it has considered this mode of exploitation to be part of a stagnant, noncapitalist economy. The theory is therefore unable to explain the rapid capital accumulation that has taken place in the South since the late nineteenth century. By recognizing that capitalist production relations depend on and reflect the relative power of capital and labor as social classes, the Marxian framework opens up the possibility that the process of capital accumulation may be able to continue on the basis of a number of possible modes of exploitation and is not confined to the Fordist strategy of capital-intensive, high-wage production that the new social historians see as uniquely capitalist.

Marx's analysis of capitalist development identifies two analytically distinct (though not necessarily historically distinct) modes of exploitation under capitalism. The most basic and, in terms of the historical development of capitalism, the earliest is to lengthen the working day without increasing wages and without changing the nature of the labor process so that surplus labor time increases absolutely. This strategy, the production of absolute surplus value, corresponds with the initial introduction of the factory system and the "formal" subsumption of labor under capital, and it depends upon State* power to provide the necessary pool of "free" labor power. In addition, the achievement of increases in $s/v$ by prolonging the working day beyond the point that would produce an equivalent to the value of the worker's labor power, and frequently by extending formerly independent producers to or beyond their absolute physical limits, provides the initial basis for later, mature capitalist development.[21]

This strategy is limited historically, however. In the first place, it is physically destructive to labor power itself and therefore can be carried out only in a situation in which labor power is cheap and abundant, that is, where there is a large pool of surplus labor. In addition, class formation and the production of absolute surplus value tends to require the direct intervention of the State: "During the historical genesis of capitalist production . . . [the] rising bourgeoisie needs the power of the state, and uses it to 'regulate' wages, i.e., to force them into the limits suitable for making a profit, to lengthen the working day, and to keep the worker himself at his normal level of dependence."[22]

---

* In view of the fact that the territorial units of the United States are called states, the following convention will be used for reasons of clarity: "state" will refer to the geopolitical units within the United States, for example, North Carolina, while "State" refers to the entire political apparatus of capitalist society.

Such a coercive strategy, particularly when it involves the use of family labor to reduce average labor costs, generates worker opposition. It also generates opposition from the most progressive capitalists who come to favor limitations on the production of absolute surplus value as a way to guarantee a stable, self-reproducing supply of labor power as a basis for costly and risky capital investments.

In Britain by the second half of the nineteenth century this combination of forces had succeeded in gaining legal limitations on the length of the working day and the exploitation of female and child labor.[23] Since that time, exploitation has taken the form of the production of relative surplus value. This mode of exploitation relies on increasing the productiveness of labor per unit of time by altering or improving the worker's tools or his mode of work, or both, and therefore represents the "real" subsumption of labor under a new, specifically capitalist production process.[24] By intensifying all, or some, aspects of the labor process, this strategy increases the rate of exploitation by reducing the amount of labor time necessary for the reproduction of labor power and increasing the amount of surplus labor time. In addition, if the impact of this increased productivity spills over into the production of consumer goods and reduces their value, the rate of exploitation may be increased further.[25]

For the capitalist such an increase in $s/v$ achieves two things. First of all, it allows him to reduce the necessary labor time embodied in each commodity, thereby reducing unit production costs. As long as he maintains this productive advantage over competitors, he can continue to sell at market prices and realize "surplus profits" (that is, profits above the industrial or social average). Alternatively, he can reduce prices below those existing in the market in order to undersell his competitors, eliminate those who are not able to respond with their own productivity increases, and expand his own share of the market; or, he can both realize surplus profits *and* increase his market share by a lesser reduction in price.

Second, while the rate of surplus value has increased, the living standards of the worker have not necessarily deteriorated. In fact, if wage levels remain unchanged, and if productivity increases occur in the production of wage goods, real wages will increase. The task of increasing $s/v$ no longer involves a zero-sum game. In such a situation, working class political opposition has to become much more sophisticated in order to be effective, since the ability to combine increases in $s/v$ with increased real wages obscures the more direct indicators of the contradictory nature of capitalist social relations. The expansion of capital and increases in productivity become the most important lever for the capitalist in raising $s/v$ and replacing absolute wage reductions and increases in the length of the working day. As a result, the production of relative surplus value has been the major historical response to the limits set by the class struggle and state legislation on the length of the working day and on harsher forms of physical exploitation in the earlier period.[26] As such, it is the basis for the Fordist strategy of accumulation. Yet the introduction of this mode of exploitation does not eliminate the possibility of historical and spatial variations in the rate of surplus value (and therefore in the living standards of workers), as the competitive market theorists suggest. Nor does it necessarily eliminate the role of the State, coercion, and other extraeconomic factors, as the new social historians suggest. For Marx, the relationship between capital and labor remains an historically variable political relationship, expressed in variations in the ratio of the paid to the unpaid parts of the working day, regardless of the mode of exploitation that is dominant at a particular time.

In contrast to competitive market theory, therefore, the Marxian framework can explain variations in wages and general social and material conditions, even in situations in which the technical compositions of capital have become equalized. In addition, this framework can overcome the central flaws in the new social history of southern development: its inability to treat the southern mode of exploitation as capitalist exploitation, and its tendency to define mature capitalism in terms of a depoliticized process of collective bargaining that necessarily leads to high wages and high standards of living. In the first place, some of the characteristics of the southern labor process can be treated as components of the early stages of *capitalist* development, based on the production of absolute surplus value and the use of State power to create and regulate labor power and the conditions in which it is consumed. Second, there is no requirement, even where the production of relative surplus value dominates, that the Fordist regime of accumulation will result in precisely the same form in one place as in another, or at all. Whether it does or not, and whether the characteristics of the earlier phase of capitalist development disappear or are carried over into the production of relative surplus value, is contingent upon the relative political strengths of capital and labor as social classes and, as the British case suggests, the existence of "progressive" capitalists with an interest in expanding the consumption levels of the working class.

*The Marxian framework*
*and the problem of southern development*

From the Marxian perspective the South's apparently paradoxical combination of high rates of capital accumulation and persisting low levels of social and material development ceases to be a paradox. Instead, it becomes a theoretically intelligible result of the development of capitalist production relations in a specific sociopolitical context. And as capital penetrates more and more formerly peripheral regions both within the advanced capitalist economies and in the Third World, such configurations are becoming increasingly common. This section of the introduction provides a brief sketch of the changing functions of peripheral regions in capitalist development and the logic for capital of interregional relocation, and it redefines the problem of southern development from a Marxian perspective.

Historically, those areas that were first to develop the general conditions in which capitalist development could occur (the most important of which, as was suggested above, is the existence of a large pool of "free" labor power) quite rapidly became centers of large-scale capital investment and industrial production. These spatial concentrations of relatively efficient capitalist production generated increasing demand for supplies of the essential means of production, such as raw materials, and for food to feed their rapidly growing industrial labor forces. At the same time the increasingly efficient production of cheap commodities provided the means for penetrating external regions (at both the national and international levels) and for converting them into satellite markets and regions of raw materials production for the relatively advanced areas.[27] Control of political and commercial relations allowed these advanced areas to benefit in an unequal exchange—the trading of efficiently produced, low-value manufactured goods for high-value natural resources within a national and international division of labor.

The historical subordination of these national and international peripheries to the needs of capital in the advanced areas does not necessarily prevent them from accumulating capital, however, as was once argued by theorists of "underdevelopment." Writing on the potential for capitalist development in the Third World, Charles Bettelheim has described the logic underlying the development of industrial capitalism in some of these areas most succinctly:

> The low wages in the countries with poorly developed productive forces and the low individual prices of production that may result from these low wages, make it possible, given certain conditions, for some of the countries, when they employ a technique that is more "advanced" than before, to realise differential profits. What this means is that low wage countries can achieve exceptionally low costs of production when they use relatively modern techniques, and thus . . . realise especially high current prices. This may have considerable practical consequences and enable some countries that are poor to begin with, if they are situated in favourable conditions . . . to embark upon large-scale industrialization.[28]

Capitalist development is possible in the Third World, according to Bettelheim, because it is possible for capitalists who locate production processes in these areas to sell at the social (in this case international) average while producing at local costs that are lower than the social average. Compared with capital in comparable sectors in the advanced areas, Third World capital can produce an above-average rate of surplus value that, if it can be realized, can generate excess profits and an above-average rate of expansion.

A similar logic applies with respect to regional development within the advanced capitalist countries. In the United States the historical, cultural, social, and political differences that have fragmented the country along regional lines also provide capital with the ability to combine relatively advanced production techniques with lower regional production costs to produce a significant competitive advantage in the production of surplus value. Conceivably, these specific regional conditions of production may permit increases in the production of either absolute or relative surplus value (or both), although it would seem likely that the latter would be more important in a context such as the contemporary United States.[29]

As later chapters will demonstrate more fully, the textile industry's relocation to the southeastern states provides a good illustration of this logic as it has been exercised within the United States. By the late nineteenth century productive conditions in New England, where the industry had emerged, were beginning to present the region with serious difficulties. The textile industry at this time was fragmented, unstable, and highly competitive, producing cheap, unsophisticated commodities. It used a production process that was mechanized, but one in which major technological breakthroughs were rare, and which therefore embodied a high and relatively irreducible degree of labor intensity. As the New England area industrialized and diversified, the textile industry found it more and more difficult to compete for labor power and capital with its relatively capital-intensive neighboring industries that were more productive and could pay higher wages. Since the industry could not increase its rate of surplus value by means of technological changes, its only other option was to try to reduce the value of labor power by lowering wages and increasing the intensity of work. Because of the nature of the New England labor market, however, this strategy was not feasible on a large scale. To begin with there was a relatively high degree of competition for labor power. Second, relatively progressive labor legislation in some of the New England states limited increases in the use of female and child labor and extensions in the length of the working day.

It was at this point, particularly in the last decade of the nineteenth century, that the textile industry began its southward migration. In the South, using existing techniques in the production of lower count, coarser textiles, large increases in the rate of surplus value could be produced in a context that provided a large, unskilled, impoverished labor force, restricted labor market competition, and offered no unions and no effective restrictions on the use of female and child labor or on the length of the working day. Textile wages were kept low by wages existing in southern agriculture, a sector that contained a vast pool of surplus labor power. In addition, in such a setting many workers were not "pure" wage earners. Wage labor in the early southern textile industry was seen by many, initially at least, as providing a necessary supplement to the main agricultural source of income and was often used to withstand temporarily adverse conditions in cash crop markets while subsistence production continued.[30] As a result of all these regionally specific conditions, there was a significant downward modification in the relationship between wages and the cost of reproducing labor power, which permitted the production of a higher average rate of surplus value than was available in the New England states.

According to competitive market theory, once such a process of capital accumulation has begun, it must ultimately end in regional convergence as new capital increases competition for labor power and equalizes regional wage levels and other production conditions. If capital and labor are regarded as active social agents locked into a real, historical, and contradictory class relationship, however, and not as dehumanized factors of production subject to the inexorable laws of the market and of technical development, one finds that this deterministic view of the consequences of capital accumulation is unwarranted.

Much has changed of course in the South since the late nineteenth and early twentieth centuries. Other industries have followed the lead of textiles in relocating in the South, large-scale capital accumulation has occurred as a result, wages and incomes have increased, labor market competition has become stiffer, and unionization drives have been undertaken. Yet despite these developments, southern capital has been able to resist the pressures that competitive market theory predicts will eliminate regional competitive advantages and has been able to maintain its above-average rate of surplus value in the long term. Table 1.1, which compares rates of surplus value for the United States, the Northeast, and the South from 1929 to 1978, demonstrates this nonconvergence quite clearly. In each of these years the South has had a significant advantage over the northeastern industrial core of the United States. From 1939 to 1973 the pattern is relatively stationary, with an average differential of 28.3 percent in favor of the South. In 1974 there is a sudden increase in this advantage to forty-nine percent, coinciding with the onset of the post-Vietnam War depression. From 1976 to 1978 the South's advantage appeared to be reverting to its former pattern.

Table 1.1. Rates of surplus value $(s/v\%)$[a] and distribution of new capital investment (NCI) in manufacturing: United States, northeastern, and southern states, 1929–78.

| | United States $(s/v\%)$ | Northeast[b] $(s/v\%)$ | NCI in NE as percentage of U.S. total | South[c] $(s/v\%)$ | NCI in South as percentage of U.S. | Population of South as percentage of U.S. |
|---|---|---|---|---|---|---|
| 1929 | 131 | 100 | — | 152 | — | |
| 1939 | 113 | 110 | — | 136 | — | |
| 1947 | 102 | 94 | — | 125 | — | |
| 1954 | 107 | 96 | 55.6 | 116 | 18.4 | 24.2 (1950) |
| 1958 | 110 | 103 | 55.0 | 131 | 21.1 | |
| 1963 | 124 | 116 | 51.6 | 149 | 21.6 | 24.2 (1960) |
| 1967 | 132 | 124 | 50.8 | 149 | 25.8 | |
| 1972 | 137 | 127 | 48.9 | 155 | 26.9 | 24.6 (1970) |
| 1973 | 143 | 129 | 49.6 | 164 | 28.3 | |
| 1974 | 152 | 134 | 45.7 | 183 | 30.0 | |
| 1975 | 148 | 132 | 42.4 | 180 | 31.3 | 26.0 (1975) |
| 1976 | 157 | 143 | 41.2 | 184 | 34.2 | |
| 1977 | 165 | 151 | 40.5 | 191 | 31.5 | |
| 1978 | 164 | 151 | 43.4 | 187 | 30.2 | |
| | | | | | | 27.1 (1980) |

*Sources*: Rates of surplus value and distribution of new capital investment were calculated from data in: U.S. Department of Commerce, Bureau of the Census, *Census of Manufactures, 1972* (Washington: USGPO, 1975), vol. 1, 47–57; ———, *Annual Survey of Manufactures, 1975* (Washington: USGPO, 1977), Statistics for States, vi, vii, 3–5, 25–27, 59–63, 103, 104, 125–28, 161, 162, 181, 182, 201, 202, 219, 221; ———, *Annual Survey of Manufactures, 1976* (Washington: USGPO, 1978), vi, vii; ———, *1977 Census of Manufactures*, Subject Series, General Summary (Washington: USGPO, 1981), 1–15 to 1–27; ———, *Annual Survey of Manufactures, 1978–9* (Washington: USGPO, 1983), 1–6. Population data from: ———, *Statistical Abstract of the United States, 1982–3* (Washington: USGPO, 1983), 10–12.

a. For a discussion of the method of calculating the rate of surplus value, see appendix.

b. Connecticut, Illinois, Indiana, Massachusetts, Michigan, New Hampshire, New Jersey, New York, Ohio, Pennsylvania, Rhode Island, Wisconsin.

c. Alabama, Arkansas, Florida, Georgia, Louisiana, Mississippi, North Carolina, South Carolina, Tennessee, Texas, Virginia.

Table 1.1 also provides an indication of one of the important effects of this differential ability to produce surplus value: the South's ability to rapidly expand its share of capital investment. Between 1954 and 1978, while the Northeast's share of new capital investment was falling by 12.2 percent, the South's share increased by 11.8 percent (−14.4 percent and 15.8 percent, respectively, if 1976 is taken as the cutoff point). Since

Table 1.2. Technical composition of capital:[31] United States, Northeast, and South, 1977

|  | Technical composition of capital (in thousands of dollars) |
| --- | --- |
| United States | 21.5 |
| Northeast | 19.8 |
| Connecticut | 15.1 |
| Illinois | 21.3 |
| Indiana | 28.0 |
| Massachusetts | 13.2 |
| Michigan | 22.0 |
| New Hampshire | 13.6 |
| New Jersey | 18.6 |
| New York | 15.5 |
| Ohio | 22.8 |
| Pennsylvania | 21.4 |
| Rhode Island | 11.3 |
| Wisconsin | 18.3 |
| South | 25.8 |
| Alabama | 28.2 |
| Arkansas | 19.2 |
| Florida | 20.1 |
| Georgia | 19.2 |
| Louisiana | 66.2 |
| Mississippi | 17.5 |
| North Carolina | 18.2 |
| South Carolina | 23.5 |
| Tennessee | 19.9 |
| Texas | 38.5 |
| Virginia | 20.8 |

*Sources*: Calculated from data in U.S. Department of Commerce, Bureau of the Census, *1977 Census of Manufactures*, Subject Statistics, General Summary (Washington: USGPO, 1981), 1–103 to 1–105, and vol. 3, pts. 1 and 2.

1967 the southern share has consistently exceeded its share of the U.S. population—by over eight percentage points in 1976.

These trends in new capital investment, together with all the other components of the interregional restructuring of capital,[32] have created a situation in which the South has begun to outstrip the Northeast in terms of the technical composition of capital. According to table 1.2, the money value of assets per employee in manufacturing in 1977 was $21,500 for the United States, $19,800 for the Northeast, and $25,800 for the South. Even if Texas and Louisiana are omitted from the southern figure on the grounds that their oil- and gas-based industries are in a sense "exceptional" in terms of the capital intensity of production, the southern average, at $20,700, remains higher than that in the Northeast.

It is possible to restate the southern "developmental paradox" in a way that is no longer paradoxical: the southern combination of high rates of capital accumulation, low wages, and retarded social and material development are the result of the ability of southern capital to extract an above-average rate of surplus value from southern workers. This ability has not been diminished by the regional convergence that has occurred in the technical composition of capital, rather, it (and the social relations of production upon which it is based) has survived despite this convergence.

### North Carolina as a case study

Such is the broad picture. Yet despite the fact that the South is often presented as the nation's last relatively homogeneous region,[33] one should resist the temptation to take aggregate analysis too far. After all, such an aggregate analysis can reveal little about the concrete historical processes that have produced a particular pattern of capitalist development in each state. This study will be restricted, therefore, to an analysis of capitalist development in a single state: North Carolina. No claim is being made here that North Carolina is in any way "typical" of the South. In many respects it is not, as succeeding chapters will suggest. Yet for the purposes of this study it is a particularly useful state upon which to focus.

Table 1.3 compares rates of surplus value in North Carolina with those for the United States and the Northeast. As in the case of the South generally, rates of exploitation in North Carolina are consistently higher than those for the Northeast. North Carolina's advantage here is more modest and (with the exception of 1954) more stable than that of the South generally, however, averaging 21 percent for the entire 1929–78 period.

Despite its relatively modest dimensions, North Carolina's above-average rate of surplus value has given the state a disproportionate share of new capital investment, which reached over four percent of the U.S. total in 1972 and 1973 (when North Carolina accounted for about 2.5 percent of the U.S. population). Although the state's share has fallen since then, it still attracts a share of new capital investment that exceeds its population share, as it has done consistently since 1963. As a result of this ability to attract capital, the North Carolina economy ranked tenth in the United States in 1977 with $14.4 billion in manufacturing assets (3.3 percent of the U.S. total).[34] Between 1950 and 1977 value added by manufacture in the state increased from $1.9 billion to $18.1 billion (again tenth in the United States), or from 2.1 percent to 3.1 per-

Table 1.3. Rates of surplus value: United States, Northeast, and North Carolina, and North Carolina's share of new capital investment (NCI), 1929–78.

| | United States $(s/v\%)$ | Northeast $(s/v\%)$ | North Carolina $(s/v\%)$ | NCI in North Carolina as percentage of U.S. total | Population of North Carolina as percentage of U.S. total |
|---|---|---|---|---|---|
| 1929 | 131 | 100 | 266 | — | 2.57 (1930) |
| 1939 | 113 | 110 | 132 | — | 2.70 (1940) |
| 1947 | 102 | 94 | 122 | — | 2.68 (1950) |
| 1954 | 107 | 96 | 100 | 1.58 | |
| 1958 | 110 | 103 | 125 | 2.00 | 2.54 (1960) |
| 1963 | 124 | 116 | 139 | 2.76 | |
| 1967 | 132 | 124 | 137 | 3.09 | 2.50 (1970) |
| 1972 | 137 | 127 | 147 | 4.10 | 2.53 (1972) |
| 1973 | 143 | 129 | 153 | 4.07 | |
| 1974 | 152 | 134 | 156 | 3.27 | |
| 1975 | 142 | 132 | 158 | 3.32 | |
| 1976 | 158 | 143 | 164 | 3.19 | |
| 1977 | 165 | 151 | 174 | 2.87 | 2.58 (1977) |
| 1978 | 164 | 151 | 178 | 2.74 | 2.60 (1980) |

*Sources*: As for table 1.1.

cent of the U.S. total.[35] And between 1950 and 1980 the state's manufacturing labor force increased by ninety-six percent, from 418,000 to 820,000, or from 2.7 percent to 4.0 percent of the total U.S. manufacturing labor force. In 1980 only seven other states had a larger manufacturing work force.[36]

In addition to this rapid economic expansion, North Carolina's economy has also undergone a significant degree of diversification, as tables 1.4 and 1.5 indicate. The traditional dominance of textiles has been reduced significantly during the postwar period, in terms of both employment and value added by manufacture. Since the 1960s in particular there has been significant growth in relatively capital-intensive sectors such as rubber, chemicals, metal products, machinery, and electrical goods and electronics. In 1947 these industries accounted for 5.4 percent of value added by manufacture in North Carolina. In 1977 they accounted for 30.3 percent.

Despite this rapid capital accumulation, diversification, and increased demand for labor power, there is little evidence that manufacturing wage rates are converging. Table 1.6 indicates in fact that average hourly earnings in North Carolina were higher relative to the U.S. average in 1950 than they presently are. Even for the period of the early 1970s, when new capital investment in North Carolina was at its highest, there

Table 1.4. Structure of employment in North Carolina manufacturing, 1947 and 1977

| | 1947 | | 1977 | |
|---|---|---|---|---|
| | Number employed | Percentage employed | Number employed | Percentage employed |
| All manufacturing | 381,480 | 100.0 | 765,300 | 100.0 |
| Food and kindred products | 16,716 | 4.4 | 39,100 | 5.1 |
| Tobacco products | 32,452 | 8.3 | 23,400 | 3.1 |
| Textile mill products | 210,350 | 55.1 | 245,300 | 32.1 |
| Apparel | 16,644 | 4.4 | 77,100 | 10.1 |
| Lumber and wood products | 31,087 | 8.1 | 32,600 | 4.3 |
| Furniture and fixtures | 27,858 | 7.3 | 78,900 | 10.3 |
| Paper and allied products | 7,859 | 2.1 | 19,400 | 2.5 |
| Printing and publishing | 5,297 | 1.4 | 15,700 | 2.1 |
| Chemicals | 9,490 | 2.5 | 33,000 | 4.3 |
| Rubber products | — | — | 21,900 | 2.9 |
| Leather products | 1,623 | 0.4 | 4,300 | 0.6 |
| Stone, clay, and glass products | 5,555 | 1.5 | 15,800 | 2.1 |
| Primary metal industries | 2,028 | 0.5 | 5,900 | 0.8 |
| Fabricated metal products | 2,822 | 0.7 | 26,300 | 3.4 |
| Machinery | 3,954 | 1.0 | 33,000 | 4.3 |
| Electrical machinery | 5,023 | 1.3 | 40,100 | 5.2 |
| Transport equipment | 1,231 | 0.3 | 11,300 | 1.5 |
| Instruments | 43 | 0.01 | 8,400 | 1.0 |
| Miscellaneous | 969 | 0.3 | 7,600 | 1.0 |

Sources: U.S. Department of Commerce, Bureau of the Census, *Census of Manufactures, 1947* (Washington: USGPO, 1949), vol. 3, 452–54; U.S. Department of Commerce, Bureau of the Census, *Census of Manufactures, 1977* (Washington: USGPO, 1981), vol. 3, pt. 2, 34–11 to 34–18.

is little evidence of any significant upward trend. In 1977 North Carolina's average hourly earnings figure ranked last among the American states, despite the fact that it was among the ten largest industrial states in the nation.

North Carolina appears to be a particularly good case study of the "southern" pattern of capitalist development. It is a state that ranks among the top ten American manufacturing states in terms of capital, value added, and manufacturing labor force. Like the South as a whole, it has experienced substantial convergence, increasing its personal income per capita from 37 percent of the national average in 1880 to 81.4 percent in 1982.[37] Yet the state maintains an average hourly wage

Table 1.5. Structure of value added in North Carolina manufacturing, 1947 and 1977

| | 1947 | | 1977 | |
|---|---|---|---|---|
| | Amount (in millions of dollars) | Percent | Amount (in millions of dollars) | Percent |
| All manufacturing | 1,646.7 | 100.0 | 18,230.6 | 100.0 |
| Food and kindred products | 78.4 | 4.8 | 977.7 | 5.4 |
| Tobacco products | 258.0 | 15.7 | 2,113.8 | 11.6 |
| Textile mill products | 846.3 | 51.4 | 4,267.4 | 23.4 |
| Apparel | 43.9 | 2.7 | 851.9 | 4.7 |
| Lumber and wood products | 84.1 | 5.1 | 583.8 | 3.2 |
| Furniture and fixtures | 102.4 | 6.2 | 1,299.5 | 7.1 |
| Paper and allied products | 47.4 | 2.9 | 715.7 | 3.9 |
| Printing and publishing | 25.4 | 1.5 | 362.2 | 2.0 |
| Chemicals | 58.6 | 3.6 | 1,663.7 | 9.1 |
| Rubber products | — | — | 618.1 | 3.4 |
| Leather products | 10.8 | 0.7 | 63.7 | 0.3 |
| Stone, clay, and glass products | 19.5 | 1.2 | 436.1 | 2.4 |
| Primary metal industries | 6.5 | 0.4 | 277.8 | 1.5 |
| Fabricated metal products | 11.9 | 0.7 | 927.8 | 5.1 |
| Machinery | 17.4 | 1.1 | 958.3 | 5.3 |
| Electrical machinery | — | — | 1,351.3 | 7.4 |
| Transport equipment | 5.2 | 0.3 | 312.9 | 1.7 |
| Instruments | 0.2 | 0.01 | 276.4 | 1.5 |
| Miscellaneous | 2.9 | 0.2 | 157.2 | 0.9 |

*Sources*: U.S. Department of Commerce, Bureau of the Census, *Census of Manufactures, 1947* (Washington: USGPO, 1949), vol. 3, 452–54; U.S. Department of Commerce, Bureau of the Census, *Census of Manufactures, 1977* (Washington: USGPO, 1981), vol. 3, pt. 2, 34–11 to 34–18.

rate that has been below 75 percent of the U.S. average since the early 1950s and shows few signs of increasing significantly. It is therefore an economy in which capital has been able to maintain an above-average rate of exploitation throughout a period of rapid expansion and capital accumulation.

The remainder of this book will be devoted to an historical analysis of the southern pattern of capitalist development. To anticipate briefly, persistently low wage levels and above-average rates of surplus value in North Carolina are the result of an historical process of class conflict in which the state's working class has been politically and economically weak and, as a result of the way in which industrialization has taken place, socially and geographically fragmented. The inability of the working class to exert sustained pressure on capital and its political represen-

Table 1.6. Average hourly earnings of production workers in manufacturing industries: United States and North Carolina, 1950–78

|  | United States | North Carolina | N.C./U.S. |
|---|---|---|---|
| 1950 | $ 1.46 | $ 1.10 | 75.3% |
| 1952 | 1.71 | 1.23 | 71.9 |
| 1954 | 1.83 | 1.27 | 69.4 |
| 1958 | 2.19 | 1.48 | 67.6 |
| 1963 | 2.53 | 1.72 | 68.0 |
| 1967 | 2.92 | 2.07 | 70.9 |
| 1970 | 3.43 | 2.48 | 72.3 |
| 1972 | 3.95 | 2.83 | 71.6 |
| 1975 | 5.04 | 3.67 | 72.8 |
| 1977 | 5.89 | 4.29 | 72.8 |
| 1978 | 6.37 | 4.66 | 73.2 |

*Sources*: U.S. Department of Commerce, Bureau of the Census, *Annual Survey of Manufactures, 1949–50* (Washington: USGPO, 1952), 68; ———, *Annual Survey of Manufactures, 1952* (Washington: USGPO, 1954), 66; ———, *1963 Census of Manufactures*, vol. 3, Area Statistics (Washington: USGPO, 1966), 34–5; ———, *1977 Census of Manufactures*, Subject Series, General Summary (Washington: USGPO, 1981), 1–2, 1–23; ———, *1978–9 Annual Survey of Manufactures* (Washington: USGPO, 1983), 1–6.

tatives has in turn allowed capital to achieve a high degree of social control and to preserve local conditions conducive to an above-average rate of exploitation, even during periods of large-scale capital relocation from other American regions.

Subsequent chapters focus on a series of broad questions about this historical process suggested by the Marxian framework outlined above. First of all, if above-average rates of exploitation reflect a particular balance of class forces, what are the origins of this pattern of class relations? Under what historical conditions were capital and "free" labor formed in North Carolina, and how did these conditions shape the production of surplus value? In considering these questions chapter two focuses on the historical process of proletarianization that occurred in North Carolina and also describes the rudimentary efforts of farmers and textile workers to resist this process of social transformation.

Second, once the social relations of capitalist production had been established in the state and had in turn given rise to conditions of production that were particularly favorable to capital, why did the entry of new capital not increase labor market competition, drive up wages, and eliminate these initially favorable conditions? Chapter three provides an analysis of the large-scale relocation of the U.S. textile industry to North Carolina and other southeastern states and argues that this process of relocation did not disrupt the social relations of production in North Carolina, but rather it reinforced them. Consequently, capital was able to maintain an above-average rate of exploitation and expand rapidly, even during the depressed conditions of the 1930s. Chapter three also discusses changes in strategies of exploitation that occurred during the 1920s and 1930s and examines the period of intense class struggle that these changes generated.

Third, what role has been played by the various levels of the State in the development of capitalism in North Carolina? Chapter four presents a brief discussion of a number of ways of looking at the relationship between the State, capital, and regional development, and also discusses the approach to "southern politics" taken by mainstream political science. It provides a brief outline of a Marxian interpretation of the capitalist State that guides the discussion of the role of the State in North Carolina. Chapter five goes on to develop some of the themes discussed in chapter three in the concrete context of North Carolina. It describes the development of a State that has played a decisive role in preserving an above-average rate of surplus value in North Carolina: by attracting "external" capital; by providing the social, political, and economic conditions required to facilitate exploitation and capital accumulation; by containing class conflict; and by limiting the possibility of "external" intervention, either in the form of the unionization of the state's workers, or in the form of federal social and economic regulation.

Finally, chapter six describes the contemporary tendencies at work in the North Carolina economy and the continuing role of state economic development policy in preserving the conditions in which exploitation can occur—in a context of increasing relocation, accumulation, and diversification of capital. It describes the means by which capital is still able to maintain a low-wage, predominantly rural, and unorganized working class as the basis for its excess profits. It also discusses the emerging contradiction between an economic development policy committed to the maintenance of labor market characteristics considered essential for the survival of the state's traditional industrial base and the sometimes conflicting interests of increasingly mobile national and international capital in relatively high-wage, often unionized manufacturing sectors.

# 2

# The Origins of Industrial Capitalism
# in North Carolina

According to Marx's theory of wages, wage levels depend in part upon the habits and expectations that formerly unfree workers bring to their newly acquired status as free wage laborers. These habits and expectations depend in turn on the social relations of production and material circumstances that preceded the transition to a free wage system and also on the circumstances of the transitional period. This chapter examines the period of transition and class formation in North Carolina. It seeks to establish, as against the new social historians, that the social formation of North Carolina in the postbellum period was capitalist, but that its social relations of production were qualitatively and quantitatively distinct from those outside the South. Later chapters show how the subsequent development of capitalism in North Carolina has been built upon policies and strategies to preserve this distinctiveness, and they examine the contradictions inherent in these strategies.

The industrial working class that began to be formed in North Carolina in the post–Civil War period had its roots in the system of capitalist agriculture that was created and solidified during the same period. Agricultural proletarianization led to the formation of a pool of surplus labor that provided the basis for textile industrialization. In order to understand the social relations of production in industry, it is necessary first of all to examine this process.

*Post–Civil War southern agriculture:*
*the construction of a wage labor system*

The central task of post–Civil War Reconstruction—the creation of a free wage labor system with which neither blacks nor whites in the southern states had much experience—posed as profound a problem in North Carolina as in other former slave states. While North Carolina's plantation ruling class was smaller than that in other southern states,[1] it relied heavily on slave labor in agricultural production. In 1860 34,658 North Carolina families (27.7 percent of the total number of families in the state) owned 331,059 slaves, who in turn constituted 33.4 percent of the state's population of 992,622.[2] After the war slavery was abolished, yet the distribution of land remained largely unchanged, given the failure of radical proposals for redistribution.[3] Farmers and planters who had previously been assured of rates of exploitation based on the provision of only a subsistence minimum to their slaves[4] now had to purchase labor power to get land back into production. Emancipation had not made it more likely that many blacks would acquire land, but the freedman's new right to sell his labor power could be expected to reduce the rate of exploitation. Emancipation thus introduced a period of struggle between planters and freedmen over the terms on which freedmen could be induced to return to the land.

Planter interests centered on efforts to return to a system that resembled slavery as closely as possible. Formal year-long contracts, gang labor, and supervision by overseers nevertheless failed to achieve the necessary results. The share wage system, in which planters contracted to pay for labor with a share of the crop at season's end, thereby guaranteeing the availability of labor for the whole period of cultivation and reducing the necessary amount of working capital, also failed to secure enough labor, as did the more coercive methods embodied in the black codes.[5] Doubts about eventual payment of shares; disputes with respect to the tasks properly covered by contracts for a particular crop; disputes about methods of payment (on an individual or gang basis); the use of barracks, overseers, and other enduring similarities with slavery all served to discourage freedmen from returning to plantation labor, thereby creating a serious postwar labor shortage.

The interests of freedmen, in contrast, centered on the creation of a new system of tenant farming on an individual or family basis that would reduce planter supervision, create the possibility of accumulation by the freedman, and maximize his ability to make independent production decisions, his own purchases, and to dispose of his own income.[6]

The freedmen's resistance, coupled with drought, crop failures, and bankruptcies in 1866 and 1867, caused planters to accede to these demands. Beginning in 1867 plantations were divided into family-sized plots of thirty to fifty acres to be operated as independent units by single black tenant families. By 1880 only 8.9 percent of agricultural land in crops in the Cotton South was still cultivated on units that could be identified as plantations.[7]

By itself such a transformation held significant potential dangers for the planters in comparison either with slavery or with the system of share wages. Under the latter system, for instance, ownership of the crop belonged unambiguously to the planter who was obligated to pay his workers according to contract. Control of the final crop and its sale and of the pace and hours of work allowed planters to maximize rates of exploitation. With the transition to single family units, however, the position of the planter became less clear. In traditional landlord-tenant relationships, ownership of the crop and responsibility for its division and sale belonged to the tenant. Legal recourse for a tenant's nonpayment of rent was provided by a landlord's lien on the tenant's crop and property, if any. Renting on "halves," in which the landlord leased land and provided tools, animals, and fertilizers, in return for 50 percent of the final crop, would, if conducted fairly, yield a rate of exploitation for the landlord of less than 100 percent and could provide some possibility of accumulation by the tenant. Again, planter control of the labor force would thus in due course be reduced.

To avoid these dangers, planters evolved a new form of tenure arrangement known as sharecropping. Sharecropping was essentially a carryover of the share wage system, adapted so as to operate with individual or family farms. Sharecropping had existed in the turpentine industry in North Carolina as early as 1837 but had no counterpart in the Cotton South before conditions demanded it in the post–Civil War period.[8] In contrast to the landlord-tenant arrangement, in a sharecropping relationship the cropper was essentially a wage laborer, working for a landlord for a specified period of time on a specified plot of land without legal right to any part of the crop until it was gathered and divided by the landlord. Cropping on halves would in theory reward the cropper for his year's labor with 50 percent of the final crop or its value. Ownership and control of the crop and its marketing, however, in a context of widespread black illiteracy and political powerlessness (especially after the demise of state governments elected under Reconstruction policies) effectively left the amount of the cropper's "fifty percent" to the landlord's discretion. That is, it reduced the share in fact to a wage.[9]

During the same period planters also faced a challenge to their labor control from supply merchants, who began to take advantage of cash and credit shortages by supplying planters and their workers with many of the supplies necessary for cotton production. In the postwar years, state legislatures elected under Reconstruction policies had passed laws giving anyone who provided workers with supplies a suppliers' lien against the proceeds of the year's crop superior to any other claim except that of the landlord for rent. As planters moved from plantation wage labor to renting, sharecropping, and supplying their own tenants and croppers, conflicts between supplier and planter inevitably arose.

Planters found themselves in an insecure position not only with respect to their liens for supplies but also to their control over the production process.

As a result, within a very few years after the appearance of share-cropping (again mostly during the early 1870s), planters in all southern states began to mobilize the power of their respective state governments behind this process of proletarianization. A series of court decisions solidified the position of sharecropper as "laborer" or servant, with no legal right of possession of crops grown under the share arrangement.[10] Since landlords had legal possession of crops until they were divided, any merchant lien for supplies against the cropper's share could not become active until after the division had been made and therefore would not touch the landlord's share. Further, since by virtue of possession the landlord could determine the real size of the cropper's share, the effectiveness of merchant liens for supplies would be jeopardized. And with respect to merchant liens for supplies provided to tenants (who retained legal possession of the crop until it was divided), planters were able to achieve legislation to extend liens for rent to cover all landlord advances and make them superior to all other liens.[11]

Because their power and profitability in the Black Belt areas were seriously limited, supply merchants were forced to do one of two things. Either they could remain in the Black Belt in an auxiliary role as suppliers to planters, who would in turn supply their own tenants, and in this role they could secure their loans with a mortgage on the planter's crops and property but could not effectively challenge planter control of the crop and its sale.[12] Or, as an alternative, many supply merchants shifted the bulk of their activities outside these areas to become suppliers to white yeoman farmers who had moved into cotton production during the period of high prices after the Civil War and were left indebted by the price collapse that began in the early 1870s.[13]

Thereafter, planters were able to consolidate their control over the cotton labor force by means of informal agreements to restrict the access of tenants to marketing facilities and by more formal actions, such as anti-enticement laws, which made it a criminal as well as a civil offense to sign a contract with a worker who was already under contract, and other laws criminalizing the breaking of contractual obligations after partial payment had been made.[14]

The system of agricultural wage labor that developed was thus peculiarly southern. Initially designed to appeal to the freedman's desire for independence in a context in which he could not effectively be controlled, it gradually became, in the period after the fall of Reconstruction governments, a system of wage labor that operated largely at the discretion of the planters. In a context of widespread illiteracy, planter control of accounts, crops, and marketing allowed planters to create a labor force whose freedom was severely curtailed by the indebtedness arising from the operation of the lien system and reinforced by the actions of the State. Planters and merchants were able to compensate for falling cotton prices in the late nineteenth century by extending cotton agriculture beyond the former Black Belt areas and by creating a system of production in which all the risks of production could be transferred to the cropper.

All southern states followed this general pattern. In North Carolina, however, the grip of planters on their tenants was formally strengthened in the 1876–77 Landlord-Tenant Act. North Carolina had recognized the legal distinction between tenant and sharecropper since 1837 and had upheld the distinction in the early postwar years. Beginning in 1868–69, however, the cropper-tenant distinction began to be amended to improve the security of landlord liens with respect to tenant crops. In the 1876–77 act this process culminated in the removal of any legal distinction between the two. Without reference to either tenant or cropper, and without mentioning third parties, the act made it a misdemeanor for the lessee to remove a crop or any part of it from the land on which it was grown without payment of rent or without the lessor's consent. Since rent could not be paid, by and large, until after the division and sale of the crop, the legal and practical status of the tenant effectively became the same as that of the cropper—a laborer.[15] In North Carolina, then, the status of tenant or sharecropper was not even preserved as a legal fiction; tenant rights to crops grown under lease were simply abolished.

It is, of course, much easier to discuss these developments at the juridical level than it is to provide quantitative empirical evidence of the effectiveness of such initiatives in proletarianizing the agricultural sector. Even though sharecropping became simply a southern version of wage labor, the terminology of tenancy and sharecropping, and not of wage labor, was retained by the Census Bureau for purposes of data gathering. Nevertheless, both recent and contemporary accounts seem to agree that by the turn of the century "considerable supervision" was exercised over the tenants, and sharecropping "increasingly . . . came to be described as merely a form of piece-rate wage labor and not a true tenancy at all."[16] As early as 1880 in North Carolina planters consistently referred to both sharecroppers and wage workers as "laborers," perhaps indicating the degree of importance they attached to these formal distinctions. In addition, the practical details of the different arrangements were often confused. In response to a question about the timing of wage payments, the Census Bureau recorded some planters as saying that they paid wages "when the cotton-crops were sold."[17]

This process of agricultural proletarianization has proved an enduring factor in North Carolina's industrialization. Table 2.1 presents a compilation of census data on the changing structure of farm tenure in North Carolina after 1880, when these types of data began to be collected. With respect to most southern states, these data are of limited value prior to 1920, since it is only at this date that sharecroppers are identified as a separate category. In the case of North Carolina, however, the abolition of the legal distinction between tenant and cropper allows us to take the tenant category as an effective indicator of the size of the expanding agricultural proletariat in the state after 1880. The number of "tenant farmers" in North Carolina increased from 52,722 in 1880 to an absolute high of 142,158 in 1935. As a percentage of the total number of farm operators, tenancy similarly increased from 33.5 percent in 1880 to a high of 49.2 percent in 1930. Table 2.1 suggests that from 1910 a large majority of these tenants and croppers were operating simply in terms of share. The number of arrangements involving the use of cash alone is limited, rising significantly only in the decade 1890–1900, probably as a result of the impact of century-low cotton prices on the profitability of the most marginal share arrangements.[18]

Furthermore, it is important to note that in North Carolina this was not simply a black proletariat. Possibly in part as a result of the 1876–77 Landlord-Tenant Act, the process of proletarianization took in large numbers of formerly independent white farmers (since they were by and large outside of the major areas of cotton production in the Black Belt). These farmers, who had to engage in cotton production as a precondition of access to the credit necessary to resume production, farmed the most marginal cotton-producing land outside the Black Belt areas. With only limited growth in the demand for cotton (chiefly the result of reduced rates of growth in British textile production and increasing British use of cotton from India and other colonies) and falling prices, these white farmers fell into the same debt trap as had the freedmen, and they were also proletarianized.

In all the years for which data are available, a majority of "tenant farmers" in agriculture as a whole were white. With respect to cotton agriculture specifically, an 1880 survey of cotton planters revealed one county in which white "laborers" dominated and twenty-seven that were dominated by blacks. In all others, the division was roughly equal.[19] However, as table 2.1 also indicates, the importance of black labor within the tenant category increased between 1900 and 1925. Black tenant labor grew by 58 percent during this period, compared to a rate of growth of 24 percent for white labor, indicating, within the general tendency of the tenant system to expand, the impact of a growing and segregated textile industry as a way out of this situation for white laborers and their families.

The postwar reconstruction of cotton agriculture described above

Table 2.1. The structure of tenure in post–Civil War North Carolina agriculture

| | 1880 | | 1890 | | 1900 | | 1910 | |
|---|---|---|---|---|---|---|---|---|
| | Number | Percent | Number | Percent | Number | Percent | Number | Percent |
| All farm operators | 157,609 | 100.0 | 178,359 | 100.0 | 224,637 | 100.0 | 253,725 | 100.0 |
| Owners | 104,887 | 66.5 | 117,469 | 65.9 | 130,572 | 58.1 | 145,320 | 57.3 |
| Tenants | 52,722 | 33.5 | 60,890 | 34.1 | 93,008 | 41.4 | 107,287 | 42.3 |
| Share-cash tenants } Share tenants } | 44,078 | 28.0 | 50,318 | 28.2 | 73,092 | 32.5 | 2,033 | 0.8 |
| | | | | | | | 80,215 | 31.6 |
| Croppers | | | | | | | | |
| Cash tenants } Others } | 8,644 | 5.5 | 10,572 | 5.9 | 19,916 | 8.9 | 20,708 | 8.2 |
| | | | | | | | 4,331 | 1.7 |
| Blacks as a percentage of total tenants | | | | | | 40.0 | | 41.1 |

*Sources*: a. 1880–1920: US Department of Commerce, Bureau of the Census, *Fourteenth Census of the United States, 1920*, vol. 6, pt. 2 (Washington: USGPO, 1922), 224–25.
   b. 1925–1940: US Department of Commerce, Bureau of the Census, *Sixteenth Census of the*

eventually resulted in large increases in the production of cotton both in the United States as a whole and in North Carolina.[20] In 1860 North Carolina had produced 145,514 bales of cotton with a market value in New York of $8,003,270.[21] In 1870, despite the disruptions caused by war and emancipation, production had recovered to 144,935 bales valued at $12,283,241. Thereafter, the figures are as follows:

|      |              |             |
|------|--------------|-------------|
| 1880 | 369,468 bales | $20,948,835 |
| 1890 | 336,261 bales | $15,938,771 |
| 1900 | 509,341 bales | $23,888,092 |
| 1910 | 706,142 bales | $52,501,658 |
| 1920 | 925,000 bales | $82,741,250 |

Because this process of expansion, which was under planter-merchant domination, was based on large increases in the number of small units farmed by labor-intensive methods, the benefits gained by the agricultural laborers themselves were limited. In 1880 wage laborers, a small

| 1920 | | 1925 | | 1930 | | 1935 | | 1940 | |
|---|---|---|---|---|---|---|---|---|---|
| Number | Percent | Number | Percent | Number | Percent | Number | Percent | Number | Percent |
| 269,763 | 100.0 | 283,482 | 100.0 | 279,708 | 100.0 | 300,967 | 100.0 | 278,276 | 100.0 |
| 151,376 | 56.1 | 132,610 | 46.8 | 115,765 | 46.8 | 128,394 | 42.7 | 132,451 | 47.6 |
| 117,459 | 43.5 | 128,254 | 45.2 | 137,615 | 49.2 | 142,158 | 47.2 | 123,476 | 44.4 |
| | | | | | | | | | |
| 468 | 0.2 | | | | | | | 1,113 | 0.4 |
| | | | | | | | | | |
| 58,819 | 21.8 | | | | | | | 41,337 | 14.9 |
| 39,939 | 14.8 | 52,419 | 18.5 | 69,091 | 24.7 | 66,393 | 22.1 | 60,300 | 21.7 |
| | | | | | | | | | |
| 9,425 | 3.5 | 7,520 | 2.7 | 9,237 | 3.3 | | | 10,720 | 3.9 |
| 8,808 | 3.3 | | | | | | | 10,006 | 3.6 |
| | | | | | | | | | |
| | 45.9 | | 45.9 | | 41.5 | | 34.5 | | 34.0 |

*United States, 1940,* vol. 1, pt. 3 (Washington: USGPO, 1942), 290–91.

c. 1945–1954: US Department of Commerce, Bureau of the Census, *1954 Census of Agriculture*, vol. 1, pt. 16 (Washington: USGPO, 1956), 10–11.

minority of the labor force in North Carolina were reported to receive from six to ten dollars per month (seventy-two to one hundred twenty dollars per year) with rations, or from thirty to fifty cents per day (ninety to one hundred fifty dollars per year) without rations. Women and children working independently received five dollars per month with board. In Pennsylvania in the same period, wage rates for tobacco laborers, which were reported to be roughly similar to those of agricultural laborers generally, ranged from $10.58 to $12.39 per month or $0.63 to $0.80 per day with board, and from $27.44 to $20.97 per month or $0.88 to $1.15 per day without board.[22] By 1900 the average annual income of laborers on farms in North Carolina was $146.75, compared with $162.88 in the South Atlantic states generally, $261.15 in Pennsylvania, $296.26 in New York, $404.49 in Massachusetts, and $288.26 in the United States as a whole.[23]

According to the testimony of William Graham, President of the North Carolina Farmers' Alliance, widely fluctuating cotton prices made

Table 2.1 (Continued)

| | 1945 | | 1950 | | 1954 | | 1959 | |
|---|---|---|---|---|---|---|---|---|
| | Number | Percent | Number | Percent | Number | Percent | Number | Percent |
| All farm operators | 287,412 | 100.0 | 288,508 | 100.0 | 267,818 | 100.0 | 190,511 | 100.0 |
| Owners | 144,450 | 50.3 | 142,085 | 49.3 | 129,239 | 48.3 | 92,261 | 48.4 |
| Tenants | 122,577 | 42.6 | 110,485 | 38.3 | 96,586 | 36.1 | 57,903 | 30.4 |
| Share-cash tenants | 949 | 0.3 | 1,462 | 0.5 | 1,785 | 0.7 | 2,110 | 1.1 |
| Share tenants | 40,481 | 14.1 | 38,805 | 13.5 | 36,051 | 13.5 | 48,636 | 25.6 |
| Croppers | 62,687 | 21.8 | 57,457 | 19.9 | 48,825 | 18.2 | | |
| Cash tenants | 7,822 | 2.7 | 4,341 | 1.5 | 3,870 | 1.4 | 2,507 | 1.3 |
| Others | 10,638 | 3.7 | 8,420 | 2.9 | 6,055 | 2.3 | 4,650 | 2.4 |
| Blacks as a percentage of total tenants | | 44.4 | | 44.4 | | 44.9 | | 43.6 |

d. 1959–1964: US Department of Commerce, Bureau of the Census, *Census of Agriculture, 1964*, vol. 1, pt. 26 (Washington: USGPO, 1967), 10.

e. 1969: US Department of Commerce, Bureau of the Census, *1969 Census of Agriculture,*

wage payments impossible for all but a few of the larger planters who owned the most productive land. We might expect, therefore, that the value of the "shares" paid to croppers and tenants were at best no higher than these meager cash wages. Responding to a census question as to whether the wage or share system was better for the laborer, most respondents naturally answered in terms of the relative ease of supervision and the likelihood of crop neglect and failure. In the handful of cases in which the question was answered directly, however, the respondents replied that it made little difference either way, "as they accumulate but little." [24]

Further, since in the cash-short southern states tenants and croppers obtained most of their supplies from supply merchants (either directly or with the planter acting as an intermediary) at inflated prices, it seems likely that, in terms of real wages, the gap between wage levels in North Carolina and other states was even wider.

Finally, as later sections will demonstrate, the expansion of cotton production into marginal land outside the Black Belt and the operation

| 1964 | | 1969 | | 1974 | | 1978 | |
|---|---|---|---|---|---|---|---|
| Number | Percent | Number | Percent | Number | Percent | Number | Percent |
| 148,202 | 100.0 | 119,386 | 100.0 | 91,280 | 100.0 | 89,367 | 100.0 |
| 70,658 | 47.7 | 75,625 | 63.3 | 57,004 | 62.4 | 48,653 | 54.4 |
| 40,115 | 27.1 | 17,872 | 14.9 | 11,304 | 12.4 | 12,966 | 14.5 |
| 2,548 | 1.7 | | | | | | |
| 30,545 | 20.6 | | | | | | |
| 3,943 | 2.7 | | | | | | |
| 3,152 | 2.1 | | | | | | |
| | 41.2 | | 19.2 | | 13.4 | | 13.0 |

vol. 1, pt. 26 (Washington: USGPO, 1972), 3.

f. 1974–1978: US Department of Commerce, Bureau of the Census, *1978 Census of Agriculture*, vol. 1, pt. 33 (Washington: USGPO, 1982), 2.

of the lien system created a large pool of impoverished white surplus labor, on which the racially segregated textile industry was able to draw as it expanded. Because of the conditions in which this pool of labor power existed, and because part-time farming permitted millworkers to supplement their incomes by growing food, mill wages remained low, and high rates of surplus value were extracted. For the farmers themselves, cotton mill labor became an available, if not easily acceptable (since it involved loss of personal freedom) means of remaining in agriculture on a part-time basis until such a time as cotton prices might begin to rise.

## The development of the cotton textile industry in North Carolina, 1820–80

The expansion of textile manufacturing as a counterpart to the production of cotton was not a post–Civil War phenomenon. It had been of interest to planters, merchants, and others in North Carolina for many years prior to the war.[25] During this period mill-building booms coincided with depressed conditions in markets for the raw cotton produced in the southern states, as planters and merchants turned to the manufacture of cotton cloth and twine as the readiest means of diversification. During the late 1820s and early 1830s, when cotton prices fell below ten cents a pound,[26] twenty mills were built in North Carolina, and several other southern states witnessed similar developments.[27] Similarly, as prices sank below ten cents again in the late 1830s and early 1840s following the Panic of 1837, a second period of mill building occurred. During this period North Carolina's textile industry grew to forty-eight thousand spindles. In 1850 the state held its first manufacturer's convention and, in 1851, its first state fair to exhibit its industrial products.[28] According to Harriett Herring, discussion of the crisis at this period centered on two points—first, that there was overproduction of cotton, and, second, that in a context of high tariffs on imported manufactured goods, increased domestic prices, and the concentration of manufacturing in New England, any remedy to the southern problem must involve "manufacture of cotton by the states that raised it."[29]

However, just as periods of mill building corresponded with depressed cotton prices, interest in mill building tended to decline as cotton prices rose. Rising production (combined with rising prices during the late 1840s and 1850s), fueled by a rapid increase in world demand for cotton, redirected investment back into land, slaves, and rail transport rather than manufacture.[30] Nevertheless, although textile manufacture was cut back somewhat during the 1850s, a certain stability had developed. By 1860 North Carolina had 39 cotton mills, 41,384 spindles, 761 looms, and 1,764 workers—all producing goods worth $1,046,000.[31] The basis for the development of some of the state's later textile centers was taking shape. Mills owned by the Battle and Fries families[32] in Edgecombe and Forsyth counties, respectively, formed the basis of later and larger developments in Rocky Mount and Winston-Salem. Cumberland, Randolph, and Alamance counties had also established stable textile production with seven, five, and five mills, respectively. The latter county witnessed the most significant prewar development with the founding of a cotton mill by Edwin Holt, using profits derived from plantation agriculture and merchandising.[33] Holt's mill used slave labor and northern machinery and for several years operated only as a spinning mill. In the 1840s, however, Holt installed looms and turned to the production of sheeting and in 1853 became the first power loom manufacturer of colored cotton cloth in the South. During the 1850s his "Alamance plaids" gained national acceptance, and in the 1860s Holt's began a process of expansion that would later make it one of the nation's largest textile empires and transform Alamance County into a leading center of the manufacture of cotton goods.

Table 2.2. The recovery of the cotton goods industry in North Carolina, 1860–80

| | (a) Esta-blish-ments | (b) Workers employed | (c) b/a | (d) Cost of labor ($) | (e) Capital ($) | (f) e/b ($) | (g) Cost of raw mater-ials ($) | (h) Value of product ($) |
|---|---|---|---|---|---|---|---|---|
| 1860 | 39 | 1,755 | 45 | 189,744 | 1,272,750 | 725.2 | 622,363 | 1,046,047 |
| 1870 | 33 | 1,453 | 44 | 182,951 | 1,030,900 | 709.5 | 963,809 | 1,345,052 |
| 1880 | 49 | 3,232 | 66 | 439,659 | 2,855,800 | 883.6 | 1,463,645 | 2,554,482 |

*Sources*: 1860: U.S. Department of the Interior, *Manufactures of the United States in 1860*, compiled from returns in the eighth census (Washington: USGPO, 1865), 437–38.

1870: U.S. Department of the Interior, Census Office, *Ninth Census of the United States, 1870*, vol. 3, Statistics on Wealth and Industry (Washington: USGPO, 1872), 553–54.

1880: U.S. Department of the Interior, Census Office, *Report on the Manufactures of the United States at the Tenth Census, 1880* (Washington: USGPO, 1883), 160–61.

Despite the destruction and disorganization caused by the Civil War, the textile industry proved its strength by its survival. Textile manufacturers, although often heavily involved in plantation agriculture as well as in manufacture, in many cases opposed secession, having "long before adopted the economic mores of the new industrial society." [34] During the war the use of a two-price system—one for gold and one for Confederate currency—allowed a quicker postwar return to production than would otherwise have been possible in the creditless postwar period. With the liberation of the plantation labor force, the difficulties involved in the resumption of agricultural production, and the decline in world cotton prices after 1868 (especially after the Panic of 1873), the relative balance between agriculture and manufacture shifted decisively. In 1867 W. F. Leak, a North Carolina planter, expressed serious concern about the effect of the possible loss of his industrial holdings, whereas before the war he would have been able to withstand their loss with little trouble.[35] After the 1873 panic, the granges of Mecklenburg, Cabarrus, Rowan, Iredell, Catawba, Lincoln, and Gaston counties (contiguous counties in the southwestern part of North Carolina's Piedmont region) began to pool funds for a venture into manufacturing. By 1878 they had accumulated ninety thousand dollars, which they planned to use to build a mill in Gaston county.[36]

*Large-scale textile industrialization
after 1880*

This reordering of economic priorities resulted in steady, if unspectacular, growth in the cotton goods sector in the period between the end of the Civil War and 1880. (See table 2.2.) By 1870 the industry had recovered to almost prewar levels. Between 1870 and 1880 there was a net increase of sixteen mills, the average number of workers per mill rose by 50 percent, capital stocks rose from $1.031 million to $2.855 million, capital/labor ratios rose from $705.5 per capita to $883.6 per capita, and total production increased from $1.345 million to $2.554 million. By 1880 North Carolina had forty-nine mills, which were located primarily in the prewar textile centers and used mostly local raw materials. They were owned for the most part by the same planter families—Schenck, Fries, Holt, Lineberger, Morehead, Odell, Leak, Battle, Patterson, Cameron, and Murchison—who had owned mills before the war.[37] With the increasing futility of attempting to increase the production of surplus value in cotton agriculture in conditions of increasing overproduction and plummeting cotton prices, planters were firmly committed to the textile industry as their main source of expanded profits. Further, with the failure of the electoral strategy embodied in the 1876 Compromise and after the fall of Reconstruction governments had reduced the need for white solidarity, the continued proletarianization of small white farmers led to the emergence of open class conflict between planters and agrarian radicals; in this situation, the virtues of industrialization as a political strategy to defuse white unrest became increasingly evident to the state's planter ruling class.[38]

In the late 1870s and early 1880s, however, a number of obstacles appeared in the path of such an expansion of the industrial labor force into textiles. To begin with, this expansion would require a relatively large amount of capital that was not readily available within the still small-scale textile industry itself or within southern agriculture. Second, the squeezing of the agricultural proletariat did not necessarily guarantee the availability of a sufficiently large and stable labor force for textile industrialization.

*Sources of capital*
*for textile industrialization*

The task of providing large amounts of capital for the expansion of the textile industry created a number of problems for millowners in the early 1880s. From a purely economic point of view, external capital was vital. Not only was the availability of capital within North Carolina severely limited, but the state's chief economic resource, cotton, was falling steadily in price. Since the expansion of cotton production only contributed to falling prices, future returns from agricultural investment would be limited. Further, if North Carolina textiles were to compete in national markets, it was necessary to acquire the latest in textile machinery.

In the aftermath of the Civil War, however, investment by northern-owned capital frequently met with opposition. Many of those exposed to the creed of the "New South" since the Civil War saw industrial development and diversification as the most effective means to achieve the "redemption" of the South. Industrialization therefore had to be, or at least had to appear to be, indigenous in origin.[39] The northern states had won the war, but they could not be allowed to win the subsequent peace.

Textile industrialists responded pragmatically to these contradictory signals, using both local and external sources of capital in practice, while publicizing the role of the former and minimizing that of the latter. A major promotional effort by chambers of commerce, daily and weekly newspapers, and itinerant industrial evangelists publicized the benefits of pooling the profits and savings of small Piedmont communities and larger towns to organize cotton mills.[40] In 1873 the editor of the Greensboro (N.C.) *Patriot* indicated that charitable orders, the Patrons of Husbandry (Grange), and similar voluntary associations might provide the organizational base upon which to encourage, create, and solidify local industries.[41] The aim of such an approach was to confer the badge of civic virtue on mill building. Investments, often paid for in large numbers of small installments, were presented as part of the wider campaign for the improvement of the South, and specifically to encourage the habits of thrift, accumulation, and investment and to help unify local white communities as joint "proprietors."

Capital raised in this way formed only a part of the picture, however. Frequently, such local subscriptions formed only seed money, designed to test the viability and profitability of cotton mill production in a particular area. Thereafter, succeeding mills would be built by a smaller number of large investors. For the latter, whose mills tended to be larger, external financial participation was crucial. A typical strategy was for local entrepreneurs to raise as much capital as possible locally, providing at least for a mill building and other basic infrastructural requirements, and then to ask northern textile machinery manufacturers to provide machinery in return for a share in the stock of the newly formed company. Commission agents in New York and other commercial centers would provide additional capital (frequently working capital) in return for stocks, or, more frequently, in return for being granted the mill's agency contract. The Newberry Cotton Manufacturing Company in South Carolina, for example, grew out of a canvass of the local community, a subscription to the capital stock by a northern investor, credit for the purchase of machinery extended by a northern manufacturer, and the promise of additional machinery from a neighboring cotton mill in exchange for stock in the new enterprise.[42] Broadus Mitchell estimates that mills could raise between 40 and 50 percent of their total capital needs from these external sources, with machinery manufacturers (who were themselves undergoing a period of rapid innovation, cost reduction, and competition and were therefore eager to expand old and to capture new markets), generally taking more stock than the commission houses.[43]

The tobacco industry, which also began to expand rapidly in North Carolina after 1880, provided capital for textile industrialization in a number of ways. In Durham, North Carolina, for instance, the first textile mill, the Durham Cotton Manufacturing Company, was created in 1884 with a capital stock of $130,000 by Julian Carr, whose money came from his interests in the Blackwell Tobacco Company. Tobacco money also provided the basis for the foundation of a mill also in Durham, by the Duke family, to produce the type of cloth used to make bags for smoking tobacco. The same family was also a large investor in other textile towns, such as Roxboro, Concord, Greensboro, and Spray.[44] Less directly, the rapid expansion of the Duke tobacco empire freed the capital of the less efficient competitors for textile industrialization. In 1900 the Hanes brothers sold their tobacco company in Forsyth County in order to invest in hosiery and knitting mills.[45] In addition, the continued expansion of textile production, especially after 1910, precipitated a major movement of capital by the Duke family into the generation of hydroelectric power from the Piedmont rivers, providing cheap power and additional infrastructure for industrialization.

Over time, as the industry expanded, the relative importance of local capital in the form of pooled savings of small retailers, professionals, and farmers tended to decline. Many smaller, community-based mill projects were flimsily financed, poorly managed, and unable to compete with later and larger operations. Further, even those operations that could compete by restricting labor costs posed the threat of instability and overproduction to the industry as a whole and became early targets of larger corporations as frequent periods of depression forced the rationalization of production and management.[46] The mills that survived despite these adverse conditions increasingly fell into the hands of larger investors (often owners or co-owners of other mills) who had played central roles in their organization.[47]

While the community of "proprietors" in North Carolina rapidly shrank in size, the influence of external capital continued. This influence was exerted chiefly by commission houses. Unlike the machinery manufacturers, who realized their holdings in the southern mills as soon as possible in order to continue their own plans for expansion, the commission houses retained their stock and agency agreements and continued to take a major interest in the expansion of the industry and its output. While this relationship between millowner and commission agent was essential for the creation of a large number of mills, it had other long term effects on the organization of the industry itself, stemming from the commission agents' ability to control the marketing of the industry's finished product. Since commissions were based on sales volume, the commission houses had a vested interest in maximizing production by the firms with which they had contracts. They did this by misrepresenting prices, using excess stocks to depress prices and maximize sales, and by making permanent agreements (i.e., regardless of market conditions) with buyers to the disadvantage of producers. In this way they exacerbated existing tendencies toward overproduction and low prices.[48] In the absence of any control of final market sales, the only way that producers could resist this tendency and raise prices would be by reducing production. This was not an available strategy, however, in a highly competitive industry with a large number of small companies, dispersed ownership, and a high and relatively irreducible level of labor intensity in production. In addition to the necessity for any capitalist business enterprise based on borrowed capital to maintain "business confidence" and the profits required by the millowners themselves for the accumulation of capital, the commission houses' control of sales and market prices therefore added a further factor into the need for high rates of exploitation and profit in the southern mills. A prior problem, however, was the need for a large and stable labor force upon which the industry could expand and to do so in such a way as to provide rates of exploitation high enough to satisfy the demands of the industry's various sponsors.

## The formation of a textile working class

Unlike the millowners, who regarded the mills as a permanent means to generate profits and accumulate capital, their employees, with roots in agricultural production, did not. Especially in the early years, they tended to see cotton mill labor as a form of temporary relief. Mill workers, having earned small amounts of cash to pay debts or to tide them over from one season to the next, would often return to agriculture. Scarcity of working capital, an unwillingness to disrupt the agricultural labor force (and, therefore, local cotton supplies) by creating competition for jobs, and the need to maximize rates of exploitation in order to be able to compete in northern markets and attract northern capital ruled out the use of wage increases to achieve labor force stability. So although the market price for cotton remained low, resistance to the pace, continuity, and discipline of factory labor, and the lack of significant material gains from it, persuaded large numbers of millhands to maintain their ties with agriculture.[49] Similar problems had been encountered in attempts to use free white labor in the prewar cotton mills of William Gregg at Vaucluse and Graniteville, South Carolina. However, although Gregg's efforts to limit turnover and improve efficiency through wage increases and the use of a mill village had failed, the restricted size of these prewar operations ensured that there was always enough labor to maintain production.[50] If postwar textile industrialization was to be carried out on an extended scale, this could not be guaranteed.

The campaign to resolve these twin problems of mobilization and stabilization took both ideological and material forms. Ideologically, in their efforts to publicize the benefits of the textile mills, textile industrialists used many of the themes that had been developed by New South propagandists since the Civil War and that were simultaneously being used in the campaign to attract capital. Central to these was the New South critique of the social and economic effects of slavery.[51] According to this analysis, not only did the introduction of slavery lead to cotton monoculture and underinvestment in other industries, but more important it drove a wedge into the white race, creating a social and economic gulf between the planter class and the rest of the white race as the latter were marginalized by the spread of the plantation system during the 1840s and 1850s. In the post–Civil War period the credit system forced these whites into cotton production and therefore into competition with black labor for credit, supplies, and land. Black laborers however were most accustomed to cotton production and (so the argument ran) were generally satisfied by very low levels of consumption. Furthermore, whites had to work land less suitable for cotton production. For all these reasons white labor could not effectively compete with blacks.

The campaign to expand textile production after 1880 was thus presented as a major element in the New South program of social betterment — to reunify the southern white family, rehabilitate the "poor white," and protect him from the competition of cheap black labor.[52] From this point of view, the fact that the mills were highly profitable was purely incidental and secondary to the social function of the movement.[53] Broadus Mitchell's analysis of textile industrialization reflects this ideology:

the white population of the South is homogeneous and always has been so. There is no distinction in blood between employers and employees. The inauguration of the industry, in point of capital and labor alike, took place within the southern family. It made for an intimacy which at first rendered impossible and which continues to retard division between factory owners and workers according to economic interest . . . when the poor whites entered the mills, they reentered the life of the South. As cotton culture had blocked progress, so cotton mills, while not dispelling the certainty of painful readjustments, opened the way to a rational economic future.[54]

The mill community was thus presented as a family within which, through contact with gainful and disciplined industrial employment, millworkers could gain full equality within the white race.[55] Left undeveloped and impoverished by their prior experiences, however, they were defined initially as "children" within this family and would remain under the paternal and watchful eye of the owner as they progressed toward adulthood.[56] By providing mill housing, credit in company stores, and religious, educational, and social facilities, the millowners were taking the first step toward re-creating the white community. The idea that the textile industry was part of a larger plan of agricultural and industrial diversification in the New South's economic war against the North added sectional commitment by those not directly involved, and it ensured favorable publicity from newspapers, the pulpit, politicians, and other ideologues of the New South. The very fact that textile industrialization was taking place predominantly in the Piedmont region of the Southeast (that is, away from the major areas of prewar slavery and cotton production) and that it was a segregated industry testified to the "civic" motives of the planter-industrialists.[57] Even the use of child labor "was not avarice then, but philanthropy, not exploitation, but generosity and cooperation and social-mindedness."[58]

Needless to say, the emerging reality of textile industrialization was determined not so much by a desire for civic betterment (although this was a factor in the ability of the textile industrialists to gain widespread public support), but by the desire to stabilize a factory labor force, to preserve planter control of the black labor force in cotton agriculture, and to maximize available rates of exploitation and profit in both areas.

The central institution, or collection of institutions, designed to achieve these purposes was the mill village. Mill villages, or more generally, company towns, have traditionally and necessarily been a favored form of organization in the transition from agricultural to industrial capitalist production in North America.[59] The particular circumstances in which the textile industry emerged in North Carolina and the southern Piedmont region generally, however, gave these villages a character somewhat of their own; this unique character was determined primarily by the length to which millowners went to control labor and maximize the production of surplus value.

To begin with, many mill villages were constructed so as to be socially and geographically isolated institutions, sometimes located on private land just outside municipal limits, and often in completely rural areas in order to minimize the local tax bill, limit social intercourse between the millworkers and the larger community, and to facilitate the attraction of rural labor. In a largely agricultural society in which movement into a mill village by indebted yeomen or tenant farmers indicated failure and inferiority and encouraged the mistrust of land-owners, the social separation of mill village from local society tended to solidify over time. According to Frank Tannenbaum's 1924 study of the social effects of mill village life, even where several mills and villages coalesced into a larger community or existed within a larger, nonmill community, the

> mill population is in a world apart. It does not play with the com-munity. It does not mix with it. It does not intermarry, it does not work with it. The children do not play baseball together, and in one instance an attempt to establish a common camp had to be given up on account of opposition to having the other children associate with the mill children. This is so general a fact in the mill section of the South that it is recognized as a caste system. The mill people are at the bottom of the scale.[60]

As a result of this social and geographical isolation, few workers who entered the textile industry on a full time basis were able to leave it. Although there was significant mobility among textile workers, it was overwhelmingly mobility between mill villages.[61] Alternative forms of industrial labor were limited, and the high cost of northward migra-tion left millworkers who did not own their own land with the alter-natives of remaining within the "sealed world of the textile industry"[62] or attempting to survive within cotton agriculture. Since some land-lords refused to lease land to former millworkers, even this alternative was not always available.[63] Where corporate paternalism was relatively successful, and where alternative sources of employment were limited, average length of employment tended to increase over time.[64]

Nevertheless, the expansion of the textile industry in its early years was so rapid that agriculture continued to form the social context within which millwork and village conditions were experienced. In addition to the large numbers of part-time farmers continuing to work in the cot-ton mills to supplement their incomes, very few full-time mill village dwellers were far removed from agriculture. Of Jennings J. Rhyne's sample of 1,923 cotton millworkers, 71 percent (1,365) were born in North Carolina, about half of these were born in Gaston county (in which the study took place), and about three-quarters were born in Gaston and its contiguous counties. Eighteen percent of the sample were born in South Carolina, 4.4 percent in Georgia, and 3.4 percent in Tennessee. Some 62.1 percent of the parents of the millworkers had been or were farmers, and 51 percent of the workers themselves had once farmed, representing a mixture of "poor whites," indebted yeoman farmers, and "mountaineers." Only 18.1 percent of millworkers had parents who had also been millworkers.[65] In addition, even if the links between workers and agriculture were totally severed, rural mill villages often incorporated land to allow the cultivation of food crops in and around the village. In this way they reduced the level of wages necessary to reproduce labor power and simultaneously increased the rate of exploitation.

Other elements of the "sealed world" were also designed to ensure the most favorable possible conditions for the exploitation of labor. Company housing was provided on condition that not only the head of the household but the whole family, including children, worked in the mill. In 1900, 57.7 percent of the total labor force of 30,273 in the cotton goods sector was female or child labor.[66] This housing practice, together with the deliberate misadvertising of labor needs, allowed millowners to maintain a relatively permanent pool of surplus labor in the mill villages to meet needs generated by the industry's frequent changes in market conditions.[67] The provision of housing close to the mill also enabled millowners and managers to exercise social and moral control.[68] Being fired for immorality, absenteeism, expressing dissent about village life and its rigors, or other activities considered to be unbecoming of the mill community involved the loss of housing (as well as job).

Efforts to control the political, economic, and spiritual lives of the millworkers extended far beyond these measures, however. Numerous studies of the southern textile industry testify to the extent of this control effort.[69] Provision and control of schools, churches, recreational facilities such as parks and baseball teams; the provision of credit and supplies at company stores; nurseries, social and community centers; medical facilities; community political organizations; and welfare and counseling services, all extended the influence and control of the owners over virtually all aspects of mill village life. Most commonly, the provision of rudimentary educational facilities and churches formed the core of the social control efforts in the villages on the grounds that "an investment in the affections of those employed is always as good as any money put in machinery."[70] For some millowners it was a "business necessity to begin at the bottom with day nurseries, kindergartens, primary departments, [a] . . . nursing and medical department if we were ever to develop a nucleus of capable and efficient workers."[71] In addition, building schools, providing or supplementing teachers' salaries, and establishing night courses were measures designed to create the promise of upward mobility and to increase worker loyalty.[72] Many churches were also built with mill money and almost all received financial aid, often in the form of salaries or salary supplements for preachers. Attendance at fundamentalist church services was high; there workers were warned of the dangers of eternal damnation and were promised better things in the next life. According to Liston Pope, "the churches . . . set out to mold transplanted farmers into stable, contented, sober citizens and industrial workers [by the] inculcation of personal virtues [and the] provision of a center of community integration other than the mill itself, and emotional escape from the difficulties of life."[73] More particularly, and therefore possibly more importantly, as the industry grew, churches became an important channel of upward mobility. In addition to long service in the mills, demonstration of community loyalty by becoming a church officer or a Sunday school teacher became a necessary precondition for promotion to such mill positions as overseer or superintendent.[74]

Finally, if all these constraints failed, as they periodically did, and if the millworkers voiced their discontent with their poor conditions of life by contemplating or engaging in strikes, millowners could always exploit the racial fears of their white workers by threatening the use of black labor in the mills in order to restore order. Although the ideology both of the New South in general and of the cotton mill campaign in particular presented the segregation of the textile industry and its location in the Piedmont region of the Southeast as part of the plan to save the white race from competition with black labor, the latter continued to play an important role in relations between millowner and millworker. For one thing, the mills' location in the North Carolina Piedmont did not involve a total separation from blacks. Gavin Wright's regional disaggregation of the Cotton South in 1860 indicates that the most significant difference between the Piedmont and the Central and Coastal Plain areas to its east was not in terms of the proportion of the population who were slaves (43.1 percent in the Piedmont as opposed to 52.2 and 47.8 percent, respectively, in the other two regions), but rather in terms of the size of farms and of slaveholdings, both of which were significantly larger in the two eastern areas.[75]

Further, for the millowners' part, the commitment to maintain a segregated textile industry appears to have depended on the availability of a sufficiently large white labor force and the profitability of racial blackmail. In the 1890s, as the southern textile industry began to expand rapidly, it gradually became clear that the Piedmont's immediately available labor supply was limited, and labor shortages began to appear.[76] In response, southern mill managements began to test the widely held view that black labor was not suitable for factory production and to find out if wages generally could be reduced as a result of its use.[77] Attempts to use black labor were made in mills at Rome and Griffin, Georgia and in three mills at Charleston, South Carolina. In addition, two mills were established by blacks, at Columbia, South Carolina, and at Concord, North Carolina, the latter manned totally by blacks except for managerial personnel and partially supported by the Duke family.[78] Although all of these mills failed, this was not obviously due to any deficiencies of the black workers. Some of the mills had proved unprofitable in the past when white labor had been used, and all found it difficult to raise sufficient amounts of capital. Southern millowners continued to take the position that the use of black labor was a possibility, undoubtedly because of its practical value when it came to maintaining the rate of exploitation of white labor. These threats of and practical experiments using black labor would be used periodically throughout the history of the textile industry (especially in periods of labor shortage and political unrest) until it became racially integrated in the 1960s.

## Wages, exploitation, profits, and growth

For North Carolina's textile industrialists, the complex structure of constraints placed upon the textile labor force—social and geographical isolation and the paternalistic control of the mill village community— was worthwhile only insofar as it allowed effective control of labor, wage levels, and the maximum production of surplus value in the wider economic and political context within which it had to operate. That it was worthwhile can quickly be appreciated. Because they were determined primarily by conditions in cotton agriculture, in the late nineteenth and early twentieth centuries wage rates and hours in the North Carolina cotton goods industry were low and long. According to census data, in 1880 the average annual wage (that is, the total wages bill divided by the average size of the labor force) in the cotton goods industry was $136.03 compared with a range in agriculture of $90 to $150 without board. By 1900 the former average had risen to $169.37 per year compared with $146.75 in agriculture. In the same years the average wages in the Massachusetts cotton good industry were $258.19 and $351.06, respectively.[79] During the late 1880s and 1890s mill laborers worked largely the same hours as did agricultural laborers— from dawn to dusk—although the range of social services available to workers in some of the mill villages was probably greater than those in cotton agriculture. After the turn of the century all southern states had hours laws. These were at best loosely enforced, however, and, even then, the laws allowed millowners to work their laborers an average of eight hours per week longer than their counterparts in New England.

Table 2.3 presents data on the distribution of cotton millworkers in the United States and North Carolina by the number of hours worked for 1909. North Carolina had 12.5 percent of the nation's cotton millworkers but accounted for 61.1 percent of those working more than

Table 2.3. Distribution of cotton mill workers in the United States and North Carolina by number of hours worked, 1909

| | Total number of workers | Less than 48 hours | 48–54 hours | 54 hours | 54–60 hours | 60 hours | 60–72 hours | 72+ hours |
|---|---|---|---|---|---|---|---|---|
| **United States** | | | | | | | | |
| Number | 378,880 | 304 | 2,879 | 571 | 190,998 | 119,226 | 64,687 | 215 |
| Percentage | 100.0 | 0.001 | 0.008 | 0.002 | 50.4 | 31.5 | 17.1 | 0.001 |
| **North Carolina** | | | | | | | | |
| Number | 47,231 | | | | 52 | 7,499 | 39,680 | |
| Percentage | 100.0 | | | | 0.001 | 15.9 | 84.0 | |

Sources: U.S. Department of Commerce, Bureau of the Census, *Thirteenth Census of the United States, 1910*, vol. 8 (Washington: USGPO, 1912), 323.

sixty hours per week. Under these conditions, relocating textile production in North Carolina would pay dividends in terms of the production of both absolute and relative surplus value.

While the use of average wage rates such as those above gives a general indication of the long-term movement of wages, it may also hide significant short-term trends for the labor force as a whole or equally long-term trends for smaller groups within the labor force. In the first case, it is worthwhile to note the vulnerability of the textile industry to overproduction and periods of depression that made wide fluctuations in wages commonplace. In the second case, average wages hide the fact that wage rates for certain categories of workers had a tendency to remain stationary or even decline over time, despite (or perhaps because of) increases in productivity and in the overall growth of the industry.

The special vulnerability of wage levels for skilled adult male workers in the early years of textile industrialization derived from the significance in the southern textile industry, as in plantation agriculture, of family labor. Family labor resulted in part from the textile workers' poverty, as well as from the use of mill village housing monopolies to expand the available labor force. Its use expanded dramatically with the invention of the ring spindle and improvements in the automatic loom after 1880, the combined effects of which were to allow reductions in skilled workers and (initially at least) in the intensity of work and to allow large numbers of female and child workers to enter textile production. Out of this ability to exploit a large supply of female and child labor grew the concept of a "family wage,"[80] which was used first to justify low wages for individuals in general, and second, to reduce the cost of skilled labor necessary in textile production. Over time the family wage and the wage level required to support a single adult male worker

Table 2.4. Male, female, and child wage rates in the cotton goods industry, North Carolina, 1890 and 1900[81]

|        | Labor force | 1890 wages ($) | Average ($) | Labor force | 1900 wages ($) | Average ($) |
|--------|-------------|----------------|-------------|-------------|----------------|-------------|
| Male   | 2,581       | 658,316        | 255.06      | 12,780      | 2,765,457      | 216.39      |
| Female | 3,274       | 513,338        | 156.79      | 10,364      | 1,629,036      | 157.18      |
| Child  | 2,038       | 184,801        | 90.68       | 7,129       | 732,594        | 102.76      |

tended to converge. In 1890 North Carolina reported average daily wages for skilled males as ranging from $1.00 to $2.50, for females from $0.40 to $1.00, and for children from $1.20 to $1.50. By 1905 the same categories were reported to be $0.50 to $6.00 (the latter figure was very rare), $0.30 to $1.00, and $0.25 to $1.00. In all these cases but that of children, the lower and most common end of the range had been reduced.[82] Table 2.4 presents census data that allow us to see the movement of male, female, and child wage rates more clearly. In 1890 the average wage rate for males in North Carolina was 163 percent that of females and 281 percent that of children. By 1900 these figures became 138 percent and 211 percent, respectively, largely as a result of the fall in the average rate for males.

In the context of the secular decline in the general price level from the 1870s to the 1890s,[83] real family wages probably increased despite the decline. From the point of view of the millowners, the ability to replace adult male workers with females and children in certain jobs undoubtedly increased the production of surplus value, even if market conditions in the late nineteenth century prevented its full realization. It also may have allowed millowners to be more selective in terms of their hiring procedures, permitted better socialization of children into mill life, and reduced the average overhead cost of mill housing.

It should also be noted that although the average wage for children has risen here, the census data probably understate the largely unregulated exploitation of child labor. Some mills paid ten to twelve cents a day for child labor.[84] Many others allowed children into the mills only as unpaid helpers for their mothers and encouraged the popularity of this concession by increasing work loads. These children would doubtless fail to appear in official statistics.

After 1900, as work intensities once again began to increase and as the first generation of mill children reached adulthood, the proportion of children in the textile labor force declined. Yet the wages and jobs of older skilled adult males remained vulnerable. Many mill villages accumulated a superfluous older adult male population that was used only in times of expansion when younger workers, who were better able

Table 2.5. Rates of surplus value in manufacturing and the cotton goods sector: United States and North Carolina, 1880–1919 (U.S. figures in millions of dollars; N.C. in thousands of dollars)

|      |                            | Salaries | Wages     | Value added |
|------|----------------------------|----------|-----------|-------------|
| 1880 | North Carolina 1[a]        | —        | 439.7     | 1,090.8     |
|      | United States 1            | —        | 45.6      | 97.2        |
|      | North Carolina 2[b]        | —        | 2,740.8   | 7,004.1     |
| 1879 | United States 2            | —        | 948.0     | 1,972.8     |
| 1890 | North Carolina 1           | —        | 1,475.9   | 3,323.5     |
|      | United States 1            | —        | 69.5      | 113.1       |
|      | North Carolina 2           | 1,278.4  | 6,552.1   | 17,586.3    |
| 1889 | United States 2            | 388.2    | 1,820.9   | 4,102.3     |
| 1899 | North Carolina 1           | 587.0    | 5,127.0   | 10,986.7    |
|      | United States 1            | 7.4      | 86.7      | 162.6       |
|      | North Carolina 2           | 2,394.8  | 14,051.8  | 40,419.9    |
|      | United States 2            | 336.1    | 1,892.6   | 4,747.0     |
| 1909 | North Carolina 1           | 1,610.0  | 12,131.0  | 23,992.0    |
|      | United States 1            | 14.4     | 132.9     | 257.4       |
|      | North Carolina 2           | 6,903.5  | 34,354.6  | 94,794.5    |
|      | United States 2            | 900.3    | 3,205.2   | 8,160.1     |
| 1919 | North Carolina 1           | 5,645.0  | 49,693.1  | 131,588.5   |
|      | United States 1            | 41.8     | 368.7     | 880.7       |
|      | North Carolina 2           | 23,774.3 | 126,680.1 | 416,901.8   |
|      | United States 2            | 2,762.9  | 9,664.0   | 23,841.6    |

*Sources*: U.S. Department of the Interior, Census Office, *Report on the Manufactures of the United States at the Tenth Census, 1880* (Washington: USGPO, 1883), 10, 161–62; U.S. Department of the Interior, Census Office, *Eleventh Census of the United States, 1890* (Washington: USGPO, 1892), vol. 6, pt. 1, 75; U.S. Department of Commerce, Bureau of the Census, *Thirteenth Census of the United States, 1910* (Washington: USGPO, 1912), vol. 8, p. 582; vol. 9, 912; U.S. Department of Commerce, Bureau of the Census, *Fourteenth Census of the United States, 1920* (Wash-

to cope with increasing work loads, were not immediately available. By the 1920s Rhyne found that only 12.2 percent of North Carolina cotton mill wage earners were over forty-four years of age, compared to an average of 26.4 percent for U.S. manufacturing as a whole.[85]

It should be stressed that the analysis of wages within the textile industry can be misleading if the data are taken too literally. This limitation results from the existence of the company store and scrip system, which played a crucial part in the appropriation of surplus value and the stabilization of the textile labor force in the early days of the industry when working capital was in short supply.[86] Payment of wages

| Productive salaries | Depreciation | Surplus value | Variable capital | Rate of surplus value |
|---|---|---|---|---|
| — | 54.5 | 596.6 | 439.7 | 136 |
| — | 4.9 | 46.7 | 45.6 | 102 |
| — | 350.2 | 3,913.1 | 4,740.8 | 143 |
| — | 98.6 | 926.2 | 948.0 | 98 |
| — | 166.2 | 1,681.4 | 1,475.9 | 114 |
| — | 5.7 | 37.9 | 69.5 | 55 |
| 639.2 | 879.3 | 9,515.7 | 7,191.3 | 132 |
| 194.1 | 205.1 | 1,882.2 | 2,015.0 | 93 |
| 293.5 | 549.3 | 5,016.0 | 5,420.0 | 93 |
| 3.7 | 8.1 | 64.1 | 90.4 | 71 |
| 1,197.4 | 2,021.0 | 23,149.7 | 15,249.2 | 152 |
| 183.1 | 232.4 | 2,338.9 | 2,075.7 | 113 |
| 805.0 | 1,199.6 | 9,856.4 | 12,936.0 | 76 |
| 7.2 | 12.9 | 104.4 | 140.1 | 75 |
| 3,451.8 | 4,739.7 | 52,248.4 | 37,806.4 | 138 |
| 450.2 | 408.0 | 4,096.7 | 3,655.4 | 112 |
| 2,882.5 | 6,579.4 | 72,493.5 | 52,515.6 | 138 |
| 20.9 | 44.0 | 447.1 | 389.6 | 115 |
| 11,887.2 | 20,845.1 | 257,489.4 | 138,567.3 | 186 |
| 1,381.5 | 1,192.1 | 11,604.1 | 11,045.5 | 105 |

ington: USGPO, 1923), vol. 9, 1102; vol. 10, 158; aggregate U.S. data from U.S. Department of Commerce, Bureau of the Census, *Census of Manufactures, 1972* (Washington: USGPO, 1976), vol. 1, 3.

*Notes:* a. North Carolina 1 and United States 1 refer to the cotton goods industry in North Carolina and the United States, respectively.

b. North Carolina 2 and United States 2 refer to manufacturing industry generally in North Carolina and the United States.

in scrip and the sale of provisions by company stores at inflated prices served to reduce the actual level of wages and was used most widely in larger cotton mill towns or in communities made up of a number of mill villages, where retail competition might exist.

Given the early instability of the textile labor force, however, mill-owners frequently went beyond these measures, emulating country merchants in the systematic creation of indebtedness and dependence on the part of their workers. For instance, workers entering a mill village would frequently have their wages withheld for a payroll period. Since this period was usually two weeks, newcomers would receive two weeks'

Table 2.6. Growth of the textile labor force, 1880–1919

|  | Textile manufacturing establishments | Wage earners | Wage earners/ establishment |
|---|---|---|---|
| 1880 | 49 | 3,232 | 65 |
| 1890 | 91 | 8,515 | 94 |
| 1900 | 177 | 30,273 | 171 |
| 1909 | 281 | 47,231 | 168 |
| 1919 | 311 | 67,297 | 216 |

*Sources*: U.S. Census Office, *Twelfth Census of the United States, 1900*, vol. 8, pt. 2 (Washington: USGPO, 1902), 660; U.S. Department of Commerce, Bureau of the Census, *Thirteenth Census of the United States, 1919*, vol. 3, (Washington: USGPO, 1921), 268; U.S. Department of Commerce, Bureau of the Census, *Fourteenth Census of the United States, 1920* (Washington: USGPO, 1923), vol. 3, p. 19, vol. 9, p. 1102.

pay at the end of four weeks, by which time they would have accumulated four weeks' debts for supplies provided at the company store at increased "advance" prices. Not surprisingly, given low wages and inflated prices, this system frequently meant instant and persisting debt for millworkers.[87] In addition, lack of education among the workers probably allowed as much latitude in the reckoning of company store accounts as it did in the case of country merchants. In case workers were tempted to leave in spite of (or because of) their indebtedness, millowners instituted a pass system, under which a millworker would not be hired by an employer without the approval of his previous employer. Again, this system was used most frequently in larger communities, where labor market competition might create instability or pressure for wage increases. After 1900, as the textile industry became more stable and began a period of rapid expansion, company stores (which had become the object of worker unrest) were built less often. Nevertheless, many of the stores in the earliest mill villages continued to operate, as did those in the more isolated communities.[88]

Combined with the use of the newest automatic textile machinery, cheap, readily available raw materials, and power, and relatively restricted competition for labor in the early years, the ability to restrict textile wages to levels roughly similar to those in cotton agriculture created a situation uniquely favorable to the generation of high rates of surplus value in North Carolina's textile industry, and since this industry formed the core of the state's industrialization, in state industry generally. Table 2.5 indicates the general results of this situation. In all cases but one, North Carolina held a significant advantage in the production of surplus value over both American industry in general or the American textile industry in particular. Only in 1909 did the North Carolina and national rates in the textile industry converge.

Table 2.7. Capitalization of the cotton goods sector and manufacturing industry, North Carolina, 1880–1919

| | Cotton goods sector | | | Manufacturing industry | | |
|---|---|---|---|---|---|---|
| | Capital ($) | Wage earners | Capital/ wage earner ($) | Capital ($) | Wage earners | Capital/ wage earner ($) |
| 1880 | 2,855,800 | 3,232 | 883.6 | 13,045,639 | 18,109 | 720.4 |
| 1890 | 10,775,134 | 8,515 | 1,265.4 | 32,745,995 | 33,625 | 973.9 |
| 1899 | 33,012,000 | 30,273 | 1,090.5 | 68,283,005 | 72,322 | 944.2 |
| 1904 | 57,413,000 | 36,356 | 1,579.2 | 141,000,639 | 85,339 | 1,652.2 |
| 1909 | 96,993,000 | 47,231 | 2,053.6 | 217,185,588 | 121,473 | 1,787.9 |
| 1919 | 268,322,984 | 67,297 | 3,987.2 | 669,144,096 | 157,659 | 4,244.2 |

*Sources*: U.S. Census Office, Twelfth Census, 660–61; U.S. Census Office, *Report on Manufactures, 1880*, 170; U.S. Bureau of the Census, *Thirteenth Census*, 912; U.S. Bureau of the Census, *Fourteenth Census*, 1102, 1120.

Although the extent to which these high rates of surplus value were translated into profits is not completely clear, the rapid growth of the industry after 1880 suggests that profits and rates of capital accumulation were indeed high. Broadus Mitchell estimates that in the 1890s and early 1900s, when profit rates in the United States as a whole were calculated at 5.83 percent and the average rate of dividends in New England was 7.7 percent, "experience in the Carolinas showed that mills, on all classes of goods made there, could have made a profit of from 10 to 30 percent." [89] In periods of prosperity, with new equipment, cheap labor, and as yet only limited competition in the Southeast, "it was not unusual for mills . . . to make 30 percent to 75 percent profit." [90] According to Melton McLaurin, a 15 to 20 percent per annum return on capital investment was generally expected by southern textile manufacturers during the late nineteenth century. In one case one hundred shares in the Dan River Mills of Danville, Virginia, which expanded from a single factory of 6,000 spindles and 260 looms in 1882 to seven factories with 67,650 spindles and 2,772 looms in 1901, increased their value to 288 shares of preferred and 55 shares of common stock in the same period. If sold at par in 1901, they would have returned 26.7 percent per annum to the investor. [91]

Between 1880 and 1919 the North Carolina textile industry grew rapidly. During this period the number of mills increased by 543 percent, employment by almost 2,000 percent, and the number of wage earners per establishment by over 230 percent. (See table 2.6.) In addition, in 1919 the smaller knit goods sector accounted for 121 mills, $29.4 million in capital, 10,216 workers, and produced goods valued at $29.8 million. In 1919 these two industries together accounted for roughly 49 percent of the state's total of 157,658 wage earners. Only

Table 2.8. Concentration of cotton goods production, North Carolina, 1909–19

| | Number of establishments | | | Number of wage earners | | |
|---|---|---|---|---|---|---|
| | 1909 | 1914 | 1919 | 1909 | 1914 | 1919 |
| **Value of products (in thousands of dollars)** | | | | | | |
| Less than 20 | 10 | 5 | — | 124 | 78 | — |
| 20 to 100 | 78 | 53 | 6 | 3,761 | 2,381 | 134 |
| 100 to 500 ⎱ | | 198 | 113 | ⎱ | ⎱ | 9,299 |
| ⎰ 184 | 184 | | | ⎰ 34,868 | ⎰ 38,697 | |
| 500 to 1,000 ⎰ | | 23 | 107 | ⎰ | ⎰ | 17,269 |
| 1,000+ | 9 | 14 | 85 | 8,478 | 12,547 | 40,595 |
| All classes | 281 | 293 | 311 | 47,231 | 53,708 | 67,297 |
| **Percentage distribution** | | | | | | |
| Less than 20 | 3.6 | 1.7 | — | 0.3 | 0.1 | — |
| 20 to 100 | 27.8 | 18.1 | 1.9 | 8.0 | 4.4 | 1.2 |
| 100 to 500 ⎱ | | 67.6 | 36.3 | ⎱ | ⎱ | 13.8 |
| ⎰ 65.5 | 65.5 | | | ⎰ 73.8 | ⎰ 72.1 | |
| 500 to 1,000 ⎰ | | 7.8 | 34.4 | ⎰ | ⎰ | 25.7 |
| 1000+ | 3.2 | 4.8 | 27.3 | 18.0 | 23.4 | 60.3 |
| All classes | 100.0 | 100.0 | 100.0 | 100.0 | 100.0 | 100.0 |

*Sources:* U.S. Bureau of the Census, *Thirteenth Census*, 905; U.S. Bureau of the Census, *Fourteenth Census*, 604.

the lumber and timber products industry, with 2,762 establishments and 22,728 wage earners (an average of 8 wage earners per establishment), the furniture industry, with 107 establishments and 7,910 wage earners (average 74), and the cigar and cigarette industry, with 18 establishments and 11,683 wage earners (average 649) and $98.6 million in capital, showed a significant presence.[92]

Table 2.7 shows the rapid increase in capital per worker in the cotton goods sector and in manufacturing generally between 1880 and 1919. In 1919 the figure of $3,987.2 representing capital per worker in cotton goods in North Carolina compares reasonably well with the national cotton goods figure of $4,285.4.[93] Much of the difference may be accounted for by the greater capital cost of private power production from coal in the older areas of cotton goods production in New England compared with the ability of the southern mills to purchase cheap hydro electric power from the Southern (later Duke) Power Company.[94] The fact that in 1919 the capitalization of the cotton goods sector lagged behind that of manufacturing generally is probably due to the high capitalization of the cigar and cigarette industry, which was, at $8,440 per wage earner, roughly twice the state average.

| Value of products (in thousands of dollars) | | | Value added by manufacture (in thousands of dollars) | | |
|---|---|---|---|---|---|
| 1909 | 1914 | 1919 | 1909 | 1914 | 1919 |
| 114.2 | 82.1 | — | 30.3 | 13.3 | — |
| 5,237.4 | 3,646.8 | 403.6 | 1,476.9 | 1,013.7 | 155.2 |
| | 47,234.4 | 39,244.4 ⎫ | | | 15,041.7 |
| 51,858.9 | | ⎬ | 17,399.3 ⎫ | 20,093.7 | |
| | 15,643.1 | 77,143.2 ⎭ | ⎬ | | 30,406.0 |
| 15,469.9 | 24,137.3 | 201,577.0 | 5,086.4 ⎭ | 7,284.6 | 85,985.6 |
| 72,680.4 | 90,743.7 | 318,368.2 | 23,992.8 | 28,405.3 | 131,488.5 |
| 0.2 | 0.1 | — | 0.1 | —[a] | — |
| 7.2 | 4.0 | 0.1 | 6.2 | 3.6 | 0.1 |
| | 52.1 | 12.3 ⎫ | | | 11.4 |
| 71.4 | | ⎬ | 72.5 | 70.7 | |
| | 17.2 | 24.2 ⎭ | | | 23.1 |
| 21.3 | 26.6 | 63.3 | 21.2 | 25.6 | 65.3 |
| 100.0 | 100.0 | 100.0 | 100.0 | 100.0 | 100.0 |

a. Less than one tenth of 1 percent.

Despite the fact that the industry remained predominantly competitive, dispersed, and small-scale, the trend toward concentration of capital is evident. (See Table 2.8.) Between 1909 and 1919 the number of mills producing goods worth one million dollars or more increased from nine to eighty-five, or from 3.2 percent to 27.3 percent of all mills. By 1919 these mills accounted for 60.3 percent of all textile wage earners (18.0 percent in 1909), and 63.3 percent of the value of all textile products (21.3 percent in 1909). Of ninety-eight establishments with two hundred fifty-one or more wage earners, sixty-six were in the cotton or knit goods sectors, as were seven of thirteen with over one thousand wage earners.[95] Two hundred and ninety-six (95.2 percent) of 311 cotton mills were owned by corporations that controlled 98.1 percent of the industry's wage earners (66,045) and 98.3 percent of the value of the industry's products ($313 million).[96] These tendencies—toward concentration of capital and corporate control—appear to directly contradict Dwight Billings's assertion that North Carolina was a noncapitalist social formation.

As late as the 1920s and 1930s the ideology of the continuing cotton mill campaign remained important, however, and continued to empha-

Table 2.9. Size of the manufacturing labor force and average establishment labor force, North Carolina, 1880–1919

|  | Population | Wage earners in manufacturing | Percent | Establishments | Wage earners/ establishment |
|---|---|---|---|---|---|
| 1880 | 1,399,750 | 18,109 | 1.3 | 3,802 | 5 |
| 1890 | 1,617,947 | 33,625 | 2.1 | 3,667 | 9 |
| 1899 | 1,893,810 (1900) | 72,322 | 3.7 | 3,465 | 21 |
| 1909 | 2,206,287 (1910) | 121,473 | 5.5 | 4,931 | 25 |
| 1919 | 2,559,123 (1920) | 157,659 | 6.2 | 5,999 | 26 |

*Sources*: See table 2.6.

size the social and economic benefits of locally owned, small-scale production for local communities of "proprietors." While many cotton mills continued to be organized initially on a scale that would lend some credence to the social interpretation of textile industrialization, by 1929 the central facts about the industry were its growth and concentration. By this time, textile production was a large-scale, highly capitalized, corporation-dominated industry, competing aggressively at the national and international levels for markets and capital. With levels of capitalization roughly equal to those in the U.S. textile industry as a whole, the favorable position of southern capital with respect to wages, the length of the working day, and the availability of labor, raw materials, and power permitted production based on above-average rates of surplus value and higher than average rates of profit.

Despite this form of production, and despite the rapid expansion of the textile labor force, textile-based industrialization and the process of class formation that accompanied it did not depart significantly from the social and geographical patterns set in the early years of the cotton mill campaign. The North Carolina economy in the 1920s was still overwhelmingly agricultural. To begin with, the state's supply of proletarianized tenant farmers, who formed a large reserve army of labor for the growth of textile production, did not reach its peak in either absolute or percentage terms until the 1920s. In 1919 North Carolina's manufacturing labor force numbered 157,659, or 6.2 percent of the state's population of approximately two and a half million. In addition, the average number of wage earners per manufacturing establishment in the state as a whole was only twenty-six, despite the concentration of production in the textile and tobacco industries (see table 2.9), and a large proportion of the state's manufacturing wage earners continued to dwell in isolated rural areas. In 1919 only 862 of the state's 5,999 manufacturing establishments and 42,216 of its 157,659 wage earners were situated in cities, and of the 98 largest establishments (with 251 or more wage earners each) only 23 were located in cities.[97] In 1910 only 6.8 percent of North Carolina's population lived in cities over 10,000, and only 14.4 percent lived in urban areas of over 2,500 people.[98] In 1920 22.2 percent (568,807) of the population was classified by the Census Bureau as "rural nonfarm," that is, as living outside urban areas, but with their major source of income deriving from nonagricultural pursuits. By 1930 these figures would be 24.1 percent, or 763,209.[99]

Continuities in the size of the reserve army of labor available for the growth of textile production and in the manner in which a textile working class was formed and integrated into industrial life would continue to form the basis of the state's above-average rates of exploitation and surplus profits. They would also seriously impede the extent to which the working class could organize in opposition to these high rates of exploitation.

### Textile industrialization and class conflict

The extent of class conflict in the southern textile industry is frequently minimized. For Broadus Mitchell the philanthropic and communitarian aspects of the cotton mill campaign ruled out the possibility of class conflict so long as the industry was controlled by southerners. George Mitchell largely follows this emphasis, dating the beginnings of significant union activity in the textile industry after World War I. Harry Boyte does not consider union activity and worker unrest to be of significant proportions until the campaigns of 1929 and 1934, when the introduction of large amounts of northern capital, personnel, and management principles began to disrupt the paternalistic social and ideological control of the southern millowners. C. Vann Woodward, claiming that too much attention has been given to explanations of the absence of union activity in the textile industry, investigates instead the neglected history of unions in other southern crafts and industries.[100]

The processes of textile industrialization, class formation, and exploitation in the late nineteenth century did generate class conflict, however. Although many of the struggles of this period were of a defensive nature, involving resistance to the process of proletarianization rather than efforts to change the process of industrial production itself, they were not insignificant. In certain areas they involved textile workers, indicating that organizations of workers and others could, under certain circumstances, pose a significant political threat. These early class struggles also gave millowners a chance to experiment with and refine a number of antiunion tactics that would become important in later periods of more intense and open class struggle.

The first major challenge to the textile industry by organized labor occurred in the mid–1880s in the context of generally depressed conditions in the United States as a whole.[101] The successful strike by the Knights of Labor against Jay Gould's Southwestern Railroad system and the rapid growth in the Knights' membership in the southern states —from 475 in 1879 to 21,008, in 487 locals, in 1886—naturally spilled over into an attempt to organize the rapidly growing textile industry in which depressed conditions and wage cuts in 1884 and 1885 had begun to generate unrest.[102]

In 1884 the Knights established a statewide organization in North Carolina, comprised of a number of locals established in Charlotte, Raleigh, and Durham, and managed to elect State Master Workman John Nicholls as U.S. Congressman for the Fourth District. With a growing number of locals in the state, the Knights were able to obtain the passage of a bill creating a state Bureau of Labor. Locals grew in a few textile areas, and in several cases, they had large numbers of textile operatives as members, although the main strength of the Knights in North Carolina consisted of artisans and farmers, who were waging a defensive struggle against the effects of proletarianization in both the crafts and in agriculture. This was especially the case among the most skilled workers who were increasingly threatened by the combination of automation, proletarianization, and family labor. W. A. Fogelman, master workman of Local 8293, thought his local was strong enough to shut down the mills of owners who discriminated against union members. It seems that the Knights led only a single strike in North Carolina—in 1877 at Burlington in Alamance County, the state's oldest textile center. They participated in other forms of political activity, however, publicizing issues in the textile towns and defending members against attacks by the millowners. In addition, realizing the importance of state legislation and judicial decisions in agricultural reorganization and proletarianization, the Knights participated in electoral politics, especially in 1886, when workers' candidates ran for office across the state, with notable successes where the agrarian/textile vote was strong. Their lobbying achieved Ten Hour and Child Labor laws, both of which were later lost again. North Carolina's State Bureau of Labor was the only one of its kind in the South until the twentieth century.

In 1888, stimulated by the successes of the previous two years, the Knights in Alamance decided to fight the elections of that year with their own statewide platform, in support of the National Union Labor party at the national level. By this time the Knights had become a serious threat to political control at the state level. The state Democratic party responded to this defection with an appeal to white supremacy, a campaign associating the Knights with Republicanism and warning of the dangers of the domination of the state by Negroes, northerners, and "foreign ideas." In a context of widespread intimidation, the Knights' candidates were defeated across the state. Democratic majorities were smallest in such areas as Alamance, however, where the textile industry was most thoroughly established, where workers' ties to the land were most distant, and where the possibility of intimidation based on isolation was smallest.

A similar pattern occurred in South Carolina, and also in the more urbanized areas of Georgia, such as Columbus, Atlanta, and Augusta, where textile workers were in a less vulnerable position with respect to the millowners. The South's most militant local, 5030 in Augusta, conducted a long strike in 1886 to regain 1884 wage levels (which had been lost in the intervening depression), the abolition of the pass system, an end to antiunion discrimination, and restrictions on the use of child labor. In response, the millowners formed the Southern Manufacturers' Association (SMA) to coordinate bargaining and other actions and to resist the pressure of local merchants and retailers suffering from the decline in trade associated with the strike. After threatening a complete shutdown, the SMA began a three-month campaign of attrition, which gradually forced merchants to stop giving credit to the workers and involved large-scale evictions from mill houses and the use of strikebreakers. Because of the rapid exhaustion of the organization's strike fund, the Knights' national organization stepped in to stop the strike, and, after that, some concessions were made by the millowners. The pass system was relaxed to some extent, union members were not discriminated against when the mills reopened, and, although its practical power remained limited, the workers' organization gained tacit recognition. Nevertheless, despite the fact that the strike was the first major militant challenge to the southern millowners and raised the issues of hours, wages, child labor, and other conditions that would form the basis for later attempts at organization, the workers' political and economic dependence was little changed.

The second major challenge in the textile industry before World War I occurred in the late 1890s.[103] In 1895 the Socialist wing of the American Federation of Labor (AFL), seeking a more significant political role than had been possible under the Federation, split to form the Socialist Trades and Labor Alliance (STLA).[104] As a result of the ensuing competition for the allegiance of northern textile workers, the AFL-affiliated National Union of Textile Workers (NUTW) embarked upon a campaign to organize the southern mills. At the same time, expanded investment in larger, electrical-powered mills during the 1890s began to create shortages of both skilled and unskilled labor in the North Carolina textile industry. The inability to attract imported labor finally led to a concerted effort to recruit labor from within the southern states. In part this involved the expansion of the labor market to include areas other than the Piedmont, especially the mountain areas in western North Carolina and neighboring Tennessee. It also led to a more concerted effort by the courts of North Carolina to enforce the legal definition of tenant as laborer, legislated in 1876–77.[105] Conditions within the textile region strengthened the hand of the NUTW in its efforts to organize the southern mills but also strengthened the resolve of the millowners to resist.[106]

The major period of NUTW progress in the South took place after 1898, when the AFL sent four organizers, two of whom were textile workers, to organize the textile mills. Using the limitation of child labor as its major objective, the NUTW claimed over five thousand members in the textile industry by 1900, mostly in Georgia and the Carolinas. Attempts to achieve child legislation failed, however. In North Carolina owners avoided legislation by voluntarily agreeing to observe a sixty-six-hour week, to refuse to hire children under twelve years of age during school term, and to refuse at all times to hire children under ten. This self-imposed restriction could not be enforced, however, and it was rarely observed.[107]

Before 1900 there were no real attempts to destroy NUTW locals directly. Southern millowners, who were interested in maintaining production levels, preferred to use more subtle methods, linking the NUTW with efforts by northern manufacturers to retard the South's competitive progress or with aid for the black race. In addition, before 1900 the union's strikes were led mostly by skilled workers who were most immune to mill village sanctions, and whose support from unskilled workers was easily broken by owners who took measures such as evictions, the blacklist, and credit cutoffs. Owners found it relatively easy to split the strike force under these conditions.[108]

As the labor situation tightened in 1900, however, the NUTW took the offensive in an effort to achieve the ten-hour day. In addition, in 1900 the Boxer rebellion in China disrupted a substantial part of the foreign market for southern cotton broadcloth. Decreased exports led to calls for wage reductions. Opposition to the union's hours demands was led by the Southern Cotton Spinners' Association, formed in 1897 and comprising virtually all of the South's textile manufacturers.

Conflict emerged in the mills owned by the Cone family outside Greensboro, North Carolina. On learning that over one hundred fifty workers had joined an NUTW local, Caesar Cone closed his factory, post office, and company store, locking out the entire labor force, and began evictions, announcing that he had moved from Baltimore in order to avoid unionization and would not tolerate unions in North Carolina. As the local membership swelled to two hundred fifty, the union's strike fund began to run out, and the mills quickly reopened with nonunion labor and a "yellow dog" contract. The strike rapidly disintegrated as the Cones tightened their local control. Migrating strikers were blacklisted in Durham and other towns in the area.[109]

During the summer of 1900 strikes and lockouts occurred across North Carolina in as many as thirty mills.[110] This time Alamance County was again the most important center of strike activity. Conflict emerged at Haw River, outside Burlington, after the dismissal of a female worker for reasons unrelated to the NUTW. The resulting strike was interpreted as a direct challenge to the management, which embarked upon a townwide lockout against union members. Nearly four thousand workers refused to return to the mills under a yellow dog contract. Again, evictions, blacklisting, and the importation of strikebreakers were used. The Alamance local was forced to capitulate when the national organization withdrew support, completely shattering the union's strength in the state.[111]

Any possibility of a resurgence by organized labor disappeared as the Southern Cotton Spinners' Association conducted a lockout against the union in 1901 in Danville, Virginia, in order to prevent the union's spread back into North Carolina.[112] In 1901 and 1902 similar coordinated action broke strikes by the newly formed United Textile Workers of America (UTWA) in Columbia, South Carolina, and Augusta, Georgia.[113] This series of defeats persuaded the northern locals, which dominated the UTWA, that attempts to organize the southern mills were futile. In 1903 the UTWA adopted more stringent financial rules, voting to expel locals that were delinquent in their payments of dues. This action virtually eliminated the remaining locals in the southern states.

Workers' struggles in the late nineteenth century in North Carolina were thus largely defensive struggles against the effects of proletarianization in both agriculture and industry. For the small farmers who formed part of the basis of the Knights of Labor, the issues of the day were the spread of the credit system, indebtedness, the concentration of landownership, and the threat of proletarianization in either agriculture or industry. For those skilled textile workers who joined the Knights and provided the leadership for the unionization efforts by the NUTW and UTWA, the issues were the gradual reduction of wage rates, and, increasingly, the loss of their jobs as mechanization deskilled the production process, opening the industry to large numbers of rural, unskilled female and child workers. Nevertheless, despite the fact that their interests were in many ways divergent, and despite the adverse social conditions in which they were forced to operate, alliances between skilled and unskilled workers in the textile industry to improve mill conditions and reduce rates of exploitation did take place.

For Melton McLaurin, the involvement of the organizations in political activities was a tactical error and served to divert attention and resources away from the more vital need to establish strong business unions in the South.[114] In the context of proletarianization and deskilling, however, political involvement at the local and state levels was a perfectly rational response. Only the capture of political power at these levels could remove the legislative and judicial basis of agricultural reorganization and proletarianization or limit the devastating effects of family labor on the textile labor force by restricting the exploitation of female and child labor and the length of the working day.

If textile workers failed to develop the organizational basis from which to effectively oppose the millowners, it was not as a result of tactical errors but because of the political and social weakness of the working class itself in the context in which it was being formed. The same factors that served to depress wage levels—the size of the textile labor force (1.6 percent of the state's population in 1900: see tables 2.6 and 2.9), its social and geographic isolation, the size of the available pool of surplus labor, and the social and political dependence of millworkers on the textile mill village—also served to limit the extent of effective organization by the textile working class. Only in a few more urbanized manufacturing centers such as Burlington, with larger mills, larger concentrations of literate, skilled workers, greater competition in the labor market, and less complete dependence on millowners, could workers' organizations prove effective even in the short term. The process of textile industrialization itself, however, which involved more widespread use of automatic machines, would increasingly undermine the bargaining power of these skilled workers.

When strikes did occur, the institution of the mill village allowed millowners as a regional group to develop a battery of devices with which to counterattack—evictions, the lockout, the blacklist, the use of imported strikebreakers, as well as the more generally used southern strategy of evoking white supremacy and the threat of a black textile working class. As North Carolina's textile-based industrialization continued into the twentieth century, there would be numerous changes in the tactics used to avert the threat of unionization. Textile industrialization, and later additions to the textile base, would nevertheless continue to follow the patterns of rural isolation and social control established during these early years.

# 3

# The Relocation of the
# Cotton Textile Industry, 1895–1939:
# The Political Economy of the "Stretch-Out"

During the 1920s and 1930s the difference between rates of exploitation in the Carolina Piedmont and in New England was the crucial factor in the relocation of the cotton textile industry to the South. By 1939 there were 19.3 million cotton spindles in the southern states (6.5 million in North Carolina alone), compared with 9.7 million in the whole of New England.[1] Related parts of the textile industry, such as the dyeing and finishing of cotton cloth and the production of rayon and other synthetic goods, were also expanding rapidly in the South.

For the ailing New England cotton textile industry in the depressed conditions of the 1920s, relocation permitted a significant increase in the production of absolute and relative surplus value through increases in the number of daily hours worked, the expanded exploitation of women and children, reduced wage levels, and increases in the intensity of work. In addition, it also ushered in a period of class conflict as intense and violent as any in American working class history.

For purposes of exposition, portions of this chapter will include comparisons of factors conducive to and constraining the increased production of surplus value in Massachusetts and North Carolina. It should be kept in mind, however, that although Massachusetts was the most important New England cotton textile producing state, there was not a closed process of capital migration between the two states, and social and economic conditions in these states were not replicated exactly throughout their respective regions. During this period, textile capital left not only Massachusetts, but all the New England states, as well as others in the Northeast, and it moved not only to North Carolina, but also to other states in the Southeast. By using North Carolina and Massachusetts as case studies, this chapter attempts to highlight the more general dynamics of the process of relocation. Massachusetts is a particularly useful state for these purposes, in the sense that it was severely affected by southern competition, and a significant effort was made to document and study the processes of regional competition and relocation.

## The production of surplus value in the textile industry

In most industries the process of technical change usually takes an incremental and cumulative form, in which major technical innovations occur relatively infrequently. Consequently, in real historical situations, it is often difficult to separate technical factors in the production of surplus value (and particularly in increases in the rate of surplus value) from other nontechnical components, such as changes in the intensity of labor. Frequently, they occur together and may be related. Nevertheless, it seems to be generally accepted that one of the features that distinguishes the development of the textile industry from that of other industries is the relatively limited contribution made to this development by changes in textile technology.[2]

After the introduction of the power loom in the 1780s, it took more than a century for the industry to deal with the problems introduced by the new machinery: the frequent breaking of warp threads, which required that the machine be watched closely and stopped frequently to limit the production of defective cloth, and the manual removal and replacement of empty bobbins. Even though engineering improvements between the 1780s and 1890s increased loom speeds and their smoothness of operation, these improved characteristics set limits on the number of looms that could be operated by a single weaver, giving the industry its above-average labor intensity.

In the 1890s these limits on productivity were broken to some extent with the introduction of, and gradual improvements in, ring spinning and the Northrup battery loom. The latter automatically ejected and replaced empty bobbins and was later further improved to stop automatically when a warp broke. This permitted an important increase in the number of looms that could be operated by a single weaver. It also improved the speed and continuity of machine operation, reduced the amount of faulty cloth produced, and reduced the number of skilled workers in the industry. By the late 1940s high-speed automatic looms were 25 percent faster than the originals and automatic shifting of shuttles had been introduced, allowing the automated production of multicolored cloth. Nevertheless, the textile industry remained relatively labor-intensive. In 1947 wage costs still represented 21.2 percent of the total value of products in cotton manufacturing, compared, for instance, with 13.5 percent in chemicals and 7.8 percent in rubber.[3]

Since the 1960s a third important stage in the development of textile technology may have emerged.[4] A variety of innovations (including the increased use of computerization) originating in Eastern Europe, Italy, Japan, and West Germany have increased machine speeds, allowed several operations to be combined, reduced the need for floor space, and reduced labor requirements. Some students of the industry have suggested that this period of relatively rapid capital investment is a qualitatively new stage in the industry's development and represents a concerted effort on the part of textile capital to shake out superfluous labor and to deskill and automate the labor process.[5]

Textile production has remained relatively labor intensive, however. Between 1967 and 1977 the technical composition of capital in the American textile industry rose from $12,400 per employee to $15,500 (current dollars). The figure for all manufacturing in the United States in 1977 was $21,500, and for a capital-intensive industry such as chemicals, $70,300. Between 1963 and 1977 value added per production worker in textiles increased by 167 percent, from $7,898 to $21,063, a slightly lower rate of increase than the 172 percent average for manufacturing as a whole ($15,703 in 1963; $42,741 in 1977). Textile wage costs in 1977 were 15.3 percent of the total value of shipments, compared with a manufacturing average of 11.6 percent and 6.3 percent for chemicals.[6]

The relative technological stability of the textile industry has had a number of implications for the way in which the industry has developed. Most important for the purpose of this book, it has limited the range of options open to textile capitalists in the face of competitive pressure. At least in those long periods in between major innovations, capital accumulation by itself will not generate significant increases in the production of surplus value to the extent that it will in other industries. Traditionally, therefore, the textile industry has had great difficulty competing for labor power with other more productive capitals. In addition, it has been much more difficult for textile capital to erect barriers to entry into the industry and to eliminate existing competition. In conditions of relative technological stability it is possible for mills operating with old machinery assembled at low cost to compensate for the age of their machinery by sidestepping the costs of depreciation and obsolescence and to remain competitive for relatively long periods of time.

The concentration of capital in the textile industry is therefore much less developed than in other industries, even though individual firms have been able to achieve a relatively significant degree of market power in some specific product lines, such as in carpets. In 1977, in only thirteen of thirty subsectors of textile production did the four largest companies account for more than 40 percent of the value of shipments; in only four of these did they account for over 60 percent; and in only ten of thirty did the top eight companies account for over 60 percent. This compares, for instance, with 93 percent for the top four manufacturers in motor vehicles, 59 percent in aircraft, and 78 percent in organic fibers.[7] In 1935, during the period discussed in this chapter, the four largest producers of cotton textiles controlled only 8 percent of the total value of their industry's product, and the largest eight firms controlled only 14–20 percent.[8]

Lacking the ability to increase surplus value significantly by means of capital accumulation, the textile industry has been forced to find alternative means of achieving greater surplus value. Characteristically, this has meant that the industry has traditionally tried to find sources of cheap labor power and ways to extend the working day and to intensify labor. As New England experienced urbanization, industrialization, and unionization, the industry's early reliance on New England farm girls was replaced partly by workers from rural Quebec, and partly by newly arrived immigrant workers from Europe. Later, as labor market competition and unionization drives dried up even these sources, the industry began its process of migration to the Southeast, where labor was abundant and cheap. The southern working class was not only rural and impoverished, but it was also relatively untouched by working class political organizations such as unions. Textile capitalists were therefore able to pay wages significantly lower than those in New England, extend the length of the working day, and intensify the labor process with relatively little worker resistance in a union-free environment. The fact that workers in the Southeast were for the most part unskilled mattered little since the sectors of the industry that moved first were those producing coarser, lower count cloth—much of it for export—using the newer automatic machinery. Later, after improvements associated with ring spinning and in finer weaving operations, the South's competitive advantage became attractive for virtually all sectors of the textile industry.

*Early relocation to the South,*
*1895–99*

It is important to note at the outset that relocation, or at least the most vigorous and statistically obvious periods of relocation, coincided with periods of depression, when competition was most intense. It should be borne in mind that, as a result of this correlation, liquidation of capital was also taking place. Although much of the capital that was liquidated in New England found its way to the southern states and elsewhere, a large and possibly greater amount did not. Finally, a major part of the growth that took place in the southern states resulted from the competitive advantages enjoyed by corporations that had originated in the South.

The view that the South should compete aggressively for textile manufacturing capital had important antebellum roots that reemerged quickly after the war and was reinforced in the middle and late 1870s. Layoffs, reduced production, wage cuts resulting from the Panic of 1873, and the threat of a strike in Fall River, Massachusetts, encouraged southern propagandists in their efforts to publicize their region's competitive advantages.[9]

The first period of actual relocation began in the late 1890s, in response to the depression that followed the Panic of 1893, and that continued, with some interruptions, until the turn of the century. While mills in New England were forced to cut production, the southern mills apparently continued unaffected. Stable foreign markets for the cheap coarse cotton cloth produced in the southern states, the continuing flow of impoverished croppers and farmers into the mill villages, and the ability of textile millowners to "squeeze" their labor with relatively little internal or external interference allowed mills in North Carolina to operate at full capacity during the depressed period.[10]

The development and marketing of ring spinning and the automatic Northrup battery loom in the 1890s probably served to increase the pressure to relocate. In addition to allowing an increase in work loads, the new machinery also permitted the use of cheaper, less skilled female and child labor. In some New England states the exploitation of female and child labor had come under legislative control. As early as 1874 in Massachusetts, for instance, the state legislature had set a daily limit of ten hours on the labor of women and children. During the 1890s and early 1900s agitation by "progressive" high wage employers, unionists, and socialists threatened (and during the period 1905–11 actually achieved) further restrictions. As a result, New England cotton manufacturers did not greet the new machinery enthusiastically.[11]

Southern manufacturers were under no such restrictions, however, and could make full use of the opportunities for deskilling and work intensification afforded by the new machinery. Northern manufacturers were forced to respond to the new levels of productivity achieved in the southern states, but, unless they relocated themselves, they were unable to use the new machinery at its optimum level of effectiveness. Even with this new machinery New England manufacturers had lost ground in comparison with the competitive position they had previously enjoyed. New capital expenditures could only be fully justified in conjunction with relocation.

Southern industrial propagandists were not slow in emphasizing this and related points. During the 1890s they became much more explicit in their views that southern growth, at the expense of the New England cotton industry, was inevitable given the major differences in production conditions, and that it was futile for New England manufacturers to struggle against the economic "facts of life." In 1895 Richard Edmonds, one of the most insistent of the southern industry boosters, tried to persuade the New England Cotton Manufacturers' Association that it would be far better to foster the southward migration of the industry than let it be strangled by southern competition. According to Edmonds, New England cotton manufacturers could not possibly overcome the major southern advantage—a large and at that point mostly untapped supply of poor white workers, who were "docile, not given to strikes, and, as a class, [were] anxious to find work and willing to accept much lower wages than northern operatives." [12]

By this time a significant body of opinion in New England appeared to agree with Edmonds's analysis. The Arkwright Club summed up a study of the situation by concluding that

> labor is cheaper in the South; that the hours of labor are longer, and that there is neither any of the restrictive legislation urged among us by the labor unions, and very generally placed on our statute-books, not any prospect even of an early agitation in behalf of such restrictions. So far as we can learn, there is no disposition to organize labor unions. [13]

To make the best of a bad situation, the *Boston Manufacturers' Gazette* thought that it might be possible to establish a new regional division of labor upon which renewed growth of cotton goods production might be based. The *Gazette* recommended the transfer of all coarse cotton goods production to the Carolina Piedmont to take advantage of the region's cheap unskilled labor. It suggested that obsolescent coarse goods machinery in New England should be replaced with newer, more efficient equipment suitable for the production of finer quality fabrics that were as yet largely untouched by southern competition. [14]

In the years following 1895, as a result of depressed conditions and the new possibilities opened up by the new machinery, millions of dollars of northern capital moved southward in search of wage levels and a working day estimated by the Arkwright Club to be 40 percent lower and 24 percent longer, respectively, than those in New England. In January 1895 representatives of three of the largest corporations in Lowell, Massachusetts, appeared before the Massachusetts legislature to amend their corporate charters so as to allow them to do business in the South. During this period the Cone family opened a number of mills in and around Greensboro, and the Camerons of Pennsylvania established a mill at Weldon. As a result of relocation and local capital accumulation, the number of spindles in the southern states increased by 151 percent between 1890 and 1907, compared with 22 percent for the same period in the North.[15]

Finally, since northern cotton manufacturers relocated to the southern states in order to maximize the production of surplus value, their external investment did not result in any fundamental changes in the social relations of production in the southern textile industry. Relocation to the Carolina Piedmont allowed northern manufacturers to reestablish the complex of paternalism and mill village social control that had provided the basis of early textile growth in New England but had become increasingly difficult to maintain as the region became industrialized. New external capital therefore replicated existing southern practice.

The establishment of Roanoke Rapids in Halifax County, North Carolina, provides an example of this replication. The town, which did not exist before its mills, was named by J. A. Chanler, a New York millionaire and heir to the Astor fortune, who built the first mill there in 1895. A second mill was established in 1896, and in 1897 the two mill villages were incorporated as Roanoke Rapids. The mills' owners provided all the town's services, including police, churches, and a baseball team, set aside land where workers could grow crops to supplement their incomes, and built a canning and storage facility, a hospital, a playground, and a library. The mills were directly integrated into the local economy, in part because millowners also purchased substantial tracts of nearby land to be rented to black tenants. Rent was paid in the form of cotton to be used in the mills.[16]

*The cotton textile industry*
*moves South, 1921–39*

The large-scale relocation of the cotton textile industry to the Carolina Piedmont began in the mid–1920s. By the end of the 1930s this area had replaced New England as the center of American cotton textile production. For the purposes of this discussion, the period is important not only because of the magnitude of the relocation that took place, but because it illustrates in a relatively unambiguous way the developing relationship between the North Carolina economy and the competitive growth process in labor-intensive industries such as cotton textiles. As we have already noted, the period of relocation beginning after the Panic of 1893 involved a measure of technological progress as well as efforts to increase the rate of surplus value by intensifying work, deskilling, and extending the working day. In contrast, the period begin-

Table 3.1. Expansion of cotton manufacturing, United States, 1914–19

|  | 1914 | 1919 | Percentage change |
|---|---|---|---|
| Number of establishments | 1,328 | 1,496 | +12.7 |
| Capital ($) | 899,764,682 | 1,914,191,506 | +113.0 |
| Wage earners | 393,404 | 446,852 | +13.6 |
| Capital/workers ($) | 2,287.1 | 4,285.3 | +87.4 |
| Wage bill ($) | 152,422,599 | 368,723,712 | +142.0 |
| Average wage ($) | 387 | 825 | +113.0 |
| Value of products ($) | 701,300,933 | 2,195,565,881 | +213.0 |
| Value added ($) | 257,778,418 | 880,664,339 | +242.0 |

*Sources*: U.S. Bureau of the Census, *Fourteenth Census*, 158.

ning in the depression of the mid–1920s illustrates much more clearly the relationship between relocation and these nontechnical aspects of exploitation.

For the cotton textile industry the Great Depression began at least half a decade earlier than it did for the American economy as a whole. Severe business downturns in 1920 and 1921 and in 1924 inaugurated a decade and a half-long period of low returns and deficits. In eight of the fourteen years from 1926 to 1939—1926, 1928, 1930, 1931, 1932, 1934, 1935, 1938—the number of cotton manufacturing corporations reporting net deficits to the Bureau of Internal Revenue exceeded the number reporting net income. In 1930, 1931, 1932, 1935, and 1938 the majority reporting deficits was a large one. Between 1923 and 1930 the average market value of twenty-five textile shares fell from $144.50 to $71.48. In 1929 less than half of the southern cotton mills paid dividends, and there were many bankruptcies.[17]

Several factors contributed to the textile sickness of the 1920s— emerging foreign competition, the difficulty of regulating the relationship between raw cotton prices and patterns of demand for cotton goods, the dominance of the commission agent in the industry's fragmented structure of production and marketing, and the most important fashion change of the 1920s, the rising hemline. Most fundamental, however, was the rapid and large-scale expansion experienced by the industry during World War I. Between 1914 and 1919 the stock of capital in the cotton textile industry increased by 113 percent, the number of establishments by 12.7 percent, the number of wage earners by 13.6 percent, the value of the industry's products by 213 percent, and value added by 242 percent (see table 3.1).

With the collapse of high levels of wartime and immediate postwar demand in 1920 and 1921, the industry found itself faced with a major crisis of overproduction and excess capacity. Wartime expansion had taken place entirely within the industry's existing structure. A large increase in the dollar value of capital per worker was caused not by technological improvements but by the addition of more machines and the use of wage increases to persuade workers to accept an expansion of their work loads and increases in the speed of production; this increase was only partially offset by the introduction of shift work. At the same time large-scale expansion did not lead to any changes in the predominantly unrationalized, small-scale, and competitive nature of the industry. Faced with excess capacity and shrinking markets after 1920–21, and especially after 1924, cotton textile firms were forced to respond by finding ways to reduce labor costs, the largest single item in the cost of production.

Under normal circumstances the industry has only a limited range of options to achieve such a readjustment in production. Under conditions of technological stability, capital accumulation was not a means to reduce production costs and increase the rate of exploitation: rather, survival in cotton textiles during the period 1924–39 was dependent on the ability to increase the production of surplus value by other means. Firms were forced to persuade, cajole, or coerce workers to accept larger work loads, to work more intensively, and to produce more for less.[18]

Since cotton goods production does not involve an assembly line, speeding up the production process is not a permanently available method of work intensification. When the speedup does occur in textiles, it is usually as a result of improvements in the manufacture of textile machinery. Consequently, the intensification of work characteristically takes the form of the "stretch-out," in which workers are required to operate and supervise more machines without corresponding wage increases. In the 1920s and 1930s the ability to implement the stretch-out was the key to survival in the cotton textile industry.

The depression of the 1920s and, arising out of it, the necessity for major cost reductions, finally put an end to the temporary resistance of the New England industry to southern competition. During the earlier period New England firms had followed the advice of the *Boston Manufacturers' Gazette* by shifting production toward finer products that less skilled southern workers and the South's automatic machinery were unable to produce competitively. By 1911 virtually all of the nation's coarse cotton goods were produced in the southern states, forcing a difficult period of class conflict and economic readjustment on areas of early textile industrialization in New England.[19]

Such a strategy had provided some temporary respite from southern competition. In the long term, however, this adaptation itself only served to intensify competition within New England as an increasing number of mills squeezed into the production of an increasingly restricted range of goods. When wartime expansion turned into postwar depression, the need for cutting expenses caused the Carolina Piedmont's attractive production costs to reemerge as a topic of discussion.

The southern states continued to generate propaganda extolling the competitive advantages available in their region. As the stakes involved in southern industrialization grew, however, banks, power companies, and other major beneficiaries of industrialization began to play a larger role, and the southern publicity campaigns became more sophisticated and organized. The southern campaign in the 1920s centered on the supposed loyalty and simple needs of the southern working class, the benevolent authority of the millowners, and the friendly personal relations between the two in the southern mill communities. In combination, these factors were said to demonstrate the viability in the South of a paternalistic form of social control that had become impossible in New England, and one that assured high profits. In some cases, the regional contrast between loyalty and protest, or between low and high wages, was explained in racial or ethnic terms — that is, in terms of the contrast between the South's native-born, white, Anglo-Saxon, rural working class and New England's more volatile racial and ethnic mix. The impact on production costs of protective labor legislation, the supposed lower cost of living in the South, and southern tax laws designed to be favorable to capital were also important themes in this period.[20]

Like the southern states generally, North Carolina's advantage with respect to the production of surplus value was threefold: first, the state's continuing and increasing availability of a large supply of cheap surplus labor and only limited labor market competition; second, a cotton mill working class that was weak, largely unorganized, and isolated, with few powerful political allies; and third, the relative absence of legislation restricting the conditions under which labor could be exploited.

The size of the industrial reserve army in North Carolina has already been partially documented. It is worthwhile at this point, however, to present some comparisons between North Carolina and Massachusetts and to document more fully movements in North Carolina's supply of surplus labor for the interwar period. Table 3.2 compares the size of the urban and rural populations in the two states in 1920 and 1930 and demonstrates North Carolina's large advantage in the ability to recruit rural labor.

Within these aggregate figures, it should be further stressed that North Carolina's rural population was far more available for industrial work than was its Massachusetts counterpart. For one thing, the transition between farm and mill was far easier in North Carolina, as a result of the predominantly rural location of the state's textile industry. As

Table 3.2. Urban and rural populations: North Carolina and Massachusetts, 1920 and 1930

| | | Urban | Rural | Percentage urban |
|---|---|---|---|---|
| 1920 | Massachusetts | 3,650,258 | 202,108 | 94.8 |
| | North Carolina | 490,370 | 2,068,753 | 19.2 |
| 1930 | Massachusetts | 3,831,423 | 418,188 | 90.2 |
| | North Carolina | 809,847 | 2,360,429 | 25.5 |

*Sources*: U.S. Bureau of Foreign and Domestic Commerce, *Statistical Abstract of the United States, 1931* (Washington: USGPO, 1931), 48.

early as 1900 in Massachusetts, a large majority of the population was crowded into thirty-three incorporated cities, twenty-five of which had populations of 25,000 or more.[21]

More important were differences in the structure of tenure in the states' respective agricultural sectors. In 1930 in the whole of New England (Maine, New Hampshire, Vermont, Massachusetts, Rhode Island, and Connecticut) only 7,885 (6.3 percent) of a total of 124,925 farms were operated by tenants. In contrast, in North Carolina in 1920, 117,459 (43.5 percent) of farm operators were potentially or actually proletarianized tenants and croppers. In 1930 the figures were 137,615 and 49.2 percent, respectively. In the four major southern textile manufacturing states (Alabama, North Carolina, South Carolina, and Georgia), almost 600,000 farms were operated by tenant and cropper families.[22]

Of North Carolina's 117,459 tenants and croppers in 1920, 63,542 were white and were working under the conditions set by the 1876–77 Landlord-Tenant Act on relatively unproductive land outside the Black Belt areas. This group provided the most accessible source of cheap surplus labor during the periodic crises that afflicted cotton agriculture. It was such a crisis that provided a part of the basis of the relocation and expansion in southern cotton textile production in the 1920s. Like the textile industry, cotton agriculture experienced relative prosperity during World War I and the immediate postwar period. High cotton prices stimulated an expansion in the amount of land under cotton cultivation, as well as a limited mechanization. As demand declined in 1920–21, however, cotton prices collapsed dramatically. Between April and December 1920 the New Orleans price for cotton fell from 41.75 cents a pound to 13.50 cents. This price collapse and the subsequent movement of farmers into the mill villages, together with an almost simultaneous fall in demand for manufactured cotton goods, quickly solved the wartime problem of a tight labor market. As local accumulation and relocation led to expanded mill building in the 1920s, the ability of southern millowners to draw on this expanded pool of surplus labor kept wage increases to a minimum.[23]

Despite the recurrent crises in cotton agriculture, the beginnings of agricultural mechanization in the 1920s, agricultural emigration, and the growth of the textile labor force, the size of the agricultural proletariat continued to increase until the mid–1930s.[24] Part of the explanation for this expansion was the continued transformation of independent farmers into tenants and croppers. However, the simultaneous expansion of both the agricultural and industrial proletariat was also related to the widespread phenomenon of farm operators working part-time in the predominantly rural textile industry. Detailed data on this phenomenon are not available prior to the 1930s, although the *Census of Population*'s "rural nonfarm" category provides a possible indication.[25] The category is a very broad one, since it includes people living in communities of less than 2,500. It also includes people living in rural areas who may have supplemented an industrial wage by growing food, but who may not have simultaneously operated a farm or produced a cash crop.

During the 1930s the phenomenon of part-time farming was investigated in the *Census of Agriculture*, which reveals the following. In 1934 74,247 North Carolina farm operators (24.7 percent of the total) reported off-farm wage work. Of these, 58,913 were white farmers of whom 29,844 had off-farm work for one hundred days or more. The average number of off-farm workdays for all operators was 118. 46,544 white operators were engaged in nonagricultural work. By 1939 this number had risen to 48,543, and the average number of workdays had increased significantly.[26] Although no data are available on the precise occupations of these part-time farmers, it seems likely, given the rural nature of the industry and its domination of the North Carolina economy, that a large number of them worked in the cotton textile industry. To the extent that this was the case, employment in the textile industry also helped to keep down wage levels.

Unlike North Carolina, the Massachusetts cotton goods industry was unable to take advantage of such a favorable situation. In 1939 the six New England states reported a total of 50,033 farm operators who had part-time, nonagricultural occupations, a relatively insignificant number given the size of the region's industrial labor force and the relatively weak competitive position of textiles in the regional labor market.

After 1935 federal policies to increase farm prices by encouraging acreage reduction, concentration of landownership, and mechanization began to reduce the southern pool of impoverished tenants and sharecroppers. Efforts to limit the harmful effects of these policies on landless tenants and croppers were destroyed by the congressional representatives of the American Farm Bureau Federation.[27] As a result, between 1935 and 1940 the number of farm operators in the South was reduced by 400,000. All but 30,000 of these were tenants and croppers.[28] During the same period, North Carolina lost 22,691 farm operators, and of these, 18,692 were tenants and croppers. After 1940 the number of tenants and sharecroppers continued to decline, providing a long-term source of cheap labor for cotton textiles and other industries as North Carolina began its limited diversification.[29]

If cotton textiles in North Carolina possessed a major advantage in terms of its reserve army of labor, it also had the advantage of its own virtually unchallenged position as the dominant employer in the regional labor market. In 1919 employment in the cotton goods industry accounted for 42.7 percent of all industrial employment in the state. In Massachusetts the figure was 18 percent.[30] As a result, while wages in the Massachusetts industry were determined primarily by intense labor market competition in a diversified industrial economy, its North Carolina counterpart operated in a context of abundant labor and relatively little high-wage competition. As a result, North Carolina cotton manufacturers had a wide range within which to set wage levels in order to ensure both the continued flow of labor into the mill villages and the simultaneous establishment of a rate of exploitation that would provide a significant competitive advantage. In the event of significant worker opposition, this ability to alter wages would be restricted.

In addition to causing a major migration of tenants and sharecroppers into the cotton mills, the depression of 1920–21 also provided the means to defeat the United Textile Workers' Association's postwar campaign for the forty-eight-hour week. This victory allowed southern textile manufacturers a free hand with which to tailor wage levels to the depressed conditions of the 1920s and institute increases in work intensity. In contrast, strikes in Massachusetts during the same period were largely successful in achieving the rollback of wage cuts instituted during 1920–21.

Between the defeat of the National Union of Textile Workers (NUTW) and UTWA southern organizing effort in 1902 and World War I, the cotton mills of North Carolina experienced a long period of relative quiet. In general, during this period southern unionism was confined to a small number of craft organizations in the larger towns. After 1915, however, the strength of the UTWA among millworkers began to increase. The high profitability of expanded wartime production for government orders persuaded mill managements to concede wage increases in order to quickly expand the labor force, introduce shift work, and maintain continuous production. About forty southern locals gained union charters, and workers were able to force the reinstatement of discharged union members in a number of successful strikes.[31] A majority of southern millowners maintained their normal level of hostility, nevertheless.

On the basis of these gains, as the war came to a close, the UTWA began to exert pressure for a forty-eight-hour week. In 1919 a three-month strike by fifteen hundred millworkers in Charlotte, North Carolina, won a reduction in the workweek, incorporation of wartime bonuses in wages, free rent for the strike's duration, and a pledge of nondiscrimination against union members. The Charlotte strike was followed by strikes in eleven other Piedmont communities, and these were settled in a similar fashion. By September 1919 the UTWA claimed forty-three locals and forty thousand members in North Carolina alone.

These gains by millworkers proved to be as impermanent as the postwar boom. From late 1920 into the spring of 1921, the southern industry gradually curtailed operations and cut wages by 30 to 50 percent. Despite the depressed condition of the industry and warnings from the UTWA that it could provide only limited support, strike action was unanimously approved by forty of the locals. On June 1, 1921, nine thousand workers walked off the job. Under no pressure to produce, the millowners simply closed their mills and waited for the strike to collapse. When union support began to run out, the *Southern Textile Bulletin* orchestrated a campaign of antiunion propaganda, accusing "northern" union leaders of betraying the workers by withholding the material support due to them in return for union dues.

By the end of August 1921, under pressure from a combination of depression, lockout, lack of union support, the *Bulletin*'s campaign, and the presence of the state militia in major strike centers such as Kannapolis and Concord, the strike collapsed. Wage cuts remained in effect, guarantees of reinstatement were refused, and the UTWA ended its campaign. By the end of 1921 not a single cotton mill local was left. Temporary gains in the tobacco industry in Durham and Winston-Salem by the International Tobacco Workers' Union (ITWU) were also lost. In addition, many existing craft organizations in the South began to suffer as southern chambers of commerce and other open shop organizations began to implement the "American Plan" across the region.[32]

Perhaps more important, however, were the longer term effects of the *Bulletin*'s antiunion campaign. According to the campaign, the major concern of northern union organizers in their attempts to organize southern workers was to limit the South's competitive advantage, and, therefore, also the relocation of industry from the Northeast. Unionization was thereby presented as directly limiting the expansion of jobs in the South. When the going got tough, however, northern organizers had misled and deserted the southern members in order not to weaken their northern organizations. While the impact of this supposed desertion did not rule out further attempts at unionization, there is some evidence that it left lingering doubts in the minds of many southern mill-workers about the usefulness of external aid in their struggle with the millowners.[33]

Although fragmented, the Massachusetts working class provided much stiffer opposition to postwar changes than their Southern counterparts. In the early part of the twentieth century, the state could not be said to have a unified labor movement. Nevertheless, nearly every town had independent unions, often loosely federated into city central labor unions. Immigrant workers, who were increasingly important in the textile industry in the late nineteenth century, generally stayed outside union organizations, preferring to organize along ethnic lines. During the industrial crises, these organizations performed all the essential trade union support functions, however, and often cooperated with unionized strikers.[34] Defensive strikes against wage cuts, changes in working conditions, or the introduction of cheaper ethnic labor were frequent, especially after 1908. As a result, management use of ethnic competition to reduce wage levels became increasingly difficult. After 1910 the anarcho-syndicalist Industrial Workers of the World (IWW) had considerable success recruiting immigrant workers into industry-wide organizations. Therefore, despite a fragmented and limited labor movement, between 1900 and 1912 Massachusetts ranked third in the United States in terms of both its annual average number of strikes (97) and the average number of workers involved (39,000).[35]

The Lawrence strikes of 1912 and 1922 illustrate the obstacles facing New England textile capital in its efforts to increase the production of surplus value in a diversified industrial economy.[36] During the first decade of the twentieth century, a combination of ethnic and working class militancy, pressure from radicals and socialists, and the reformist sentiments of progressive employers interested in restricting low-wage competition had resulted in a period of significant social reform legislation between 1905 and 1908. In 1909, when a fifty-six-hour workweek went into effect, employers adjusted wage rates to maintain approximately the same weekly wage. When the fifty-four-hour limit went into effect in January 1912, however, in the face of stiff southern competition, they refused to repeat this. Although centered at Lawrence, the ensuing strike also involved mills at Lowell, New Bedford, and Boston and included a total of almost one hundred thousand workers, most of whom were in cotton textiles.

Since only twenty-five hundred workers in Lawrence belonged to craft unions affiliated with UTWA, the IWW provided the organizational basis for the strike. Although the IWW failed in the longer term, the Lawrence strike was a success in terms of accomplishing the immediate goals of the workers themselves. Efforts by employers and public officials to coerce the strikers into submission succeeded only in increasing support for the strike. The politically isolated Lawrence employers were forced to come to a settlement that included wage increases of from 5 to 25 percent, additional pay for overtime, reform of the bonus system, and a pledge of nondiscrimination against the strikers. To avoid further conflict and limit IWW gains, similar wage increases occurred throughout New England.

The settlement of the Lawrence strike possibly spelled the end of the untrammeled use of ethnic competition as a means of raising rates of exploitation. During the war, increased demand and rising prices made such strategies unnecessary. Between 1914 and 1919 hours were reduced from fifty-four to forty-eight per week, and wages increased by 178 percent. During late 1920 and early 1921, depression forced the predominantly unorganized Massachusetts workers to accept a 22.5 percent pay cut. In January 1922, however, they resisted an attempt to cut wages by a further 20 percent. The resulting strike began in the Pawtucket Valley and involved eighteen thousand workers in Massachusetts alone. In contrast to the situation in North Carolina the previous year, textile capital in Massachusetts found it impossible to break the strike, which ended in partial victory for the workers. In June 1922 the Board of Conciliation and Arbitration of the Massachusetts Department of Labor and Industries was authorized by the state legislature "to bring about an amicable settlement of the industrial conflict" and to investigate the business and financial aspects of the industry in order to assess the extent of the threat of southern competition. On June 23 strikers rejected an employer proposal to submit the wages question to a three-member mill-appointed committee in exchange for a return to work. On August 22 the same employer announced that work would be resumed under the wage scale in operation prior to the strike. Similar compromises occurred in the other strike centers.[37]

North Carolina and Massachusetts differed also in the extent to which they had developed protective labor and other forms of social legislation. During the nineteenth century, Massachusetts had pioneered child labor legislation (1836), instituted the first state factory inspection system (1866), and was the first state to limit the working day for women and minors to ten hours (1874). In addition, the state was also the first to establish a Bureau of Labor Statistics, the first to compel corporations to pay workers weekly, and the first to forbid the payment of wages in scrip.[38] Between 1905 and 1908 the Massachusetts legislature passed an eight-hour law for all employees doing government work, strengthened the system of factory inspection with respect to health and child labor violations, and prohibited night work for women and children. In 1911 a system of workmen's compensation was created, a minimum wage commission was founded to oversee the wages of women and minors, and legislation was passed establishing the fifty-four-hour week and eight-hour day.[39] Although minimum wage laws for female labor were ruled unconstitutional by the Supreme Court in 1923, the Massachusetts law survived.[40] In addition to the overnight ban, by 1922 working hours for women and minors were limited to forty-eight per week and nine per day.[41]

In North Carolina progress was much more limited. Efforts by the Knights of Labor, the American Federation of Labor (AFL), and agrarian radicals to introduce child labor restrictions during the early stages of proletarianization and industrialization proved to be as permanent as the other activities of these organizations in the state. Questionnaires on the use of child labor, distributed by the state Bureau of Labor Statistics, were ignored by the millowners.[42] After 1900, however, the issue of child labor assumed more direct importance in state politics. Implicit in the Democratic party's strategy to disenfranchise black voters in 1900 was a commitment to minimize the impact of the literacy test on whites by improving the state's minimal system of public education. Despite the new political importance of education for whites, efforts to restrict child labor in the mills led most frequently to concealment rather than change. A federal Bureau of Labor study in 1907 (after the North Carolina legislature had adopted a twelve-year age limit) revealed that of the total number of children employed in the state's textile mills, 8.6 percent were under twelve and were employed illegally. This figure did not include those under that age employed legally through legal exemptions. In addition, the investigators were convinced that with a reliable method of establishing age, the number employed illegally would be found to be much higher. Of 4,091 southern mill children studied, 24.6 percent of the six–eleven age group were working, as were 87.8 percent of the twelve–thirteen age group and 96.2 percent of the fourteen–fifteen age group. In North Carolina 53.8 percent of mill children were illiterate.[43]

After 1907, largely in an effort to avert the threat of independent factory inspection, North Carolina's millowners embarked on what was essentially a program of self-regulation. In 1907 a law sponsored by the cotton manufacturers was introduced into the legislature. It purported to strengthen the commitment to eliminate the employment of children under twelve, and it also forbade the employment of those aged twelve and thirteen, except in an "apprenticeship" capacity and then only after a minimum of four months of school attendance in the preceding twelve months. Since the bill was sponsored by the manufacturers, there was no difficulty in securing its passage. In practice, however, "apprentice-ship" was interpreted as "learning" and the employment of twelve year olds continued largely as before.[44]

In 1916 the passage of the Keating-Owen Act, which eliminated goods produced by child labor from interstate commerce, threatened to bring about a significant level of federal inspection. This threat, and a further effort to achieve the same ends by the use of federal tax law, was defeated in the Supreme Court in cases initiated in western North Carolina by David Clark, editor of the *Southern Textile Bulletin*.[45] Nevertheless, North Carolina's textile manufacturers again responded by strengthening their machinery of self-inspection. An act of 1919, again sponsored by the state's manufacturers, required children between eight and fourteen years old to attend school for the entire six-month term, except where problems of distance, poverty, or mental or physical deficiencies intervened. In addition, children under sixteen were not to be employed between nine P.M. and six A.M.

A more important feature of this legislation, however, was that the responsibility for administering child labor law was taken away from the state commissioner of labor and given to the newly formed State Child Welfare Commission, composed of high-level officeholders serving on a voluntary basis. Further, the ability of employers to present a parent-signed certificate showing a child to be of legal age was to be accepted as prima facie evidence that millowners were obeying the law. Finally, legal exemptions allowed boys between twelve and fourteen to be employed when school was not in session, on Saturdays, and after school, and the law did not apply to agricultural labor or domestic service. By and large, such a system could be effective only to the extent that the millowners wanted it to be. Nevertheless, in 1920 inspectors found 738 violations in four thousand inspections, and they pursued three hundred prosecutions.[46]

Progress in areas other than child labor was equally limited. Female labor remained undifferentiated from that by males until 1937; that is, it was subject to the same sixty-hour maximum workweek, with no limitations on night work. Only in 1937, under pressure from federal fair labor standards requirements and after the relocation of the cotton textile industry was assured, did the state differentiate female from male labor. Females were restricted to nine hours a day and forty-eight hours per week and males to ten hours a day and fifty-five per week. At the same time, a minimum age of sixteen was set for industrial work. Night work for females continued to be allowed, except for those under eighteen.[47]

What ultimately determined the relative importance of the various openings left by North Carolina's system of labor law in the 1920s was the depression in which the textile industry found itself and the type of adaptations that had to be made in order to survive and to maintain a competitive advantage over New England. In conjunction with lower wages and the intensification of work, the ability of southern textile capital to operate a night shift using cheaper female labor provided a significant lever in increasing the production of surplus value.[48]

Having an abundant supply of cheap labor after the 1920–21 agricultural collapse and having averted the postwar threat of unionization, southern textile manufacturers were able to respond to depression in the industry as a whole by reducing real wage levels, intensifying work loads, shortening the day shift, and also maintaining the second night shift introduced during wartime expansion. In this way, both overhead and labor costs could be significantly reduced. Since workers were paid on an hourly basis, production could be stopped if conditions required it.[49] Mill village dependence and the fact that by the late 1920s these conditions were generalized throughout the southern textile industry ensured that workers would not leave in search of other employment.

It was this pattern of intensive exploitation, coupled with periods of unemployment, that explains the somewhat paradoxical situation in which, in the 1920s, southern textile workers worked on average fewer weekly hours than did their northern counterparts.[50] In Massachusetts it proved to be impossible for cotton manufacturers to maintain the second shift since in that state women were not allowed to work between six P.M. and six A.M. An all-male shift would have reduced northern overheads but still would not be competitive with its relatively unregulated southern counterpart. As a result, manufacturers in Massachusetts were forced to operate with a single shift, higher labor costs, and higher overheads, while their southern competitors flooded cotton goods markets with cheaper products. Beyond this, as the crisis of the middle and late 1920s deepened into the Great Depression, it is possible that the shorter average hours in the southern states allowed policies of work intensification to be instituted in a more effective manner.

*Wages and exploitation,*
*North Carolina and Massachusetts,*
*1919–39*

It is impossible to present a precise account of the way in which the various factors outlined above contributed to North Carolina's competitive advantage over the New England cotton textile states. For instance, while it is known that the stretch-out was enforced relentlessly during the late 1920s,[51] its impact on production and rates of exploitation cannot be accurately estimated. For one thing, the output of the cotton

Table 3.3. Average annual wage rates in the cotton goods industry: North Carolina and Massachusetts, 1910–39

| | North Carolina | | | Massachusetts | | | Wage differential (N.C. as percentage of Mass.) |
|---|---|---|---|---|---|---|---|
| | (a) Wage earners | (b) Wage bill ($) | b/a ($) | (a) Wage earners | (b) Wage bill ($) | b/a ($) | |
| 1910 | 49,171 | 12,130,608 | 246.70 | 111,252 | 45,117,069 | 405.54 | 61 |
| 1919 | 67,297 | 49,134,506 | 730.11 | 122,499 | 109,902,503 | 897.17 | 81 |
| 1921 | 66,136 | 41,398,350 | 624.26 | 106,337 | 96,547,054 | 907.93 | 69 |
| 1927 | 95,786 | 66,149,690 | 690.60 | 90,875 | 88,089,667 | 969.34 | 71 |
| 1931 | 73,508 | 42,014,080 | 571.56 | 46,990 | 38,868,889 | 827.17 | 69 |
| 1937 | 104,457 | 72,476,760 | 693.84 | 44,719 | 38,232,448 | 854.95 | 81 |
| 1939 | 109,975 | 74,981,789 | 682.93 | 37,923 | 31,645,862 | 834.48 | 82 |

Sources: U.S. Bureau of the Census, *Thirteenth Census*, 490; U.S. Bureau of the Census, *Fourteenth Census*, 638–39, 1121–22; U.S. Department of Commerce, Bureau of the Census, *Biennial Census of Manufactures, 1921* (Washington: USGPO, 1924), 1422, 1460; U.S. Department of Commerce, Bureau of the Census, *Biennial Census of Manufactures, 1927* (Washington: USGPO, 1930), 1361–65, 1387; U.S. Department of Commerce, Bureau of the Census, *Biennial Census of Manufactures, 1931* (Washington: USGPO, 1935), 1224, 1251; U.S. Department of Commerce, Bureau of the Census, *Biennial Census of Manufactures, 1937* (Washington: USGPO, 1940), part 1, 1365–70, 1395; U.S. Bureau of the Census, *Sixteenth Census, Manufactures, 1939*, vol. 3, 424–33, 748–51.

textile industry is only systematically accessible in terms of its market value (either as total product value or as value added by manufacture). This in turn is dependent on the market price at which the goods sell. This information cannot be used, therefore, to assess the differential impact of the stretch-out since, in the determination of price, it also incorporates the impact of cheaper labor, the strategy of underselling to expand markets, and the effects of the commission houses. Nevertheless, it is possible to indicate the general effects of all these factors combined in wage levels, rates of exploitation, and the extent of industrial relocation during the period.

Table 3.3 presents data on average wage levels in the North Carolina and Massachusetts cotton goods industries between 1910 and 1939. The average cotton goods wage in North Carolina is consistently lower than that in Massachusetts. Nevertheless, variations in these figures illustrate some of the points mentioned above. By the end of World War I, the wage differential had narrowed considerably. Between 1910 and 1919 wages in both states had risen by roughly 490 dollars, but by 1920 the differential had increased again. As a result of the depression of

1920–21 and the defeat of the UTWA's campaign in the same years, nominal wages fell in North Carolina. In Massachusetts, on the other hand, cotton textile workers were able to maintain their average wage levels, and, even though nominal wages in North Carolina began to rise once again after 1921, living standards generally declined during the 1920s relative to those in the North. According to Frank Stricker, real weekly earnings of cotton workers fell by 12 percent in the South between 1923 and 1929, compared to a 4 percent decrease in the North.[52] By 1931 wages in Massachusetts had begun to decline under the impact of the Great Depression and southern competition, and in North Carolina wage levels had fallen even further, to a level 22 percent below those of 1919. Thereafter, the wage differential begins to move once again in favor of North Carolina, both as a result of the impact of depression and relocation on wage levels in Massachusetts and an improvement in the North Carolina situation. By 1939 the average wage level in North Carolina was still below that of 1919 (−7 percent), although the drastic fall in prices after 1929 probably helped to improve the situation. Throughout this period, the cotton goods wage labor force grew steadily—1931 was the only exception. The overall growth rate in the North Carolina cotton goods labor force during the period was 66 percent. During the same period, the cotton goods labor force in Massachusetts decreased by 64 percent.

In using average wage figures, one faces the difficulty that this measure possibly overlooks significant variations between occupations within the industry. Abraham Berglund's regional and occupational breakdown for 1928 (table 3.4), however, suggests that while there was internal variation, it did not involve cases in which the differential worked in favor of the northern states.[53] The most skilled and highly paid group of cotton millworkers—loom-fixers—were still paid roughly ten dollars per week less in the southern mills than in New England.

In North Carolina in 1928, the average hourly wage rate was $0.317, compared with $0.405 in Massachusetts—a differential of 22 percent. For a full-time week of sixty and forty-eight hours, wages would be $19.02 and $19.44, respectively. That is, working full time, workers in North Carolina could take home almost as much pay as their northern counterparts. Southern cotton millworkers worked on average fewer weekly hours than their counterparts in the North. As I have suggested, this was the result of southern textile capital's ability to intensify work and use cheap labor in a double shift system. Because it caused frequent periods of unemployment, this system of production served to reduce average wages and widen the regional weekly wage gap. The Berglund data above reflect the impact of reduced hours caused by periodic unemployment. According to the federal Bureau of Labor Statistics in data

Table 3.4. Average actual weekly earnings by cotton goods occupations and sex: southern states and New England, 1928

| Occupation | South | New England | South as percentage of New England |
|---|---|---|---|
| Cord tenders and strippers (male) | 10.28 | 17.93 | 57 |
| Drawing frame tenders | | | |
| Male | 9.91 | 15.68 | 63 |
| Female | 8.13 | 12.89 | 63 |
| Speeder tenders | | | |
| Male | 13.65 | 21.12 | 65 |
| Female | 11.48 | 15.59 | 74 |
| Loom fixers (male) | 18.38 | 28.43 | 65 |
| Slasher tenders (male) | 14.57 | 23.69 | 62 |
| Frame spinners | | | |
| Male | 6.76 | 17.51 | 39 |
| Female | 8.49 | 14.91 | 57 |
| Trimmers or inspectors (female) | 9.30 | 12.07 | 77 |
| Weavers | | | |
| Male | 13.57 | 19.60 | 69 |
| Female | 12.05 | 17.71 | 68 |

Sources: Weekly wage rates excerpted from Abraham Berglund, George T. Starnes, and Frank T. de Vyver, *Labor in the Industrial South: A Survey of Wages and Living Conditions in Three Major Industries of the Industrial South* (Charlottesville, Va.: Institute for Research in the Social Sciences, University of Virginia, 1930), 88–90, table 22. Figures in third column rounded to nearest 1 percent.

presented to the Senate Committee on Manufactures, variations in the amount of available work reduced the average weekly earnings of North Carolina cotton millworkers in 1928 to $12.23 per week, compared with $16.47 per week in Massachusetts.[54]

For the millworkers, the combination of long hours, heavy work loads, and low wages meant abject poverty, and, for many, sickness and disease. In a study of the cost of living in northern and southern mill towns in 1919 and 1920, the National Industrial Conference Board reported that in order to achieve an average minimum American standard of living in 1920, a family of five (man, wife, and three children) would require $1,267.76 in Fall River, Massachusetts, $1,347.09 in

Pelzer, South Carolina, $1,399.60 in company housing in Charlotte, North Carolina, and $1,527.67 in noncompany housing in the same city.[55] In Fall River this would require a steady weekly income of $24.38. In the southern cases it would require $26.80, $27.66, and $29.34, respectively. In North Carolina in 1920 this would require at least two average weekly wages and more as the 1920s progressed and wages fell. Given high rates of unemployment (particularly among higher-wage male workers), a gradual decline in the availability of work for children as agricultural conditions swelled the pool of cheap surplus adult labor, and declining real wages during the 1920s, it seems unlikely that this requirement could be met.

What resulted was a regional standard of living during the 1920s and 1930s that was based on inadequate housing, an undeveloped system of education, cheap, flimsy clothing, and a protein-and-vitamin-deficient diet based on corn, with small amounts of pork as the major source of animal protein.[56] Part-time farming and mill village kitchen gardens, used to bridge the gap between the workers' earnings and subsistence levels, often contributed to these dietary deficiencies, the major consequence of which was the disease known as pellagra.[57]

For southern textile capital, the ability to reduce wages and implement the stretch-out was the key to high rates of surplus value and, ultimately, to the ability to attract large amounts of new capital. By exploiting the region's cheap and abundant labor supply, its relatively undeveloped system of labor legislation, and by using cheap hydroelectric power and the most recently available automatic machinery, southern manufacturers were able to achieve a significant reduction in production costs. In 1922 the Massachusetts Department of Labor and Industries found that the cost of producing identical standard print cloth was 28.0313 cents per pound in Massachusetts and 19.2464 cents per pound in North Carolina, a difference of 31 percent. The largest item of difference involved was the cost of labor—17.4048 cents per pound in Massachusetts, 9.4273 cents per pound in North Carolina.[58]

Rates of surplus value during the entire period reflect this important competitive advantage, in both periods of prosperity and of depression (table 3.5). In 1939, at the end of a long period of depression, rationalization, and relocation, the rate of exploitation in the North Carolina cotton goods industry was over twice that in Massachusetts. In the cotton broad woven goods division, North Carolina's rate was 278 percent of that in Massachusetts and, in cotton thread, 394 percent. Only in the more specialized production of narrow fabrics did Massachusetts manage to hold on to its advantage.

By 1939 the South's competitive advantage had resulted in a major regional shift in the location of the cotton textile industry. Between the

Table 3.5. Rates of surplus value in the cotton goods industry: North Carolina and Massachusetts, 1919–39 (in thousands of dollars)

|  |  | (a) | (b) | (c) |
|---|---|---|---|---|
|  |  | Salaries | Wages | Value added |
| 1919 | North Carolina | 5,644.9 | 49,134.5 | 131,588.5 |
|  | Massachusetts | 9,351.6 | 109,902.5 | 237,012.2 |
| 1921 | North Carolina | 5,423.5 | 43,198.4 | 76,803.6 |
|  | Massachusetts | 7,835.4 | 96,547.1 | 160,104.3 |
| 1927 | North Carolina | 6,494.2 | 66,149.7 | 125,789.8 |
|  | Massachusetts | 7,895.0 | 88,089.7 | 139,075.1 |
| 1933 | North Carolina | 2,958.0 | 45,295.0 | 82,275.0 |
|  | Massachusetts | 2,332.0 | 31,110.0 | 47,414.0 |
| 1937 | North Carolina |  |  |  |
|  | Broad goods | 3,472.8 | 49,578.4 | 83,052.6 |
|  | Narrow fabrics | 98.1 | 255.4 | 532.9 |
|  | Yarn and thread | 2,267.9 | 22,643.0 | 40,974.7 |
|  | Total cotton goods | 5,838.8 | 72,476.8 | 124,560.2 |
|  | Massachusetts |  |  |  |
|  | Broad goods | 2,356.2 | 29,566.4 | 45,513.5 |
|  | Narrow fabrics | 538.3 | 2,017.8 | 3,877.0 |
|  | Yarn and thread | 1,159.2 | 6,648.2 | 10,607.5 |
|  | Total cotton goods | 4,053.7 | 38,232.4 | 59,998.0 |
| 1939 | North Carolina |  |  |  |
|  | Broad goods | 4,849.9 | 50,744.2 | 117,829.0 |
|  | Narrow fabrics | 111.3 | 318.0 | 722.3 |
|  | Thread | 122.3 | 546.7 | 1,875.2 |
|  | Yarn | 2,682.7 | 23,372.9 | 45,009.9 |
|  | Total cotton goods | 7,766.2 | 74,981.8 | 165,436.4 |
|  | Massachusetts |  |  |  |
|  | Broad goods | 2,299.8 | 23,487.6 | 36,343.6 |
|  | Narrow fabrics | 547.8 | 2,242.1 | 5,206.0 |
|  | Thread | 378.5 | 2,178.0 | 3,705.9 |
|  | Yarn | 592.5 | 3,738.3 | 6,343.3 |
|  | Total cotton goods | 3,818.6 | 31,646.0 | 51,598.8 |

Sources: U.S. Bureau of the Census, Fourteenth Census, 636–45, 1120–23; U.S. Bureau of the Census, Biennial Census, 1921, 1420–27, 1460–63; U.S. Bureau of the Census, Biennial Census, 1927, 226, 315; U.S. Department of Commerce, Bu-

| (d)<br>Productive<br>salaries | (e)<br>Depreciation | (f)<br>Surplus value | (g)<br>Variable<br>capital | (h)<br>Rate of sur-<br>plus value (%) |
|---|---|---|---|---|
| 2,822.5 | 6,579.4 | 73,052.1 | 51,957.0 | 141 |
| 4,675.8 | 11,850.6 | 110,583.3 | 114,578.3 | 97 |
| 2,711.8 | 3,840.2 | 28,853.2 | 44,110.2 | 65 |
| 3,917.7 | 8,005.2 | 51,634.3 | 100,464.8 | 51 |
| 3,247.1 | 6,289.5 | 50,103.5 | 69,396.8 | 72 |
| 3,947.5 | 6,953.8 | 40,084.1 | 92,037.2 | 44 |
| 1,479.0 | 4,113.8 | 31,387.2 | 46,774.0 | 67 |
| 1,166.0 | 2,370.7 | 12,767.3 | 32,276.0 | 40 |
| 1,736.4 | 4,152.6 | 27,585.2 | 51,314.8 | 54 |
| 49.1 | 26.6 | 201.8 | 304.5 | 66 |
| 1,134.0 | 2,048.7 | 15,149.0 | 23,777.0 | 64 |
| 2,919.4 | 6,228.0 | 42,936.0 | 75,396.2 | 57 |
| 1,178.1 | 2,275.7 | 12,493.3 | 30,744.5 | 41 |
| 269.2 | 193.9 | 1,396.1 | 2,287.0 | 61 |
| 579.6 | 530.4 | 2,849.3 | 7,227.8 | 39 |
| 2,026.9 | 2,999.9 | 16,738.8 | 40,259.3 | 42 |
| 2,425.0 | 5,891.5 | 58,768.3 | 53,169.2 | 111 |
| 55.7 | 36.1 | 312.5 | 373.7 | 84 |
| 61.2 | 93.8 | 1,173.5 | 607.9 | 193 |
| 1,341.4 | 2,250.5 | 18,045.1 | 24,714.3 | 73 |
| 3,883.1 | 8,271.8 | 78,299.7 | 78,864.9 | 99 |
| 1,149.9 | 1,817.2 | 9,888.9 | 24,637.5 | 40 |
| 273.9 | 260.3 | 2,429.7 | 2,516.0 | 97 |
| 189.3 | 185.3 | 1,153.3 | 2,367.3 | 49 |
| 296.3 | 317.2 | 1,991.5 | 4,034.6 | 49 |
| 1,909.3 | 2,579.9 | 15,463.6 | 33,555.3 | 46 |

reau of the Census, *Biennial Census of Manufactures, 1933* (Washington: USGPO, 1936), 152, 169; U.S. Bureau of the Census, *Biennial Census, 1937*, 287, 359; U.S. Bureau of the Census, *Sixteenth Census*, 424–33, 748–51.

Table 3.6. Cotton goods manufacturing: North Carolina and Massachusetts, 1919–39

| | (a) Establishments | (b) Wage earners | b/a | Cost of labor (in millions of dollars) | Value of products (in millions of dollars) | Value added (in millions of dollars) |
|---|---|---|---|---|---|---|
| **1919** | | | | | | |
| North Carolina | 311 | 67,297 | 216 | 49.1 | 318.4 | 131.6 |
| Massachusetts | 191 | 122,499 | 641 | 109.9 | 596.7 | 237.0 |
| **1939** | | | | | | |
| North Carolina | 341 | 109,795 | 322 | 74.9 | 324.3 | 165.4 |
| Massachusetts | 121 | 37,923 | 313 | 31.6 | 99.3 | 51.5 |

Sources: U.S. Bureau of the Census, Fourteenth Census, 638–39, 1120–21; U.S. Bureau of the Census, Sixteenth Census, 424–25, 728–29.

summer of 1923 and the end of 1924 alone, approximately $100 million of northern capital moved south for the purpose of purchasing or building southern mills.[59] Between 1921 and 1929, while 2.5 million spindles were being scrapped nationally, fifty-one mills with over 1.3 million spindles and complementary machinery moved south.[60] Table 3.6 gives a general indication of the results of this process. By 1939 Massachusetts had lost 37 percent of its cotton mills, 70 percent of its wage earners, and the state's mills produced cotton goods with a value equal to only one-sixth of their 1919 value. The average number of wage earners per mill had fallen from 641 to 313. During the same depressed period, the rationalized and reorganized North Carolina industry had gained thirty mills, increased its labor force by 63 percent, and increased both its product value and value added.[61] In addition, the size of the average North Carolina mill had increased from 216 workers to 322. By far the greater part of the liquidation of textile capital during the 1920s and 1930s occurred in New England. Bankruptcies of smaller, less efficient mills within the South were more than compensated for by the migration of New England capital and local capital accumulation.[62]

In addition to cotton goods production, the process of limited diversification continued. Along with 109,795 cotton goods workers in 1939 (40 percent of the state's manufacturing labor force), there were 44,578 (16.6 percent) employed in the hosiery sector, 4,287 (1.6 percent) in knit goods, 3,416 (1.3 percent) in dyeing and finishing, and 14,958 (5.5 percent) in the production of rayon goods. Together, these textile sectors accounted for roughly 66 percent of the state's manufacturing labor force. The labor-intensive furniture industry accounted for a further 17,070. The cigarette industry, with a labor force of 15,375, continued to be the only significant element of large-scale, capital-intensive production. In all these industries, wages continued to be set by those factors that determined wages in the cotton goods sector and by the dominance of the cotton goods sector itself. Within the hosiery group, workers enjoyed roughly a 20 percent higher wage rate than did cotton goods workers generally, at an average of $813 per year. In knit goods, dyeing and finishing, and rayon, average wages were $593 (−14 percent), $770 (+13 percent), and $768 (+13 percent), respectively. In the cigarette industry, very high levels of productivity in a highly capitalized production process in conjunction with wage levels only slightly higher than those in other industries in the state (average $903, 32 percent higher than in cotton goods) provided the basis for a rate of exploitation of 659 percent.[63]

## Stretch-out and class conflict, 1929–37

So far in this chapter, and for purposes of exposition, I have emphasized the weakness in North Carolina of working class opposition to increases in the production of surplus value. This should not be interpreted to mean, however, that no such opposition existed. The defeat of the UTWA in 1920 and 1921, and the emergence during the twenties of a systematic effort by southern chambers of commerce, banks, power companies, and, increasingly, state governments to eliminate unionism and attract capital did indeed inaugurate a period of dormancy in southern labor organization.[64] By the late 1920s, however, the very success of the southern strategy of accumulation, based on the stretch-out, wage cuts, and the double shift, created conditions conducive to the reemergence of prounion sentiment.[65] Further, as the mill towns and villages and the mill corporations themselves expanded, the increased use of managers, superintendents, and efficiency experts increased, as did the size of the mill town middle classes—doctors, lawyers, and retailers, in addition to the above—who were dependent on the continued profitability of the mills. The emergence of a socially and geographically separated "uptown" in the mill communities became a major focus of worker hostility.[66]

During the second half of the 1920s tentative efforts at union organization began in the Piedmont region. Most notable was the formation of the Piedmont Organizing Council (POC) in January 1928 in Durham, North Carolina. The POC launched a program of monthly meetings in industrial communities. The largest of these meetings, in June 1928 at Winston-Salem, had 450 delegates and led to the creation of a similar organization, the Tidewater Labor Conference in Virginia.[67]

It was the textile workers' revolt of 1929, however, that provided the major spur to what was perhaps, until recently, the most significant period of class struggle in the history of the southern textile industry. In addition to the 1929 revolt, this period also witnessed the AFL organizing drive of 1930, the 1934 textile general strike, and the Committee of Industrial Organization (CIO) drive of 1937.

Although the 1929 revolt spread to numerous textile centers in North and South Carolina and in Georgia, the major battles took place during the spring and summer of that year at Elizabethton, Tennessee, and at Gastonia and Marion, North Carolina. The histories of these revolts are well known and need not detain us here.[68] It is worthwhile to stress a number of central points, however. First, despite several apparent differences between the three strikes—between the corporations involved, between the communities in which they operated, and between the types of organizations to which the workers turned—[69] the central issues in all three cases were the mills' strategies of cost-cutting and the severity of the exploitation to which these strategies gave rise.

The basic element in these strategies was the stretch-out.[70] Although the stretch-out occurred in its most extreme forms in the newer, more automated mills that had been laid out in the 1920s specifically to facilitate such increases in work loads, and although there was early opposition from the more paternalistic of the southern millowners, the competitive situation in the late 1920s universalized the practice. Corporate secrecy limited the availability of data on the extent of the stretch-out, yet some indications are available. According to Ethelbert Stewart, U.S. commissioner of labor statistics, "instead of a weaver operating 30 or 36 looms, as was true only a few years ago, plants are now built in banks of 90, 100, 110, and I have been informed of one mill where a weaver is expected to look after 118 looms."[71] Similarly, the U.S. Senate report cited above indicates that work loads of eighteen looms at the end of the war had increased to as many as one hundred twenty-four looms by the end of the 1920s.[72] The stretch-out implemented by Cone Mills in Greensboro in the 1920s eliminated one quarter of the company's skilled weavers. They were replaced by a smaller number of unskilled battery fillers, mostly young boys and girls who were, of course, paid significantly lower wages.[73]

Perhaps as important as the ability to "stretch" workers, however, were the practices used to limit or reduce wage levels. In Elizabethton, by a combination of layoffs of older male workers, the misrepresentation of wages, and the use of mill housing rents the management had achieved a reduction in wage levels. According to Margaret Bowen, secretary of Local 1630, UTWA at Elizabethton, most of the labor force, which was 40 percent female, was between sixteen and twenty, with

very few over thirty-five years of age.[74] According to another Elizabethton worker, the nature and intensity of the work was at least partly
responsible for this situation: "at thirty-five you're old in the mill. They
begin to lay you off or put you on sweepin'."[75] Although she was
promised $16.00 per week to work in the Elizabethton mill, Bowen
actually received $10.08, which was raised to $10.65 after several
months. From this she had to pay five dollars per week for rent, four
people to a room, one dollar per week for transport, and a dollar and
forty cents per month for insurance.[76]

Similarly, in Gastonia the Manville-Jenckes management reacted to
overproduction, depression, and the emergence of competition from tire
fabric plants built by the tire companies themselves by introducing a
stretch-out without consultation, extending payment by piecework, replacing high-wage labor, and implementing two 10 percent wage cuts.
By early 1929, the Loray mill's labor force had been reduced from 3,500
to 2,200.[77]

In Marion conditions were even worse. According to the Federal
Council of Churches, living and working conditions in Marion's mills
were "unbelievable." Young female workers worked for the first thirty
days as unpaid "apprentices," then for a further four months at five
cents per hour, twelve hours a day, sixty hours a week. Children were
employed illegally. In the late 1920s, with the stretch-out gradually
tightening, average wages were eight to ten dollars per week.[78] After
surveying housing conditions in Marion, Sinclair Lewis described the
typical mill house as "a box (on stilts) with an unscreened porch. It has
three living rooms and a kitchen. In each of the living rooms there are
normally two double beds. In these double beds, there sleep anywhere
from two to five people, depending on their ages."[79] These houses
rented for twenty cents per room per week, or three dollars and twenty
cents per month. In Marion itself, similar houses rented for ten dollars
per month on the open market, so that the mill's subsidy to up to twelve
economically active persons was six dollars and eighty cents, or as little
as 14.2 cents per person per week. Despite millowners' assurances about
the significance of their housing policies and subsidies in the calculation
of standards of living, Lewis concluded that actual wages could be
taken as a relatively accurate indicator.[80]

Second, the workers' demands clearly reflected their struggle against
mill village exploitation. In all three cases, workers struck against the
stretch-out, low wages, the exploitation of women and children, and
housing costs and conditions. In Gastonia, under the direction of Fred
Beal of the National Textile Workers' Union (NTWU), workers developed a comprehensive set of demands that included the elimination of
piecework, a minimum twenty-dollar weekly wage, a forty-hour, five-

day week, abolition of the stretch-out, equal pay for equal work for women and children, free baths and improved mill toilet facilities, a 50 percent reduction in rent and lighting charges, and union recognition.[81]

Finally, the extent to which the corporations regarded the strategy of cost-cutting as nonnegotiable (and the extent to which the components of the strategy of textile industrialization had been taken over by the various levels of the State) is illustrated by the corporation's (and the State's) response to the strikes. The viciousness of these responses was similar in all cases, regardless of whether the strikes were led by the NTWU, which was affiliated with the Communist party, or by the UTWA-AFL. According to Irving Bernstein, it took only three minutes for the local Manville-Jenckes representative to reject all of the Gastonia strikers' demands.[82]

In all three strikes, mill executives, "uptown" communities, and local public officials coordinated campaigns against the strikers, which included sweeping legal injunctions, issued usually without even a hearing, and various forms of violence and intimidation. Newspaper campaigns characterized the strikes as communist insurrections against the State and private property and as attempts to destroy the system of racial segregation.[83] In Gastonia local police attacked a tent colony for evicted workers, the NTWU strike headquarters was demolished, and a twenty-nine-year-old mother of five was murdered. According to Heywood Broun, "the officials of Gastonia have been . . . no more than the hired musketeers of the millowners."[84] Local churches played an important role in maintaining social control and defeating the strike.[85] In Marion an attack on fleeing strikers by local police resulted in six dead and twenty-five severely wounded. All the dead had been shot in the back.

Again, in all three cases, state-level officials intervened. In Elizabethton strikers were faced by eight hundred state police and deputy sheriffs, who were paid directly by the mills and equipped with National Guard uniforms in contravention of federal laws governing the conditions under which such equipment might be issued. Patrols reported to the mills' superintendents rather than to their officers, and they were fed in the mill cafeteria. In Gastonia, O. Max Gardner, governor of North Carolina and himself president of a cotton manufacturing corporation in adjacent Cleveland County, seized upon a minor picket line scuffle between strikers and local police and sent in five companies of state militia, including cavalry and a howitzer battery. State troops were also used in Marion.

Finally, the local and state judicial system attributed the widespread violence of the period solely to the strikers. Weimar Jones summed up his analysis of eight major cases of violence in the three strikes as follows:

Of eight slain in the three states, seven were strikers; the only murder conviction was of strikers for the death of an officer. In two of the major cases, strikers were accused and convicted; and in one, officers (some of them mill-paid) were accused and acquitted. That is the record for the major cases. The percentages are the same in the dozens of minor ones. In every case where strikers were put on trial strikers were convicted; in not one case where anti-unionists or officers were accused has there been a conviction.[86]

The combination of private and public opposition was enough to defeat the strikes in all three cases. In Elizabethton the strikers agreed to return to work under existing conditions, and management agreed not to discriminate against union members. One thousand workers were blacklisted. In Gastonia and Marion the strikes collapsed in the midst of the legal and extralegal campaigns against the workers and the organizations. The only successful strikes during the period were in South Carolina, where workers rejected aid from "outside" unions. By appealing to the remaining paternalism of the employers and the state government, the workers were able to achieve a state government investigation into working conditions and a minor relaxation of the stretch-out.[87]

If the largely spontaneous and for the most part poorly organized revolt of the textile workers in 1929 failed to achieve significant changes in the nature and extent of exploitation in the mill villages, neither did the subsequent AFL organizing campaign of 1930.[88] In line with general AFL practices in the 1920s, and taking encouragement from the growing liberal opposition to working conditions in the textile industry, wage levels, and the apparent ease with which the millowners broke the law, the AFL chose to organize the corporations in effect rather than the workers. Having rejected the militant campaign advocated by southern delegates to the AFL National Convention in October 1929, the Federation embarked upon a campaign emphasizing the threat of communism and the benefits of union-management cooperation, reduced and rationalized production, controlled expansion, and increased working class purchasing power.[89]

Not surprisingly, since fierce competition worked entirely to their benefit and since they had little trouble recruiting the necessary cheap labor, the southern manufacturers would have nothing to do with any of the AFL's efforts. By September 1930, thirty-one textile locals had been formed, but none had achieved either recognition or any other sources of bargaining power. Employers simply fired union members. The effective culmination of the campaign was a strike beginning in late September 1930 in Danville, Virginia, by the Riverside and Dan Mills against a wage cut and the imposition of the stretch-out. The strike's pattern followed that set in the 1929 revolt almost to the letter.

In January 1931, after the mill management had begun evictions and imported strikebreakers under the protection of one thousand National Guardsmen, the strike collapsed.[90]

The textile general strike of 1934 also followed the pattern established in 1929, despite apparently significant institutional and legal differences.[91] The creation of the cotton textile industry's Code of Fair Competition No. 1 under the 1933 (federal) National Recovery Act (NRA) failed to address the issues most pressing to cotton millworkers, north and south. Although it provided for a minimum weekly wage of twelve dollars in the southern states and thirteen dollars in the North (in order not to destroy all of the southern competitive advantage), cleaners, outside employees and, significantly, "learners" were exempt. The workweek was set at forty hours with a two-shift limit but with no minimum number of hours. The Cotton Textile Industry Committee, headed by George Sloan (who also headed the private Cotton Textile Institute) was given the responsibility of administering, in addition to wages and hours, section 7(a) of the NRA, which guaranteed collective bargaining. The issue of the stretch-out was to be dealt with by committees established in each mill, or failing that, state industrial relations boards, or, failing that, the tripartite Cotton Textile National Industrial Relations Board, which was in turn effectively run by Sloan. In practical terms, Sloan made no effort to control the stretch-out, and he interpreted section 7(a) as limiting representation and bargaining rights to the employees of particular mills. Company unions were the most common outcome of this interpretation. By September 1933, UTWA membership was estimated at forty thousand, but this was not accompanied by increased bargaining rights.

At first, the code and the threat of a federal 4.2 cents per pound processing tax on raw cotton combined to lift output and employment. Expanding inventories and the resulting fall in production, however, quickly led employers to begin to chisel away at the code's provisions. This was especially the case in the South, where enthusiasm for the Cotton Textile Institute and the code was at best lukewarm.[92] Wages in all categories were cut to the minimum, large numbers of workers were reclassified as "learners," and there was a general increase in the stretch-out. In May 1934 the workweek was reduced from eighty to sixty hours for two shifts, reducing the code minimums in effect to $9 and $9.75.

Prior to this reduction, the NRA was perceived as doing little to help the workers in their struggles. With it, however, the NRA and its institutional offshoots had become clearly implicated on the side of capital. By June 1934 the UTWA reported a membership of 270,000 workers. On July 16, 20,000 workers in twenty-four Alabama mills walked out.

On Labor Day, September 3, 1934, they were followed by 65,000 workers in North Carolina and by an additional 175,000 in the remaining textile states on the following day. A few days later the total number of strikers was reported at 376,000.

The conduct of the strike, as well as its genesis, was also largely unaffected by the NRA and its institutional appendages. What differentiated the strike from earlier (and later) efforts was its size and the extent of its organization, by both the workers and employers. What finally forced the UTWA to accept arbitration, which represented an unambiguous defeat for the workers, was the fact that the union had little choice. Under little pressure to produce, millowners merely had to wait for the strike to collapse. In the meantime, they made sure that it would collapse by importing labor spies and armed guards, evicting workers from mill housing, and engaging in a coordinated and largely successful effort to persuade local and state authorities to intervene on their behalf. Workers were evicted from public housing, removed from public relief, and again terrorized by local police and state militias. Deaths occurred in both North and South, and southern governors dispatched a total of ten thousand National Guardsmen, forcing the UTWA to abandon its tactic of using "flying squadrons" of strikers to maintain picket lines and keep mills closed.

In the final analysis, the only issue settled by the White House–appointed Winant arbitration committee was that the strike ended. Union recognition was dismissed as "not feasible." Wage levels, regional differentials, and the stretch-out were to be studied. In addition, the agreement put an end to only one side of the conflict. By demobilizing the workers, it removed the only guarantee that the employers would keep their promise to rehire without discrimination. As a result, three hundred and thirty-nine mills (two-thirds of them in the South) refused to rehire, and permanently evicted, strikers. The new, theoretically neutral Textile Labor Relations Board placed the burden of proof of discrimination on the workers. Once again, southern workers had been comprehensively defeated and returned to the state of terror induced by the stretch-out since the second half of the 1920s.

The final effort to organize southern cotton millworkers during this period occurred in 1937–38, under the leadership of the Textile Workers' Organizing Committee (TWOC), which was formed when the CIO absorbed the UTWA in March 1937.[93] The UTWA had been expelled from the AFL in 1936. As was the case in 1934, the existence of federal legislation guaranteeing the right to bargain collectively (this time, the Wagner National Labor Relations Act of 1935) failed to aid the organizing campaign. After an impressive start in the spring of 1937, which led to wage increases of up to 10 percent for 44,000 workers in the Carolinas, the onset of renewed depression in September forced a number of TWOC locals to accept wage cuts. Employers simply ignored the Wagner Act, and relied on well-tried methods of union busting—discharge of union members, evictions, denial of company store credit, mobilization of the local power of the State, the church, the press, and the Klan, and, as usual, violence and intimidation. The TWOC unsuccessfully tried to avoid charges of communism and "Yankee" interference by hiring southern union organizers.[94] By levying neither initiation fees nor union dues until after a contract was signed, they also tried to avoid charges that they were trying to cheat the workers.

Little headway could be made, however. By early 1939 the union claimed only twenty-seven agreements covering 27,000 southern workers, 7 percent of the region's 350,000 millhands.[95] By 1946 the Textile Workers' Union of America (TWUA), which emerged from the TWOC, had considerable bargaining strength in woolens, synthetics, silk, hosiery, carpets, and other sectors of the textile industry. With respect to the southern cotton textile industry, however, it had largely failed. At the peak of its strength at this time, after a period of wartime expansion, the TWUA together with the remnants of the UTWA (AFL) represented only about 20 percent of southern cotton and rayon workers and had made no significant inroads into the region's major textile corporations such as Burlington, Stevens, Cannon, and Deering-Milliken.

*The impact of capital accumulation and relocation
on the social relations of production
in North Carolina*

Rather than undermining the existing social relations of production in North Carolina in the 1920s and 1930s, capital accumulation (from both local and "external" sources) served to reinforce them. As the cotton textile industry fell behind in terms of its ability to compete with newer, more capital-intensive industries, relocation to the Carolina Piedmont and the preservation of the particularly favorable balance of class forces in that region became of vital importance. Further, the rapid growth of individual cotton textile corporations and of the industry as a whole in the region provided a major stimulus to growth in a number of other, related areas, such as banking and hydroelectric power generation. To the extent that these related sectors were dependent on the continued growth and profitability of the region's major industry, the forces committed to the preservation of the status quo were strengthened.

Finally, the growing political power of textile capital and the increasing commitment of the State to the strategy of textile industrialization are indicated by the relatively new but steadily expanding direct role of the various levels of the State in relations between capital and labor. Efforts by workers to increase their bargaining power and to effect changes in the nature and extent of their exploitation were opposed and defeated by powerful combinations of public and private power.

In the post–World War II period, the maintenance of existing social relations of production would become the cornerstone of the state's industrial development strategy. The pattern set by the cotton textile industry in the 1890s, 1920s, and 1930s—relocation of the most labor-intensive, technologically backward capital to escape high-wage labor market competition and to maximize opportunities for increasing the production of surplus value—would be repeated on a number of occasions in the postwar period, although they would not always result in the same degree of regional concentration.

# 4

## Capital, Exploitation, and the State
## in North Carolina:
## Theoretical Considerations

It should be clear by now that the State has played an important role in
the development of capitalism in North Carolina. This role has been
seen in the construction of the legal foundations of proletarianization,
the creation of a racial division of labor, and in efforts to resist the
spread of unions. So far, these interventions have been considered only
insofar as they have been essential to the historical narrative. If the role
of the State in the creation and preservation of North Carolina's distinctive mode of exploitation is to be more fully appreciated, it must be
given more systematic consideration. This chapter attempts to come to
grips, at a broad theoretical level, with the relationship between capitalist exploitation and the State in order to provide a framework for the
historical discussions of the State and State policy in chapters five and
six. Before beginning this discussion and for purposes of comparison
and clarification, it is worthwhile to look at a number of alternative
perspectives on the State.

*Politics and the State in southern development:*
*the competitive market model, the new social history,*
*and mainstream political science*

In the competitive market model of regional growth it is the market
that ensures the optimal allocation of resources and guides the process
of regional convergence. Given this feature, the proper role of the State
in competitive market theory is necessarily a limited one. The State
must protect the legal equality and contractual rights of the owners of
the factors of production, adjudicate disputes, and intervene when the
market fails because of externalities or monopoly distortions. In other
words, it must ensure the continued operation of the market and no
more. It is a "rulemaker and umpire." [1] If the State fulfills these require-

ments, the market will ensure that resources are efficiently allocated and that the process of interregional convergence will occur. If it goes beyond these tasks, it runs the risk that it too will introduce distortions that may lead to the misallocation of resources and to inefficiencies. According to Milton Friedman (in part eight of the American Public Broadcasting System's "Free to Choose"), the power of this model is borne out by the rapid growth of the southern states of the United States, where capitalism has been relatively "unfettered" by State-induced distortions.[2]

As chapters two and three have shown, the State has indeed intervened in at least one of the rapidly growing southern states. But it has intervened not to limit exploitation (which seems to be what Professor Friedman fears most) nor to preserve formal-legal equality and contractual rights, but rather to create and preserve social conditions favorable to the production of an above-average rate of exploitation. Where necessary this has involved the State in actions to deny contractual rights to certain groups of people. And, consequently, while there has been interregional convergence in technical compositions of capital, there has been significantly less convergence when measured by indicators of the general welfare.

The competitive market model's most crucial failing with respect to the role of the State is not just that it is empirically incorrect in this case. Rather, it is that the model does not have the explanatory power to deal with any State intervention, regardless of its beneficiaries, that goes beyond that required to maintain the market. This is because, as was suggested earlier, the model restricts its definition of the market to include only final market transactions between formally equal individuals and treats as exogenous all those noneconomic factors that determine their content. Together, these restrictions prevent competitive market theory from dealing with political inequalities and class struggles that have their source in unequal property ownership and that determine the form of the State and the content of State policy. The only kind of State that competitive market assumptions allow (and can explain) is a socially neutral State that operates in the interest of the whole of society by maintaining the market. In this respect, it is instructive to read Marx's analysis of the idea of a neutral State in his *Critique of Hegel's Doctrine of the State*, which was written in the 1840s, but which remains relevant today.[3]

Unlike the competitive market model of capitalist development, the new social history accepts the view that production relations in the post–Civil War South were political relations. According to this view, political power at the State level was used by planters to create and strengthen the postwar system of labor control and to resist challenges from merchants and from farmers' organizations. Yet the authors associated with this perspective present State action in a theoretical context that denies that the southern mode of production was capitalist. Although they attempt to outline alternative theories of this mode of production, its class dynamics are poorly specified. Consequently, if the new social historians are unable to analyze the links between southern production relations and capital accumulation, they cannot deal theoretically with the relationship between these production relations and the State. Rather their emphasis is on showing empirically how the State was dominated by planters and operated to further their interests. The major failing of this type of analysis is that it abstracts the State from its social context in the relations of production and treats it simply as an "instrument" in the hands of a particular social class. The limits of State action imposed by class conflict are left unspecified, as are the sources and the nature of variations in its policies and other interventions.

If the above general approaches to regional development are incapable of developing a satisfactory theory of the role of the State, so is "mainstream" political science. The most influential theory of politics and the State in the South, both in the past and contemporaneously, is that developed by V. O. Key in the late 1940s. For Key and others who follow his emphasis, it is the regional fixation with the specific issue of race that is at the heart of the South's distinctive political behavior and the structure and policies of the southern states.[4]

According to Key, the Compromise of 1876 returned the southern states to the control of white conservatives, whose power base lay in the southern Black Belts (plantation counties). Having experienced black political power during Reconstruction, these conservatives proceeded to construct a one-party political system in the South. In this way, they hoped first to prevent the remobilization of black voters by the Republican party, and second to create the largest possible united bloc of southern congressmen to defend (at the federal level) the region's authority over racial matters. Internal social and economic differences that structured political conflict prior to the Civil War were systematically blotted out as planters and their allies appealed to white racial solidarity and loyalty to the Democratic party.[5]

Thereafter, Key argues, white Democratic rule based on the application of various forms of social pressure and violence to dissenters of both races continued, interrupted only by the short-lived Populist revolt of the 1890s. The latter, which again raised the specter of black political power, caused southern Democrats to respond by excluding blacks from access to political power. By disenfranchising blacks, they created a more secure political basis for generalized racial segregation, white supremacy, and Democratic political control of both the southern states and their federal representatives. Consequently, from 1876 onward, "the predominant consideration in the architecture of southern political institutions has been to assure locally a subordination of the Negro population, and externally, to block threatened interference from the outside with these local arrangements."[6]

Externally, Key argues, southern politics was concerned almost exclusively with defending the region's racial practices against federal interference. Internally, the institutionalization of racism, the elimination of party competition, and the establishment of the white Democratic party primary as a focus of political conflict transformed southern politics into factional politics. The struggle between contending factions within the party was constrained by the need to maintain the party's essential racial solidarity. As a result, conflicts were confined to local issues based on localized support and to questions of patronage and personality, within a system based on corrupt, malapportioned electoral systems designed to serve planter interests, and on widespread political apathy among poor whites.[7] Subordinated to the issue of race, southern politics provided no incentive for the adoption of programmatic positions on fundamental political or economic issues and consequently inhibited the growth of stable organizations either in power or in opposition.[8]

For Key, therefore, the southern fixation with race ultimately ruled out institutionalized and regular political conflict. It is the function of conflict in a healthy capitalist system (by which Key means the rest of the United States) to maintain a responsive ruling class, stimulated and strengthened by continual challenge. In the southern states, however, the "upper bracket . . . goes unchallenged," and "develops privileges and repressions destructive of mass morale and often restrictive of the potentialities of the productive system."[9] The southern states have developed no system or practice of political organization and leadership adequate to deal with their problems.[10] The region's social and economic backwardness and its isolation from mainstream United States are thus maintained.

According to Key, the case of North Carolina is a partial exception to this general theory. This state had achieved more honest and more stable factional politics, a more "virile and balanced economy," and greater racial harmony than its southern neighbors.[11] Key argues that this was so for two reasons: first of all, the state's smaller planter class was less able to impose its white supremacist views on the state than was the case elsewhere; and second, and perhaps as a result, an "aggressive aristocracy of manufacturing and banking" had been able to play a more prominent role in the state's development.[12] Thus, accord-

ing to Key, the general impact of race on the southern State has prevented it from carrying out the functions required of it by the southern
economy. The State therefore acts as a barrier to capitalist development.
But in North Carolina the State has been able to play a relatively more
effective role because of the weakness of the planters and therefore of
the influence of race. Assuming that industrial capital has been less
dependent on the manipulation of racial differences than have planters,
the state's "progressive plutocracy," argues Key, has been able to overcome the racial constraints on State action.

There are a number of inconsistencies in the relationship between
Key's general theory and its modification in the case of North Carolina.
If the state's planter class was relatively weak, North Carolina nevertheless experienced a bitter white supremacy campaign in which the
Democrats recaptured the state from a Populist-Republican coalition,
and after which they proceeded to disenfranchise black voters.[13] In
addition, Key does not explain how or why bankers and industrialists,
who participated in these campaigns, could immediately thereafter become "progressive." Nor does he explain why they should relax their
long-term concerns about the crucial issues of taxation and public expenditure in order to provide free public education for all, including the
blacks so recently disenfranchised.[14]

Key's theory of the racial origins and functions of the southern State
severely limits our ability to understand the complex roles played by
both the State and race in capitalist development in North Carolina.
This theory defines the role of the State in terms that are both ahistori-
cal and atheoretical. The southern fixation with race is abstracted from
its context in the totality of the region's social relations of production,
and particularly from its links with strategies of exploitation. Key's
analysis simply links the manipulation of racial divisions with the desire
of southern planters to preserve white supremacy at the political level.
One might infer that this desire is not without a material basis, but Key
does not explicitly investigate such a possibility.

In both its weaker and its stronger versions, Key's theory is also misleading. As chapters two and three have shown, the State has been a
positive factor in capitalist development not only in North Carolina
but also in the other textile states. In addition to providing the essential
basis for a profitable capitalist agriculture, its role in labor control, in
the production of surplus value, and in capital accumulation has benefited not only textile capital but also other capitals that have been drawn
to the region.

None of this is intended to suggest that the issue of race is unimportant. On the contrary, many of the struggles emerging from capitalist
development in North Carolina have been played out in racial terms.

Rather, what is being suggested is that the importance of race and the manner in which it comes to be organized and articulated at the level of the State cannot be understood through a theory that severs its historical and theoretical links with the struggle over material production.[15] As a result, the structure and role of the State itself cannot be adequately understood in terms of Key's theorization.

### The state in Marxian political economy

Since the onset of sustained economic crisis in most Western capitalist countries beginning in the late 1960s, there has been a tremendous growth in the literature on the capitalist State, much of which emerges from Marxist assumptions. Some progress has been made. On the other hand, in much of this literature the limited but distinctive contributions of Marx to the analysis of the role of the State in capitalism have been obscured or lost altogether. In their place, there has emerged an approach to the State that relies on a fusion of Marxist terminology with the kind of reasoning used in functionalist sociology and political science rather than in historical materialism. From this perspective the State is seen as an authoritative structure that performs, for capital, a series of functions that are defined as being essential for the reproduction of the capitalist system. In order for the state to be able to perform these functions—which usually involve the regulation of economic and social relationships in order to promote capital accumulation and social cohesion—the State must be "relatively autonomous"; that is, in order to be able to further the long-term interests of capital in general, the State must be able to act independently of particular capitals and, when necessary, of the economic level as a whole.[16]

This perspective is inadequate for a number of reasons. First, in an effort to construct a Marxist political theory, (that is, a theory of capitalist states generally) the functional requirements of capital are usually derived from an analysis of the capitalist mode of production at its most abstract level, rather than from a consideration of capitalist production in real historical situations. The possibility that different social contexts can give rise to variations in strategies of exploitation and accumulation and in patterns of class conflict, and that these may in turn give rise to variations in the extent and content of State intervention, is ignored in the interest of deriving theoretical generalizations. The price of this approach is "conceptual stretching." The categories of functional Marxism (accumulation, legitimation, coercion, and social cohesion) become so broad that it is often very easy to fit a specific State action into any or all of them, with the result that they become analytically useless.

Second, the concept of relative autonomy effectively severs the links between the State and even this abstract model of capitalist development. Once the functional requisites of capitalist reproduction have been derived, the relationship between the State and capital is relegated to the status of a defensive covering generalization that, following Engels, "on the whole the economic movement gets its way." [17] The problem of the capitalist State is thus abstracted from its social context and treated as a specifically political problem, thus duplicating the fragmentation of capitalist social relations that is characteristic of bourgeois social thought.

Third, to define the capitalist State in terms of the functional requirements of capitalist reproduction does not *explain* the role of the State. To begin with, it does not even adequately define the role of the State unless it can be shown that only the State can perform such functions, that all its acts are functional, and that without them capitalism will suffer unpleasant consequences. Yet the success with which the State carries out its functions will presumably vary with historical conditions. The degree of functional success needed to maintain capitalism must therefore be specified, or the theory becomes tautological: what the State does contributes to the reproduction of capitalism, while the persistence of capitalism must mean that the State is performing its required functions. Further, it seems entirely possible that certain States under certain conditions may be dysfunctional; that is, for a variety of reasons they may be incapable of, or even impede, action necessary to ensure capitalist reproduction.[18] In these cases, their structure and functions may have to be transformed, or, if this is not possible, other entities, such as class organizations, cartels, or international organizations, may be required to pick up the slack.

More important than these problems, however, is the fact that to define the functions of the State is not to explain them, even if all the above conditions are met. Functional analysis cannot explain how the State develops, or why its forms, structures, and practices differ in different capitalist societies.

In general, this radical functionalism fails because it closes off the very kind of historical analysis that is necessary to analyze the relationship between capitalism and the State in concrete social situations. It diverts attention away from historical questions and toward abstract questions of functional logic such as those mentioned above.[19] As a result, it confines empirical Marxist research on the State to the task of filling functional pigeonholes with the relevant examples of State action, occasionally amending a functional category, or perhaps adding a new one. Consequently, like the competitive market model, it cannot generate categories that permit the conceptualization and explanation of variations in State policy either over time or in different social contexts. It is therefore of little use in explaining the particular pattern of State intervention that has played such an important role in creating and maintaining an above-average rate of exploitation and accumulation in North Carolina.

The above discussion suggests, among other things, that a general theory of the capitalist State may be difficult to develop within the Marxian framework and that, if one is developed, its usefulness will be limited. This should not be taken to mean, however, that the Marxian framework cannot provide a useful set of methodological principles or concepts to aid in the analysis of the capitalist State. Indeed, these basic principles can be found in Marx's fragmentary writings on historical materialism and the State. These principles can be distinguished from the functionalist approach discussed above in that they rest on a historical mode of explanation in which the State is not seen as a relatively autonomous entity operating in the interests of capital but rather as a product and constituent part of specific historical patterns of exploitation, accumulation, and class conflict. This involves consideration not only of Marx's abstract model of the capitalist mode of production, but also its specific historical manifestations in concrete social relations. According to Marx,

> the specific economic form, in which unpaid surplus-labour is pumped out of direct producers, determines the relationship of rulers and ruled, as it grows directly out of production itself, and, in turn reacts upon it as a determining element. Upon this, however, is founded the entire formation of the economic community which grows up out of the production relations themselves, thereby its specific political form. It is always the direct relationship of the owners of the conditions of production to the direct producers—a relation always naturally corresponding to a definite stage in the development of the methods of labour and thereby its social productivity—which reveals the innermost secret, the hidden basis of the entire social structure, and with it the political form of the relationship of sovereignty and dependence, in short, the corresponding specific form of the state.[20]

The most important feature of the "direct relationship of the owners of the conditions of production to the direct producers" under capitalism is that it is a relationship of exploitation, in which the surplus product of the wage laborer is appropriated as surplus value by capital. It is also therefore a relationship of class struggle. The extent and modes of State action therefore cannot simply reflect the economic and political needs of capital alone or the abstract logic of capitalist competition, as the functionalist argument often suggests. Rather, they are determined by, and determine in a reciprocal fashion, contradictory class forces in the struggle over the distribution of the social product.

The State is thus a result of the history of class struggle while at the same time a participant in it. It must secure the conditions necessary for capital accumulation in a context of class conflict and by means that are themselves conditioned by class conflict. The capitalist State therefore is an object of class struggle, which cannot only be used to further the interests of capital, but which is also potentially a threat to those interests. What appears from the functionalist perspective as the "relative autonomy" of the State can therefore be seen as a reflection of the fact that the reproduction of capital must be achieved within a context of contradictory class pressures.

Beyond these general methodological principles, there is little else that can be said about the capitalist State on the basis of Marx's abstract discussion of the capitalist mode of production. In order to inject content into the role of the State and to understand its historical and spatial variations, it is necessary to analyze the concrete historical development of capitalism in specific contexts with different precapitalist class structures, cultural, ethnic, and racial compositions, and different traditions and values. As Marx goes on to say, the fact that the role of the State is determined in large part by the exploitative social relations of capitalist production "does not prevent the same economic basis—the same from the standpoint of its main conditions—due to innumerable different empirical circumstances, natural environment, racial relations, external historical influences, etc., from showing infinite variations and gradations in appearance, which can be ascertained only by analysis of the empirically given circumstances."[21] This does not reduce the Marxian political economy of the State to an atheoretical study of history, however. Rather, it simply requires that the analysis of the capitalist mode of production be concretized in the material conditions of life, much as it was by Marx in *Capital*. The task of a Marxian analysis of the capitalist State is to discover, in the analysis of concrete historical situations, the connections between the development of capitalist production and exploitation, class struggle, and the structure and policies of the capitalist State.

Bob Jessop has recently proposed two concepts which, although not new, are useful in this context: the concepts of "accumulation strategy" and "hegemonic project."[22] The utility of these concepts lies in their potential for establishing links between the logic of the capitalist mode of production and the concrete class struggles that occur in real social contexts and for providing substantive coherence in dealing with the capitalist State.

For Jessop, an accumulation strategy defines not only a strategy of exploitation and growth but also the various social and political conditions necessary for its implementation. Thus an accumulation strategy must take account of, among other things, the relations between capitals and the balance of class forces between capital and labor. These, of course, vary significantly with historical conditions. The Fordist strategy of accumulation, for instance, is based not only on the economic dominance of certain highly productive capitals but also on the relative political power of organized labor in these sectors.

If an accumulation strategy provides a stable framework within which competition and conflict can be fought out (and limited), and if consequently the strategy is accepted more or less by the subordinate classes involved (if in other words it permits the development of a notion of the "general interest"), then it can be said to be hegemonic.

The broad outlines of the accumulation strategy implemented in North Carolina have already been indicated; this strategy depends on the ability of capital to combine relatively advanced production techniques with below-average costs of production to generate an above-average rate of surplus value. Within this strategy the State's primary role has been to guarantee the social conditions that allow this higher-than-average exploitation to occur. Because of this, the State's direct role in regulating productive relations has remained much more central than it has in other regions of the United States where the emergence of Fordist wage relations permitted "the silent compulsion of economic relations (to set) the seal on the domination of the capitalist over the worker."[23] Chapters five and six (in part) attempt to document the various dimensions of this intervention during the twentieth century.

The nature of this accumulation strategy raises questions that are theoretically and historically anterior to the analysis of the State's long-term role in capital accumulation, however, and that require consideration of large-scale efforts in the late nineteenth century to use the State to resist proletarianization and exploitation. During this period, capital accumulation required the simultaneous uprooting of large numbers of white farmers from their traditional occupations and life-styles and their subjection to an intensive labor process that pushed them to their physical limits. In addition, it proletarianized their wives and children, paid them inadequate wages, and imposed upon them all the social constraints of mill village life. Such a strategy is hardly capable of creating a long-term basis for hegemony in terms of material rewards and characteristically gives rise to resistance. The case of North Carolina is no exception, as chapters two and three have demonstrated.

What is exceptional in the case of North Carolina (compared not only with earlier cases of capitalist development but also with many contemporary cases in the industrializing Third World) is that this accumulation strategy and the class conflict which it generated occurred in the context of democratic political forms imposed on the southern states after their defeat in the Civil War. On the one hand, therefore, capital accumulation in North Carolina required that the State "regulate" wages—that is, "force them into the limits suitable for making a profit, . . . lengthen the working day, and . . . keep the worker himself at his normal level of dependence." [24] On the other hand, the emergence of class struggle from within this strategy threatened the ability of capital to use the State for these purposes. From the point of view of North Carolina's relatively small group of planter-industrialists, a way had to be found to use the State to regulate the social relations of production while at the same time insulating it from the political consequences of this role.

In late nineteenth-century North Carolina this was not a simple task, and the period between Reconstruction and the turn of the century was dominated as much by class struggle at the level of the State as at the point of production. Until the 1890s capital was able, within certain limits, to maintain control of the State. During the 1890s, however, an interracial coalition opposed to the domination of planter-industrial capital and the process of proletarianization captured the State, threatening to undermine the social and political basis of capital accumulation.

This threat was averted by capital between 1898 and 1900 in a series of moves that redefined the social, political, and legal limits of political practice and the role of the State, limits that lasted at least until the passage of the 1965 Voting Rights Act. The most important component of all this was the political institutionalization of white supremacy and the destruction of black political influence by means of a series of qualifications to vote. In defining the substance and organization of politics and the State as a defense against the threat of "Negro domination," capital in effect excluded a large portion of the State's proletariat from political power and seriously impeded resistance (including resistance to proletarianization and exploitation) from white workers that might split the "white family." It also thereby duplicated, on a grander scale, the racial component of mill village paternalism that presented textile industrialization as a crusade for the social and moral rejuvenation of the white race.

The transformation of North Carolina politics between 1898 and 1900 can therefore be seen as the culmination of, and for capital the "final solution" to, a period of intense class struggle. The segregation and disenfranchisement of blacks was not an end in itself, as Key suggests. Rather, it was a means, first of all, to insulate the State from the class struggle in order that it could be used more effectively to guarantee conditions for capital accumulation. And second, it was a way of providing the strategy of accumulation in North Carolina with a limited basis for hegemony that could not be provided by material means.

These racial restrictions on political activity cleared the ground for the State's role after 1900 as guarantor of the social and political basis for the production of an above-average rate of surplus value. They also made it possible for capital in North Carolina to control the State's representatives at the federal level in Washington. As the twentieth century progressed, the State's role in protecting North Carolina's productive relations from "external threats" would become as important as its role in defeating internal ones.

Historically, the U.S. federal government has been the principal focus for "progressive" capital in the United States in its search for protection against "unfair competition" in the production of surplus value (that is, the ability to extract higher rates of surplus value). Even prior to the New Deal,[25] this movement had begun to press for the standardization of products in certain industries and for the provision of greater uniformity in regulations between states. By the time of the New Deal, these concerns were expanded as "progressive" elements of capital and elements within the Democratic party and the labor movement began to press for the regularization of wage levels, hours, conditions of labor, and labor relations. These initiatives at the federal level presented, at least potentially, a threat to the strategies of exploitation in the South. As the next chapter demonstrates, the role of southern congressmen in limiting and opposing this threat was crucial to the continued viability of these strategies.

# 5

# Capital, Exploitation, and the State
# in North Carolina:
# From the Civil War to the New Deal
# and Beyond

*Class conflict and the emergence of a*
*capitalist State in North Carolina, 1868–1900*

Although a variety of political organizations emerged in opposition to the interests of planter-industrialists during the late nineteenth century, the general dimensions of class conflict at the level of the State remained relatively stable. The material basis of this conflict was the ongoing processes of proletarianization and exploitation. On the basis of the conflicting interests of planter-industrialists on the one hand and freedmen and small white farmers on the other, two opposed conceptions of the structure and role of the State emerged. These first became evident in the struggle over Reconstruction.

Effective Republican control of North Carolina under the 1867 Reconstruction Act lasted only until 1870, when both houses of the state legislature were captured by the conservatives, a loose coalition of secessionist Democrats and Whigs who opposed the enfranchisement of blacks. Nevertheless, the Reconstruction Constitution of 1868 incorporated significant changes in the structure and role of the State.

In addition to abolishing slavery, providing for universal manhood suffrage, and eliminating the property qualification for voting and for election to the state senate, the 1868 constitution made fundamental changes in the structure of local political control. Prior to the Civil War, county government had been carried out by a county court of justices of the peace, appointed for life by the governor on the recommendation of the county's representatives in the general assembly. This court not only tried cases but appointed county officers, levied taxes, and exercised broad administrative powers and social and economic controls. Justices of the peace were generally the largest land- and slaveowners, and their control at the county level was frequently passed down from generation to generation within the same family. The ability of the largest planters to control law and politics at the county level was a crucial element in labor control under plantation slavery.[1]

In response to the desire on the part of both upland white farmers and freedmen for greater freedom from planter domination, the 1868 constitution abolished the county court system and replaced it with the township-county commission form of local government and provided for the popular election of all county officials.[2] In addition, the Republicans saw the State as a means to reduce inequality. The 1868 constitution provided for a system of public education, with free tuition for those between the ages of six and twenty-one. Counties were to be divided into school districts, each of which had to have at least one school running for a minimum of four months a year. The system was to be governed by a board of education comprising the governor, the newly created superintendent of public instruction, and a number of other elected officials. More important, to reduce inequalities, finance was to be controlled at the state rather than the local level. The proceeds from a uniform property tax and other supplementary funds collected at the state level would be distributed to each county in proportion with its school-age population. An equal amount was to be spent on each child, regardless of race.[3]

The Republicans also embarked upon a program of infrastructural development. During 1868 and 1869, a total of about $7.5 million in state bonds was issued, the proceeds of which were to go to aid private railroad companies to repair and rebuild war-damaged equipment and to extend their operations. The Republicans believed that such expenditures would encourage immigration and economic growth and that the resulting increases in the state's tax base would allow the debts to be serviced.[4]

These changes created a State that posed a direct threat to the interests of planters and confirmed their fears about the long-term consequences of the enfranchisement of North Carolina's propertyless blacks. As chapter two demonstrated, their postwar efforts to reestablish production and accumulate capital in a context of chronic capital shortage depended on their ability to maximize the production of surplus value. This, in turn, required a high degree of political and economic control at the local level. It also required that taxation on property be minimized. By democratizing local government and law enforcement, the new constitution limited the planters' ability to control their labor. In addition, the expansion of State activities into education and infrastructural development caused a significant increase in State expenditures. Between 1868 and 1870 the State debt increased by 100 percent to $32 million, the bulk of which was a result of the failure of railway bonds to generate growth, the collapse of bond prices, and the misuse of funds by railway officials.[5]

Resulting tax increases fell largely on the State's only significant form of property—land. In public, planters complained that these increased taxes were used to line the pockets of lawyers and railroad officials and were wasted if used to educate freedmen. Perhaps more important, however, were the unstated objections of planters—that increased educational expenditures might result in a reduced labor supply, a further erosion of planter control, and a reduced ability to accumulate.

Like conservatives elsewhere in the South, North Carolina's planter-industrialists responded to this political and economic squeeze in a variety of ways. Some former Democrats sought to moderate change during the late 1860s by becoming Republicans. Those who remained conservatives fought the new constitution on the grounds that it turned government over to the propertyless, implying that it was property ownership rather than race that was the basis of their complaints. When this strategy failed to split the black vote, planters used economic pressure, boycotting black workers unless they voted correctly.[6]

Ultimately, the conservative recapture of the state required a more extensive and coordinated campaign. Evidence of bribery in the votes for railroad bonds allowed Conservatives to attribute the mounting state debt to the corruption of government by the propertyless and by blacks. Violence and intimidation by the Ku Klux Klan caused large numbers of poor whites to return to the conservative fold and kept many blacks away from the polls in 1870. In addition, the failure of the Republican program of economic development caused many former Whigs with industrial and commercial interests to desert to the conservatives. Strengthened by these additions, the conservatives won majorities in both houses of the state legislature in 1870.[7]

Thereafter, conservative forces began to reconstruct a State more consonant with the requirements of capital. First of all, in 1871 the system of educational financing was overhauled. Funds for education were to be derived from a property tax, set at a uniform rate across the state and supplemented by the proceeds of a poll tax. Most significantly, in order to eliminate the possibility of redistribution, the proceeds from each county were to be used in that county. In addition, because the poll tax was uniformly set and could be differentially enforced at the local level, a significant degree of regressivity was introduced into the system. If the revenues were inadequate to maintain the constitutional four-month term, county commissioners were prohibited from levying additional taxes. The commitment to low taxes was thus given precedence over educational provision. And in 1875 a racially segregated educational system was established by constitutional amendment.[8]

Thirty other amendments were added to the constitution in 1875. Democracy at the local level was destroyed and replaced by a system of centralized control resembling that under slavery, in which local political power was monopolized by property owners. Henceforth, justices of the peace were to be appointed by the conservative-dominated general assembly. They would in turn appoint county commissioners. In addition, most other county offices were made appointive.[9]

Finally, having taken complete control of the State with the Democratic victory in the 1876 gubernatorial election,[10] North Carolina's planter-industrialists were able to begin to use State power to increase rates of exploitation and capital accumulation. As we have seen, the Landlord-Tenant Act of 1876–77 was a major initial step in this direction in that it provided the legal and political basis for the creation of an impoverished wage labor force. In 1879 the State's "dishonest" debts in railroad bonds were repudiated, as was the interest on its "honest" debt. The honest debt was itself scaled down from $43.8 million to $6.5 million, in a move which, according to Hugh T. Lefler and Albert R. Newsome, "rendered more feasible the financing of a program of state development."[11]

Throughout the period of full Democratic control from the late 1870s to 1894 (when the Democrats lost control of the state legislature to a coalition of Populists and Republicans), there was only modest growth in real public expenditures, and the rate of growth gradually declined during the period. Moreover, as was the case throughout the South at this time, the taxation system was highly regressive, depending heavily on the poll tax and the general property tax. Together, these taxes accounted for almost half of state government revenues in 1877; they increased to almost 70 percent in 1882 but returned to the 50 percent level by 1892. The burden of the general property tax in North Carolina, as in other southern states, fell disproportionately on small property. Unlike a number of its counterparts, North Carolina did not make formal provisions for property tax exemptions for new capital entering the state. Nevertheless, according to C. Vann Woodward, the tendency either to undervalue significantly or to exempt completely the property of railroads, utilities, and manufacturing capital was a characteristic component of efforts in all southern states to attract capital, regardless of events in legislative assemblies. Meanwhile, almost every piece of property owned by blacks, however insignificant, was taxed.

In addition to the general property tax, North Carolina also levied other specific taxes on business, but these accounted for a relatively small proportion of revenues during the period under discussion, rising from 8.6 percent in 1877 to just over 16 percent in 1882 but falling back again to under 12 percent by 1892.[12]

From 1870 to the early 1890s, the Democratic party ruled North Carolina in the interests of capital. The economic and racial policies of the post–Reconstruction Democrats provided a fertile soil within which textile capital could grow and upon which a campaign to attract external capital could be based. As a result, "the industrial growth of North Carolina in the 1880s and 1890s was reflected in the growth of the Democratic party, into whose ranks came many lawyers, textile mill-owners, and railroad magnates. While the leadership of the party was not captured by the industrial or capitalist element until the 1890s, its presence gave the party in the 1880s a 'procorporation' attitude which was further enhanced by 'machine' politics."[13]

Throughout this period the relationship between State and capital was a symbiotic one. Party leaders and public officials, who were for the most part large landowners, often also held free rail travel passes, served as lobbyists and legal counsels for railroads, textile companies, and other corporations, and frequently held stock in these businesses.[14] Far from adopting a laissez-faire attitude to capitalist development,[15] the Democratic State intervened aggressively to facilitate proletarianization, labor control, and low wages. A laissez-faire attitude was adopted only in areas where the possibility of regulation existed. On the major national labor issues of the late nineteenth century—railroad regulation, the control of monopolies, and the limitation of the working day and child labor, as well as on the "local" social and economic consequences of proletarianization—the State was inactive.

Since the post–Reconstruction Democratic State was a capitalist State that presided over a coercive process of proletarianization and exploitation of whites as well as blacks, it could not represent the triumph of white racial solidarity in the way that Key and others have suggested.[16] Despite Democratic efforts to reorganize political conflict around the issue of white solidarity, the influence of the class struggle continued to be felt in a number of ways. The most significant and most enduring source of opposition to the domination of capital through the Democratic party came from upland white farmers in the western part of the state, who were traditionally Republican and hostile to the power of the planters. In addition, the Republicans were able to maintain the allegiance of large numbers of blacks who were being proletarianized. In the gubernatorial elections of 1880, Kousser has estimated that 60 percent of adult black males voted Republican, while only 17 percent voted Democratic and 14 percent abstained. For 1884 the estimates are 74 percent, 20 percent, and 2 percent, respectively. As a result, between 1880 and 1896 Democrats were never able to win more than 54 percent of the vote in gubernatorial elections. Between 1876 and 1888, from a total electorate of approximately 250,000, the Democratic margin over the Republicans varied from six thousand to twenty thousand. Turnout, stimulated by this conflict, remained high, varying from a low of 78.4 percent in 1892 to a high of 85.7 percent in 1888. Only in the elections of these years did black nonvoting rise above 30 percent.[17]

The struggles arising from the process of class formation also generated political conflicts within the Democratic party. During the late 1880s, as conditions in agriculture deteriorated, a number of insurgent farmers' organizations emerged as pressure groups within the Democratic party. The Farmers' Association, a network of local clubs within a statewide network, had some success with this strategy, when in 1887 they were able to persuade the state legislature to create an agricultural college. In the industrializing Piedmont region, the association was both challenged and stimulated in 1887 by the Knights of Labor, who sought support from both black and white farmers for an independent political strategy. Such a strategy was defeated, however, when the Democrats charged that the Knights were dominated by Republicans and blacks, causing many white farmers to withdraw their support.[18]

In January 1888 the Farmers' Association was absorbed by the Farmers' Alliance, a more aggressive organization that advocated cooperation in marketing and supply as a means to counter the effects of the lien system and falling commodity prices, and which appealed predominantly to the interests of smaller planters, white yeoman farmers, and the more stable tenants. Neither the most impoverished tenants and sharecroppers nor the larger planters were recruited, nor were blacks. The alliance provided aid to blacks in establishing a Colored Alliance, but contacts between the two organizations remained limited.[19]

Critics of the alliance movement and its later transformation into the Populist party have made much of the internal contradictions within the movement. According to these critics, the failure to achieve lasting social and economic reforms (either as the alliance or as the Populist party) can be put down to the fact that its leadership consisted of relatively prosperous, if relatively small, planters. From an economic point of view, the interest of these planters in maintaining the system of exploitation was, ultimately, stronger than its interest in an alliance with small farmers and tenants to resist impoverishment and proletarianization. In turn, the interest of small farmers and tenants in improved crediting and marketing facilities could do little to alleviate conditions for the black sharecroppers of the Colored Alliance, who had been reduced to the status of wage laborer by the Landlord-Tenant Act, and who therefore stood at the very foot of the chain of exploitation. Consequently, relatively minor concessions by the Democratic power structure could divert or fragment the insurgent organizations.[20]

This argument correctly focuses on the central weaknesses of the alliance and the Populists. The dominant process at work during this period of capitalist development in North Carolina was proletarianization, the precondition for the formation of a textile working class, for the production of surplus value, and for capital accumulation. Because of textile industrialization, the process of proletarianization in agriculture in North Carolina was perhaps more extensive than elsewhere in the South. As a result, it increased the threat of proletarianization for white yeomen farmers and small planters. Constrained politically by the state's racial practices, the white insurgent coalition that emerged was composed of class fractions whose contradictory positions in the process of production outweighed their (sometimes) common interest in changes in the credit system, tariff policy, freight rates, marketing, and electoral politics. Further, because the Colored Alliance was composed largely of tenants and croppers, racial and economic cleavages overlapped, making cooperation between the two organizations doubly difficult.[21]

This argument does not mean, however, that the Populists did not constitute a real threat to planter-industrial domination, proletarianization, and capital accumulation, and it does not mean that political participation by the alliance was a tactical error. As far as the latter is concerned, the alliance/Populist political insurgency was above all a response to the direct role of the State in proletarianization and capital accumulation. What needs to be emphasized is that the processes of class formation and capital accumulation not only generated an opposition that was defensive and beset by internal contradictions, but they were initiated by a planter-industrial class that was, as we have seen, politically and economically weak. Control of the State was a precondition for success, but this control was fragile, despite Democratic manipulation of racial fears. During the late 1870s and 1880s the Republican alliance of upland white farmers and blacks provided a persistent challenge to planter control through the Democratic party, a challenge that was contained only with difficulty. So long as the State was directly involved in proletarianization and capital accumulation, the Democratic claim that their party controlled the State in the interests of the white race was not convincing.

As in the rest of the South, the initial radicalism of the North Carolina alliance was weakened in a number of ways: by the collapse of its cooperative supply and marketing institutions in the deteriorating economic conditions of the early 1880s; by the struggle to free itself from the hold of the Democratic party (which took place prior to the

1892 elections) and the unwillingness of many alliancemen to desert the "Party of the Fathers"; by the conservatism of many of its remaining leaders (Lawrence Goodwyn refers to Marion Butler, leader in North Carolina from 1892, as the "most reluctant Populist of them all"); by the Democratic counteroffensive, which included both attempts at cooperation and social and cultural ostracism; and by the alliance's entry into a Populist national "shadow" movement whose roots lay outside the alliance's cooperative organizational network and political culture.[22]

Yet despite all these difficulties, and despite an expanded Democratic effort to restrict voting by illiterates and to brand the Populists as traitors to white supremacy, the Democrats failed to enforce party and racial discipline in the 1892 elections. Although turnout declined from 85.7 percent in 1888 to 78.4 percent in 1892 and the Democrats won both houses of the legislature and the governorship, the Populists (with 17.1 percent) and Republicans (with 33.4 percent) accounted for a majority of the votes cast.[23]

This warning was ignored by the Democrats, who continued to ostracize the dissenting farmers after 1892. In a context of collapsing prices and a speedup in the process of proletarianization caused by the Panic of 1893, the Democrats refused to address farmers' grievances and continued their policies to aid capital. In addition, they amended the alliance's charter to prohibit its cooperative business activities.[24]

For the 1894 elections the Populists negotiated a cooperative agreement with the Republicans. Both parties supported a single ticket on which both were represented, both would share public offices, and both would stand on a common platform of reforms in tax laws, election laws, county self-government, a nonpartisan judiciary, and expansion of public services. The Democratic platform consisted exclusively of national issues and the commitment to white supremacy. The "Fusion" coalition won virtually all the elective state and congressional offices and won control of both houses of the legislature by large majorities. In 1896, using the same strategy, the Fusionists again won both houses. In addition, the Republican party elected a governor in a race in which all three parties nominated their own candidates.

Many of the Fusion reforms of the 1890s repeated those of the Reconstruction period.[25] The registration law of 1889, which discriminated against illiterate voters, was repealed and replaced with what J. Morgan Kousser considers to be the fairest and most Democratic election law in the post–Reconstruction South. This law provided for election judges, nominated by each party, to monitor vote counting; a voting place for every three hundred fifty voters to prevent deliberate counting delays; limited registrars' powers to make disqualification of voters more difficult; and it placed the burden of proof on the challenger in case of vote challenges. To facilitate voting by illiterates, the 1895 law allowed colored ballots and party symbols on ballot papers. As a result, compared with 1892, turnout in 1896 rose by 49,696 votes, of which only 9,767 went to the Democrats. Black turnout increased from 64 percent to 87 percent. Fusion majorities in both houses were increased. Despite population increases, the 1896 turnout figure was not exceeded until women voted in 1920.

Second, the 1875 county government law was repealed and replaced by a system that returned the selection of county officials and justices of the peace to local electorates. Once again, local political control and the enforcement of the lien laws was jeopardized. In eastern counties with large black populations, blacks gained political office in some cases.

Third, public services were again expanded. State appropriations for public schools were increased by twenty cents per one hundred dollar property value, a sixty-cent poll tax, and a further state allocation. Between 1896 and 1900 the proportion of state funds going to black schools increased by six percentage points. In 1897 the position of county superintendent of schools, a post that had been abolished in the Democratic cost-cutting measures after Reconstruction, was restored. Every school district was required to vote on the issue of local school taxes (which the Democrats had prohibited) every two years until the taxes were approved, and an appropriation of fifty thousand dollars was made to aid schools in those districts that voted favorably. Appropriations to the University of North Carolina were increased. In addition, training institutions for local schoolteachers were established, and expenditures for charitable and correctional institutions were increased. As a result of all these measures, the proportion of State expenditures going to education increased from 6.4 percent in 1892 to 10.6 percent in 1897. Perhaps even more significant, the fastest-growing source of state government funds in these years was the category of "specific business taxes" mentioned above. Between 1892 and 1897 contributions from this source increased from 11.7 percent to 18.2 percent.

Fourth, to reduce farmer indebtedness, the legal rate of interest was reduced from 8 to 6 percent per annum. The alliance's business charter was restored, and property in the state was revalued upward to increase the tax base. The powers of the State Railroad Commission were enlarged.

Finally, a number of further reforms were called for and discussed, although they were not implemented: the repudiation of municipal bonded debts, which had been used in some cities and towns to provide incentives for external capital; further increases in school taxes; a system of reformatories and apprenticeships; court reform; and railroad reform. Republican Governor Daniel L. Russell inaugurated a discussion of the relationship between the needs of external capital and the public good in the State. He promised to repossess the North Carolina Railway, leased in 1895 by outgoing Democratic Governor Elias Carr to J. P. Morgan's Southern Railway Company, claiming that transportation systems were a public good and should be publicly owned and controlled.[26]

The Fusion governments of 1895 and 1897 failed to implement their more polemical and radical promises, such as the breakup of trusts, large banks, and railroad monopolies. Yet the significant political and social reforms that were carried out, their consequences with respect to political mobilization, and the fact that such issues as public ownership became the subject of political discussion were sufficient to galvanize capital in North Carolina into opposition. In this opposition, capital was aided by the growing fragility of the Fusion coalition. Disputes about the distribution of patronage and the election of a U.S. senator in 1897 increased the frictions caused by contradictory class interests within the coalition. Moreover, the 1896 election had clearly benefited the Republicans more than the Populists, who confused voters by supporting the Democratic party at the national level and the Republicans at the state level.[27]

It is clear that the main reason for the Democrats' narrow 52.8 percent majority in 1898 lay elsewhere. Threatened by the Fusion reforms, and the rhetoric of Governor Russell, capital solidified in support of the Democrats. The Democrats in turn campaigned in 1898 on a platform that consciously attempted to combine the appeal to white supremacy in response to the threat of "Negro domination" with policies to facilitate capital accumulation, while simultaneously proposing education expansion, action against governmental corruption, and the popular election of U.S. senators in order to bid for support from Populist farmers.[28]

The reconciliation of these three political thrusts and of the political forces concerned was not achieved without difficulty. In particular, the Democrats had to reassure capital that the reintegration of the Populist insurgents, the impact of this insurgency within the party itself, and the stepped-up campaign of white supremacy would not result in any diminution in efforts to encourage capital accumulation. Furnifold Simmons, the North Carolina State Democratic chairman, sent former Governor T. J. Jarvis to secretly visit bankers, railroad officials, and manufacturers to solicit funds and other aid in return for a promise that taxes on capital would not be increased for at least two years.[29]

Postelection opinion confirmed the success of these efforts. According to the *Charlotte Observer*,

the businessmen of the State are largely responsible for the victory. Not before in years have the bankmen, the millmen, and the businessmen in general—the backbone of the property interest of the state—taken such sincere interest. They worked from start to finish, and furthermore they spent large bits of money in behalf of the cause. . . . When Democratic rallies were held, mills and shops were shut down so that the operatives could attend the speakings.[30]

For the electorate, however, the material interests that provided the incentive for such a role were obscured. According to A. Eugene Holton, chairman of the Republican Executive Committee, "the defeat of the Republican party was charged to the negro, but the negro was only the torch light which the voters have observed, while the tar beneath, which produces the light, has been obscured."[31] For Holton, the business counterattack was a result of: the reduced legal interest rate, which represented a loss of 2 percent on approximately fifteen million dollars in North Carolina's banks and on loans extended by the banks; the threat of repudiation of municipal bonds, which were often held by those corporations whose expansion or relocation they were designed to facilitate; and the 1897 revaluation of the stock of property and capital. Again, according to the *Observer*, "with the assurance of a legislative change of policies which the Democrats were ready to give to ensure success, it was an easy matter for the Democrats to raise unlimited means with which to carry on an effective campaign."[32]

Finally, business interests also participated in other aspects of the campaign. The Red Shirt Clubs, which were responsible for large-scale intimidation of both black and white voters in the eastern half of the state (and, in Wilmington, for a full-scale local "revolution" that overthrew the legally constituted city government, caused large numbers of blacks to leave the city, and left ten blacks dead) were "composed of respectable and well-to-do farmers, bankers, school teachers and merchants—in many cases the best men in the community."[33]

Following the 1898 victory, the Democrats moved to undo the reforms enacted by the previous two Fusion legislatures. County government was again turned over to the general assembly, allowing it to revert to control of capital at the local level. In order to placate former insurgent farmers, the legislature appropriated one hundred thousand dollars for public schools, made the commissioner of agriculture an elective office, and replaced the Railroad Commission with a three-man corporation commission empowered to supervise railroads, banks, telephone and telegraph companies, street railways, and express companies. The commission's three members were to be appointed by the governor.[34]

More important, however, the Democrats realized that the degree of political control necessary for continued capital accumulation could not be guaranteed given the existing political structure. Their experiences since the Civil War demonstrated the fragility of political control in a situation in which significant white Republican support continued in the western part of the state, and in which blacks continued to be able to vote. Democratic policies could not serve as a basis to attract the votes of black tenants and sharecroppers, and electoral manipulation and white supremacy had been shown to be an unsure basis for control in the depressed conditions of the 1880s and 1890s.

Therefore, in order to obtain the necessary degree of control, the Democrats moved to eliminate blacks permanently from North Carolina politics. Josephus Daniels, editor of the *Raleigh News and Observer* and a major figure in the 1898 white supremacy campaign, was sent to seek advice from other southern states that had responded to the farmers' revolt by disenfranchising black voters. The 1899 legislature subsequently passed a constitutional amendment containing requirements that any applicant for voter registration must have paid his poll tax and must be able to read or write any section of the state constitution. A "grandfather clause," included to strengthen the white supremacist interpretation of disenfranchisement, provided that "no person who was entitled to vote on or before January 1, 1867, or his lineal descendent, should be denied registration by reason of his failure to possess the educational qualifications, provided that he shall have registered prior to December 1, 1908." [35]

In order to assure the amendment's popular endorsement, the Democrats also reformed the election laws instituted by the Fusionists. The appointment of election officers was taken from local democratically elected officials and placed in the hands of a state election board chosen by the legislature. All voters were required to reregister, and the discretionary powers of registrars were widened. Finally, a law that provided for separate ballot boxes for different political offices and prohibited the counting of wrongly distributed ballots was passed. The only way an illiterate voter could vote was by having his ballots arranged in order by someone who could read. Constant reordering of the boxes eliminated this possibility. In 1900 approximately 19 percent of the state population and 53 percent of blacks were illiterate. [36]

Finally, the racial violence that had been responsible for the Democrats' 1898 victory was once again evident. The Democratic candidate for governor in 1900, C. B. Aycock, branded opponents of the amendment as "public enemies," and the Red Shirts openly intimidated voters of both races. Alfred M. Waddell, a former Democratic congressman from Wilmington, told an election eve crowd to "go to the polls tomorrow, and if you find the Negro out voting, tell him to leave the polls, and if he refuses, kill him, shoot him down in his tracks." [37]

Compared with 1898 the Fusionist vote fell by 25 percent in 1900, its support virtually disappearing in areas of black concentration. Total turnout fell from 85.4 percent in 1896 to 74.6 percent. The disenfranchising amendment was approved by 59 percent of those who voted. The thirty-one Piedmont and western counties in which the amendment was defeated had populations that were predominantly white. Of eighteen counties with a black population majority not one defeated the amendment. County votes for the amendment were positively correlated (0.41) with county per capita white wealth. For every increase of one thousand dollars in white per capita wealth, there was a 12.4 percent increase in the white vote for the amendment.[38]

*The political and economic impact*
*of disenfranchisement*
*and the role of the State after 1900*

The exclusion of black workers from political participation allowed plantation capital in North Carolina to strengthen its control over the black labor force. The link between black disenfranchisement and production is perhaps best expressed by a Mississippian, whose state had in 1890 pioneered the disenfranchisement of blacks,[39] and who warned that "If the Negro is permitted to engage in politics, his usefulness as a laborer is at an end. He can no longer be controlled or utilized. The South has to deal with him as an industrial and economic factor, and is forced to assert its control over him in sheer self-defense."[40] By disenfranchising blacks, the Democrats created a State whose form paralleled in many ways the form taken by the industrial exploitation of whites. After 1900 racial exclusion, combined with the threat of racial competition, provided part of the basis of capitalist domination both in textile production and at the level of the State. The newly segregated State represented both an extension and a reinforcement at the political level of a major element in North Carolina's relations of production.

Moreover, disenfranchisement also allowed a further penetration of racial divisions into these social relations. In the system of social segregation that came to be known as Jim Crow, many forms of social intercourse between the races were prohibited.[41] More significantly, however, this period also saw the extension of racial segregation in the economy. According to William Chafe, between 1870 and 1900 almost 50 percent of skilled workers in Greensboro, North Carolina, were black. They included brickmakers, carpenters, foundry workers, and railway employees. After 1900, however, blacks were progressively excluded from these occupations. In lumber, woodworking, and furniture factories, black labor was replaced with white agricultural labor. White women replaced blacks in the tobacco industry. The local office of the Southern Railway Company fired all black conductors, engineers, and firemen. By 1910 not a single black was listed as a factory worker.[42]

The political exclusion of blacks was significant beyond its impact on black politics and black labor. By assuring Democratic control of the state legislature, exclusion of blacks strengthened the control of planter-industrial capital at the local level. The political and legal basis of agricultural proletarianization was stabilized, and the link between agricultural impoverishment and the rate of surplus value in the textile industry was preserved. By eliminating the political threat to agricultural production, disenfranchisement also strengthened capital's control of the textile labor force.

Disenfranchisement also had a direct political impact on white workers. A significant part of the propaganda campaign that preceded disenfranchisement had been based on the premise that the exclusion of blacks would rejuvenate the two-party system. No white votes would be lost as a result of the literacy test. Rather, the removal of blacks from politics, so the Democrats argued, would allow increased freedom of expression and dissent by whites, since the threat of "Negro domination" would no longer exist. Supporters of both parties would therefore benefit, and the state's white leaders would be able to deal more effectively with the social and economic problems besetting the state's white population.

In fact, black disenfranchisement had exactly the opposite effects. First, the elimination of the party's black support virtually eliminated any hope of a Republican victory at the state level. Between 1900 and the 1920s the number of Republican state senators averaged two or three (out of fifty), while the number of representatives averaged five or six (out of one hundred twenty).[43] Consequently, after 1900, with secure majorities in both houses of the U.S. Congress, the national Republican leadership reverted to the "southern strategy" it had last used after the Hayes presidential victory in 1876. Efforts to mobilize the black and white poor in the South were terminated and replaced with efforts to compete for the support of capital by promising tariff protection and infrastructural improvements. Convinced that the black vote was henceforth unimportant or dangerous or both, the Republicans, like the Democrats, excluded blacks from the party. Thereafter, political conflict between planter-industrial capital and small farmers and tenants occurred only sporadically. Since the Democratic party was the only political organization with a chance of achieving political power, this conflict necessarily had to focus on the party's nominating elections and was therefore constrained by the fact that the party was, in practical terms (although not formally), an all-white organization.[44]

Second, white political activity was also reduced by black disenfranchisement. It is not clear to what extent this can be attributed to the collapse of party competition or to the direct effect of the literacy test. What is certain is that the disenfranchisement of whites was not an unintended consequence of efforts to disenfranchise blacks. Powerful interests in North Carolina saw in disenfranchisement an opportunity to destroy the political power of white workers and to establish in power "the intelligence and wealth of the South." In the southern states generally, the late 1890s saw a resurgence of antidemocratic theorizing.[45] Significant perhaps, the struggle over disenfranchisement coincided with the NUTW's campaigns for the ten-hour day and the regulation of child labor.

The extent of the reduction in white political activity is difficult to determine. North Carolina Democratic leader, Furnifold Simmons, admitted that seventeen thousand whites lost their votes because of the poll tax alone. Republicans guessed the figure to be as high as forty thousand. Assuming that no blacks voted (which is probably unrealistic, since the use of the literacy test was left to local discretion and was probably dependent on local conditions), J. Morgan Kousser estimates that the fall in white turnout between 1896 and 1904 was 23 percent. In the 1908 election for governor, under the same assumption, Kousser estimates total turnout at 52 percent and white turnout at 73.6 percent. Since some blacks probably voted (especially in counties outside the Black Belt), actual white turnout was probably lower than this figure suggests.[46]

Whatever the initial impact of the poll tax and literacy test on white voters, their long-term impact was to eliminate the possibility of effective opposition to the domination of capital through the Democratic party. Consequently, in the long-term, political participation atrophied. Between 1920 and 1946 (that is, after the enfranchisement of women and including the New Deal period of electoral realignment and mobilization at the national level), the average turnout in Democratic primaries for governor and senator was 42.8 percent and 35.3 percent, respectively, at general elections (that is, coinciding with elections to the state legislature), and 20.6 percent and 19.9 percent otherwise. If no blacks had voted, these figures would have represented, respectively, 58.5 percent, 48.4 percent, 28.1 percent, and 27.2 percent of the white voting age population.[47] In 1976, when 396,000 black voters (54.8 percent of the black voting age population) were registered to vote after the civil and voting rights "revolution," only 43.7 percent of the state's voting age population voted in the election for governor. Between 1960 and 1976 an average of 49.4 percent voted for president and 39.6 percent for U.S. representatives.[48] In other words, the disenfranchisement of black voters provided the basis of a long-term political demobilization. This in turn became the central basis of capital's control, through the Democratic party, of exploitation and accumulation in North Carolina.

Events in North Carolina can thus be seen to parallel, in a general way, those occurring in the United States as a whole in the 1890s and 1900s. In his discussion of the momentous changes in party and electoral politics that occurred in this period, E. E. Schattschneider notes that "both sections became more conservative because one-party politics tends strongly to vest political power in the hands of people who already have economic power. Moreover, in one-party areas (areas of extreme sectionalism) votes decline in value because the voters no longer have a valuable party alternative."[49] Similarly, for Walter Dean Burnham, the "chief function of the fourth party system" (1896–1931) was the "substantially complete insulation of elites from attacks by the victims of the industrializing process, and a corresponding reinforcement of political conditions favoring an exclusively private exploitation of the industrial economy."[50]

On the other hand, it would be an error not to recognize that sectionalism, one-party dominance, and political demobilization proved to be much more extensive and durable in the South, primarily as a result of the region's racial component. As Key demonstrates, average turnouts in elections for governor and senator from 1920 to 1946 in New York state were, at 56 percent and 60 percent, respectively, substantially higher than those in North Carolina.[51] In presidential elections from 1920 to 1976, inclusively, the average turnout in North Carolina was 45.2 percent, in New York 64.6 percent.[52]

Within North Carolina, variations from a pattern of low county-level turnout figures were associated with pockets of persisting Republican strength in the western part of the state. In eighteen counties (of a total of one hundred) in which the Republicans won at least 40 percent of the vote in the 1940 election for governor, average turnout was 66.6 percent, compared with a statewide average of 41.4 percent.[53]

There is no such variation related to the extent of industrialization. The existence of a large and expanding textile working class in a number of counties did not result in high levels of working class political activity, despite the conflicts of the late 1920s and 1930s. As we have seen, textile industrialization operated within a system of production relations established in agriculture. The production of surplus value in the textile industry, as in agriculture, was achieved within a social structure characterized by social and geographical isolation and disorganization and political and economic dependence. Neither the southern Democratic party nor the Republicans attempted to appeal to the interests of southern workers after 1900.

Formal political activity was missing consequently from most textile mill villages and towns. In the mill villages visited by Frank Tannenbaum, "the people have no political life. They do not vote. They are not interested in politics."[54] Jennings S. Rhyne's larger sample of both workers and villages uncovered wide variations in political activity. Not surprisingly, since milltown political offices were in most cases part of the larger paternalistic structure, few millworkers held political office. Of 487 male family heads studied, 60 percent voted either regularly or occasionally. This figure does not necessarily contradict Tannenbaum's observations, since Rhyne curiously failed to study the political participation of women (perhaps because it was negligible). The 60 percent male rate also included wide variations, however. In one mill, only 29 percent voted; in another 86 percent. In general, voting was positively associated with home ownership and negatively related to the rate of mobility. Some 81.8 percent of homeowners in the sample voted regularly or occasionally. The more stable the labor force and the more freedom from mill village control, the greater the political activity.[55] Stable employment, home ownership, and freedom from social and economic constraints were not generally characteristic of North Carolina's industrial labor force. In addition, the electoral mobilization and realignment caused at the national level by New Deal policies had little impact in North Carolina.

In 1940 there were twelve North Carolina counties with five thousand or more textile wage earners. They accounted for a total of 121,675 textile wage earners, 29.5 percent of the total labor force in all occupations in the twelve counties. Blacks accounted for 21.1 percent of their total population, less than the statewide figure of 27.5 percent. Yet turnout in these counties, at 42.4 percent in 1940, was virtually identical with the statewide figure of 41.4 percent. The five largest textile counties — Alamance, Cabarrus, Gaston, Guilford, and Rowan — with 74,756 textile workers (39.7 percent of their combined labor force), some of the state's largest textile centers, and a combined black population that was only 18 percent of the total had a turnout rate of 41.8 percent.[56]

The State that emerged in North Carolina after 1900 reinforced the social and economic control of planters and textile industrialists and played an important role in containing periodic threats to proletarianization, exploitation, and capital accumulation. It also allowed the cost of expanding State activities in a number of areas to be passed on to the state's working class through a regressive system of taxation. The ability to realize surplus value within North Carolina was thereby restricted, but the social and economic conditions under which surplus value was produced were preserved.

The State's most important function in the period after 1900 was to preserve the relations of exploitation that were the basis for capital accumulation in North Carolina. As earlier chapters indicated, lien laws were used to proletarianize both black and white farmers, providing an expanding pool of wage laborers for both agriculture and the textile industry. State labor policy was designed to allow the textile industry to regulate itself with respect to the use of child and female labor and the length of the working day. As industrialization continued and the dimensions of class conflict widened, maintenance of the relations of exploitation increasingly involved the direct use of State power. Local justices of the peace made injunctions against strike action freely available to capital when workers rebelled. Finally, the use of troops against workers in 1919, 1921, 1929, and 1934 destroyed a number of unionization campaigns in order to keep workers at their "normal level of dependence."

Beyond this role as overseer of the process of exploitation, the State's activities were limited. Since capital accumulation was based on the existence of a large and expanding pool of impoverished surplus labor and since the levels of skill and education needed in most jobs in the textile industry were low or nonexistent, State expenditures to increase the social wage or to increase productivity were unnecessary and potentially counterproductive. Consequently, for a long period after 1900, the State confined itself to a role that kept public expenditures and tax levels as low as possible.

Political considerations sometimes allowed partial exceptions to this general rule, however.[57] The expansion of the State education system after 1900, which had been promised by the Democrats during the campaigns of 1898 and 1900, was a case in point. During the disenfranchisement campaign, it was charged that the Democrats' proposed literacy test would disenfranchise large numbers of illiterate whites as well as the black population. The Democrats responded by promising expanded educational facilities for whites, along with a "grandfather clause" that would protect illiterate white voters until it expired in 1908. These were presented as part of a long-term campaign whose aim, given the elimination of troublesome black political participation, was to create equality within the white race. The Democratic educational policy was therefore an essential element in the broader appeal for racial solidarity against the Populists and Republicans. It also allowed the Democrats to co-opt a small but vocal group of "progressive" middle class reformers that had emerged within the "New South" movement but had been given little opportunity to participate in the actual construction of southern capitalism thus far. After 1900 this group allied itself with the Simmons-Aycock Democratic political machine. Working within the limits set by the racial, political, and economic constraints on the development of capitalism and State policy, this group became the Democratic mouthpiece for the educational aspects of their strategy. It also functioned as an important link with external "progressive" educational funding organizations, such as the Rockefeller-dominated General Education Board.[58]

Despite this expansion, which increased the proportion of state government expenditures going to education in 1902 to 26.9 percent, educational policy continued to be constrained by the requirements of capital accumulation. Educational control and financing, still based on the system established in the 1870s, were situated for the most part at the county level, in order not to conflict with the imperatives of proletarianization and the production of surplus value. Since there were wide variations in the counties' abilities to support educational facilities, it became increasingly difficult to argue that educational expansion was leading to equality among whites. The system of educational financing was highly regressive. Blacks paid higher taxes for education than did whites, poor whites paid higher taxes than rich whites, and the law was designed to prevent any redistribution between "rich" and "poor" counties. After 1900 the ratio between per capita expenditures on education for blacks and those for whites fell by 53 percent in ten years, and there was increasing inequality between per capita expenditures in rich and poor counties.[59]

The establishment of a State Equalization Fund in 1901 and a four-month minimum school term in 1907 perhaps helped to reduce educational inequalities between counties (for whites) to some extent. State expenditures continued to be constrained, however, by the requirements of capital accumulation. In a context of proletarianization and rapidly increasing inequality, education was first and foremost a mechanism of labor discipline and social control. Since agricultural proletarianization was facilitated in part by widespread black and white illiteracy, education that went beyond the inculcation of basic values of discipline and obedience to authority was potentially counterproductive. Further, until the 1920s, when depressions in agriculture and the textile industry necessitated the imposition of the stretch-out, the need for child labor in the textile industry limited the possibility of educational reform. Laws to limit the use of child labor by requiring a minimum level of education left many loopholes and other devices to the discretion of capital, and only a small number of textile occupations required more than a bare literacy. Teachers, as providers of discipline rather than education, were neither well-trained nor highly paid, and the quality of public school education remained low.

The logic of State educational policy was transformed in the period after World War I, however. Social and economic conditions in the 1920s led to a significant increase in the number of unemployed children, especially in the industrializing Piedmont region. During this decade, North Carolina's population increased by six hundred thousand. Simultaneously, the agricultural depressions of 1920–21 and 1924 expanded the pool of adult surplus labor available to the textile industry and drove down wages. By the middle of the decade, while the industry was experiencing depression and increased competition at the national level, a high rate of exploitation in the southern states was causing extensive interregional migration of capital. The imposition of the stretch-out was facilitated by this expanded pool of labor power, and in turn both permitted and required (since it drastically increased the intensity of work) a reduction in the use of child labor. Increasing numbers of unemployed children necessitated increased educational expenditures both for practical reasons—the work discipline and social control formerly provided by the mill had to be replaced—and because the paternalistic ideology of the mill villages demanded that they should not be left idle. Beginning in the 1920s, therefore, the school gradually began to take over from the mill the task of reproducing the social relations of production in North Carolina.

During the 1920s only the wealthiest counties with expanding urban and industrial property values were able to cope with these "new" educational requirements while at the same time maintaining acceptably low tax rates. In 1928 all but one of ten counties that received no State equalization funds were urban and industrial counties.[60] For the rest of the counties, whose property tax bases were mostly in land (the value of which was at best stable during the 1920s), increasing expenses could not be met without increased tax rates, and the advantages of educational expansion were by no means clear. If anything, increased education raised the possibility of labor shortages in the rural counties where child labor was still crucial in agricultural production. Consequently, educational expansion and educational finance became objects of struggle between counties, between the county and state levels of government, and between agricultural and industrial capital. Increased State expenditures were necessary to support expansion in the rural counties but implied the need for increased revenues at the state level. Such increases were only feasible politically if they could be achieved by means other than State taxes on landed property, if they did not lead to a reduction of political and social control at the local level, and if they did not interfere with exploitation and capital accumulation in the textile industry.

During the 1920s it proved impossible to meet all these requirements simultaneously.[61] While control of education remained at the local level, responsibility for expansion and finance was gradually transferred to the state level. Yet, despite a variety of attempts to create new taxes, to revalue the state's property, and to rationalize the educational system in order to cut costs, it proved to be impossible to find a politically acceptable way of meeting all the conflicting demands in this area. For example, in 1929 the state legislature defeated a proposal by the governor to transfer responsibility for the entire educational system and its financing to the state level and to guarantee an eight-month school term.[62] Although this proposal would have allowed a drastic reduction in county property taxes and a large reduction in educational costs through the creation of a uniform statewide system, it was defeated as a result of opposition from the representatives of the eastern agricultural counties on the grounds that it would drastically reduce the size of the agricultural labor force.

The struggle over educational policy and finance in the 1920s was duplicated in the area of highway construction. An efficient and cheap system of transportation was essential if North Carolina's competitive advantage in production costs was to be maintained. In addition, as textile industrialization continued, the mills began to rely more heavily on rural laborers and part-time farmers. Consequently, easy access by road to the mills from the surrounding areas became increasingly important. As in the area of education, however, progress was limited. Responsibility for highways was also situated at the county level, and the quality of roads varied accordingly. In many cases, the construction of roads was determined on the basis of political patronage rather than economic necessity.[63]

During the 1920s a system of state roads was created to link county seats and major towns. By 1930 North Carolina had become the "good roads" state and had accumulated a vast public debt in the process. Yet the deficiencies of the county-based system of secondary roads continued to cause difficulties in an economy in which a very large proportion of production took place in rural areas and in which increasing numbers of children had to be transported to increasingly large and distant schools. As in education, a rurally dominated state legislature defeated proposals for the rationalization of the highway system and the transfer of responsibility to the State level.

It was the depression, beginning in late 1929 and lasting throughout the 1930s, that finally broke these political stalemates. In turn, the change permitted the State to intervene more effectively in the areas of schooling and highway construction in order to respond more effectively to the needs of capital in these areas. By the end of 1930, not only were the educational and highway systems failing to perform as required, but their inefficient administration and the difficulties involved in generating new revenues had caused the combined state and local debt to rise to $535 million, the annual cost of which was roughly forty million dollars out of a total revenue that had averaged one hundred million dollars in the three previous years. As the depression deepened, falling land values, the crash in security values, increasing difficulty in realizing surplus value, and rising unemployment reduced the likelihood that this level would be equaled in the short term. Counties that relied heavily on land as the base for property taxes were unable to maintain schools and roads. At the end of 1930, delinquent property taxes amounted to $7.5 million, and 150,000 pieces of property were involved in tax sales. The formation of the North Carolina Tax Relief Association signaled the beginning of a large-scale tax revolt.[64]

It was in this context that North Carolina became the pioneer (in the United States) in the centralization of State power that was a precondition for an effective reorganization of State policy. The legislative program proposed by Governor O. Max Gardner in 1931 had as its basis a study by the Brookings Institution, which recommended first that political centralization was essential to provide the services necessary in a modern economy and to eliminate inefficiencies, and second, that taxes on property, and especially on real property, had to be reduced. Not all of Gardner's proposals were successful. His attempt to make all but three (governor, lieutenant governor, and auditor) of the state's thirteen administrative offices appointive rather than elective failed, as did a proposal to consolidate counties into larger units. In other important areas, however, the legislature had little choice but to agree with Gardner's initiatives.[65]

First, a law transferred responsibility for all roads, including forty-six thousand miles of secondary roads, to the State. All county equipment, supplies and labor were to be turned over to the State Highway Commission. All prisoners sentenced to sixty or more days in jail were to be turned over to the commission for work in highway maintenance. In 1933 the commission took complete control of prison administration, and by 1936 the state's prison system was entirely self-financed by the sale of labor power to the commission.[66]

Second, a Local Government Act was passed establishing a Local Government Commission to regulate the mobilization of funds by the counties for infrastructural purposes and to ensure adequate protection against waste and misuse.[67]

Third, the rationalization of State administration, begun sporadically during the 1920s,[68] was expanded in order to strengthen the governor's role as the "General Manager of the business corporation of the government."[69] Executive agencies with powers of oversight and coordination were created in the areas of purchasing, standardization of contracts and purchases, and personnel. New executive departments (of banking and insurance, and labor) were established, the latter to facilitate the gathering of data rather than to perform any regulatory functions.

In addition, responsibility for providing the minimum six-month school term was transferred to the State, allowing a drastic program of reorganization and cost reduction to be implemented.[70] Since education was an important mechanism of political and social control and work discipline at the local level, opposition to a complete transfer of control continued. The system established in 1931 maintained a significant degree of local control. Rural school committees and boards of trustees in school districts retained their control over teacher selection and, in the latter case, the power to appoint school superintendents. County boards of education retained control of administration, the election of county superintendents, school organization, transportation, and general school business. In addition, counties were allowed to mobilize additional funds for the extension of the school term. While taxation of property for the six-month school term was prohibited, county boards could supplement any item of expenditure from special taxes or from money for the extended term. In other words, if the approval of county commissioners and the State Board of Equalization could be gained, funds for extending the school term could be diverted from other local functions.[71]

The most important struggle during the 1931 legislature was over the problem of raising the revenues necessitated by State centralization and the loss of property tax revenue. Here, agreement between industrial and agricultural capital in the state legislature proved difficult to reach. Prior to 1931, most tax reform proposals had focused on the benefits of a constitutional amendment to allow lower tax rates to be set on intangible property in order to increase the amount declared for tax purposes. These proposals made little headway in a state legislature that was dominated for the most part by real property and that was unwilling to legislate a reduced property tax rate for holders of stocks and bonds.[72] In the face of this stalemate, two major proposals appeared in 1931. The first called for a general 1 percent sales tax on all retail sales, and the second for a series of "luxury" sales taxes—20 percent on tobacco and cigarettes, and 10 percent on soft drinks, cinema admissions, gun shells, and a number of other items.

Opposition to the luxury sales tax and to attempts to increase taxes on corporations was organized by Duke Power lobbyists such as Clyde Hoey, by Standard Oil and Carolina Power and Light lobbyist James Pou, and by lobbyists from the American and R. J. Reynolds tobacco companies. The general version of the sales tax was opposed by the State Merchants' Association, by the state's few labor organizations, and by both large and small agricultural capital, whose tenant supply business would be affected. The latter also led opposition to a suggestion that the new school law should be repealed and replaced with a law that was feasible within the property tax–based system of finance that had existed prior to 1931.[73]

After a series of long and acrimonious debates, amid charges of bribery and attempted bribery against Reynolds, both sales tax versions died in the state senate, and the issue became deadlocked. In order to prevent the collapse of the entire package of political and administrative reforms, a temporary arrangement was worked out that reduced property taxes by $12.16 million, 20 percent of total property tax revenue in 1930.[74] In order to make up for this reduction, the state gasoline tax was increased and a new license tax was levied on wholesale and retail sales. Corporation franchise taxes on capital and surplus and undivided profits, on the assessed value of railroad equipment, and on the gross sales of public utilities were increased. In addition, corporation and individual tax rates were increased.

In practice, the only gains from these changes resulted from the increased gasoline and license taxes and from savings that resulted from reorganization. Any increased revenue that might have resulted from corporate franchise and income tax increases was offset by reduced taxes on property, approximately 33 percent of which was owned by corporations. Changes in individual income tax rates and brackets had only a limited effect in the depressed conditions.[75]

This arrangement, while meeting the essential requirements of agricultural and industrial capital, was insufficient to meet costs. The 1931–32 budget was in deficit by seven million dollars, and a deficit of thirteen million dollars was predicted for 1933–34.[76] In this situation, a number of proposals were made for raising additional revenues. First, the Brookings Institution warned that a general sales tax was regressive and would deepen the depression by reducing consumer demand and that a luxury tax on cigarettes and tobacco was not politically feasible. The only plausible alternative was to reduce the number of income tax exemptions in order to increase the number of taxpayers.[77] Second, a University of North Carolina tax study urged further property tax reductions and efforts to increase corporation taxes, to amend the tax system in order to reach intangible property, and to adopt a luxury sales tax as a crisis measure.[78] Third, the North Carolina Tax Commission recommended no new taxes but rather a more extensive and intensive program of cost cutting.[79]

Neither the new governor, J. C. Blucher Ehringhaus, nor the state legislature endorsed the Tax Commission's proposals. Further attempts at reorganization and centralization were made. The State Board of Equalization was replaced by the State School Commission, the highway and prison departments were merged, and the Corporation Commission was replaced by a three-man, appointive Utilities Commission.[80] Yet it became evident that any effort to retreat in the areas of education, highway construction, and debt service would have serious consequences for the state's ability to attract capital and to undertake further infra-structural projects and might, in addition, reduce support for the reform package. The political and economic barriers to increased taxes on capi-tal and to the luxury sales tax were equally significant. Consequently, with Ehringhaus committed to an eight-month school term and to the elimination of the state's 15 percent property tax, debate during the 1933 legislature focused once again on the general sales tax.

The R. J. Reynolds Tobacco Company was again prominent in the campaign to adopt the general sales tax.[81] In the legislature, the main supporters of the proposal were W. M. Hendren, a Reynolds attorney, in the Senate, and Robert M. Hanes, a major Reynolds stockholder, in the House. Outside the legislature, the proposal was advocated by S. Clay Williams, the president of Reynolds, and a corps of lobbyists maintained in Raleigh by the company. Opposition to the sales tax, "the badge of a bankrupt state," was again led by the State Merchants' Association.[82]

The combined Ehringhaus proposal—to expand education, elimi-nate property taxes, and avoid increasing taxes on capital—was suffi-cient to fragment opposition and to secure the passage of a 3 percent sales tax on all goods sold in the state. The minimum school term was extended to eight months, the state property tax was dropped, and teachers' salaries were reduced by 32 percent.[83] Because mass consump-tion levels in the state were low, the sales tax had to be highly inclusive. Only a few necessities, such as flour and meat, were excluded.

The two major arguments against the sales tax—that it would re-duce demand and deepen the depression, and that it was regressive and unjust—proved to be hopelessly ineffective in this struggle. North Carolina was a state whose importance to capital lay in its large pool of cheap surplus labor, the weakness of its working class organizations, and, consequently, in its above-average rate of exploitation. The realiza-tion of surplus value, on the other hand, did not depend on consump-tion levels within the state. The most important commodities produced in North Carolina—cotton and other textile goods, tobacco, cigarettes, furniture, and lumber—were produced for national and international mass consumption markets. Consumption levels within North Carolina played only a small part in the strategy of capital accumulation. By offering rewards in educational expansion and reduced property taxes, it was possible for the Ehringhaus administration to split opposition to the sales tax proposals and to impose a disproportionate share of the costs of an expanded state and more extensive state policies on the state's agricultural and industrial workers. Almost 42 percent of the increase in state revenues ($18.3 million) between 1929 and 1935 re-sulted from the sales tax, and 38.3 percent from increases in the gasoline tax, which would become increasingly regressive as automobile owner-ship spread. Increases in corporate franchise tax revenues accounted for a further 16.5 percent, but this figure must be weighed against corporate savings from property tax reductions. In 1935 taxes on retail sales (15 percent), beer (0.7 percent), gasoline (34.0 percent), and automobile licenses (15 percent), accounted for almost 65 percent of a total revenue of approximately fifty-one million dollars. The corporation franchise tax provided 13.1 percent of 1935 revenues compared with 11.25 per-cent in 1929, and individual and corporate income taxes provided 14.7 percent compared with 23.5 percent in 1929.[84]

The system of state and local taxation continues to be highly regres-sive, although on a much expanded scale. The most regressive item in state taxation, the sales tax on purchased food to be prepared at home, was lifted in 1941 but replaced in 1961 during the administration of the "liberal" Governor Terry Sanford in order to finance further educational expansion. In 1968, in order to permit a reduction in property taxes, counties were allowed to levy an additional 1 percent sales tax. As a result, in 1973–74, according to James A. Wilde, 21.7 percent of total state and local revenues (of approximately $2,340.5 million) resulted from the sales tax.[85] This tax currently does not apply to farm ma-chinery and industrial equipment, and highly priced consumer durables, such as automobiles, boats, and aircraft, are taxed at lower rates. The basic exemptions for income tax purposes (two thousand dollars for a married couple) have remained the same since the tax was introduced and have therefore become increasingly regressive. In 1973–74 personal income tax provided 21.5 percent of total state and local revenues.

According to Wilde, the state and local tax system in North Carolina is regressive regardless of whether the cost of corporate income taxes and property taxes alternately falls on consumers or capital owners.[86] If they are assumed to fall on consumers, tax rates are highly regressive, ranging from 23.1 percent on money incomes of less than $1,150 to 5.2 percent on incomes over $57,500. If it is assumed that the corporate tax bill is shared equally between owners and consumers, the rates are 19.7 percent and 8.6 percent, respectively.

There is some debate as to the impact of variations in business tax rates on the relocation of capital generally. According to Robert New-man, variations in corporate tax rates account not only for a portion of the relocation of industry to the South but also have an influence on the distribution of capital within the South. Barry Bluestone and Bennett Harrison, on the other hand, suggest that this variable is much less important in the relocation decisions of corporations than variations in wages, unionization, and the social wage. Nevertheless, their calculation of effective state and local business tax rates reveals that whereas the U.S. and northeastern averages equal 1.69 percent and 1.92 percent of total sales, respectively, the southern average is 1.09 percent, and the rate for North Carolina is 0.98 percent.[87]

Whatever its long-term impact, the imposition of a more regressive tax regime generated relatively little popular resistance. Since a large proportion of individual workers were able to supplement their incomes by producing food, since mill village control remained effective, and since most workers were excluded from political participation, capital and the State were largely insulated against the political consequences of this tax reorganization. For their part, textile workers were forced to concern themselves with the simultaneous but perhaps more important consequences of the stretch-out and wage reductions that provided the background for the 1934 general strike. In 1936 the Shelby machine was able to defeat an internal Democratic challenge based on the repeal of the sales tax and increased corporation taxes, and it nominated and elected its third consecutive governor, Clyde Hoey.[88]

Equally important for the preservation of the conditions of exploitation, especially during the 1930s, was the role of the state's representatives at the federal level in resisting attempts to regulate conditions of production, competition, and exploitation. In North Carolina, as in the southern states generally, the disenfranchisement of blacks and the destruction of electoral competition formed the basis for a virtual Democratic monopoly of elected representatives to the U.S. Congress. Between 1900 and 1920 only three North Carolina delegates to the U.S. House of Representatives were Republicans, and there was no Republican senator. Between 1910 and 1920 the state delegation to the House was completely Democratic.[89] Further, because successive Democratic political machines were dominated by capital, the range of needs to which congressmen had to respond was relatively narrow. Consequently, the political longevity of congressmen from North Carolina and the South was high.

Congressional continuity, in turn, enabled southerners to accumulate seniority and hence a disproportionate degree of political power within the congressional committee system. With Democratic majorities in the House from 1912 to 1919 and in the Senate from 1914 to 1919, southerners controlled the most important committees. North Carolina provided the chairmen of the powerful Finance and Rules committees (Furnifold Simmons and Lee Overman, respectively) in the Senate during these years. In the House, North Carolina provided the Democratic leader, Claude Kitchin, the chairman of the House Rules Committee, E. W. Pou, and the chairman of the Judiciary Committee,

E. Yates Webb.[90] All but two of the fourteen major Senate committee chairmanships, and all but two of thirteen in the House were held by southerners in 1914.[91]

On the basis of this disproportionate political power, much of the legislation enacted under the administration of Woodrow Wilson (1913–21) was of direct benefit to southern capital. Tariff reforms reduced the protection given to northern manufactures, reducing the prices for manufactured goods and machinery upon which the southern states depended. Southerners also supported a graduated federal tax on large incomes, reasoning that it would have most impact on the wealthy northeastern states. The Federal Reserve Act included provisions for regional reserve banks, and for short-term farm credit facilities. The Cotton Warehouse Act of 1914 provided for federal licensing of warehouses to improve their stability. The Federal Farm Loan Act of 1916 established twelve regional banks to make long-term loans to farmers on the security of their land. The Smith-Lever Act of 1914 provided federal grants-in-aid for county agricultural extension agents, and the 1916 Bankhead-Shackleford Federal Highways Act established federal aid on a dollar-matching basis for highway construction.[92]

On the other hand, limited efforts to enact "progressive" social reforms met with opposition from southerners. Opposition to the 1916 Keating-Owen Child Labor Act was centered in the southeastern textile states, although congressmen from other parts of the South supported it.

Efforts to establish workmen's compensation and to restrict the length of the working day found little southern support.[93] In 1914 the Commission on Industrial Relations, a federal commission representing the interests of the nation's largest corporations and charged with the task of investigating and promoting the idea of "responsible" unionism, proposed to hold hearings in the South. This attempt was averted after heavy southern pressure in Congress that resulted in reduced appropriations for the commission. Only a single southern hearing was held — in Dallas in 1914.[94]

*The State and national economic regulation: the impact of the New Deal in North Carolina and the South*

During the Wilson administration, pressure for economic regulation was limited. Capital, under the umbrella of the National Association of Manufacturers, remained hostile for the most part. Further, if southern congressmen were not always unanimous in their condemnation of those efforts that did occur, this was because the courts and the constitutional doctrine of states' rights in the area of production and labor legislation remained the strongest defense of regional production relations. As chapter four indicated, attempts to pass federal child labor legislation failed in the courts and led to a long but equally fruitless attempt at constitutional revision.

A much more significant threat to production relations in North Carolina and the South occurred during the depression of the 1930s. Federal policies designed to contain the social and political effects of this crisis (increasingly open class warfare and the emergence of militant organizations such as the CIO and the Unemployed Leagues) and to provide the economic basis for eventual recovery had to confront the political problems posed by the existence of differing regional modes of exploitation, rates of surplus value, and strategies of capital accumulation. Welfare and social security payments, for instance, threatened to sever the links between agricultural impoverishment and the necessity of textile mill wage labor, while the establishment of a minimum wage threatened to reduce or even eliminate regional wage differentials. Similarly, proposals to rationalize and reduce production and to restrict competition by regulating hours and the exploitation of female and child labor threatened other components of the southern competitive advantage. For southern capital, all efforts to limit competition were a threat, since the region's production relations gave it a competitive edge that could not be matched by the industrial states.

In the event, the potential dangers of federal economic regulation for capital accumulation in North Carolina and the South failed to materialize unambiguously. The political power of southerners within the national Democratic coalition, and more particularly within the congressional committee system, proved to be the crucial factor. After a decade of Republican control of Congress, Democratic electoral victories in the elections of 1930 and 1932 gave the party majorities in both houses of Congress and brought southern committee seniority back into play. In 1933 nine of fourteen major Senate committees were chaired by southerners, and twelve of seventeen in the House. Southerners also occupied powerful positions within the Democratic party. In the Senate Joseph T. Robinson of Arkansas was floor leader until 1937, when he was succeeded by Alben Barkley of Kentucky. In the House the Democratic floor leaders were successively Joseph Byrns of Tennessee, William B. Bankhead of Alabama, and Sam Rayburn of Texas. Each also became House speaker in turn, in 1935, 1936, and 1940.[95]

This disproportionate southern congressional strength persisted throughout the 1930s. In 1940 thirteen southern states that, because of disenfranchisement, contributed about 10 percent of the U.S. voting population, were able to elect approximately 25 percent of the U.S.

Congress. In the crucial House and Senate Rules committees, which determined whether and when major pieces of legislation come to the House and Senate floors, six out of nine Democrats in the fourteen-man House committee were southerners, as were five out of eight Democrats on the Senate committee. In addition, southern Democrats chaired numerous other important committees, including the Senate Agriculture, Appropriations, and Finance Committees, and the House Banking, Agriculture, and Ways and Means committees.[96]

Southern Democrats also gained strength from their high degree of cohesiveness. During the 1930s and 1940s southern Democrats on the average voted together to a greater extent than did other Democrats or Republicans. In policy areas relevant to the defense of southern production relations (labor standards, labor relations, work relief, racial issues, education, and agriculture), southerners tended to vote with the Republicans.[97] Their solidarity on these issues and their tendency to ally with the Republicans derived from the necessity of defending the South's regional competitive advantage against the threat of federal regulation, and from the degree to which productive relations in the textile industry resembled those in agriculture. Consequently, significant conflicts did not occur within the southern bloc between the interests of the countryside and agriculture on the one hand, and those of the towns and industry, on the other. Southern congressmen opposed efforts to provide relief, welfare payments, and minimum wage levels because they would affect both agriculture and industry. Since the mode of exploitation in agriculture was crucial to the continued formation of an industrial working class, it was in the interests of textile capital to oppose improvements in the welfare of tenants, sharecroppers, and small farmers. Policies that would reduce racial inequalities or encourage the organization of labor also met with united opposition.

The political power of southerners, both as a necessary part of the Democratic New Deal coalition and in their later open opposition to New Deal reforms, was reflected in four major areas of New Deal social and economic policy: work relief and social security; "fair" labor standards; agricultural reforms; and labor-management relations.[98]

*Work relief and social security*

Federal New Deal policy in work relief and social security included a variety of temporary schemes, including the Federal Emergency Relief Administration (FERA), the Civil Works Administration (CWA), and the Works Progress Administration (WPA), as well as the permanent system of programs established by the 1935 Social Security Act. In all cases, these programs were designed with the intention of not disrupting southern production relations or impeding the production of surplus value.[99] The policy that relief should not exceed existing labor standards was established by FERA, the New Deal's first general relief agency, and was continued, at least in theory, by its successors. In order to gain southern support, or at least to limit appropriations, regional differentials were built into relief payment regulations. For instance, the Emergency Relief Appropriation Act of 1935 specified that the work relief "security wage" was to be higher than that for nonwork relief but lower than prevailing wage levels, so as not to compete with private enterprise. Consequently, the security wage varied with the local market wage. Farm laborers hired for work relief in the southern states were paid fifteen dollars per month, while professionals in New York City were paid ninety dollars per month. The range of WPA payments for all southern occupations was twenty-one to thirty-one dollars, compared with forty to ninety-four dollars in the Northeast. It was estimated that these levels of relief in the Northeast provided from 39.5 percent to 76.8 percent of the cost of an "emergency" level of existence. The southern states, with over 25 percent of the total U.S. population, received only one-seventh of total FERA expenditures and less than one-sixth of combined FERA, CWA, and WPA expenditures. In addition, the southern states themselves contributed relatively little to the programs. In the United States as a whole, the federal contribution to FERA was 62 percent, while in all the southern states but Texas it reached over 80 percent, and in some cases, over 90 percent. Relief programs were, in addition, closed or reduced during the southern harvesting season, and, since relief was usually not given without prior consultation with planters and millowners, relief was often used as a political weapon against dissident organizations, such as the Southern Tenant Farmers' Union (STFU) or the UTWA.

Despite all these precautions, however, it was never possible to protect southern production relations entirely. This was particularly the case in agriculture, where wages and living standards were lowest. After the beginning of the "Second New Deal" in 1935, many southerners, especially displaced farmers and the unemployed, did benefit, and they managed to reduce the degree of control exercised over them by others. Moreover, by this time, the increasing pace of rationalization and mechanization in agriculture was reducing the demand for agricultural labor power, making it less necessary for the largest planters in North Carolina to resist federal intervention as fiercely as they once had. Nevertheless, in general, southern planters, industrialists, and their representatives at all levels of the State prevented relief programs from ever being used systematically to reduce or eliminate the South's locational advantages with respect to the production of surplus value.

The permanent system of social security (which included Old Age Insurance, Unemployment Insurance, and Aid to Families with Dependent Children, or AFDC) established in 1935 was designed to follow similar principles. Southern congressmen pressed for narrow coverage and state control of administration, fearing once again that nationally uniform payments would undermine the southern competitive advantage, and that a system supervised by the federal government would compete with local Democratic organizations as dispensers of patronage, undermine local social control, and open relief rolls to blacks.

Consequently, the Social Security Act's original wording—that relief could not be denied if the age and need requirements were met—was altered to the much looser requirement that relief could not be denied on grounds of citizenship, thus giving the states freedom to discriminate according to local political, economic, and racial requirements. The implementation of unemployment insurance schemes was left to the states, whose participation was encouraged by a special federal 1 percent payroll tax, 90 percent of the proceeds of which would go to the states if they implemented such a program, and which would otherwise revert to the federal treasury. Beyond this, states were able to adopt any level of benefit they wished, specify their own eligibility rules, set waiting periods, and limit maximum benefit periods.

The rest of the act's programs—provisions for the aged, blind, and orphaned—were also turned over to the states, with federal grants-in-aid supplementing matching state expenditures. Like unemployment insurance, the programs were also synchronized with local conditions of production:

> Since 1935, each state legislature has utilized its broad license under the Social Security Act to design welfare legislation and administrative procedures to accommodate local economic interests. . . . What explains the diversities, as well as the similarities (of relief practices), is not the vicissitudes of local morals and local politics, as critics sometimes charge, but the objective of regulating the giving of aid so that it meshes with the varying manpower requirements of local economic enterprises.[100]

Between 1935 and 1939 nearly all the states enacted legislation to create parallel state schemes. Federal matching funds significantly expanded the patronage capacities of southern Democratic political machines and enhanced racial inequalities and social control. Because local production relations determined the administration and implementation of the programs, wide variations occurred across the nation. Coverage was generally low, since agricultural workers (and, after 1939, workers in the processing, packaging, and distribution of agricultural products) were excluded. Despite widespread poverty, in December 1940 five southern states had fewer than one thousand families in the AFDC programs. By southern standards, North Carolina (with ten thousand cases) did well, perhaps because of its widespread white poverty and the relatively smaller percentage of the population that was black. Overall, in 1939–40, the percentage of the total labor force in employment covered by unemployment insurance was 27.4 percent in the southern states, compared with 50.6 percent in ten nonsouthern states.[101]

Benefits were also low. In 1939 the national average weekly compensation for unemployment was $10.13, compared with $5.88 in North Carolina. In addition, the duration of benefits was usually shorter in the South. In North Carolina "voluntary" unemployment resulting from strike action was a grounds for disqualification. Because of the limitations imposed on unemployment insurance coverage, an additional burden was placed on the other welfare programs. Because states were required to provide matching funds for these programs, welfare provisions in the southern states were not given high priority, and state tax systems were highly regressive, these welfare programs were by and large inadequate, and their cost fell most heavily on the poor.[102]

Significant regional variations remain a central feature of the American public welfare system.[103] In 1977 the average monthly AFDC payment per family in the South was $117, 49.2 percent of the U.S. average and 43.8 percent of the northeastern average. In North Carolina the average payment was $154, 64.7 percent of the U.S. average.[104] In the same year, the average weekly unemployment insurance payment in the south was $68, 86.1 percent of the U.S. average and 81.9 percent of the northeastern average. The average payment in North Carolina was $67, 84.8 percent of the U.S. average.[105] Manufacturers' nonpayroll labor costs (for social security and other nonmandatory programs) per employee in 1977 averaged $2,700 for the United States as a whole, $3,045 in the Northeast, $1,941 in the South and $1,525 in North Carolina.[106] In the same year, and for the same groups of states, total nonpayroll labor costs represented deductions from surplus value of 14.4 percent, 16.3 percent, 10.8 percent, and 10.3 percent.[107]

Both bourgeois and radical writers accept that these variations in the social wage play an important role in the relocation of industry. For all fifty states (plus Washington, D.C.) the correlation coefficients between the above three indicators of the social wage (average monthly AFDC payments, average weekly unemployment insurance payments, and manufacturers' nonpayroll labor costs per employee) in 1977 and the percentage change in manufacturing employees from 1967 to 1980 are −0.30, −0.29, and −0.43. For a restricted universe of twenty-five northeastern and southern states, they are −0.76, −0.73, and −0.58.[108]

*Regulation of the conditions of labor*
*and exploitation*

The federal effort to stabilize the national economy by setting standards of "fair competition" in, for instance, the 1933 National Industrial Recovery Act (NIRA) came into direct conflict with the southern strategy of capital accumulation.[109] In North Carolina and other southern textile states in particular, the ability of capital to appropriate above-average amounts of surplus value formed the basis for both local accumulation and the relocation of capital from New England. Southern capital interpreted NIRA and the labor codes (which attempted to regulate hours, wages, and the exploitation of female and child labor) as an attempt to restrict the region's competitive advantages and to stop further relocation. In 1933 the Southern States Industrial Council (SSIC) was formed "to protect the South against discrimination" and endorsed precode wage differentials.

Congressional opposition from southern Democrats, led by Harry F. Byrd and Carter Glass of Virginia, Thomas P. Gore of Oklahoma, and Millard E. Tydings of Maryland, failed to defeat the legislation in the crisis conditions of 1933 but ensured that the NIRA (and therefore the codes) permitted labor standards and other conditions of production to vary according to both industrial sector and regional location. Consequently, as the worst of the 1933 crisis receded, restrictions were gradually relaxed. The principle of industrial self-regulation allowed the Cotton Textile Institute to largely ignore the stretch-out, which could be more effectively implemented in the South.[110] Because of this, the fact that minimum wage levels were not effectively enforced and the fact that workers who could be reclassified as "learners" were entirely exempt, the formal reduction in the regional wage differential from 38.5 percent to 15.9 percent that resulted from the code meant little in practice, either for levels of competition or for the extent of exploitation. Even if it could have been enforced, there was little in the textile code to prevent textile capital from compensating for the reduction in the wage component of their competitive advantage by increasing other components, such as the intensity of work or mechanization (as happened in the tobacco industry). By the time the U.S. Supreme Court ruled the NIRA to be an unconstitutional encroachment on the states' right to regulate labor in May 1935,[111] the act made little difference to the ability of textile capital to appropriate surplus value or to the ability of the southern textile states to attract external capital.

Nevertheless, at the national level, pressure to regulate conditions of labor continued. Legislation could not be achieved until 1938, however, by which time the Supreme Court's opposition to federal intervention had been muted, and southern congressmen had been persuaded to undertake more open political opposition to New Deal policies. The Fair Labor Standards Bill included provisions for minimum wages, maximum hours, and a five-man board to raise standards as required, if prior collective bargaining had not already achieved minimum levels. Southern Democrats saw this bill, like the NIRA, as a threat to their regional competitive advantage and a surrender to organized labor. Southern congressional opposition was centered in the House Rules Committee, where Representatives Eugene E. Cox of Georgia, Howard W. Smith of Virginia, Martin Dies of Texas, William J. Driver of Arkansas, and J. Bayard Clark of North Carolina, along with three Republicans, formed an anti-bill majority on the fourteen-man committee.

Outside Congress, opposition to the bill was led by the SSIC, which represented the South's major industrial capital, particularly its textile, lumber, and paper industries. The argument of the anti-bill forces was a simple one. According to David Clark, editor of the *Southern Textile Bulletin*, "the day that the Wage-Hour bill is held constitutional by a packed United States Supreme Court is the day that will mark the end of states' rights in the United States, and bring near the end of our form of government and the establishment of a dictator." [112]

A Senate version of the bill, passed in 1937, had provided for a five-man independent board and allowed for regional differentials. Another version of the bill, which exempted agricultural and fisheries workers but did not permit regional differentials, passed the House in 1937. The Republican and southern Democratic majority on the House Rules Committee, opposed in principle to any legislation, refused to vote the House bill out of committee. In 1939, however, a liberal Democratic primary victory in Florida, in the midst of a renewed economic downturn, and Gallup poll evidence that a majority of southerners supported action with respect to wages and hours forced the committee to vote out the bill. The bill that finally emerged from the House-Senate Conference Committee contained major exemptions and a great deal of regional and sectoral discretion in order to gain the required southern support.

The 1938 Fair Labor Standards Act (FLSA) established sixteen as the minimum age for work in mining and manufacturing in interstate commerce, and eighteen as the minimum for dangerous occupations. The maximum workweek was set at forty-four hours until October 23, 1939, forty-two from then until October 23, 1940, and forty thereafter. Hours of labor in excess of these standards were to be paid at not less than one-and-a-half times the regular rate. A large number of exemptions to these standards and to minimum wage provisions were allowed, however; these included seasonal labor, interstate services and retailing, fishing, agriculture, handling, processing and distribution of agricultural produce, local newspapers, and local transportation. The North Carolina working class was particularly hard hit by the processing exemption, which affected twenty-four thousand black workers in tobacco drying and stemming. An exemption for learners again generated a major industrial reclassification, although the number of companies claiming this exemption declined until 1949, when an increased minimum wage caused a further increase.

The act's minimum wage target—forty cents per hour in all industries operating in interstate commerce—was to be approached only very gradually, with acceptable minima of twenty-five cents until October 23, 1939, and thirty cents until October 23, 1945. After this seven-year breathing space, the minimum wage had to be at least forty cents, except where otherwise decided by industrial advisory wage boards that were required to take account of competitive conditions and the effect of transportation, production, and living costs. Minimum wage rates were to be as high as was "economically feasible." Guidelines for economic feasibility included a requirement that wage rates should not lead to reduced employment. In addition to learners, less-than-minimum wages could also be paid to apprentices, messengers, and handicapped workers.

Despite these loopholes, a disproportionate number of violations in the ensuing years occurred in the southern states. With 18 percent of all FLSA-covered workers in 1949, the southern states produced 31 percent of all minimum wage violations, and 40 percent of all child labor violations. In North Carolina 59 percent of all investigated establishments were in violation of basic FLSA provisions. Violations were disproportionately concentrated in the manufacture of food, textiles, and paper, and in transportation. In addition, because of the weakness of North Carolina's working class, the proportion of suits brought by employees, as opposed to federal inspectors, was lower than in the United States as a whole. M. H. Ross's conclusion was that "the FLSA has not basically altered [regional] wage differentials in most industries."[113]

### The rationalization of agricultural production

In industry efforts to limit competition and rationalize production had, for a number of reasons, involved attempts to regulate wages, hours, and other conditions of production. The same pattern did not emerge in agricultural policy.[114] Policies to reduce acreage and production, to eliminate surpluses, to raise or subsidize commodity prices, and to increase the capital intensity of production far outweighed efforts to regulate the impact of these changes on the vast southern pool of impoverished agricultural labor. Since wage labor in southern agriculture was to some extent disguised, agricultural reforms did not include attempts to regulate wages. As a result, southern agricultural capital wholeheartedly supported, and participated in, the formation and implementation of New Deal agricultural policy.

Attempts to remedy the crisis in agriculture included a number of devices to limit production and increase prices. The 1933 Agricultural Adjustment Act (AAA) was basically a system of voluntary acreage reduction for which farmers would receive compensation to restore them to "parity"—that is, to the level of purchasing power enjoyed by farmers during the agricultural "golden age" from 1908 to 1919 (1919 to 1929 for tobacco). The seven basic commodities to which this program applied included the southern staples of cotton, tobacco, and rice. The AAA also included federal authority to subsidize exports and to arrange marketing agreements between growers and processors.

In cotton production the AAA was followed by an emergency plow-up in 1933, which eliminated an estimated four million bales and compensated farmers to the tune of one hundred twelve million dollars. Crop destruction had only a limited impact on price levels, however. A further response was the creation, again in 1933, of the Commodity Credit Corporation (CCC) under the Reconstruction Finance Corporation. The CCC, sponsored by Oscar Johnston, the AAA finance director and manager of the British-owned Delta and Pine Land Company, one of the South's largest cotton plantations, was designed to use federal loans to buy up cotton when its market price fell below a certain minimum. For 1933 this minimum was set at ten cents per pound. The CCC's programs were later extended to include wheat, tobacco, peanuts, corn, and other commodities. In 1939 the CCC was transferred to the federal Department of Agriculture, where it achieved permanent status as the cornerstone of the agricultural price support system.

In 1934 the Bankhead Cotton Control Act introduced direct federal quotas on cotton production—ten million bales in 1934, and ten and a half million in 1935. All sales in excess of this level were to be taxed at 50 percent.

In tobacco the situation was even more chaotic. In August 1933 tobacco markets in the southeastern states opened with prices at ten cents, seven cents below "parity," and they were promptly closed at the request of the growers. During a three-week market holiday, the AAA, under pressure from North Carolina governor Ehringhaus, among others, signed up virtually all growers for acreage reductions in 1934 and negotiated a marketing agreement with buyers at a level close to parity. The Kerr-Smith Tobacco Control Act of 1934, similar to the Bankhead Act, supplemented voluntary reductions with a system of quotas.

These policies generated little opposition from southern capital. The actual administration of agricultural policy at the local level was carried out by the Department of Agriculture's Extension Service, whose former, mostly educational tasks were shelved in order to allow it to carry on its new functions during the crisis. Because the extension service was dominated at the local level by the largest planters, they achieved a high degree of control over the distribution of AAA benefits. The American Farm Bureau Federation (AFBF), the largest national farmers' organization, moved quickly during the 1930s to increase its relatively small southern membership. As a result, southern planters were integrated into an organization aggressively committed to the expansion of federal intervention in agriculture. For all practical purposes, the Agricultural Extension Service and AFBF were practically synonymous. Southern congressmen were therefore invariably vocal in their support of extensions in the acreage reduction and price support systems, and most New Deal agricultural legislation bears the name of southern congressional sponsors.

That is not to say that there was no opposition from within the southern states. There was some opposition, but it came mainly from ginners, merchants, brokers, and those involved in transportation and distribution, who were concerned with the volume of cotton handled rather than with its production cost and market price. In the textile industry, opposition came largely from New England manufacturers. The most important southern manufacturers' organization, the American Cotton Manufacturers' Association, resolved in 1935 that the AAA "must be guarded, treasured, and made permanent."[115] For southern textile capital, acreage reduction, and mechanization raised the cost of cotton (at least for those who did not control their own supply), but it also increased the flow of cheap labor into the textile industry, facilitating the imposition of the stretch-out. Those manufacturers who had moved into the production of rayon (which was not subject to a processing tax) gained the benefits of both stable prices and the stretch-out.

Consequently, when in January 1936 the regulation of agricultural production by federal quotas and the processing tax was declared unconstitutional by the Supreme Court,[116] southern capital opposed the decision. Within weeks, the legislation involved was replaced by the Soil Conservation Act, which provided benefits for withdrawing land from production for purposes of soil conservation. In 1938, as a result of a large harvest in 1937, the second Agricultural Adjustment Act was passed. This act virtually reestablished the whole of the 1933–36 legislation but did not include quotas, acreage allotments, or processing taxes.

Throughout the 1930s the effects of both depression and rationalization in agriculture were felt primarily by the large southern pool of impoverished wage laborers in the tenancy and sharecropping systems. Gordon Blackwell's data on eight hundred twenty-five displaced tenant farm families in North Carolina indicates a high rate of displacement in the depressed conditions of 1930–32, a lower rate in 1933, and an increase again in 1934—"doubtless due to the acreage reduction program of the AAA."[117] The terms of the general plow-up in 1933 specified that tenants and croppers were to be compensated in accordance with their crop shares, so that displacement was not a major problem. Rather than plowing up the land of their tenants and croppers, planters plowed up their own crops to make sure that generous federal benefits did not go to their laborers and reduce labor control. The normal operation of the AAA left tenants and croppers entirely at the mercy of the planters, however. To begin with, AAA contracts could be legally written so as to reduce the tenant's share of federal benefits well below his formal crop share. Beyond this, the AAA lacked the organization required to be able to enforce its own formal rules. Its local administration, through the extension service, was dominated by the planters and the policies of the AFBF generally, and could not be effective if it went against their interests.

In any case, the function of the AAA was to reduce agricultural production and increase farm prices, rather than to tamper with the social relations of southern agricultural production. Consequently, it was a simple matter for planters to ensure control of AAA benefits, to increase the intensity of production on a reduced amount of land, and to make the necessary adjustments in the size of their labor forces. Formal acreage reduction contracts in 1934–35 provided croppers and tenants with only 11 percent and 15 percent of total benefits. In reality they probably received far less. Frequently, when signing contracts, the planters simply "forgot" to mention their tenants. Or, if this was not possible, planters could demand payment of old debts, or more simply, they could raise rents by the amount of the tenant's AAA check. By these means, large numbers of tenants were displaced. Attempts to enforce formal AAA requirements that acreage reductions be spread equitably and that normal numbers of tenants and other employees be maintained were for the most part unsuccessful. As a result, southern agriculture began a process of transition away from the sharecropping and tenancy systems, toward a more formal system of wage labor.

The AAA facilitated this transition by allowing land to be taken out of production, by increasing the amount of cash available to planters for the payment of wages, and by requiring, at least formally, that benefits be shared with tenants and croppers but not with wage laborers. In the case of North Carolina, the early stages of this transition do not show up in the census data; probably because displacement from the largest plantations was obscured by the effects of continuing proletarianization through new formal "tenancy" agreements at the boundaries of the system. By 1940 the absolute decline in the number of tenants and croppers is evident. (See table 2.1.)

The human costs of the recentralization of southern agricultural production were enormous. Between 1932 and 1934–35 alone, the number of acres planted to cotton fell from 35 million to 26.5 million. Man-hours in cotton production fell from almost 3,000 million to 2,250 million, and the cash return to labor declined by a similar proportion. Relief expenditures in the South expanded rapidly, but for many displaced tenants and croppers (particularly, but not only, for blacks) this means of support was unavailable. During the 1930s, therefore, as the transition to a system of wage labor continued, the pool of migratory casual laborers and part time sharecroppers, which had begun to expand in the 1920s, expanded much more rapidly. By 1940 this group, working intermittently for daily wages of between fifty cents and a dollar, had expanded to about 850,000 in the Southeast alone. In 1935 a majority of southern farmers had been resident on the same farm for only a year or less.

Efforts to deal with these laborers' problems in the early years of the New Deal were limited. In 1933 Senator Bankhead of Alabama included a provision in the National Industrial Recovery Act authorizing a twenty-five million dollar appropriation to finance a program of subsistence homesteads that would restrict the drift of impoverished farmers to the cities. Significantly, many of these communities sprang up close to industrial centers and in reality became a federally subsidized means of allowing industrial workers to supplement their incomes by growing food. This limited program had more impact in allowing the reduction of industrial wages during the depression than it did in alleviating agricultural problems.

More significant was the establishment of the Division of Rural Rehabilitation and Stranded Populations under FERA, which provided distress loans to enable farmers to stay off the welfare rolls and undertook the establishment of rural communities, some of which resembled those provided for in the NIRA, but most of which were subsidized farming communities.

Beginning in 1935 the pressure of an impending presidential election and political threats from the left in the form of Huey Long's radical welfare and taxation proposals and the activities of the socialist Southern Tenant Farmers' Union (STFU) precipitated significant changes in both the organization and the scale of the effort to deal with the farmers' distress. In 1935 the Resettlement Administration centralized earlier efforts at rural rehabilitation, land-use planning, and resettlement communities, and it experimented with cooperative and collective farming. Most of its efforts occurred within the existing agricultural social structure, however, and were designed to provide loans and grants for supplies and equipment. In the same year, a bill to authorize a $1,000 million program to finance land purchases by former tenants and croppers passed the Senate but died in the southern-dominated House Agriculture Committee. In 1936 the president appointed a Special Committee on Farm Tenancy that reported in 1937 in favor of a new body to facilitate tenant land purchases and encourage private farm ownership and family farming. The Bankhead-Jones Farm Tenant Act of July 1937 provided for purchase loans at three percent over forty years. Ten million dollars was to be made available in the first year, twenty-five million dollars in the second, and fifty million dollars per year thereafter. The Resettlement Administration was transformed into the Farm Security Administration (FSA) and was given responsibility for the new program.

The FSA, as "the residual legatee of nearly every human problem of rural life that was not solved by increasing the prices of a few 'basic commodities,'"[118] had responsibility for a variety of programs. It was heavily oriented toward the southern states, where the dislocations caused by depression and agricultural reform were greatest. The FSA staff contained many southern liberals, and almost 40 percent of its rehabilitation funds were spent in the South. The bulk of its activities, like those of the Resettlement Administration, were in rural rehabilitation. These activities posed no direct threat to southern production relations. In certain areas, however, its activities threatened to limit local planter prerogatives. Its provision of low interest loans for supplies and credit competed with local sources of credit. Its efforts to supervise and educate "client" families, discourage single-crop agriculture, encourage self-sufficiency, diversification, and land-use planning, reduce farm debts, and improve tenure arrangements all served to reduce dependence on the cash crop and lien systems. The FSA farm ownership program, which was most strongly established in legislation and which had more potential to change southern production relations, accounted for only a small part of the organization's total activities. Nevertheless, it was this—the availability of aid to farmers of both races and the experiments in cooperative agriculture—that contained the most direct potential threat to the control of the planters in the AFBF.

The AFBF's attack on the Farm Security Administration as part of its campaign to strengthen its grip on the Department of Agriculture, did not focus explicitly on the substance of FSA policies, however. This was not because of any sympathy on the part of the AFBF for the southern agricultural proletariat. There is little evidence that the AFBF considered their plight as anything more than a useful tool for increasing the amount of federal money going into southern agriculture. Rather, what the AFBF and southern planters objected to in the FSA was the fact that its policies and expenditures were out of their control. No matter what its policies and mandate, if the FSA, like the AAA, could be controlled through the extension service–AFBF network, its funds, like those of the AAA that were designated for tenants and croppers, could be put to the use of agricultural capital.

The FSA had no roots within the agricultural establishment and did not serve the interests of agricultural capital, except possibly insofar as it responded to political unrest. Although it operated within the Department of Agriculture, the FSA was uniquely the project of a few liberal reformers within the Roosevelt administration. As a "poor man's Department of Agriculture,"[119] it had its own administrative structure at the county and local levels. It was opposed because it dealt directly with the southern poor, rather than doing so through capital or the Democratic party, and it therefore posed a direct threat to the system of social control that formed the basis of capital accumulation in the South. Counterproposals to the 1937 Special Committee Report by Edward O'Neal of the AFBF clearly illustrate this opposition.[120] For O'Neal, the committee's report was acceptable only if the laws it proposed were administered by the secretary of agriculture through the extension service and if county and regional administrators and eligibility boards were appointed by the secretary from lists supplied by the state directors of extension services.

Between mid-1941 and 1946, the FSA was under permanent seige by the AFBF. The major battles, as one might expect, were fought in the congressional committees in which southern power was at its greatest, and particularly in the House Committee on Appropriations. In addition, the FSA was investigated, first of all, by the Byrd Committee, a joint committee on nonessential governmental expenditures (that could more appropriately be described as a committee set up to use the wartime emergency to destroy as much of the New Deal as possible) chaired by the anti–New Deal senator from Virginia. This committee's evidence and findings were also made available to the House and Senate appropriations committees. Second, the FSA was also investigated specifically by a House agriculture subcommittee chaired by Representative Cooley from the fourth district of North Carolina, who would later chair the full House Agriculture Committee. It was this investigation that signaled the beginning of the end of the FSA. In late 1942 it was placed under the War Food Administration and its activities were severely curtailed, and in 1943 its appropriations for the following year were withheld. In 1946 the agency was liquidated, and its acceptable parts were carried on by the Farmers' Home Administration (FHA), which in practice became an agency to assist war veterans to purchase farms.

During the same period, the Bureau of Agricultural Economics, which threatened the AFBF's virtual monopoly of agricultural policy formation, suffered the same fate largely at the same hands and was reduced to its present-day role as a gatherer of agricultural data.

### The regulation of labor-management relations

New Deal labor relations legislation did not pose a direct threat to production relations in North Carolina or elsewhere in the South.[121] Neither the 1933 National Industrial Recovery Act (NIRA) nor the 1935 (Wagner) National Labor Relations Act (NLRA) guaranteed the ability of workers to organize, and neither outlawed the most effective anti-union strategies.

Section 7(a) of the NIRA established the legal right of workers to organize and to bargain collectively, but it did nothing to compel employers to sign agreements. Beyond the fact that section 7(a) appeared to suggest governmental support for the principle of unionization, only the efforts of workers themselves could assure such an outcome. Constrained by their own economic dependence and political weakness, and by competition from a vast pool of impoverished agricultural workers, southern textile workers possessed few means to construct lasting organizations that would allow them to negotiate the conditions of their own exploitation. Even when undertaken on such a vast scale as the 1934 textile general strike, efforts at working class organization achieved little.

Company unions were the most common outcome of the NIRA. Although they had become more sophisticated since the employee representation plans of the 1920s, they continued to be a product of, and to reflect, management policy. Their major function was to direct workers' efforts into social and other activities rather than into issues arising from production. Consequently, company unions had little impact on the extent of management control or on working and living conditions. In the southern textile industry, employers felt little pressure to go even this far.

Like the NIRA, the NLRA protected the right of employees to bargain collectively, through representatives of their own choosing and without employer interference. In addition, it became unfair labor practice for employers to interfere with the choice of bargaining agents; organize, dominate, or support any labor organization; discriminate in hiring or tenure; discharge for giving evidence under the act; and refuse to bargain collectively with the employees' chosen agenda. A National Labor

Relations Board (NLRB) was set up, to which cases of unfair labor practice were to be appealed. Agricultural and domestic workers were exempt from NLRA provisions. Because agricultural capital was not directly affected, and because it was thought that the NLRA, like the NIRA, would be invalidated by the U.S. Supreme Court, congressional opposition to the NLRA was weak. The probability of court action also restricted the act's effectiveness. Expecting invalidation, employers simply refused union recognition. Again, company unions, which the act did make illegal, were the most important result, although they had to become increasingly independent of direct employer intervention in order to comply with the act's requirements.

By and large, even after the NLRA was ruled to be constitutional in 1937,[122] the situation remained roughly the same as it had been prior to the passage of the act. Effective union organization and bargaining depended on working class strength and militancy. In some mass production industries in the Northeast (such as steel, automobiles, rubber, and mining), strong, militant, and, occasionally, radical workers' organizations were established. In the southeastern textile states, little progress could be made however. Despite the operation of the NLRA, the CIO southern organizing drive that began in 1937 made few substantial gains.

Although the threat of unionization was averted in 1934 and 1937, and although the textile working class remained economically dependent and politically demobilized, southern textile capital had reason to fear renewed efforts at unionization. Internally, the mechanisms used by textile capital to create and maintain low wage levels and high rates of exploitation in a labor-intensive industry—particularly the stretch-out—would continue to push textile workers toward labor organizations as their only hope of social change. In addition, to the extent that southern capital's strategy of capitalist development continued to be successful in attracting capital from the more industrialized and unionized Northeast, it would be increasingly in the interest of both workers and labor unions in that region to see the southern states unionized. Unionization was therefore likely to continue to have both internal and external sources. As a result, southern capital supported efforts to amend the NLRA after 1937 in order to increase the freedom of capital to combat unions, to hold their growth at existing levels, and to prevent their growth outside the major industrialized states. These efforts were coordinated by the National Association of Manufacturers (NAM), which, after 1937, was forced to drop its prior argument that the NLRA was unconstitutional and to begin to campaign actively for its amendment.

An initial effort to amend the act occurred as a result of a series of congressional hearings in 1938 and 1939 into the operation of the National Labor Relations Board. A bill was introduced containing most of the proposed amendments of the NAM and the U.S. Chamber of Commerce—removal of the implication in the preamble to the act that the denial of organizing rights by employers was the major cause of strikes; protection of "freedom of speech" by employers in unionization drives; provisions for employer requests for representation elections; and separation of the judicial and prosecutorial functions of the NLRB. The bill passed the House but died in the Senate in 1940. In addition to this bill, there were two hundred seventy-nine other bills and legislative proposals for changes in national labor policy between 1936 and 1947 that were sponsored by over one hundred different senators and representatives. Most of these were attacks on the principles of the NLRA, and most were similar to major NAM criticisms. Pressure for restrictive legislation was particularly strong in the House of Representatives and came from traditionally conservative southern Democrats and from eastern and midwestern Republicans.

Before 1947 the effects of the NAM's campaign were to be seen mainly at the state level, where the legislative trend after 1937 was toward the regulation of unions and the weakening of NLRA safeguards. In 1939 laws restricting coercion or intimidation by unions were passed in Wisconsin, Pennsylvania, Michigan, and Minnesota, and in 1943 twelve states, mostly in the South and Southwest, passed laws restricting a variety of union activities. "Right-to-work" amendments to state constitutions—outlawing collective bargaining agreements or union security—were passed in Arkansas and Florida in 1944, and in Arizona, Nebraska, and South Dakota in 1946. In early 1947 an expanded drive for such restrictions, led by the NAM, led to a variety of legislative and other restrictions in thirty states. Fourteen states—seven in the South—passed right-to-work laws. In the rest of the states, restrictions were imposed on picketing, boycotts, and other union activities.

In North Carolina the struggle of Local 22 of the Food, Tobacco, Agricultural and Allied Workers' Union against policies of racial segregation, competition, and speedup carried out by the R. J. Reynolds Tobacco Company, and a wider CIO organizing drive in 1946–47, formed the background to the state's adoption of a right-to-work law. In order not to jeopardize the rapid capital accumulation that was taking place in the immediate aftermath of World War II (nine hundred new plants and almost five hundred expansions during the period 1945 to 1947), Governor R. Gregg Cherry requested that the state legislature ensure that North Carolina should remain strike-free during 1947, and that, if necessary, legislation should be passed to secure this goal. On February 5, 1947 the state legislature passed a right-to-work law that banned the closed shop and other forms of union security and the compulsory dues checkoff.

It was the election of Republican majorities in both houses of Congress in 1946 that guaranteed federal action to amend the NLRA. On the day the 80th Congress convened in January 1947, seventeen bills dealing with federal labor policy were dropped into the House hopper. Between then and June 1947, when the Taft-Hartley Act became law over the president's veto, labor policy was the major congressional preoccupation. The amendment of the NLRA proceeded swiftly. In the twenty-five–member House Committee on Education and Labor, the four southerners in the ten-man Democratic delegation—Graham A. Barden of North Carolina,[123] Ovie C. Fisher and Wingate H. Lucas of Texas, and John Stephens Wood of Georgia—voted with the solid Republican majority. In the Senate committee, southern Democrats also supported the majority—Allen J. Ellender of Louisiana by voting with it, and Lister Hill of Alabama by abstaining. A split in the Republican senators led to a more moderate Senate bill, however. The four-man Democratic delegation to the ten-man conference included Ellender and Barden, both of whom were known for their strong antiunion and anti-NLRA views. Consequently, the stronger House version of the bill prevailed.

By acceding to most of the demands made by the NAM in the period between 1937 and 1946, the Taft-Hartley Act significantly changed labor law. Coverage was amended in order to exclude foremen and supervisors, who were to be regarded as a necessary and integral part of management. The definition of "unfair labor practices" on the part of employers was loosened to allow "free speech" for employers, so long as this did not involve the use of threats or reprisals. More important, employer statements were to be excluded as evidence of unfair labor practice. The clause forbidding employer domination of labor organizations remained, but independent organizations could not be denied a place on a representation ballot. All agreements to require the hiring of union members only—the closed shop—were declared invalid. Other forms of union security were valid, as long as the union was a legally recognized bargaining unit and the security agreement was established by a majority of all workers concerned. However, in order to ensure that individual states could preserve established conditions of production, section 14(b) of the act allowed that, if greater restrictions on union security existed in state law, they were to prevail over federal law.

In addition, a number of restrictions were placed on union labor practices. Some of these were left so vaguely defined as to increase greatly the amount of litigation necessary in unionization efforts. "Coercion" and "restraint" of workers by a union were declared to be unfair labor practices, as was the refusal to bargain in "good faith." Because of their vagueness, these restrictions opened up the possibility that unions could be held responsible for the actions of their members, that peaceful picketing could be restricted as an unfair restraint, or that good-faith bargaining could be so interpreted as to put pressure on union bargainers to make concessions. Secondary boycotts and sympathetic strikes were banned as unfair labor practices and were subject to mandatory injunctions and priority of handling by the NLRB.

The Taft-Hartley Act amendments did not seriously alter relations between unions and employers in industries and regions where unions were well-entrenched, although they did tend to restrict unions' freedom of action. The act's major impact was to provide even greater obstacles to the organization of the working class in areas in which workers were already weak. By providing greater freedom of speech and action for employers and requiring employer coercion to be legally proven by means other than employer statements themselves, the ability of employers to coerce and dominate unorganized workers was expanded. In 1952 the Eisenhower NLRB ruled that employer speeches warning of the possibility of plant closures and the relocation of capital were noncoercive. In addition, procedural and definitional vagueness allowed employers' legal representatives to develop techniques to protract NLRB hearings in order to allow the orchestration, usually by third parties, of antiunion campaigns. State right-to-work laws, by making union security clauses illegal, prevented unions from requiring membership or payment of dues in order to benefit from union-negotiated improvements in wages and working conditions. Where these laws apply, it is not economically rational for an individual to join a union, since he or she will gain the benefits of the union's activities in any case.

Studies of labor relations in the southern textile industry and in North Carolina in the 1950s clearly illustrate the impact of the Taft-Hartley amendments to the NLRA. In 1949 and 1950 in North Carolina, more charges of unfair labor practices were presented to the NLRB than in any previous period. Yet despite this increase, the number of worker petitions for representation elections fell steadily from two hundred fifty-nine in 1947, to one hundred thirteen in 1948, ninety-eight in 1949, and sixty-three in 1950. Further, in the elections that were held, the percentage of union victories also fell — from 71 percent in 1947 to 65 percent in 1948, 58 percent in 1949, and 52 percent in 1950. Successful unions also tended to gain a progressively smaller number of new members. Finally, because of legal vagueness, both legal and illegal resistance to worker organization by employers increased. Of the last one hundred thirty-four representation elections held under the Wagner NLRA, seven were board-ordered as a result of legal disputes. Of the first one hundred thirty-two under the Taft-Hartley NLRA, fifty-six had to be ordered. Conscious that the resources and the punitive powers of the NLRB were limited, employers became increasingly willing to resist, knowing that even if found guilty of an unfair labor practice, the length of the legal and administrative process would cause the unionization drive to falter or would create conditions in which the drive could be actively undermined.

The right-to-work movement, the latest stage in the long-standing opposition of employers' groups such as NAM to unionism and social reform and a direct descendant of the open shop and American Plan movements of the early twentieth century,[124] remains a potent force in the development of American capitalism. The present National Right-to-Work Committee was formally created in 1955 by E. S. Dillard, president of the Old Dominion Box Company of Charlotte, North Carolina, and Fred A. Hartley, Jr., former congressman and cosponsor of the 1947 Taft-Hartley Act. It has supervised efforts to extend the geographical base of right-to-work laws at regular intervals, usually corresponding with periods of recession or depression. Three states enacted such laws in the recession of 1953–54 (Alabama, Mississippi, and South Carolina) and one during the recession of 1957–59 (Kansas). In addition, similar but unsuccessful efforts occurred in 1958 in California, Colorado, Idaho, Ohio, and Washington. Louisiana adopted a right-to-work law in the aftermath of the 1974–75 recession.[125] In the fall of 1978 similar efforts failed in Missouri and New Mexico.[126]

Despite the movement's failure to capture a major industrialized state outside the South, a total of twenty states now have right-to-work laws (see figure 5.1). Eleven of these states are the former Confederate southern states, and they accounted for almost 82 percent (61.3 million) of the total population in the right-to-work states in 1980.[127] In the same year the rate of union membership as a percentage of total non-agricultural employment was 14.1 percent in the right-to-work states, compared with 25.2 percent for the United States as a whole.[128] In 1977 the average hourly wage for production workers in manufacturing in the right-to-work states was $5.00, slightly less than 85 percent of the U.S. average of $5.89.[129]

*Capital, the State, and exploitation*
*in North Carolina*

In order to ensure its control of the processes of class formation and exploitation, capital in North Carolina created a one-party State that systematically excluded a large proportion of the state's working class from access to political power. Most immediately, this strengthened capital's control of political power and law enforcement at the local level, and it removed the political threat of interracial coalitions opposed to the process of proletarianization and the production of surplus value.

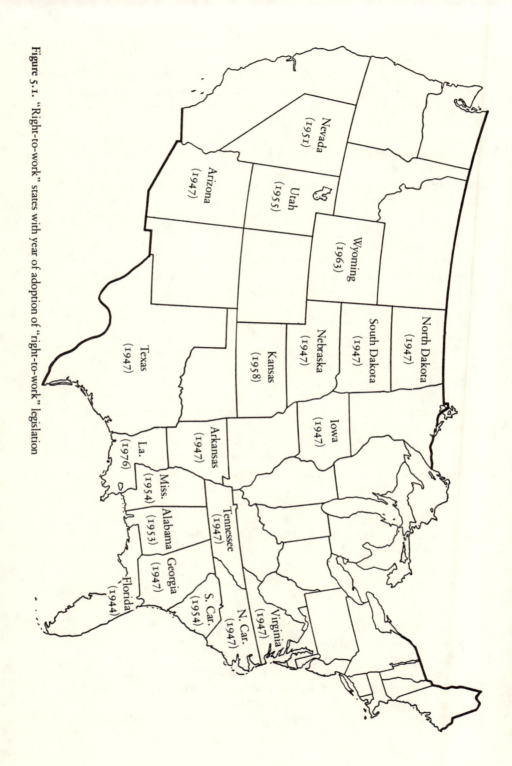

**Figure 5.1.** "Right-to-work" states with year of adoption of "right-to-work" legislation

Nevada
(1951)

Arizona
(1947)

Utah
(1955)

Wyoming
(1963)

South Dakota
(1947)

North Dakota
(1947)

Nebraska
(1947)

Kansas
(1958)

Iowa
(1947)

Texas
(1947)

Arkansas
(1947)

La.
(1976)

Miss.
(1954)

Alabama
(1953)

Tennessee
(1947)

Georgia
(1947)

Florida
(1944)

S. Car.
(1954)

N. Car.
(1947)

Virginia
(1947)

Having effectively eliminated political opposition, direct intervention by the Democratic State in the process of exploitation continued and grew during the twentieth century.

Other long-term consequences followed. Since the production of surplus value could continue virtually unregulated, and since a large pool of surplus agricultural labor was available to meet the requirements of a rapidly expanding textile industry, the dominant mode of exploitation in North Carolina continued to accommodate both agricultural and industrial capital. At the political level, textile and other industrial capitals were able to expand their influence through the office of the governor and were able to play an increasingly important role in the expansion and reorganization of State activities. State expansion and reorganization did not disrupt production relations in North Carolina, however. Rather, while permitting the provision of the essential infrastructure for rapid capital accumulation, these changes served to reinforce the economic dependence and political weakness of the North Carolina working class, thereby contributing to the reproduction of relations of exploitation. During the depression of the 1930s, a disproportionate share of the costs of these expanded activities was passed on to the working class through a regressive system of taxation. Because capital in North Carolina realized its surplus value largely outside the state, the reduction in mass consumption levels within North Carolina that resulted from these changes was the least unacceptable option in a crisis situation.

Finally, the structure of the capitalist State in North Carolina provided a virtual monopoly of elected representatives at the federal level for the state Democratic party. The politically powerful southern Democratic bloc in Congress was able to maintain local and state control of major New Deal policies. Southern capital was consequently able to reap the financial and political benefits of federal efforts at economic stimulation and regulation, while the potential costs, in terms of the disruption of southern production relations and restrictions on the ability to produce surplus value, were minimized. In areas in which this control was not possible, such as in the provision of agricultural relief, the offending legislation was weakened or destroyed. Consequently, the mode of exploitation that had provided the basis for capital accumulation in, and relocation to, North Carolina in the interwar period underwent only limited changes during the crisis of the 1930s, and it continued to form the basis for capital accumulation in the post–World War II period.

Such changes as did occur during the crisis of the 1930s represented only minor adjustments in patterns of labor control and exploitation. For instance, the sale of mill housing, which began in 1938 in the context of uncertainty caused by the debate over the FLSA, was not only a response to the struggles of the 1930s, which had focused to some extent on mill village paternalism, but an adjustment that perhaps served to preserve or expand the southern competitive advantage rather than to restrict it.[130] For one thing, large-scale agricultural unemployment was providing a rapidly expanding pool of impoverished labor for the textile industry. In such a situation, the relative contribution of the mill villages to labor control became less apparent.

In addition, the method of sale virtually guaranteed control for a further ten years and perhaps more. In most cases, houses were sold for sums between eight hundred and one thousand dollars (which was in most cases far in excess of their real values) with a 10 percent down payment and a weekly wage deduction of $2.50 per week per house for seven to ten years. The purchases were therefore dependent on continued mill employment and provided an additional incentive to workers not to engage in union activity. From the point of view of capital, the ability to make a large weekly deduction from wages provided a significant guaranteed advantage over the ten years, during which a high rate of capital accumulation could occur. Assuming two workers per house, at a 1939 average annual wage rate of $683, the annual housing deduction of $127 represented a deduction from wage levels of almost 10 percent and a further increase in the South's competitive advantage over New England.[131] In addition, corporate property taxes would be reduced. Consequently, the main reason that workers agreed to these purchases was because they were compelled to do so. In most cases, they were simply notified that their choice was to buy or to leave the mill village and their job.[132] The transfer of ownership, or potential ownership, of mill houses to millworkers was a device to increase rates of exploitation and to preserve the regional competitive advantage, and not an indicator of their decline.

## 6
## State Economic Development Policy
## and the Pattern of
## Postwar Industrialization

The strategy of capital accumulation that transformed North Carolina into the center of U.S. textile production in the 1920s and 1930s did not take place without criticism. In addition to the periodic rebellions by textile workers against the stretch-out and wage cuts, the process of capitalist development also generated criticism from other sources.

In particular, during the 1930s sociologists and economists associated with the University of North Carolina began to question a strategy of capital accumulation that led to a high degree of dependence on a few low-wage industries (textiles, lumber, and furniture), which produced for the most part cheap finished or semifinished goods for national markets. According to these scholars, dependence on agricultural production was the major cause of unequal exchange between North Carolina and other regions, the drainage of capital to the more productive regions of the United States, and the "colonial" status of the southern economy. In the industrializing southern states like North Carolina, however, capital accumulation was reinforcing, rather than changing, this status.[1] The "chamber of commerce" style of development and "competitive regionalism" were attracting primarily low-wage, labor-intensive industries and were impeding the South's ability to move from "absentee exploitation" toward a more "self-contained development," balanced growth, and improved living standards.[2] If the region was to achieve these goals, a more rational, planned approach to capital accumulation was required.[3] If necessary, this approach should incorporate a willingness to turn away capital in these low-wage sectors that were already overrepresented in the region.[4] At the very least an attempt should be made to move away from dependence on the production of raw materials and semi-processed goods by attracting capital in the finishing and distribution of textiles, the processing of food, and the manufacture of components for other, nonsouthern industries. Generally, the southern states should attempt to develop newer industries with high levels of productivity, profits, and wages.

Some of the failings of this type of regional analysis and strategy have already been discussed—in particular, its view that industries that are more modern, more capital-intensive, and more profitable will necessarily create higher wages and improved living standards and reduce regional economic inequalities. What needs to be emphasized here, however, is the inadequacy of this approach as a political strategy. It relies implicitly on the State as the only logical planning agency, yet, as we have seen, during the 1920s and 1930s, the State had played a major role in the chamber-of-commerce strategy of capital accumulation. State policy was committed to the preservation of precisely those social conditions that allowed the extraction of the largest possible amount of surplus value, guaranteed the continued competitiveness of the state's existing economic base, and attracted those "types of manufacturing [which] are hard-pressed in their present locations." [5]

Because of this limitation, the academic critics of capital accumulation in North Carolina were unable to do much to change the process. Between 1935 and 1947 a number of such critics, including Howard Odum, Rupert Vance, and Harriet Herring, were appointed to the North Carolina State Planning Board, a body formed in 1935 using funds from the federal government's Public Works Administration and the National Planning Board. [6] The board's planning program, which was the only condition of eligibility for these funds, included a number of specific components, such as land-use studies, a ten-year public works program, and the integration of transportation networks. The board was given little political power, however, and was kept entirely separate from the State Department of Conservation and Development, which continued its normal industry-hunting functions. Beyond serving as a forum for discussion, data gathering, and as a precondition for federal patronage, the board's concrete achievements were few. As wartime demand created economic expansion, the board came increasingly under attack, was reorganized in 1943, and was abolished in 1947 on the grounds that it simply duplicated work that was already being done more effectively by agencies of the State. [7]

By this time, the whole notion of planning had undergone such a transformation that it was barely recognizable. John Van Sickle's concept of "liberal planning," for instance, consisted of nothing more than the complete removal of all barriers to the free mobility of capital—minimum wage laws, collective bargaining, "excessive" social security and unemployment insurance payments—and the provision of necessary information on tax levels, land-use, labor law, labor markets, and natural resources. [8] In other words "planning," to Van Sickle, signified nothing more than a more systematic effort by State and private agencies to achieve exactly what they had in the past—the continued and expanded reproduction of productive relations that allowed the production of an above-average rate of exploitation in order to attract "hard-pressed" capital from other regions.

## Postwar economic development policy

Official State economic development policy in the postwar period has incorporated, as rhetoric, many of the proposals made during the 1930s and 1940s for changes in the pattern of capitalist development.[9] In particular, it has stressed the need to recruit new industries, to create new jobs for those being "rationalized" out of agricultural production, and to reduce dependence on the production of raw materials and semi-finished goods. It has also emphasized the need to increase the state's per capita income in relation to other states and the potential social and economic benefits to be gained by creating a more diversified and productive industrial mix.[10] In addition, a variety of agencies and services have been established through the period, not simply to attract and accommodate capital, but also, again at least publicly, to aid communities to achieve "orderly and attractive industrial development."[11]

In practice, however, the strategy of industrial expansion adopted in the postwar period has more closely resembled Van Sickle's conception of planning than it has the proposals of Odum, Herring, and Vance. Efforts to attract new, more capital-intensive production have taken place within a set of political and economic constraints imposed by the need to maintain the state's labor-intensive economic base and to provide for its expansion. In the view of Luther Hodges, "the role of state government here . . . is, first, to encourage homegrown enterprise, and second, to attract prospective industries to North Carolina."[12] State economic policy has been formulated in such a way as to minimize the potentially disruptive impact of new capital accumulation (increased labor market competition, higher wages, and the threat of unionization) on the production of surplus value by preserving, as far as possible, existing social relations of production.

This effort has taken two forms. In the first place, the state's right-to-work law, the Taft-Hartley amendments to the National Labor Relations Act that sanctioned it, and a high degree of freedom from external interference with the conditions of production continue to underpin the state's industrial strategy. Under most conditions, these commitments are expressed through the promise of "sound government" and a state legislature that is "conservative" in the areas of labor and wages.[13] Occasionally, however, a more direct commitment is necessary. In an address to the North Carolina Textile Manufacturers' Association in 1963, Governor Dan Moore assured capital of continued State support against the efforts of the Johnson administration to repeal section 14(b) of the Taft-Hartley Act (which gives concurrent jurisdiction to states in the area of union security, provided only that state law is more restrictive than federal law) and to federalize the unemployment insurance system.[14] For Governor Moore active state assistance in restricting union security was essential to the growth of "free enterprise," while the federalization of the unemployment insurance system "would force upon us the manner in which we would spend these funds, and would also dictate to us the amount of unemployment insurance taxes which we must collect from the employers of North Carolina."[15] Similarly, the AFL-CIO campaign to amend the NLRA in the late 1970s led Governor Jim Hunt, who campaigned in 1984 as a "southern liberal" for a seat in the U.S. Senate, to make public once again the State's commitment to a union-free environment. At a meeting with business leaders at the Winston-Salem home of textile industrialist Gordon Hanes, Hunt reassured textile capital of his support for the right-to-work law and the existing level and distribution of taxes, while at the same time promising the state's banks and power companies a continuing and expanding program of industrial recruitment.[16]

For most of the period after World War II the existence of legal restrictions on union security has been an effective barrier to unionization in North Carolina. As a later section of this chapter shows, this and the increasing legal complexity of the National Labor Relations system have transformed the conflict over the rate of exploitation and the struggle for unionization from an often violent political and economic task into a predominantly legal one, without in any way increasing the probability of the workers' success. Nevertheless, the direct, coercive intervention of the State in relations between capital and labor has not disappeared.

The 1958 strike at the Harriet-Henderson mills in Henderson, North Carolina, was in this respect reminiscent of the conflicts of the 1920s and 1930s.[17] The only real difference was that, in this case, the strike was caused not by an attempt to unionize the mills, but by the company's efforts to destroy a fourteen-year-old local of the TWUA by refusing to renew contract clauses that called for the arbitration of grievances and a compulsory dues checkoff. The strike, which became in effect a three-year-long lockout against the union, was one of the longest and most violent strikes in U.S. history, involving over one thousand workers, open violence (including the bombing of workers' homes), and at times nearly one-fifth of the state's police force. The state police and units of the National Guard, reinforced on occasion by regular army units, maintained fixed bayonets and were given authority by the state legislature to arrest without warrant, to protect strikebreakers imported from Virginia, and to enforce injunctions against picketing. In addition, a special judge and prosecutor were sent to establish a strike court, at which unionists and sympathizers were sentenced to hard labor on road gangs and to heavy fines. In addition, during the strike nearly three hundred thousand dollars in bail bonds was exacted from almost two hundred union members in order to increase pressure on the union.

Between February and May 1959 the special strike court heard ninety cases — twelve charges against seven strikebreakers, four charges against two foremen, and seventy-four charges against twenty-nine union members. The strikebreakers were found not guilty on eight of the twelve charges, two other charges were declared "nonsuited," one strikebreaker was found guilty of speeding, and the last charge was left "pending further action." One foreman was found guilty of disorderly conduct and the other of assault with a deadly weapon. The record in both cases showed "sentence to be given later." Of the twenty-nine unionists, two were found not guilty and the rest received fines and "hard labor" sentences of up to twenty-one months. Eight top union officials, including Boyd Payton, TWUA director for the Carolinas, were later sentenced to four to ten years on charges of conspiracy to dynamite a textile plant on the evidence of a paid State Bureau of Investigation informer. All were later paroled or pardoned, but the damage to the union was already done. The strike officially ended in mid-1961, by which time the mills were operating on a three-shift basis, five days a week, using strikebreakers. According to Michael Myerson, the strike, the first real test of the right-to-work law in North Carolina, had "an anaesthetic effect on textile organizing in North Carolina which has not yet worked off completely."[18] And while the Henderson strike provides the major example of direct State action against workers' organizations in the postwar period, it has not been the only one. Intimidation of strikers by sheriffs, local police, and state troopers remains a characteristic part of North Carolina's "strikebreaking apparatus."[19]

Like the commitment to defend a union-free environment, the second component of North Carolina's postwar strategy of industrialization also follows from the need to maintain an above-average rate of surplus value. It has been State policy to continue the pattern of decentralized industrialization established earlier in order to perpetuate the fragmentation and dispersion of the state's working class, to minimize competition for labor, and therefore to preserve low wage levels and a high rate of exploitation.[20]

The target to which new capital has been guided in the postwar period has been the state's large, underemployed agricultural labor force.

The decline in North Carolina's farm population, beginning with the depression of the 1930s and the New Deal agricultural policies, did not begin to show up in the census data until 1940, some years after it had become evident throughout the rest of the South. Even then, between 1940 and 1950, the reduction in farm population was only 17 percent, from 1,659,000 (larger than all other states but Texas) to 1,377,000. This percentage reduction was lower than both the southern and national averages in the 1940s. Consequently, by 1950 North Carolina's farm population was only slightly smaller than it had been in 1920, and it had become the largest in the nation.[21]

During the 1950s, while farm population was declining, the number of farms and the number of acres under cultivation both increased. Since the former increased at a faster rate than the latter, average farm size actually declined during the decade. In 1950 it stood at sixty-seven acres, compared with the U.S. average of two hundred thirteen.[22] During the 1950s average farm size began to increase slowly, but the decade also witnessed a rapid increase in the number of farms under ten acres.[23] Generally, therefore, North Carolina's farms remained small and unremunerative, and a large proportion of their operators continued to need additional sources of income. In 1949, 97,109 (33.7 percent) of the state's 288,473 farm operators reported that they had taken additional, off-farm work, and 77,861 (27 percent) reported that their off-farm earnings exceeded the value of the agricultural products they had sold.[24] Since these data refer only to farm operators, and not to their families, it would seem reasonable to assume that off-farm work was even more extensive.

The rate of decline of the farm population continued to be lower than the rate for the South generally until the 1960s, when it matched the southern average but remained lower than the rate in South Carolina, Georgia, Alabama, and Mississippi.[25] This slow decline, combined with its very large initial base, has meant that North Carolina's agricultural labor force has remained throughout the postwar period an important source of labor power for new capital. In 1970 it stood at 463,000 and was exceeded by only Texas, Illinois, Minnesota, and Iowa. In 1982 there were roughly 88,000 farms in North Carolina, with an average acreage of 126 acres, slightly over 29 percent of the U.S. average of 433 acres. Only Rhode Island, Connecticut, and Massachusetts had a smaller average farm size. In 1978 27.4 percent of North Carolina's farms had sales valued at less than twenty-five hundred dollars and 56 percent had sales with a value less than ten thousand dollars. In 1970 31,865 rural farm families (32 percent of the total number of such families) had total incomes (from both agriculture and off-farm work) less than 125 percent of the federal government's poverty level.[26]

The availability of this large pool of impoverished agricultural laborers for work in new industry has provided the focus for the State's postwar campaigns to attract external capital. Characteristic themes in these campaigns have been: the availability of female labor, the advantages of continuing agricultural rationalization and mechanization on the one hand, and of chronic rural underemployment on the other; the effectiveness of social control mechanisms and of the State's industrial training programs; the intergenerational stability of the state's honest, patriotic, native-born (white) labor force; its discipline and willingness to furnish a "full day's work for a fair day's pay"; and its unfamiliarity with labor organizations and unwillingness to engage in strikes.[27] For specific audiences, additional attractions might be presented. For instance, in an address before the Southern Garment Manufacturers' Association in 1955, Governor Luther Hodges stressed that North Carolina was already a major textile producer and was experiencing rapid growth in the production of synthetic fibers. The core of his address, however, was a description of the state's small town and rural proletariat, its reserve agricultural labor force, and its efficient highway system. Together, these allowed industry "to locate away from congestion and at the same time to draw upon a large and industrious labor supply that is mostly rural. They are stable people who generally live on farms or in the country where they can gather some extra income and additional independence from some kind of farming."[28]

State policy in North Carolina remains committed to this pattern of decentralized capitalist development and to the maintenance of an industrial working class with one foot in agriculture. In a major policy statement in the early 1970s, the State Department of Administration established the "creation of a network of smaller urban centers [as] the key idea in a settlement pattern for shaping the growth and location of population within the state."[29]

Postwar efforts to encourage such a pattern have consisted essentially of two components. First of all, the State has maintained an array of agencies, divisions, departments, and programs designed to mobilize and publicize economic resources and to attract capital to the state. Throughout the postwar period, the departments of Conservation and Development, Natural and Economic Resources, and Commerce have, at various times, maintained subdivisions and agencies devoted to collecting data on product and labor markets, available manufacturing space, and site information, and providing on-the-job training, liaison with other State agencies and local industrial development organizations, and assistance to local organizations in their own industry-hunting activities. In 1977 four separate divisions within the Department of Commerce were devoted to economic development. The Business Assistance Division was responsible for all of the above functions, and it also operated a business clearinghouse, which was designed to bring potential buyers and sellers together in mergers, acquisitions, or joint ventures. In addition, the Industrial Development Division (IDD) employed sixteen full-time industrial recruiters whose role was to "sell" North Carolina to corporate executives looking for new locations with particular socioeconomic characteristics.[30] The IDD performed the same functions with respect to foreign capital, while the Travel and Tourism Division was responsible for, among other things, attracting capital in the tourism industry. In 1978 a Small Communities Economic Development Division was established to "attack the problem of too few communities being fully prepared for industrial development and attempt to direct industry to those communities as they reach a higher degree of readiness."[31]

In some cases, the State has given a direct role in the campaign to attract capital to corporations with an interest in furthering and shaping the process of industrialization. In 1955 the state legislature authorized Governor Hodges to create a corporation to raise funds from the state's financial institutions in order to make long-term loans (that might not otherwise be made by individual institutions) to companies expanding or relocating in North Carolina. The initial one million dollar capital stock of the North Carolina Business Development Corporation was raised by the sale of shares to private corporations. The state's two major power companies, Carolina Power and Light and Duke Power, the major beneficiaries of the program of industrial expansion, contributed $50,000 and $100,000, respectively, making them the largest shareholders. Smaller purchases, of $15,000 and $25,000, respectively, were made by the Cone family and the Burlington Foundation (a division of Burlington Industries), reflecting in part the textile industry's interest in attracting capital in industries that provided markets for textile products or supplied the industry with its raw materials or machinery (the apparel and household furniture industries in the first case, and the textile machinery and synthetic fiber industries in the second) and in part the perceived need to share in the control of an important part of the industrialization campaign. Banks, insurance companies, and other financial institutions provided loan capital totaling four million dollars.[32]

Ultimately, however, what has been crucial to the industrialization of North Carolina (not only in the sense that it has occurred, but that it has done so with only a limited effect on production relations and rates of exploitation) has been the ability to mobilize the state's pool of surplus rural labor and to ensure that new capital accumulation does not disrupt existing patterns of labor control and wages at the local level.

The second component of the State's industry-hunting policy has therefore been to help organize and finance local industrial development organizations in such a way as to preserve local discretion over final location decisions. For Hodges, in order for industrialization to proceed with a minimum of disruption, it was necessary that "the final job of selling an industry on North Carolina [was] left to the people at the local level."[33]

In most cases, however, the "final job" has been carried out not by the "people," nor by organizations politically responsible to the people. Rather, most of the local industrial development organizations established in North Carolina since the 1950s have been private organizations, such as chambers of commerce, whose prime concern has been to preserve those local conditions that they see as being essential for the health of existing capital. This has been the case particularly in former textile company towns and in other areas that are politically and economically dominated by textile capital. Since 1961 it has been possible for cities, counties, or groups of cities or counties to create public economic development commissions with full-time staffs and access to public funds. Since these organizations would be politically accountable to city or county commissions and their electorates, however, their emergence has been slow and uneven. In some cases, where these political considerations have appeared to be less significant, private organizations have simply asked county or city commissioners to designate them as the official development agency in order that they might use public funds.[34] By and large, therefore, the use to which State agencies and programs are put in facilitating capital accumulation and the determination of the types of new capital that are locally acceptable are left to the discretion of established capital and of the local bankers, retailers, and other businessmen who are dependent on its continued viability.

The most important consequence of State policy during the postwar period is that it has attracted to North Carolina primarily labor-intensive, low-wage industries seeking to escape unionization, labor market competition, and higher wages in other regions. Higher-wage, unionized companies wishing to expand or relocate into North Carolina without conforming to local political and economic requirements (despite the clearly stated message of State promotional material) often receive an unfriendly reception in the state.

It is impossible to assess accurately the amount of capital or the number of jobs lost to workers in North Carolina as a result of this opposition to the entry of high-wage or unionized production. There are a number of reasons, however, to suggest that its impact has been of major proportions. First of all, this kind of opposition has been documented throughout the postwar period. In their analysis of the economic reorganization of "Petropolis" (Durham, North Carolina) in the 1950s, Robert Agger and his colleagues noted that a number of leading industrialists "remained opposed to new industry because of the possibility that there would be increased competition for available labor and higher labor costs."[35] Similarly, in the late 1960s, Roy Sowers, Jr., director of North Carolina's Department of Conservation and Development, discussed a number of such cases and the general problem of local businessmen who "want to set the labor standards of a new industry" because of the fear that their employees "will leave their jobs to accept the higher-paying jobs new industries offer."[36]

Second, during the 1970s, with capital perhaps more generally mobile than at any previous time, a number of concrete cases of successful opposition to new capital have been documented. In 1974 the Xerox corporation canceled plans to locate a plant employing fifteen hundred to two thousand unionized workers in Raleigh, North Carolina, as a result of pressure from the Raleigh Chamber of Commerce.[37] In the following year, Raleigh, whose chamber of commerce has a written policy against recruiting companies that do not agree to resist unionization, also turned down the Miller Brewing Company.[38] In late 1977 an attempt by the Brockway Glass Company of Pennsylvania to locate a bottling plant at Roxboro in Person County was rejected by the Person County Economic Development Commission.[39] In this case, the plant would have created three hundred unionized and relatively high-wage jobs in a small rural community and would have disrupted the low-wage, nonunion environment upon which local manufacturers, banks, and retailers depended. According to the *Wall Street Journal*, the rejection of Brockway (which finally located in Danville, Virginia) "illustrates a little-known but widespread attitude in the South; fearful of unions and competition for local labor, community leaders in many areas have quietly been spurning northern companies eager to move into the sunbelt."[40]

An executive of the Fantus Corporation, a Dun and Bradstreet subsidiary specializing in industrial site selection, estimated that "literally scores" of such cases occur each year, particularly in the textile-dominated Carolinas.[41] Few such cases come to light, however. The cost of public awareness can be high. In the first place, public knowledge of the tight social control exercised by established capital might scare off other more acceptable capital. In addition, the last thing that capital wants to do is to generate issues that might become politicized and give rise to efforts to organize the state's working class. In the Brockway case, although the Person County Economic Development Commission was successful in its efforts, widespread public debate and criticism had a chastening effect. In a similar case in Cabarrus County, four thousand workers held a rally in Concord to demand that the Philip Morris Company be allowed to go ahead with plans to build a one hundred million dollar cigarette factory that would eventually employ over two thousand workers and pay wages considerably higher than the area's average. In the face of this public protest, the Cannon Mills Corporation (whose eight textile mills, fourteen thousand workers, and the state's last remaining unincorporated company town [Kannapolis] dominate Cabarrus County, and which was the chief obstacle to the project) was forced to drop its opposition.[42]

For these reasons, it is likely that local economic development organizations will attempt to keep the process of relocation and site selection out of public scrutiny and that the scale of the opposition to unionized or high-wage production will remain unknown. For D'Arcy Bradsher, vice president of the Roxboro branch of the Central Carolina Bank and Trust Company and a member of the Person County Economic Development Commission, "the worst mistake we ever made was asking to be recognized as a public agency."[43] After it was required to make public its rejection of Brockway's overtures, the commission resigned en bloc to continue its activities as a private body.

Experiences such as these have led some commentators to speculate that the conflict between state-level officials committed to capital accumulation and job creation and those who wish to maintain a low-wage economy and limit labor market competition at the local level might give rise to State action that seeks to limit the local power of private capital.[44] Despite former Governor Hunt's promise to continue to attract "good jobs with good pay," and "to fight those industrialists who don't want it," the likelihood of State action to reduce the level of local discretion seems small.[45] At one level, at the end of his final term, Hunt remained as firmly committed to the State's antiunion policy as any of his predecessors. Generally, as long as industries such as textiles, apparel, and furniture, which depend on low wages, a nonunionized labor force, and the ability to produce high rates of surplus value, continue to dominate North Carolina's economy and politics, State action to restrict the power and profitability of these capitals remains unlikely, regardless of the personal preferences of State politicians. Limited efforts during the 1960s and 1970s to dilute local opposition to new capital by encouraging the formation of multicounty planning units and economic development commissions have had little effect.[46] For both the *News and Observer* and the *Wall Street Journal*, therefore, the lesson to be taken from these conflicts in site selection is not that they represent an important contradiction in North Carolina's strategy of industrialization, but simply that they are unfortunate events that need to be avoided. The way to avoid repetitions of the Person and Cabarrus cases in the future is for the corporations and State agencies that match companies and new locations to take greater care in the process of site selection and to ensure that incompatibilities do not occur. In other words, greater care must be taken to ensure that local productive relations are not threatened by "new" capital.[47]

This remains the major practical problem of State development policy in North Carolina. In 1981 the Hunt administration supported a twenty-four million dollar appropriation for the establishment of a microelectronics research center in the Research Triangle Park. According to its sponsors, this appropriation would be "seed" money that would attract to the state other companies engaged in semiconductor manufacturing. The state's campaign to influence public opinion has presented the semiconductor industry as a high-wage, high-growth industry that will improve the state's per capita income level. The administration's critics are less optimistic, however. They point out that most corporations in this area have well-established research operations and will be unlikely to need further expansions, having moved beyond the research stage and into mass production. The production of semiconductors is a highly routinized process, using mostly unskilled or semiskilled (and mostly female) labor. Its average hourly wage is lower than that in the rest of the electronics sector and is roughly comparable to the average hourly wages in textiles, apparel, and furniture. After a period of rapid growth and prosperity, this industry is currently experiencing a crisis of overproduction and is engaging in a price war. What the major corporations are looking for, therefore, is a way to make reductions in production costs. Given these circumstances, the most likely response by the industry is to continue to internationalize its production, in order to take advantage of extremely low labor costs in parts of Southeast Asia and Latin America. If North Carolina does expand in this area, it seems reasonable to assume that the industry will be more interested in preserving the state's established production relations rather than in dissolving them.[48]

## The pattern of postwar capitalist development

The most important effect of State economic development policies and the local political power of established capital has been the creation of the pattern of industrial expansion that was outlined briefly in the introduction. North Carolina's productive relations and high rate of exploitation have provided the basis for the continued expansion of its labor-intensive, low-wage industries—textiles, apparel, and furniture—which were already established or were being established during the interwar period. Despite being badly hit by the depression of 1974–75,[49] these three industries accounted for almost 37 percent of the 407,000 new manufacturing jobs created in North Carolina between 1947 and 1978, and for over 51 percent of total manufacturing employment in the latter year. (See table 6.1.) Furthermore, newer, more capital-intensive production expanding or relocating in North Carolina in search of reduced production costs has tended to reinforce the pattern of decentralized rural development established by these earlier industries. Consequently, despite large-scale industrial expansion and a limited diversification in the postwar period, the productive relations on which the profitability of these labor-intensive industries depend have been maintained. North Carolina's decentralized, low-wage, nonunionized economy continues to provide the foundation for an above-average rate of exploitation.

Since World War II North Carolina has claimed an increasing proportion of total U.S. textile employment. In 1947 17.1 percent (210,000) of the American textile labor force was in North Carolina, while in 1978 the figure was 28.2 percent (243,000). Despite postwar growth and diversification, the textile industry in 1978 still provided jobs for over 30 percent of all the manufacturing employees in the state. (See table 6.1.) In the same year, North Carolina's four largest corporations — Burlington Industries, Cannon Mills, J. P. Stevens, and Cone Mills — were textile corporations.[50]

As in previous periods, the effect of an above-average rate of exploitation has been felt in two ways. In the first place, it has provided the basis for a high rate of capital accumulation for that part of the textile industry already established in North Carolina. Second, it has served as a major attraction for the remaining "external" textile companies. Both of these sources have made significant contributions to postwar textile expansion.

The case of Burlington Industries provides perhaps the best (but not the only) example of the first case.[51] Established in 1923, Burlington Mills (as it was known until 1955) grew rapidly during the depressed 1920s and 1930s into one of the South's largest textile corporations, producing mostly rayon goods. During World War II, Spencer Love, the founder and major shareholder in Burlington, served as director of the Bureau of Textiles, Leather, and Clothing of the War Production Board.[52] With a guaranteed source of profits from wartime cost-plus contracts, Burlington, like many other textile corporations, began a process of forward integration that was designed to free the corporation from the hold of its commission agents, to enable it to control the conversion of its products into finished goods, and to therefore take even greater advantage of the cost-plus formula. Between 1940 and 1948

Table 6.1. Manufacturing employees by industrial sector, 1947 and 1978 (absolute figures in thousands)

| Sector | 1947 | Percentage | 1978 |
|---|---|---|---|
| Food products | 16.7 | 4.4 | 39.8 |
| Tobacco products | 32.5 | 8.3 | 21.6 |
| Textile products | 210.4 | 55.1 | 243.4 |
| Apparel products | 16.6 | 4.4 | 78.0 |
| Lumber and wood | 31.1 | 8.1 | 32.2 |
| Furniture | 27.9 | 7.3 | 82.8 |
| Pulp and paper | 7.9 | 2.1 | 19.0 |
| Printing and publishing | 5.3 | 1.4 | 16.7 |
| Chemicals | 9.5 | 2.5 | 32.6 |
| Petroleum | | | |
| Rubber and plastics | | | 24.4 |
| Leather | 1.6 | 0.4 | 3.9 |
| Stone, clay, glass | 5.6 | 1.5 | 16.7 |
| Primary metals | 2.0 | 0.5 | 6.6 |
| Fabricated metals | 2.8 | 0.7 | 29.0 |
| Nonelectrical machinery | 4.0 | 1.0 | 34.8 |
| Electric machinery | 5.0 | 1.3 | 43.7 |
| Transport equipment | 1.2 | 0.3 | 13.1 |
| Instruments | | | 8.8 |
| Miscellaneous | 1.0 | 0.3 | 8.2 |
| All sectors | 381.5 | 100.0 | 789.1 |

Sources: U.S. Department of Commerce, Bureau of the Census, *Census of Manufactures, 1947*, vol. 3 (Washington: USGPO, 1950), 452–54; U.S. Department of

Burlington Mills acquired twenty-four other firms and expanded into the hosiery business to compete with established hosiery manufacturers such as Hanes. In the process, Burlington became the largest producer and seller of finished synthetic fiber in the United States. During the textile depression of 1949, Burlington's size, relative efficiency, and the competitive advantage afforded by producing in North Carolina allowed Love to initiate the industry's first postwar price-cutting war in an effort to eliminate competition. In 1960 Burlington (by now Burlington Industries) entered the carpet business by acquiring James Lees and Company of Philadelphia and, in a further effort to eliminate the most marginal producers, gave crucial support to the proposal for a one dollar per hour minimum wage in North Carolina. (The average hourly wage in the North Carolina textile industry in 1960 was $1.51.)[53] In 1962 sales reached one billion dollars for the first time. In 1966 Burlington

| Percentage | Absolute change | Percentage of total absolute change | Percentage of U.S. employment in sector 1947 | Percentage of U.S. employment in sector 1978 |
|---|---|---|---|---|
| 5.0 | +23.1 | 5.7 | — | 2.6 |
| 2.7 | −10.9 | | 29.0 | 36.5 |
| 30.8 | +33.0 | 8.1 | 17.1 | 28.2 |
| 9.9 | +61.4 | 15.1 | 1.5 | 5.9 |
| 4.1 | +1.1 | 0.3 | — | 4.5 |
| 10.5 | +54.9 | 13.5 | 8.8 | 17.2 |
| 2.4 | +11.1 | 2.7 | 1.7 | 3.0 |
| 2.1 | +11.4 | 2.8 | 0.7 | 1.6 |
| 4.1 | +23.1 | 5.7 | 1.5 | 3.6 |
| 3.1 | +24.4 | 6.0 | | 3.3 |
| 0.5 | +2.3 | 0.6 | — | 1.6 |
| 2.1 | +11.2 | 2.7 | 1.2 | 2.6 |
| 0.8 | +4.6 | 1.1 | 0.2 | 0.6 |
| 3.7 | +26.2 | 6.4 | 0.3 | 1.8 |
| 4.4 | +30.8 | 7.6 | 0.3 | 1.6 |
| 5.5 | +38.7 | 9.5 | 0.6 | 2.3 |
| 1.7 | +11.9 | 2.9 | 0.1 | 0.7 |
| 1.1 | +8.8 | 2.2 | 0.02 | 1.5 |
| 1.1 | +7.2 | 1.8 | 0.2 | 1.8 |
| 100.0 | +407.6 | 100.0 | 2.7 | 3.8 |

Commerce, Bureau of the Census, *Annual Survey of Manufactures, 1978* (Washington: USGPO, 1983), 6-190–6-192.

entered the furniture business with the acquisition of Globe Furniture of High Point, North Carolina, and by 1976 Burlington was North Carolina's largest corporation, with seventy-two plants and thirty-seven thousand workers in the state, and it was the world's largest textile corporation.

The second case is perhaps best illustrated by the example of J. P. Stevens and Company, Inc.[54] Prior to World War II the core of the Stevens operation had been its New York commission house, J. P. Stevens and Company, which had contributed large amounts of capital during earlier periods of textile expansion in the South and consequently controlled a large amount of southern production. In addition, a second branch of the family owned the M. T. Stevens Company, which owned ten mills in New England producing mostly woolens and worsteds.

Like Spencer Love, Robert Stevens, chairman of the Stevens commission house, gained access to wartime government orders, serving as a colonel and deputy director of purchases in the Army Quartermaster Corps and directing more than fifty million dollars in government orders to J. P. Stevens.[55] In 1944 26 percent of all government orders in cotton textiles went to Stevens and three other large commission houses. For the Stevens companies, however, the war years presented a challenge as well as an opportunity for guaranteed high profits. In the first place, the federal government's cost-plus formula for contract work was encouraging textile manufacturers to escape from the domination of the commission agents (including Stevens') and to establish selling and distribution departments within their own vertically integrated companies. By so doing, they threatened the large and stable supply of semi-finished textile goods on which the commission agents depended for their profits. Second, the M. T. Stevens Company became a target during the early 1940s for the CIO's organizing campaign. By 1945 five of the company's ten mills had been unionized.

For both sides of the family, therefore, the direct acquisition of southern textile mills seemed to be the solution to their differences. Consequently, in 1946, the two branches of the family business merged with eight other southern textile companies (including former North Carolina Governor O. Max Gardner's Cleveland Cloth Mills), which had formerly simply been clients of the Stevens commission house. The transaction, valued at over fifty million dollars gave the Stevens family a 40 percent holding in the new, expanded company (J. P. Stevens and Company, Inc.), which now owned twenty-eight mills, nineteen of which were nonunionized southern mills. In addition, the merger added to the company a group of southern directors with an intimate knowledge of southern textile production and strong links with the economy and politics of the Piedmont Carolinas.

During the postwar period the new company gradually closed down its unionized New England plants, replacing them as needed with southern plants that were subjected to programs of rationalization, speedup, and behavior modification in production, and of social reorganization elsewhere (including the elimination of mill housing and other forms of corporate welfare). By 1980 Stevens, the second largest U.S. textile producer, had eighty-one plants in the United States, sixty-one of them in North and South Carolina.

The trends toward corporate concentration and a greater degree of integration between the various branches of textile production were not limited to a small number of companies, however. Rather, these trends were widespread during wartime and the postwar years. Selling agents and industrial consumers of textile products (such as the apparel and rubber tire industries) began to acquire textile mills in order to guarantee supplies of the particular goods they needed. Textile mills not only bought out other textile mills in order to expand production, but they also moved into the finishing, selling, and distributing sectors of the industry,[56] and also into the apparel industry. Between 1940 and 1947 five hundred forty-two firms in the U.S. textile and apparel industries either merged into, or were acquired by, other firms.[57] During roughly the same period, cotton yarn and cloth mills accounting for almost 4.5 million spindles changed hands. Almost a quarter of these were acquired by newly formed companies, 8 percent by textile machinery manufacturers, 18 percent by other cotton mills, 15 percent by apparel companies, 5 percent by other industrial users, 6 percent by cutters, and 15 percent by selling agents.[58] Between 1943 and 1947 in North Carolina alone, ninety mills with 1.6 million spindles and 23,000 looms (26 percent of the textile machinery in the state) changed hands.[59]

This period of rapid corporate concentration had a number of significant implications for the textile industry. First, it decisively altered the competitive, fragmented structure of mill ownership. By October 1948 the five largest textile corporations in the South controlled 19 percent of total southern textile employment. The forty-two largest companies, each with over three thousand employees, controlled 58 percent of all spindles and 60 percent of all looms. Further, only seven of these forty-two companies had retained their former vulnerable position with respect to commission agents. Before World War II brokers and commission agents accounted for 45.1 percent of all distributed sales of cotton broad goods. In February 1946 75 percent of sales took place through the same integrated organizations that produced the goods.[60] Although by no means matching the oligopolistic structure of the more capital-intensive sectors of manufacturing industry, these changes led to an increase in the industry's potential for controlling production and prices and for the production and marketing of specialized finished product lines and created a more stable basis for further expansion and concentration in the postwar period. In 1977, by which time the textile industry had become a predominantly southern industry, relatively high levels of concentration had developed in a number of sectors. For instance, according to the *Census of Manufactures*, the share of total shipments accounted for by the top four companies was 39 percent in the cotton weaving mills sector, 42 percent in synthetics weaving, 67 percent in carpet weaving, 60 percent in synthetics finishing, 57 percent in thread mills, and 80 percent in tire cord and fabric.[61]

Second, as the example of Stevens indicates, corporate concentration was associated with the continued flight of northern textile capital to the southern states. Higher rates of exploitation in virtually all the subdivisions of the textile industry (see table 6.2), the absence of unions, and, consequently, a greater degree of freedom with respect to changes in wage levels and the conditions of production provided large integrated southern companies such as Burlington with a potential for capital accumulation that could not be equaled by northern capital. The relative success of the TWUA-CIO northern organizing campaign and the expansion of southern producers into hosiery and synthetics made further relocation of capital inevitable.

As in previous periods of relocation, the consequences of such interregional contrasts are best seen during periods of depression. The southern textile industry weathered the depression of 1948–49 with relatively little damage. A disproportionate number of the 225,000 textile workers (17 percent of the textile labor force of March 1948) unemployed in mid-1949 were in New England, and they were concentrated in weaving and in the production of woolens and worsteds (which accounted for over one-third of the region's textile industry). The southern industry, on the other hand, relied less on the declining woolens and worsteds sector. By mid-1950 125,000 workers had been reemployed, but the remaining 100,000 or so, again disproportionately in the North, were left unemployed as a result of relocation and the effects of integration and rationalization.[62] Consequently, while the industry as a whole was undergoing a process of rationalization and concentration, the process took place mostly at the expense of workers in the Northeast. In the southern states, in contrast, the industry continued to expand. Between 1939 and 1951 the North Carolina textile industry expanded from 695 plants, 181,000 workers, and products with a value of approximately $550 million to 1,047 plants, 230,000 workers, and sales of $2,688 million. Although the largest gains were in the production of synthetic fibers, the woolens and worsteds sector also expanded. Despite the depressed conditions of 1948–49, North Carolina registered an increase in textile employment of approximately twenty thousand between 1947 and 1951.[63]

Partly because of the increasing integration of textile and apparel production, and partly because the production of apparel is, like textile production, a low-wage, labor-intensive process, the apparel industry has also become a predominantly southern industry during the postwar period. Between 1950 and 1974 the South's share of employment in the apparel sector increased from 17 percent to over 44 percent. Between 1958 and 1972 New York City alone lost 18 percent (68,000) of its apparel-producing jobs.[64] In North Carolina employment in this industry increased from 16,600 in 1947 to 78,000 in 1977 or from 4.4 percent to 9.9 percent of the total North Carolina manufacturing labor force. (See table 6.1 above.)

As in the textile industry, the most central cause of the relocation of

Table 6.2. Rates of surplus value in the textile industry: North Carolina, the rest of the United States, and New England, 1947 (figures in millions of dollars)

| | (a) Payroll | (b) Wages | (c) Value added | (d) Productive salaries (a−b*0.5) | (e) Depreciation (c*0.05) | (f) Surplus value (c−b−d−e) | (g) Variable capital (b+d) | (h) Rate of surplus value (f/g) |
|---|---|---|---|---|---|---|---|---|
| **North Carolina** | | | | | | | | |
| SIC 22[a] | 417.6 | 377.6 | 846.3 | 20.0 | 42.3 | 406.4 | 397.6 | 102 |
| 221 | 13.1 | 11.2 | 23.2 | 1.0 | 1.2 | 9.8 | 12.2 | 80 |
| 222 | 106.7 | 97.7 | 209.7 | 4.5 | 10.5 | 97.0 | 102.2 | 95 |
| 223 | 182.5 | 167.3 | 405.8 | 7.6 | 20.3 | 210.6 | 174.9 | 120 |
| 224 | 2.3 | 2.0 | 4.6 | 0.2 | 0.2 | 2.2 | 2.2 | 100 |
| 225 | 94.2 | 83.8 | 164.1 | 5.2 | 8.2 | 66.9 | 89.0 | 75 |
| 226 | 11.2 | 9.1 | 22.7 | 1.1 | 1.1 | 11.4 | 10.2 | 112 |
| 227 | 2.4 | 2.2 | 5.6 | 0.1 | 0.3 | 3.0 | 2.3 | 130 |
| 229 | 5.1 | 4.4 | 10.6 | 0.4 | 0.5 | 5.3 | 4.8 | 110 |
| **United States (−N.C.)** | | | | | | | | |
| 22 | 2,415.1 | 2,070.3 | 4,476.6 | 172.4 | 223.8 | 2,010.1 | 2,242.7 | 90 |
| 221 | 441.6 | 382.8 | 763.1 | 29.4 | 38.2 | 312.7 | 412.2 | 76 |
| 222 | 193.9 | 172.5 | 350.4 | 10.7 | 17.5 | 149.7 | 183.2 | 82 |
| 223 | 755.3 | 682.8 | 1,531.2 | 36.3 | 76.6 | 735.5 | 719.1 | 102 |
| 224 | 62.7 | 50.5 | 106.0 | 6.1 | 5.3 | 44.1 | 56.6 | 78 |
| 225 | 396.2 | 328.1 | 686.9 | 34.1 | 34.3 | 290.4 | 362.2 | 80 |
| 226 | 207.7 | 167.0 | 336.6 | 20.4 | 16.8 | 132.4 | 187.4 | 71 |
| 227 | 155.1 | 128.8 | 325.0 | 13.2 | 16.3 | 166.7 | 142.0 | 117 |
| 229 | 147.6 | 114.5 | 285.5 | 16.6 | 14.3 | 140.1 | 131.1 | 107 |
| **New England (Connecticut, Maine, Massachusetts, New Hampshire, Rhode Island, Vermont)** | | | | | | | | |
| 22 | 708.7 | 610.8 | 1,245.1 | 49.0 | 62.3 | 523.0 | 659.8 | 79 |
| 221 | 285.3 | 251.9 | 504.1 | 16.7 | 25.2 | 210.3 | 268.6 | 78 |
| 222 | 35.7 | 29.8 | 65.0 | 3.0 | 3.3 | 28.9 | 32.8 | 88 |
| 223 | 189.1 | 169.8 | 346.4 | 10.0 | 17.3 | 149.3 | 179.8 | 83 |
| 224 | 25.2 | 20.5 | 39.3 | 2.4 | 2.0 | 14.4 | 22.9 | 63 |
| 225 | 22.3 | 17.4 | 38.9 | 2.5 | 1.9 | 17.1 | 19.9 | 86 |
| 226 | 52.3 | 42.3 | 76.9 | 5.0 | 3.8 | 25.8 | 47.3 | 55 |
| 229 | 37.5 | 28.4 | 70.5 | 4.6 | 3.5 | 34.0 | 33.0 | 103 |

*Source*: U.S. Department of Commerce, Bureau of the Census, *Census of Manufactures, 1947*, vol. 3 (Washington: USGPO, 1950), pp. 122, 263, 281, 381, 452–4, 547, 609; U.S. Department of Commerce, Bureau of the Census, *Census of Manufactures, 1954*, vol. 1 (Washington: USGPO, 1957), pp. 4–23.

a. The Standard Industrial Classification (SIC) codes for the textile industry in 1947 are as follows: 22, textile mill products; 221, woolens and worsted products; 222, yarn and thread mills; 223, cotton and rayon broad woven goods; 224, narrow fabric mills; 225, knitting mills; 226, finishing; 227, carpets; 229, miscellaneous textile mill products.

apparel capital during the postwar period has been its relatively irreducible labor intensity. Although certain peripheral operations such as
needle positioning, thread cutting, pleating, hemming, and pattern cutting have been subject to automation and speedup, the level of mechanization in the industry remains low, and the sewing machine remains
central for most operations. Apparel production therefore remains a
highly labor-intensive process. In 1971 the total capital invested per
production worker in this industry was nine thousand dollars, less than
25 percent of the average for manufacturing as a whole. Difficulties in
the handling of the industry's raw materials, the relative rareness of long
production runs, and a very low threshold for entry make mechanization a risky business for all but the largest firms producing the most
standardized goods for the most stable markets (such as, for instance,
Levi-Strauss). In 1977 the United States had 26,505 establishments
producing apparel, the vast majority of which were single-unit companies. Well over 50 percent of these establishments (14,572) employed
fewer than twenty workers.[65]

These characteristics have caused the apparel industry, like textiles,
to search for sources of cheap labor power. Traditionally, apparel has
employed large numbers of female workers and has gradually eliminated the most skilled, and therefore the most highly paid, workers by
creating a minute division of labor in which workers are each set to
perform particular tasks, usually using a specially adapted sewing machine. The most intense attempts to mechanize—for example, cutting
by laser—have been directed at cutting, grading, and marking operations that require high levels of skill and experience and that have in the
past been male jobs.

While the process of deskilling has continued in the postwar period,
it has been complemented by a large-scale relocation. For the largest
firms, the search for lower labor costs has led to the creation of an international division of labor, in which the designing and cutting parts of
the production process are performed in the United States, while the
fabric is sent to be sewn abroad by cheaper, unskilled labor and then
reimported. In 1975 10.2 percent of U.S. apparel imports were produced in this way.[66]

Internationalization, however, is an option open to only a few of
the largest apparel producers. For the rest, relocation to the South has
proved to be the only feasible way of reducing production costs. As was
the case with textiles, the apparel industry locates predominantly in
rural areas, employs mostly female workers, and benefits from the
prevalence of part time farming.[67] Lower wages, longer hours, and high
levels of work intensity—conditions that provide a high rate of surplus
value—are the major advantages of such a strategy. In 1978 average
hourly earnings in apparel production were $4.08 in New York, $4.04

in Pennsylvania, $3.37 in North Carolina, and $3.38 in South Carolina.[68] Workers in the Northeast receive an average of eight days per annum paid holidays, compared with an average of six in the South. Southern apparel plants are larger, more modern in layout, and usually employ a more elaborate division of labor. In the production of men's and boy's shirts, only 40 percent of workers in the mid-Atlantic states (New York, New Jersey, and Pennsylvania) were employed in units with over two hundred fifty workers, compared to over 60 percent in the Southeast. Larger plants in the South allow the use of more efficient production methods, including the progressive bundling system, in which standardized bundles of garments flow in a logical work order from one operator to another, and which is the apparel industry's closest equivalent to an assembly line. In the Southeast, 65 percent of workers operate under this system, compared to 52 percent in the mid-Atlantic states.[69]

Finally, the availability of cheap labor also explains the rapid expansion of furniture production in North Carolina. Between 1947 and 1977 employment in furniture production has increased from 27,900 to 78,900, or from 7.3 to 10.3 percent of the state's labor force. By the latter date North Carolina had become "the furniture center of the nation" accounting for 17 percent of the total U.S. furniture manufacturing labor force and for 22.8 percent in household furniture.[70] Like textiles and apparel, the furniture industry is a dispersed industry, dominated numerically by family firms. In 1977 there were 10,235 different furniture establishments in the United States. Only 3,588 (35.1 percent) had over twenty employees.[71] In 1967 only twenty-seven companies had annual sales of more than ten million dollars.[72]

Unlike textiles and apparel, the bulk of the shift in furniture manufacturing after the depression of the 1930s was achieved primarily as a result of southern expansion rather than relocation. Nevertheless, the logic of this regional shift is similar to that in those industries. Like apparel and textiles, furniture production is characterized by a relatively irreducible labor intensity. The most skilled jobs are being slowly eliminated by mechanization and the furniture labor force remains for the most part semiskilled or unskilled. It is also becoming an increasingly female labor force (16.9 percent in 1966 and 27.2 percent in 1970).[73] Its wages are, on average, the lowest of all manufactured durable goods sectors, and they rank low even among nondurables. In 1978 the average hourly wage in furniture production in North Carolina was $4.27 compared with $4.92 in New York, $5.25 in Pennsylvania, and $4.70 in New Jersey.[74]

In addition to textiles, apparel, and furniture, North Carolina has experienced growth in a number of "newer" manufacturing sectors, some of which embody a significantly higher capital intensity of production

Table 6.3. North Carolina manufacturing labor force by place of residence, 1960 and 1970

| | Total | | Urban | | | |
|---|---|---|---|---|---|---|
| | 1960 | 1970 | 1960 | Percent | 1970 | Percent |
| All manufacturing | 509,193 | 704,306 | 221,802 | 43.6 | 278,092 | 39.5 |
| Furniture, lumber, and wood products | 80,749 | 88,205 | 22,259 | 27.6 | 26,739 | 30.3 |
| Primary metal industries | 3,129 | 6,560 | 1,454 | 46.5 | 2,473 | 37.7 |
| Fabricated metal industries | 6,970 | 15,613 | 3,680 | 52.8 | 7,083 | 45.4 |
| Machinery, except electrical | 12,866 | 26,190 | 6,857 | 53.3 | 13,527 | 51.6 |
| Electrical machinery | 25,231 | 37,198 | 12,917 | 51.0 | 15,677 | 42.1 |
| Transportation equipment | 5,326 | 10,625 | 2,397 | 45.0 | 3,594 | 33.8 |
| Other durables | 13,291 | 36,355 | 5,197 | 39.1 | 13,998 | 38.5 |
| Food and kindred products | 33,009 | 31,164 | 16,320 | 49.4 | 12,813 | 41.1 |
| Textiles, apparel | 254,736 | 332,463 | 109,014 | 42.8 | 125,526 | 37.8 |
| Printing, publishing | 13,062 | 15,419 | 9,292 | 71.1 | 9,834 | 63.8 |
| Chemicals | 13,547 | 22,684 | 6,631 | 48.9 | 10,149 | 44.7 |
| Other nondurables | 47,177 | 81,830 | 25,784 | 54.7 | 36,679 | 44.8 |

*Calculated from data in* U.S. Department of Commerce, Bureau of the Census, *Census of Population, 1960,* vol. 1, pt. 35 (Washington: USGPO, 1963), 178; U.S. Department of Com-

than the state's traditional industries. Six of these sectors (chemicals, rubber and plastics, stone, clay and glass products, fabricated metal products, nonelectrical machinery, and electrical and electronic equipment) accounted for 37.9 percent (154,400) of the manufacturing jobs created between 1947 and 1978 and in the latter year provided 22.9 percent of the manufacturing jobs in the state (see table 6.1). In 1976 Western Electric was the fifth largest corporation in the state, employing ninety-five hundred in four plants.[75] Nevertheless, the expansion of these industries does not represent a break with the pattern of industrialization established by their labor-intensive predecessors.

In the first place, growth has taken place predominantly in the most labor-intensive subdivisions of these sectors, or in the subdivisions, such as the production of textile machinery, that are closely related to the state's traditional industrial base (or both). For example, of the state's 33,000 chemical workers in 1977, 16,200 are employed in the production of synthetic fibers, a subsector of the chemical industry that employs a high proportion of semiskilled or unskilled production workers. The wages earned by these workers are, by the standards of the chemical industry generally, relatively low.[76] Similarly, North Carolina's elec-

| Rural nonfarm | | | | Rural farm | | | |
|---|---|---|---|---|---|---|---|
| 1960 | Percent | 1970 | Percent | 1960 | Percent | 1970 | Percent |
| 243,945 | 47.9 | 389,569 | 55.2 | 43,446 | 8.5 | 36,645 | 5.2 |
| 48,595 | 60.2 | 56,595 | 64.2 | 9,895 | 12.3 | 4,871 | 5.5 |
| 1,431 | 45.7 | 3,859 | 58.8 | 244 | 7.8 | 228 | 3.5 |
| 2,716 | 39.0 | 7,949 | 50.9 | 574 | 8.2 | 581 | 3.7 |
| 5,140 | 40.0 | 11,841 | 45.2 | 869 | 6.8 | 822 | 3.1 |
| 10,340 | 40.8 | 19,227 | 51.7 | 2,074 | 8.2 | 2,294 | 6.2 |
| 2,437 | 45.8 | 6,490 | 61.1 | 492 | 9.2 | 541 | 5.1 |
| 6,900 | 51.9 | 20,326 | 55.9 | 1,194 | 9.0 | 2,031 | 5.6 |
| 13,558 | 41.1 | 16,498 | 52.9 | 3,131 | 9.5 | 1,853 | 5.9 |
| 125,511 | 49.3 | 188,936 | 56.8 | 20,211 | 7.9 | 18,001 | 5.4 |
| 3,413 | 26.1 | 5,246 | 34.0 | 357 | 2.7 | 339 | 2.2 |
| 5,777 | 42.6 | 11,700 | 51.6 | 1,139 | 8.4 | 835 | 3.7 |
| 18,127 | 38.4 | 40,902 | 50.0 | 3,266 | 6.9 | 4,249 | 5.2 |

merce, Bureau of the Census, *Census of Population, 1970*, vol. 1, pt. 35 (Washington: USGPO, 1973), 216–17.

trical and electronic equipment industry is concentrated in light electronic assembly, which is again relatively labor-intensive, requires few skills, and pays low wages.[77] And in the transportation equipment sector, over 50 percent of jobs in North Carolina are in the parts and accessories division, which follows the same pattern. Here, the average hourly wage in North Carolina in 1978 was $5.14, compared with the U.S. average of $8.82.[78] As a result, in order to reduce labor costs, these industries have followed, as far as possible, the established pattern of industrialization, locating in rural areas, employing mostly agricultural and female labor, and observing local patterns of racial and class competition and discrimination.[79] For instance, in 1973 a new record of $747.1 million in new capital investment was established, and 22,172 new jobs were created. Leading sectors of new capital investment were chemicals, with $162.1 million, textiles, with $161.6 million, and the metal working sectors, with $102.8 million. Some 84.6 percent of this new capital and 85 percent of the new jobs created were located in rural areas or in communities of less than fifteen thousand in population.[80]

The consequence of this pattern of industrial expansion can be seen in tables 6.3 to 6.5. First of all, as industrialization proceeds in North

Table 6.4. Farm operators reporting off-farm work, North Carolina, 1949–78[a]

|  | 1949 | 1959 | 1969 | 1978[b] |
|---|---|---|---|---|
| Farm operators | 288,473 | 190,567 | 119,386 | 89,367 |
| Operators working off farms | 97,109 | 79,573 | 68,885 | 47,273 |
| Percentage | 33.7 | 41.8 | 57.7 | 52.9 |
| Operators working up to 100 days | 37,126 | 28,926 | 18,982 | 9,614 |
| Percentage | 12.9 | 15.2 | 15.9 | 10.8 |
| Operators working over 100 days | 59,983 | 50,647 | 49,903 | 37,658 |
| Percentage | 20.8 | 26.6 | 41.8 | 42.1 |
| Operators working over 200 days |  |  | 35,741 | 30,995 |
| Percentage |  |  | 29.9 | 34.7 |

*Calculated from* U.S. Department of Commerce, Bureau of the Census, *1950 Census of Agriculture*, General Report, vol. 2 (Washington: USGPO, 1953), 186; U.S. Department of Commerce, Bureau of the Census, *1969 Census of Agriculture*, vol. 1, pt. 26, section 1 (Washington: USGPO, 1972), 3, 5; U.S. Department of Commerce, Bureau of the Census, *1978 Census of Agriculture*, vol. 1, pt. 33 (Washington: USGPO, 1982), p. 3.

a. These data refer to farm operators only, not to their families or to the agricultural population.

b. In 1978, 5,251 farm operators failed to report whether they had off-farm work or not.

Carolina, the state's manufacturing labor force becomes an increasingly rural labor force. In 1976, with a population in excess of five million, North Carolina had only four cities with a population of over one hundred thousand—Charlotte, 252,000; Greensboro, 157,000; Raleigh, 137,000; and Winston-Salem, 140,000.[81] Between 1960 and 1970 the percentage of the manufacturing labor force classified as "urban" fell from 43.6 percent to 29.5 percent, while those classified as "rural non-farm" increased from 47.9 percent to 55.3 percent. In other words, North Carolina's manufacturing labor force is made up increasingly of workers who live in rural areas and on farms, but whose nonagricultural income exceeds that derived from the sale of agricultural produce. In addition, some 5.2 percent of the manufacturing labor force also sell agricultural products whose value exceeds their manufacturing income (table 6.3). This pattern (declining proportion of the population urban, increasing proportion rural nonfarm) holds up consistently for all sectors except furniture, lumber, and wood products, in which a small increase in the percentage of the labor force that is urban probably reflects the declining importance of the lumber industry. Further, the largest percentage increases in the rural nonfarm category were in the newer, more capital-intensive industries: primary metals (13.1 percent); fabricated metals (11.9 percent); electrical machinery (10.9 percent); transportation equipment (15.3 percent); and food (11.8 percent).

Table 6.5. Female employment in manufacturing, North Carolina, 1950–70

|  | 1950 | 1960 | 1970 | 1950–70 |
|---|---|---|---|---|
| Total manufacturing employment | 410,186 | 509,193 | 704,306 |  |
| Female manufacturing employment | 131,494 | 179,171 | 294,796 |  |
| Percentage | 32.1 | 35.2 | 41.9 |  |
| New manufacturing employment |  | 99,007 | 195,113 | 294,120 |
| New female employment |  | 47,677 | 115,625 | 163,302 |
| Females as percentage of new employment |  | 48.2 | 59.3 | 55.8 |

*Calculated from data in* U.S. Department of Commerce, Bureau of the Census, *1960 Census of Population*, vol. 1, pt. 35 (Washington: USGPO, 1963), 180; U.S. Department of Commerce, Bureau of the Census, *1970 Census of Population*, vol. 1, pt. 35 (Washington: USGPO, 1973), 215–17.

Second, an increasing proportion of North Carolina's farm operators have reported part-time off-farm work during the postwar period. Between 1949 and 1969 the proportion of operators working off their farms increased from 33.7 percent to 57.7 percent, while the proportion working over one hundred days more than doubled, from 20.8 percent to 41.8 percent. In 1969 almost 30 percent of all farm operators had off-farm work for over two hundred days. By 1978 the proportion of farmers reporting off-farm work and the proportion working up to one hundred days declined from 1969, perhaps because almost 6 percent of farmers failed to report the extent of their off-farm work. The percentage reporting over two hundred days of off-farm work increased significantly from 29.9 to 34.7 (table 6.4).

Third, table 6.5 indicates that, as a result of the increasing industrial penetration of rural areas, a majority of the jobs created in North Carolina between 1950 and 1970 went to women.

*Labor organization*
*in the postwar period*

In conjunction with the operation of the right-to-work law and other forms of official discouragement, an increasingly dispersed, fragmented rural working class has presented a formidable barrier to unionization. Not only has union membership remained lower than in every other state, but it has also failed to keep up with the rate of economic growth during most of the postwar period, declining as a percentage of total nonagricultural employment from 8.3 percent in 1953[82] to 7.4 percent in 1964 and 6.9 percent in 1974 before rising to 9.6 percent in 1980.[83]

Throughout the postwar period, the state's major industries have remained unorganized. In 1976 the only unions with more than five thousand members were the Communications Workers, with 17,000, the Teamsters, with 15,400, the Tobacco Workers, with 8,500, and the International Brotherhood of Electrical Workers, with 5,300.[84] From 1952 to 1970 the percentage of total working days lost in strikes varied from a low of 0.005 percent in 1960 and 1961 (in the aftermath of the TWUA's defeat at Henderson) to a high of 0.14 percent in 1955.[85] In 1970 the rate of 0.03 percent was roughly one-fifteenth of the national rate.[86]

Since the failure of the AFL (1946–47) and CIO (1946–53) postwar southern organizing drives, most efforts at labor organization in the South have been carried out by individual unions concentrating on particular industries and particular areas. In North Carolina, as one might expect, given the structure of the state economy, the most important struggles have been carried on in the textile and apparel industries by the largest national textile and clothing unions—the Amalgamated Clothing Workers' Union (ACWA) and the TWUA (which merged in 1976 to form the Amalgamated Clothing and Textile Workers' Union)—and the state's major corporations—Stevens, Burlington, and Cannon. As the above figures suggest, these efforts have met with only limited success. A TWUA drive against Burlington and Cannon that began in 1956 made some progress, but collapsed by the end of the decade in the wake of defeats at Henderson, North Carolina, and Darlington, South Carolina.[87] In the latter case, the TWUA won the right to represent the workers in collective bargaining. The response by the owning corporation, Deering-Milliken, however, was to liquidate its capital at the plants concerned and move its production elsewhere. This action convinced the union that success could be gained only if an entire corporation could be organized. Otherwise, closures could not be prevented.[88] Consequently, during the early 1960s, the AFL-CIO's Industrial Union Department and the TWUA chose to resurrect the CIO's old tactic of targeting a single leading corporation for organization. In this way they hoped to be able to concentrate resources and establish a beachhead for the unionization of the entire industry. Burlington Industries, which had fiercely resisted unionization since the 1920s and whose founder, Spencer Love, was a close political ally of the state's "progressive" governor Terry Sanford, was bypassed. Rather, the union chose to single out J. P. Stevens, which was implementing a severe program of speedup in its fifty-five mills in North and South Carolina in the early 1960s.[89]

Having opened in late 1963, the campaign to organize J. P. Stevens is still under way, and it illustrates the extreme difficulties faced by workers and unions at all stages of the unionization and bargaining processes.[90] In the first place, the social and economic context of textile production in North Carolina—a dispersed labor force in rural areas or small communities that have few alternative sources of employment and that are therefore easily dominated by capital—guarantees that the early stages of the unionization process are long and difficult. The defeat suffered by the TWUA in 1975 in a representation election at a Stevens plant in Wallace, North Carolina, provides an illustration of these obstacles. Stevens's two plants in Wallace employ about nine hundred workers, between 35 and 40 percent of the town's population. A Stevens executive sits on the town board, and the corporation is the municipal water system's largest customer, accounting for $200,000 of its annual $280,000 in revenue. In addition, Stevens regularly meets with the local business and retail community as part of its public relations efforts. In 1975 the result was that local merchants, who were clearly aware of prior examples of plant closures at Darlington, South Carolina, and Statesboro, Georgia, actively participated in the campaign by threatening prounion workers with the removal of credit and other services. Despite having enlisted a majority of the plants' workers as members, the TWUA lost the representation election, 540–404. This result was overturned by the NLRB in 1978 on the grounds that Stevens had engaged in illegal harassment of workers, and Stevens was ordered to enter into contract negotiations with the ACTWU. This order was stayed when Stevens appealed the ruling.

Second, the weakness of the National Labor Relations Act itself seriously weakens efforts at labor organization. The initial NLRB hearings regarding Stevens's illegal activities in the campaign to organize seven plants in Roanoke Rapids, North Carolina, were held in 1964, when the TWUA charged that Stevens had illegally fired prounion workers, violating section 8(a)(3) of the National Labor Relations Act. The remedies for such illegal activity are few and difficult to enforce, however. While the NLRB can order the workers reinstated and award backpay (less any wages the workers received from another job), the company can appeal the rulings in the courts, delaying action and virtually forcing the fired workers to leave the area and find alternative employment. Meanwhile, since the board has no power to issue injunctions or contempt citations, it cannot prevent the same offense from being committed repeatedly. Further, the NLRA does not allow workers to sue for civil damages. Finally, if the workers choose to strike, the same law allows employers to sue the union for damages from secondary boycotts and to request court injunctions against picketing. According to Bill Finger and Mike Krivosh,

> rather than protect workers, section 8(a)(3) functions more like a "hunting license" for southern textile executives. They can discharge employees illegally, pay peanuts in penalties several years later (if the

worker is still around), then deduct the amount as a legitimate business expense. In other words, the law itself makes firing pro-union employees a relatively inexpensive way to stifle individual expression and undercut a union drive. Exploiting that sinister aspect of the Labor Act is exactly what J. P. Stevens has done.[91]

After the failure of the 1963–64 unionization effort, and with effective strike action eliminated as an alternative by the poverty of the workers, the weakness of the union, and the advantages given to employers by the NLRA, the TWUA turned to court action in order to demonstrate its commitment to the victimized workers. Between 1965 and 1976 two hundred eighty-nine illegally fired workers received $1.3 million in backpay, and Stevens was found guilty of a lengthening list of illegal antiunion tactics.

The two major legal innovations to emerge from this period of litigation—the ability of the NLRB to throw out the result of representation elections held under unfair conditions and award bargaining rights to the union and a ruling that union officials must be able to gain access to workers inside the plants—played an important role in the TWUA victory at Roanoke Rapids in 1974 and at High Point in 1979. The unionization of approximately three thousand workers at Roanoke Rapids did not result in concrete material gains, however. Exploiting the vagueness of the NLRA requirement that employers and employees bargain in "good faith," Stevens turned the bargaining over to a professional antiunion attorney, Whiteford Blakeney.[92] The "Blakeney Formula" of bargaining is to discuss nonessential points but to refuse to talk about the crucial points, such as dues checkoff and grievance arbitration. Combined with a refusal to grant normal corporate wage increases to the workers in the recently unionized plants, this strategy is designed to make it as difficult as possible for the new union to finance itself and to establish material gains for its members. The hope is that eventually either the initial enthusiasm for the union will fade, or the union will be forced to take strike action, in which case the employer can take advantage of the NLRA's legal benefits.

In response to this strategy, in June 1976 the TWUA merged with the ACWA in order to maximize their southern strength and agreed on a strategy to force Stevens to sign a contract. This strategy had four main components—a national consumer boycott, pressure on corporations with which Stevens has interlocking directorships, an expanded southern organizing drive, and a more sophisticated and extensive legal attack.

By the late 1970s this offensive appeared to be paying dividends. The consumer boycott, joined by the AFL-CIO, a number of states, cities, and religious and civil liberties groups, appeared to be at least part of the reason for Stevens's low (compared with a number of other textile corporations) rate of increase in profits in 1978.[93] In addition, the union's pressure on Stevens's corporate allies resulted in the resignation of Stevens's chairman, James D. Finley, from the boards of Manufacturers' Hanover Trust and the New York Life Insurance Company (both of which hold ACTWU funds), and the resignation of directors of Avon Products and the New York Life Insurance Company from the Stevens board. In addition, a number of other large corporations became involved in the dispute.[94]

In October 1980 Stevens finally settled the conflict, agreeing to a 2.5-year contract covering ten unionized plants (seven in Roanoke Rapids, and three others at High Point, North Carolina, Allendale, South Carolina, and West Boyleston, Alabama) and approximately 3,200 employees.[95] Stevens agreed to pay about three million dollars in withheld wages, an 8.5 percent increase in the first year of the contract, and back payments to the union's pension fund. In addition, there was to be a union dues checkoff, acceptance of third-party arbitration in the event of disputes over working conditions, and a seniority and jobposting system to undercut the company's traditional method of promoting supervisors' "favorites." The company also agreed to offer the same contract to any union local established in a Stevens plant and recognized by the NLRB in the following eighteen months.

Despite its provision of material benefits for the unionized workers, there are a number of reasons to suggest that the achievement of this contract may not represent the major breakthrough in the organization of the southern textile industry that some union leaders have suggested. First, the wage increases that were gained simply bring wage levels in the unionized plants back to parity with the other nonunionized Stevens plants. No wage advantage for union members has been established. Second, in order to gain the contract, a number of other concessions were made by the union. During the eighteen months in which the contract was available to other successful locals, the union relinquished its crucial right of access to plant canteens, rest areas, and parking lots for union organization purposes. In addition, the union agreed to withdraw all legal charges against Stevens, to terminate its consumer boycott and campaign of corporate pressure, and, generally, to stop treating Stevens differently from other textile corporations. All of these concessions, given the inability to guarantee union security in a right-to-work state, may serve to erode the union's strength and pave the way for a corporate counteroffensive. In an interview in the summer of 1979 in which he predicted a settlement between Stevens and the ACTWU, George Hood, a professional "union-buster" who had been involved in the Roanoke

Table 6.6. Average hourly earnings of production workers by manufacturing sector: North Carolina and the United States, 1978 ($)

| | North Carolina | United States | North Carolina/ United States |
|---|---|---|---|
| 20 Food and kindred products | $ 4.70 | $ 5.96 | 79 % |
| 21 Tobacco products | 6.78 | 6.64 | 102 |
| 22 Textile mill products | 4.28 | 4.41 | 97 |
| 23 Apparel | 3.37 | 3.80 | 89 |
| 24 Lumber and wood products | 4.35 | 5.47 | 80 |
| 25 Furniture | 4.27 | 4.70 | 91 |
| 26 Pulp and paper products | 6.61 | 6.97 | 95 |
| 27 Printing and publishing | 5.74 | 6.68 | 86 |
| 28 Chemicals | 6.13 | 7.42 | 83 |
| 29 Petroleum products | | 9.12 | |
| 30 Rubber and plastics products | 5.35 | 5.64 | 95 |
| 31 Leather products | 3.83 | 3.95 | 97 |
| 32 Stone, clay, and glass products | 5.08 | 6.50 | 78 |
| 33 Primary metal products | 5.69 | 8.81 | 65 |
| 34 Fabricated metal products | 5.27 | 6.51 | 81 |
| 35 Machinery, except electrical | 5.76 | 7.08 | 81 |
| 36 Electrical and electronic equipment | 5.28 | 6.03 | 88 |
| 37 Transportation equipment | 4.95 | 8.46 | 59 |
| 38 Instruments | 5.26 | 5.86 | 90 |
| 39 Miscellaneous | 4.14 | 4.65 | 89 |
| All sectors | 4.66 | 6.37 | 73 |

*Sources*: U.S. Department of Commerce, Bureau of the Census, *1978–9 Annual Survey of Manufactures* (Washington: USGPO, 1983), 1–5, 6–190 to 6–192.

Rapids campaign, cast some light on Stevens's possible strategy in signing a contract after six years of resistance:

> I suppose their [Stevens's] thinking is they know the employees want to decertify. They feel reasonably confident that the union no longer represents a majority there.
>
> Once there's a contract, my understanding is that we would be able to, the employees would be able to, petition for a decertification election. These unfair labor practice charges would no longer block a decertification election.[96]

*Wages and exploitation in contemporary North Carolina*

The strategy of capital accumulation implemented in North Carolina in the late nineteenth and early twentieth centuries has survived despite

Table 6.7. Rates of exploitation by manufacturing sector: North Carolina and the United States, 1978

|  | | North Carolina | United States |
|---|---|---|---|
| 20 | Food and kindred products | 221 | 263 |
| 21 | Tobacco products | 737 | 532 |
| 22 | Textile mill products | 112 | 112 |
| 23 | Apparel | 110 | 113 |
| 24 | Lumber and wood products | 117 | 140 |
| 25 | Furniture | 121 | 128 |
| 26 | Pulp and paper products | 153 | 170 |
| 27 | Printing and publishing | 171 | 193 |
| 28 | Chemicals | 353 | 388 |
| 29 | Petroleum products | | 507 |
| 30 | Rubber and plastics products | 166 | 152 |
| 31 | Leather products | 147 | 124 |
| 32 | Stone, clay, and glass products | 182 | 170 |
| 33 | Primary metal products | 305 | 121 |
| 34 | Fabricated metal products | 274 | 146 |
| 35 | Machinery, except electrical | 243 | 169 |
| 36 | Electrical and electronic equipment | 249 | 171 |
| 37 | Transportation equipment | 186 | 143 |
| 38 | Instruments | 232 | 230 |
| 39 | Miscellaneous | 174 | 172 |
|  | All sectors | 178 | 164 |

*Calculated from data in* U.S. Department of Commerce, Bureau of the Census, *1978–9 Annual Survey of Manufactures* (Washington: USGPO, 1983), 1–8, 5–3 to 5–29, 6–190 to 6–194.

rapid postwar growth and diversification. In 1978 the average hourly manufacturing wage in North Carolina was 73 percent of the national average. Only in the tobacco products sector, which North Carolina dominates, was its average higher than the national average. (See table 6.6.) Consequently, the state's above-average rate of exploitation has been maintained. In 1977 this stood at 174 percent compared with 165 percent for the United States and 151 percent for the Northeast. (See table 6.7 and the introduction.) In 1978 the corresponding figures were 178 percent, 164 percent, and 151 percent.[97]

Tables 6.6 and 6.7 are notable not only because they indicate continuity in below-average wage levels and above-average rates of exploitation, but also because they indicate the extent to which recently mobile capital in sectors such as chemicals, rubber, metal products, electrical and nonelectrical machinery, and transportation benefit from this continuity. By the 1970s the long domination of the state by textile capital and the impact of State policy on wage levels and the social relations of

Table 6.8. Technical composition of capital (gross book value of depreciable assets per employee) by manufacturing sector: North Carolina and the United States, 1978 (in thousands of dollars)

|  | North Carolina | United States |
|---|---|---|
| 20   Food and kindred products | 26.7 | 27.0 |
| 21   Tobacco products | 33.4 | 33.6 |
| 22   Textile mill products | 17.7 | 17.9 |
| 23   Apparel | 3.3 | 3.2 |
| 24   Lumber and wood products | 18.5 | 19.0 |
| 25   Furniture | 8.3 | 8.7 |
| 26   Pulp and paper products | 61.5 | 53.8 |
| 27   Printing and publishing | 15.3 | 14.7 |
| 28   Chemicals | 69.0 | 80.0 |
| 29   Petroleum products | — | 186.7 |
| 30   Rubber and plastics products | 27.2 | 23.3 |
| 31   Leather products | 3.9 | 4.3 |
| 32   Stone, clay, and glass products | 37.3 | 34.4 |
| 33   Primary metal products | 34.3 | 53.5 |
| 34   Fabricated metal products | 17.1 | 17.3 |
| 35   Machinery, except electrical | 23.4 | 18.3 |
| 36   Electrical and electronic equipment | 13.0 | 14.3 |
| 37   Transportation equipment | 15.3 | 19.0 |
| 38   Instruments | 22.6 | 15.5 |
| 39   Miscellaneous | 12.1 | 10.3 |
| All sectors | 19.3 | 23.4 |

Sources: As table 6.7.

production generally have created a social context that allows these capitals to produce an above-average rate of exploitation (provided only that they are able to escape Fordist wage relations in the Northeast and overcome the political obstacles to relocation in North Carolina). The chemicals sector only *appears* to be an exception to this generalization because of the uneven nature of the relocation process. Almost half of the chemical sector's employment in North Carolina is concentrated in the production of organic fibers for the textile industry. In this division, North Carolina's rate of surplus value in 1978 was 272 percent, compared with 192 percent for the United States as a whole. By producing in North Carolina, newer capitals such as this can take advantage of interregional variations in rates of unionization, the length of the working day (or year),[98] wage levels, and the intensity of work, and can achieve an above-average rate of exploitation regardless of variations in the technical composition of capital. (See table 6.8.) The competitive advantage afforded by these production relations in North Carolina also outweighs (in all but two of these cases) additional variations in the

Table 6.9. Rates of profit[a] by manufacturing sector, United States and North Carolina, 1978

|  |  | North Carolina | United States |
|---|---|---|---|
| 20 | Food and kindred products | 22.0 | 25.3 |
| 21 | Tobacco products | 78.4 | 61.3 |
| 22 | Textile mill products | 24.5 | 25.1 |
| 23 | Apparel | 33.5 | 38.3 |
| 24 | Lumber and wood products | 23.7 | 28.7 |
| 25 | Furniture | 37.5 | 39.0 |
| 26 | Pulp and paper products | 29.3 | 33.2 |
| 27 | Printing and publishing | 61.7 | 68.3 |
| 28 | Chemicals | 56.0 | 53.9 |
| 29 | Petroleum products | — | 13.9 |
| 30 | Rubber and plastics products | 36.2 | 38.2 |
| 31 | Leather products | 38.0 | 35.3 |
| 32 | Stone, clay, and glass products | 45.7 | 46.3 |
| 33 | Primary metal products | 50.6 | 23.5 |
| 34 | Fabricated metal products | 59.4 | 39.2 |
| 35 | Machinery, except electrical | 43.0 | 48.7 |
| 36 | Electrical and electronic equipment | 64.4 | 51.9 |
| 37 | Transportation equipment | 42.0 | 27.8 |
| 38 | Instruments | 67.2 | 76.5 |
| 39 | Miscellaneous | 48.1 | 46.1 |
|  | All sectors | 38.0 | 34.0 |

*Sources*: As table 6.7.

a. Ratio of surplus value produced to the sum of constant (cost of raw materials + depreciation) and variable capital (production workers' wages + productive salaries). $(s/(c + v))$ = rate of profit $(s/(c + v))$ (%) rate of profit expressed as a percentage

cost of materials used and in capital depreciated in the production process. (See table 6.9.)

In the sector that had traditionally dominated the North Carolina economy, textiles, the wage differential is relatively small and the above-average rate of exploitation in textile production has disappeared. A significant wage advantage remains in apparel and furniture production, but the rate of surplus value in these industries is lower than their national average.

Before discussing the sources and implications of these changes, we should note that these figures are averages for entire industrial sectors. Consequently, like the 1978 statewide average of 178 percent, they may obscure significant differences between industrial subsectors and between corporations within the same sector. Further investigation reveals, for instance, that North Carolina enjoys significant advantages in the

Table 6.10. Average hourly earnings in the textile and apparel industries by major producing states, 1978 (over 20,000 production workers)

|  | Textile mill products | Apparel |
| --- | --- | --- |
| Alabama | $ 4.17 | $ 3.39 |
| Florida | — | 3.55 |
| Georgia | 4.36 | 3.39 |
| Mississippi | — | 3.39 |
| North Carolina | 4.28 | 3.37 |
| South Carolina | 4.63 | 3.38 |
| Tennessee | 4.00 | 3.46 |
| Texas | — | 3.39 |
| Virginia | 4.42 | 3.48 |
| California | — | 3.71 |
| Kentucky | — | 3.71 |
| Massachusetts | 4.69 | 4.07 |
| New Jersey | 4.88 | 4.02 |
| New York | 4.36 | 4.08 |
| Pennsylvania | 4.50 | 4.04 |

Sources: U.S. Department of Commerce, Bureau of the Census, *1978–9 Annual Survey of Manufactures* (Washington: USGPO, 1983), pt. 6.

production of narrow fabrics and in the knitting mills sector of the textile industry. Further, a number of large, modern, and integrated textile/apparel corporations have developed within these industries' predominantly competitive structures since World War II. It would seem likely that these corporations, such as Burlington, Stevens, and Cannon, should be able to make more efficient use of labor power than the industry in general and should therefore have above-average rates of exploitation. Conversely, many of North Carolina's 1,372 textile mills in 1977 (630 of which have less than fifty employees) were owned by smaller, less efficient companies whose survival is due to the low wages that have been maintained in the state, and whose lower rates of exploitation probably serve to reduce the average rate. Unfortunately, because of the way in which data are presented in corporate annual reports, it is not possible to test this hypothesis.

Having taken note of these difficulties in the use of state aggregate data, however, it remains the case that North Carolina's advantage in the production of surplus value in textiles and apparel has disappeared (table 6.7). Ultimately, it appears that this change in the state's relative position is the result of the virtual completion of the process of interregional relocation of capital, of which the early industrialization formed a part. This process has now established southern production relations as the basis of competition and exploitation in these industries and has reduced the number of sources of variation in rates of exploitation. For instance, southern textile and apparel wage rates are not only low, but they display only a limited degree of variation (table 6.10). When we compare rates of exploitation in North Carolina and the United States as a whole, therefore, we are no longer measuring the impact of variations in productive relations and strategies of exploitation but, rather, more limited variations within the same regional (southern) strategy. The national average rate of exploitation, especially in the textile industry, is now by and large a southern rate of exploitation.

Since southern production relations form the basis for exploitation in the apparel and (especially) textile industries, variations in rates of exploitation in these industries will tend to be associated with relatively small variations in the social relations of production and in capital intensity. As the first major southern textile state, North Carolina's textile employment is disproportionately concentrated in a number of the older, less mechanized subdivisions of textile production — particularly weaving and spinning — in which average rates of exploitation are relatively low. For instance, 25 percent of value added and 27.4 percent of employment in textile production in North Carolina in 1972 were in spinning of yarn and thread, where the rate of exploitation at the national level is well below that for the textile industry as a whole. In contrast, 37 percent of value added and 25 percent of employment in textile production in Georgia (which has the highest textile rate of exploitation in the United States) results from the production of carpets, the most mechanized and concentrated subdivision of textile production. At the national level this subdivision has the highest rate of exploitation in the textile mill products sector. Without this source of surplus value, the average rate of exploitation in the Georgia textile industry would fall below the national average.

In both textiles and apparel (but especially in the more labor-intensive apparel industry), a number of nonsouthern states — Massachusetts and New York in textiles, California, New York, and Massachusetts in apparel — also display above-average rates of exploitation. In both cases these high rates probably result from a combination of: smaller establishment size (see table 6.11); a consequent ability to respond more easily to short-run changes in fashion or economic conditions; easy access to urban mass markets; increasing levels of urban poverty and unemployment; the availability of small (in terms of the industries' total needs) but important pools of black, female, and immigrant labor power; and a higher proportion of "high fashion" and high-count specialty textile production, for both of which conspicuous consumption and proximity to a large high-income clientele render demand less price-sensitive. While the northeastern textile industry is now

Table 6.11. Average establishment size in the textile and apparel industries, by major producing states, 1977 (over 20,000 production workers)

| | Production workers (in thousands) | Establishments | Average |
|---|---|---|---|
| **Textile mill products** | | | |
| Alabama | 38.3 | 180 | 213 |
| Georgia | 100.3 | 691 | 145 |
| North Carolina | 219.5 | 1,372 | 160 |
| South Carolina | 124.0 | 429 | 302 |
| Tennessee | 24.1 | 171 | 141 |
| Virginia | 37.9 | 100 | 379 |
| Massachusetts | 21.4 | 277 | 77 |
| New Jersey | 19.6 | 527 | 37 |
| New York | 36.1 | 1,243 | 29 |
| Pennsylvania | 40.4 | 536 | 75 |
| **Apparel** | | | |
| Alabama | 49.0 | 345 | 142 |
| Georgia | 66.1 | 622 | 106 |
| Mississippi | 35.8 | 221 | 162 |
| North Carolina | 68.0 | 702 | 97 |
| South Carolina | 38.9 | 319 | 122 |
| Tennessee | 61.7 | 443 | 139 |
| Texas | 63.6 | 925 | 69 |
| Virginia | 33.8 | 287 | 118 |
| Kentucky | 24.7 | 156 | 158 |
| Florida | 28.1 | 1,279 | 22 |
| California | 85.2 | 4,288 | 20 |
| Illinois | 20.5 | 568 | 36 |
| Massachusetts | 35.7 | 767 | 47 |
| New Jersey | 52.4 | 1,920 | 27 |
| New York | 177.4 | 7,797 | 23 |
| Pennsylvania | 118.9 | 1,979 | 60 |

*Sources*: U.S. Department of Commerce, Bureau of the Census, *1977 Census of Manufactures*, vol. 3 (Washington: USGPO, 1981), 981.

small and its impact on the industry as a whole relatively insignificant, a relatively large proportion of the apparel industry remains in the larger northern cities in order to take advantage of these conditions.

Historically, productive relations in North Carolina have enabled textile capital to resist the pressures resulting from its own limitations (a high and relatively irreducible labor intensity and relatively high levels of competition) on the one hand and wider social and economic developments (unionization, generally high rates of capital accumulation, and labor market competition) on the other. The ability to extract an above-average amount of surplus value from the state's dispersed rural labor force has allowed textile capital in general to maintain its rate of exploitation throughout the postwar period and has permitted the larger corporations to achieve significant rates of growth.

The political and economic domination of textile capital has had a wider impact, however. For capital in the newer, more productive manufacturing sectors, North Carolina's productive relations now permit rates of exploitation that are significantly higher than their respective national averages. In the production of rubber and plastics products, primary and fabricated metal goods, machinery, electrical and electronic equipment, and transportation equipment, North Carolina's overall advantage in the production of surplus value is large and occurs in virtually all the three-digit subclassifications of these sectors. In the production of special industry machinery (North Carolina accounts for almost 20 percent of U.S. employment in the textile machinery sector) the rate of exploitation in North Carolina is over three times greater than the national average, and in the production of motor vehicle parts it is over twice as large. These above-average rates of exploitation are simultaneously an expression of the success of the strategy of industrialization adopted in North Carolina and of the major contradiction that it creates and with which it must continually deal. By maintaining a low-wage, union-free economy, it provides the basis for the making of excess profits by the most efficient capitals and therefore perpetuates and expands the threat to the labor-intensive industrial base that it must preserve.

## Contemporary tendencies
## in the North Carolina economy

If the North Carolina economy has been able to absorb new capital without affecting the extraction of above-average rates of surplus value, this does not mean that capital accumulation has had no effect on productive relations. In reality, beginning in the late 1960s the emergence of a relatively tight labor market set in motion a number of important tendencies that may eventually have a major impact on the state's economy.

The most significant and visible of these changes has been the textile industry's increasing use of black workers as textile operatives, rather than simply in their traditional roles as laborers and service workers. This process began in the mid-1960s after the passage of the 1964 Civil Rights Act and a number of executive orders concerning eligibility for government contracts. It only became numerically and socially significant, however, in the later years of the decade, as labor market competition from new industries forced capital in the labor-intensive sectors—textiles, apparel, furniture—to search for new sources of cheap labor power.[99]

This search was not achieved without some difficulty. A number of state and federal programs were established during the mid-1960s to stem the flow of black ex-farm workers and tenants out of the state and to redirect them toward the industrial Piedmont area. Success was slow and limited partly because the effects of almost a century of industrial segregation and northward mobility and partly because of the increasing ability to find employment with companies moving to the rural areas of the state.[100] Consequently, the textile corporations themselves were forced to try to deal with the problem. In April 1969 a number of textile companies, including Burlington, Cone, and Fieldcrest, for the first time expressed a strong, collective interest in, and promised expanded support for, the development of textile curricula not only in community colleges but also in high schools.[101] In addition, the larger corporations began to establish their own recruitment and training programs. Burlington Industries, for example, initiated the Burlington Education Skills Training Program (BEST) to recruit school dropouts and unemployed, unskilled ghetto dwellers into a combined classroom and on-the-job training system.[102]

Through efforts such as these, the corporations were able to break down the understandable reluctance of black workers to enter the textile industry. Between 1964 and the end of the decade, the percentage of the North Carolina textile labor force that was black increased from 5.5 percent[103] to 11.6 percent.[104] A decade later, 23 percent of J. P. Stevens employees in North and South Carolina were black, with much higher percentages in the more eastern parts of those states. In Roanoke Rapids, for example, over 40 percent of the workers in seven Stevens plants were black.[105]

Racial segregation and the use of racial fears and competition to maintain a weak and divided labor force did not end simply because blacks were allowed into the mills. Burlington, Stevens, and other companies have continued to deny the most elementary rights to black workers, reserving supervisory positions for whites only and harassing or firing workers who complain to the Equal Employment Opportunity Commission (EEOC).[106] In addition, appeals to fears of racial domination and violence remain part of the companies' antiunion propaganda arsenal, as the campaign against unionization at Roanoke Rapids demonstrates.[107]

In spite of, or perhaps as a result of, this strategy, a number of commentators have suggested that the entry of black workers into the textile labor force will significantly improve the prospect of unionization. In this view, the racial consciousness developed during the struggle for civil rights and a lack of contact with the paternalistic ideology and social constraints developed in the mill villages will make black workers more able and willing to undertake collective action to improve conditions and wages.[108] Although experience quickly showed that no differences existed between black and white workers in terms of performance and turnover, the fact that blacks continue to be considered as "undesirable employees"[109] undoubtedly reflects a certain anxiety on the part of millowners and corporate executives. The important role played by blacks in the Roanoke Rapids campaign and in organizations such as the Carolina Brown Lung Association has undoubtedly strengthened this conviction.[110]

In response to increased labor market competition, the impact of racial integration on strategies of social control and exploitation, the threat of unionization, and pressure to improve working conditions from the Occupational Safety and Health Administration (OSHA), the larger textile corporations embarked on a program of relocation and mechanization designed to reduce production costs and increase the production of surplus value. The process of relocation to areas of cheap labor has taken two forms. First, within the South textile production is gradually being moved to rural areas that can supply black labor power that is not only relatively cheap, but also relatively untouched by the radicalizing influence of the (mostly urban) civil rights movement. For the region as a whole, this means that the textile industry is becoming increasingly concentrated in the Deep South. For North Carolina it means that the industry is moving toward the eastern part of the state where the mechanization of tobacco agriculture is making large numbers of small tobacco farmers available for part-time or full-time industrial jobs,[111] and where, consequently, rates of exploitation are higher than the state average (see table 6.12). During the late 1960s Burlington Industries invested $125 million in the coastal plains region of North Carolina, where, by the end of the decade, it employed over eleven thousand workers in twenty-three plants.[112]

Second, the process of relocation is increasingly an international one. Burlington opened its first Mexican operation near Cuernavaca in 1944, replicating the major elements of the strategy of exploitation it followed in North Carolina.[113] Until 1966 the corporation's foreign labor force did not rise above two thousand. Yet by 1970 it was twelve thousand strong and was distributed among operations in a number of countries, including the Republic of Ireland, Italy, Mexico, Japan, and Brazil.[114]

Until the mid-1970s; these tendencies took place in a context of overall growth in the textile industry in North Carolina. In 1973 Burlington's total labor force reached its peak of 88,000 (77,000 in the

Table 6.12. Rates of surplus value in the 39 most eastern counties and eastern counties with towns over 25,000, 1972 and 1977 (in millions of dollars)

| | Payroll | Wages | Value added | Productive salaries | Depreciation | Surplus value | Variable capital | s/v |
|---|---|---|---|---|---|---|---|---|
| North Carolina 1972 | 4,929.1 | 3,427.3 | 11,014.5 | 750.9 | 682.9 | 6,153.4 | 4,178.2 | 147 |
| 41 eastern counties, 1972 | 863.9 | 622.3 | 2,234.7 | 120.8 | 138.6 | 1,353.0 | 743.1 | 182 |
| 8 eastern "urban" counties, 1972[a] | 344.8 | 234.7 | 1,064.2 | 55.1 | 66.0 | 708.4 | 289.8 | 244 |
| North Carolina 1977 | 7,518.5 | 5,086.3 | 18,230.6 | 1,216.1 | 991.6 | 10,936.6 | 6,302.4 | 174 |
| 41 eastern counties, 1977 | 1,447.3 | 1,045.9 | 3,937.1 | 200.7 | 212.6 | 2,477.9 | 1,246.6 | 199 |
| 8 eastern "urban" counties, 1977 | 586.9 | 407.8 | 1,802.3 | 89.6 | 97.3 | 1,207.6 | 497.4 | 243 |

Sources: U.S. Department of Commerce, Bureau of the Census, *Census of Manufactures, 1972*, vol. 3, pt. 2 (Washington: USGPO, 1976), 34–6, 34–7; U.S. Department of Commerce, Bureau of the Census, *Census of Manufactures, 1977*, vol. 3, pt. 2 (Washington: USGPO, 1981), 34–8 to 34–9.
a. Brunswick, Cumberland, Edgecombe, Nash, New Hanover, Onslow, Wayne, and Wilson counties.

United States, 11,000 overseas), as did the textile labor force of the state as a whole, at over 290,000.[115] The post–Vietnam depression of late 1974 and early 1975 drastically altered this context, however, as levels of unemployment in textiles in the state reached approximately 30 percent and corporate profits plummeted, leading to large increases in new capital investment in order to reduce production costs and increase the rate of surplus value.[116] In 1973, the last full year before the depression, Burlington Industries spent $99.3 million on new capital and calculated this to be 110 percent of depreciation. In 1976, the first full year after the worst of the depression, the corporation spent $159.7 million, 157 percent of depreciation. In 1977 the figures were $206

Table 6.13. International capital investment as a percentage of total fixed asset expenditures, Burlington Industries, 1972–77 (in millions of dollars)

|  | Fixed asset expenditures | International fixed asset expenditures | International expenditures as percentage of total expenditures |
|---|---|---|---|
| 1972 | $ 115.6 | $ 8.2 | 7.1 % |
| 1973 | 99.3 | 8.7 | 8.8 |
| 1974 | 142.5 | 12.4 | 8.7 |
| 1975 | 104.3 | 13.4 | 12.8 |
| 1976 | 159.7 | 21.3 | 13.3 |
| 1977 | 206.0 | 37.6 | 18.3 |

*Source*: Burlington Industries, *Annual Report, 1977* (Greensboro, 1977), 26–27 and passim.

million and 186 percent.[117] Although less impressive, capital expenditure figures for J. P. Stevens confirm the trend. In 1973 Stevens spent almost forty-one million dollars on new capital. In 1976 and 1977 the company spent fifty-six million dollars and fifty-seven million dollars, respectively.[118]

The bulk of these expenditures were used to buy the most modern textile technology, such as chute-fed carding machines, open-ended spinning machines, and shuttleless looms that use air or water jets to carry the yarn across the warp of the fabric. As in the past, such improvements allowed the largest corporations to combine operations, increase machine speeds and the intensity of work, and achieve significant reductions in operating floor space and labor intensity. Between 1973 and 1977, while the money value of Burlington's net sales increased from approximately $2.1 billion to $2.4 billion per annum, its labor force was reduced from 88,000 to 69,000.[119] By 1980 a further three thousand jobs had been eliminated.[120]

In the search for an increased rate of surplus value, new capital investment by the major corporations is taking place increasingly at the international level where a relatively stable environment for textile trade was created by the signing of the multifiber agreement in 1973.[121] The period between 1973 and 1977 witnessed a significant increase in the proportion of Burlington's total fixed asset expenditures that went to its international operations (see table 6.13). The logic of this combination of mechanization and internationalization can be quickly appreciated by looking at a specific instance of large-scale capital exports. In February 1978 three North Carolina textile and apparel corporations announced major investments in the Republic of Ireland.[122] Burlington announced the construction of two new plants and the expansion of two existing ones. This plan, totaling almost ninety million dollars alone, would increase Burlington's investments in the Republic to approximately two hundred million dollars and increase its Irish work force from 1,050 to 2,400. At the same time, Fieldcrest Mills of Eden, North Carolina, announced the completion of a sixty million dollar towel plant in Kilkenny that will eventually employ four hundred, and Blue Bell of Greensboro, North Carolina, announced that it had begun production at three plants employing a total of two hundred and fifty workers. In all three cases, a combination of advantages in both production and markets provided the incentive for investment. Major considerations were: the willingness of the Irish government to pay half the costs of plant construction and all the labor costs during an initial period of on-the-job training; the government's willingness to forgo taxes on profits from export sales as long as those profits remain in the Republic; the saving of 5 percent to 15 percent in Common Market tariffs by producing in the Republic rather than in the United States; and, most crucially, the Republic's plentiful and cheap supply of labor. During the late 1970s Irish wage levels were typically about half of those in the European Economic Community (EEC), and the level of unemployment was over 10 percent. In addition, the percentage of women in the labor force was low (26 percent), suggesting plenty of scope for expansion.[123]

The most important consequence of these new tendencies is that most of the jobs eliminated by mechanization by the large companies such as Burlington have been southern rather than foreign jobs. Of the 18,000 jobs eliminated by Burlington between 1973 and 1976, 15,000 were in the United States.[124] Between 1975 and 1980 Burlington closed or sold fifty-one plants in the United States, and put over one billion dollars into new capital.[125] Textile employment in North Carolina reached its peak of over 290,000 in 1973 but had fallen by over 67,800 (23.4 percent), standing at 222,200 in October 1982.[126] For the first time in the history of the North Carolina textile industry, economic depression, mechanization, and relocation are causing a contraction of the state's textile employment. This contraction, the mechanization of tobacco agriculture, and an increasing flow of poor migrants to the South from northeastern cities,[127] have in turn eased labor market conditions and the pressure of wages, providing the basis for a new period of increased exploitation and rapid capital accumulation.[128]

## Conclusion

The dominant tendency in the pattern of postwar capitalist development in North Carolina has been toward the preservation of the state's traditional productive relations. State economic policy and the political power of capital at the local and state levels facilitated the relocation and expansion of capitals whose productive requirements were identical or similar to those in the dominant textile industry, and which therefore reinforced, rather than disrupted, the status quo. Large-scale capital accumulation therefore took place without any significant increase in the political or economic strength of the working class. Because of this tendency to preserve productive relations, the textile, apparel, and furniture industries have increasingly become concentrated in North Carolina and the other southeastern states that share its characteristics. These industries have thus been able to maintain high rates of surplus value and capital accumulation.

The major beneficiaries of this tendency in recent years are companies in the newer manufacturing sectors that became increasingly mobile in the 1960s and 1970s. North Carolina's below-average wage levels and the absence of countervailing union power allow capital in these sectors to generate high rates of exploitation and regional surplus profits, increasing the state's attractiveness for capital. This, in turn, has exacerbated the fundamental problem with which state industrial policy has had to deal—the need to achieve economic growth without disrupting the productive relations on which so much of the North Carolina economy depends.

The threat of a disruption to productive relations that became evident in the late 1960s has thus far been averted. The textile industry, most crucial to the preservation of above-average rates of exploitation in North Carolina and potentially most seriously affected by this pressure, responded with large-scale mechanization and national and international relocation, replenishing, at least temporarily, its pool of surplus labor.

# 7

# Conclusion:

# Prospects for the Future

It should be clear by now that the strategy of capital accumulation implemented in North Carolina is not a solution to the social problems afflicting North Carolinians. These social problems—underemployment and overwork, poverty, ill health, racism, and a relatively restricted social wage—are not caused by exogenous factors as suggested by competitive market theory. Nor are they the result of cultural lag[1] or past mistakes by "irresponsible" southern businessmen.[2] Rather, they are both components and consequences of a strategy of capital accumulation that depends upon the production of an above-average rate of surplus value. Consequently, to base efforts to deal with these problems on the continued success of this strategy in attracting capital is contradictory, implying that problems can be overcome by the process that creates and relies on them.

Increases in the stock of capital or in capital/labor ratios do not imply, in an abstract fashion, corresponding increases in the living standards of workers. Rather, the impact of capital accumulation on the distribution of wealth and income in a particular social context depends upon the balance of class forces in that context. Any attempt to improve the standard of living of workers in North Carolina or to eliminate the gap between this standard and the U.S. average therefore requires that the balance of class forces in the state be altered.

For this to occur, social and political changes of a momentous nature must take place. Neither the likelihood nor the nature of such changes can be accurately predicted from the pattern of capitalist development thus far. On the basis of the broad social and political tendencies underlying this process, it should be possible, however, to shed some light on the likely (and less likely) sources of change. Marx's discussion of the origins of social reform in nineteenth-century Britain provides some initial clues in this respect. It suggests that progressive social change occurs as a result of: (a) the struggles of working class people to limit their exploitation and to improve their living and working conditions; and/or, (b) the actions of progressive capitalists and social reformers.[3] In both cases, it falls to the State to impose the politically or economically necessary regulations.

The history of capitalism in North Carolina suggests that the most important source of social change has been the federal level of the State, responding to a variety of reformist impulses. In the contemporary period, the U.S. Congress continues to be the site of a number of initiatives that, although designed primarily to protect northeastern states and communities from sunbelt competition and the social consequences of capital relocation and deindustrialization, would also have important consequences for North Carolina and the South. The two most important of these initiatives are attempts to reform labor law and to enact legislation to regulate plant closings.[4]

The focus of the first of these initiatives, as might be expected, has been Section 14(b) of the Taft-Hartley Act, which gives states the power to enact right-to-work laws outlawing union security agreements. In the absence of such agreements the financial and organizational stability of union locals is precarious, and efforts at further expansion are difficult. Although a labor law reform bill that included a provision to repeal Section 14(b) gained only lukewarm support from the Carter administration and was defeated in Congress in 1978, it seems likely that efforts in this area will continue. Union officials agree with corporate executives that right-to-work laws are the single most important factor in capital relocation decisions and a major threat to the labor movement.

Yet it is by no means clear that the repeal of Section 14(b) will allow unions to make significant inroads into states such as North Carolina, and it is not clear that such gains, even if they did occur, would significantly alter the overall balance of class forces. For one thing, legal changes such as this do not necessarily have a major impact on the basic social and economic conditions that also impede unionization. Even without Section 14(b), these conditions still tilt the balance of class forces decisively in favor of capital. After all, North Carolina maintained an above-average rate of exploitation throughout the 1930s and 1940s, prior to the existence of right-to-work laws and during the most significant period of unionization in American history.

In addition, even in the "strongholds" of union power in the northeastern states, union membership nowhere reaches 40 percent of the nonagricultural labor force. Even if this level of unionization could be reached in North Carolina, over 60 percent of nonagricultural workers would remain unorganized. This combination of numerical, organizational, and financial weakness with the tradition of "business unionism" (which surrenders claims to participation in corporate decision making in return for wage concessions) makes it unlikely, even if Section 14(b) were to be repealed, that unionization alone could regulate capital's most effective weapon in wringing concessions from workers and communities—the ability to relocate capital. And unions alone do not have the capacity to rebuild local and regional communities in the aftermath of such relocations.

It is for these reasons that increasing efforts have been made in recent years to supplement labor law reform proposals with legislation requiring prior notification of, and protection for workers and communities in the event of, plant closings. At the state and local levels, four plant closing laws had been enacted by August 1983—in Pittsburgh, Philadelphia, Maine, and Wisconsin.[5] More important for states such as North Carolina, however, are a series of attempts to enact federal plant closing legislation—the National Employment Priorities Act (NEPA), introduced into Congress in 1974 and again in a revised form in 1979; the Employee Protection and Community Stabilization Act of 1979; and proposed amendments to the National Public Works and Economic Development Act and the Small Business Administration Reauthorization Act.[6] Although none of these initiatives would impose severe restrictions on the mobility of capital, they have been taken seriously as signs of things to come, and capital has made a sustained effort to block their success.[7] None of the initiatives at the federal level has yet passed.

In the present political climate, with a steadily expanding bloc of southern/sunbelt right-to-work members of Congress to galvanize opposition to progressive social and economic legislation, the prospects for labor law reform and plant closing legislation at the federal level are not bright. For the time being at least, and perhaps even in the longer term, the struggle for progressive social reforms in states such as North Carolina will have to be carried out by workers within these states.

Organizing workers for this struggle will be an extraordinarily difficult task. The frequency of workers' defeats during the history of capitalist development in North Carolina and the complex of powerful social sanctions against all forms of dissent seriously impede collective solutions to pressing social problems.[8] But while the historic failure of working class struggles in southern industry has undoubtedly left its imprint on the collective consciousness of southern workers, it would be a mistake to write off the possibility of collective action on the grounds that southern workers have become fatalistic or apathetic, as the boosters of southern capitalism sometimes argue. Studies of Appalachian coal miners by John Gaventa[9] and of the Carolina Brown Lung Association (CBLA) by Bennett Judkins[10] both suggest that the relative unwillingness of many southern workers to engage in collective action is not the result of a culture of fatalism and acquiescence but is rather a rational accommodation to the high probability of defeat, based on their experience of past defeats and on their recognition of the range of forces arrayed against them:

> They're not fatalistic; they are realistic. If you have very few options, to pretend that you have is to be a fool. It is being practical to know what your options really are. . . . I think what happened in 1929 was that the outside leadership played them as fools, but equally or more importantly, the textile industry did a very good job of elevating the amount of risk. Here is the possibility of a rainbow, and here is the possibility of hell. And the textile industry made the possibility of hell much greater than the possibility of a rainbow. They brought in the troops and they killed people, and when you're not really sure about the rainbow, but you're fairly sure that you might get hurt and lose your job and maybe killed, it's just practical to not jump for the rainbow.[11]

The distinction between obedience out of fear and obedience based on resignation is an important one and provides a much more fruitful basis from which to consider the possibility of social change than do arguments about the fatalistic nature of southern culture. As Goran Therborn points out, obedience out of resignation is based on a "profoundly pessimistic view of the possibilities of change" and a belief in "the practical impossibility of a better alternative."[12] Such a characterization of the consciousness of southern workers is historically inadequate, at least if the long-term struggles of the Stevens's workers at Roanoke Rapids and the history of the Brown Lung Association are to be taken seriously.

In contrast, again following Therborn, obedience based on fear of the repressive capabilities of the powers that be is perfectly compatible with both the belief that better alternatives are possible *and* with practical attempts to achieve them during those periods when gaps appear in the "matrix of affirmations and sanctions."[13]

The studies by Gaventa and Judkins both provide indications of how it is possible to overcome this fear, to create gaps in the matrix of affirmations and sanctions, and to mobilize southern workers to collective action. According to Judkins, the growth of the CBLA into a relatively stable agency for social change in the southern textile industry is the result of a number of factors.

In the first place, as might be expected given the circumstances of those involved, it required external assistance: material assistance from volunteer organizers who had been involved in the strike against Duke

Power's mines in Harlan County, Kentucky, and from a variety of charitable, religious, and public interest organizations;[14] and political assistance in the form of the Occupational Health and Safety Act, passed by the U.S. Congress in 1970. This act established OSHA in the Department of Labor to administer the legislation and the National Institute for Occupational Safety and Health (NIOSH) in the Department of Health, Education, and Welfare to do the necessary scientific research. In 1972 thirty-one years after byssinosis had been recognized as an occupational disease and included under workers' compensation provisions in Great Britain, OSHA classified cotton dust as one of America's five most hazardous workplace substances.[15] The textile industry itself is not convinced of this, and it continues to claim that byssinosis is the result of smoking (much to the distress of the tobacco industry), to withhold information about sick workers, and, as a matter of routine, to challenge suits brought by brown lung victims before the North Carolina Industrial Commission.[16] But for the textile workers themselves, OSHA's classification of cotton dust confirmed what they already suspected and provided an important political and psychological boost to the reform movement.

Second, according to Judkins, the emergence of byssinosis as a major social issue provided additional political levers. First, it was an issue that allowed a direct attack on what remained in the late twentieth century (after the sale of most mill villages, increasing racial integration, and corporate concentration) of textile mill paternalism that claims that the welfare of textile workers is best taken care of by the industry.[17] Second, it provided a unique combination of short-term (compensation for sick, disabled, and retired brown lung victims[18]) and long-term (cleaning up the mills for future generations) incentives around which to mobilize mass support.[19] Third, brown lung was an issue that provided a target group—disabled and retired textile millworkers—that was relatively free from the matrix of affirmations and sanctions available to the textile industry and whose loyalty to the community could not be called into question.[20]

Despite the continued obfuscation, resistance, and open threats[21] of textile capital, the CBLA expanded and has become a relatively stable organization with fifteen chapters in four states, a budget of over $300,000 and a paid staff of forty.[22] In addition to its successes in gaining a series of out-of-court settlements for victims of brown lung,[23] the association has extended the boundaries of political activity among its members in ways that are by no means insignificant when considered in their social context. It has, for instance, organized mass filings of compensation claims, the storming of the North Carolina Industrial Commission, protests at southern universities and hospitals whose employees have opposed compensation for brown lung victims, and visits to Washington, D.C., to lobby the U.S. Congress and osha for more stringent cotton dust standards.[24] In addition, the fact that one of the centers of cbla activities is Roanoke Rapids, the site of the actwu's partial victory over J. P. Stevens in October 1980, may be suggestive of some "spillover" from the brown lung issue into more general working class concerns.

According to Judkins, the cbla has played an important role in increasing awareness of the possibility and benefits of collective action for social change and in developing the nucleus of what may eventually become a southern social change movement.[25] Despite these successes, however, many important questions remain to be answered. Simply stating some of them gives a sense of the difficulties involved. Can the initiatives and successes of the cbla be extended beyond disabled and retired workers who are relatively immune from sanction to encompass active textile workers, who remain vulnerable to the interregional and international relocation of capital and to the effects of technological change? Can they, in addition, be extended beyond the specific issue of occupational health to more general questions of control of the labor process and exploitation? And, most important, can they be extended beyond even these questions to the crucial social questions relating to accumulation strategies, the control of capital investment and relocation, and the role of politics and the State? The history of capitalism in North Carolina indicates the range of obstacles that must be overcome in order to generate social change at these levels. But the future will be determined not by history, but by those who have understood it and are able to use their understanding to change the present. The analysis of capitalism in North Carolina presented in this book is an attempt to contribute to such an understanding.

# Appendix

*The calculation of*
*rates of surplus value*

The rate of surplus value $(s/v)$ is defined as "surplus value" divided by "variable capital." Surplus value $(s)$ is calculated, using *Census of Manufactures* data, as follows: value added by manufacture is reduced by the amount of production workers' wages and the cost of capital depreciated during the production process. In addition, since many salaried occupations are also directly productive, value added must also be reduced by the amount of productive salaries. For present purposes, it is assumed that 50 percent of salaries are productive and therefore deductible from total value added. Variable capital $(v)$ is defined as wages plus 50 percent of salaries (again assumed to be productive). This follows the method presented in Series 4 by Ernest Mandel in *Late Capitalism* (London: New Left Books, 1975), 174–75. The higher the rate of surplus value, the larger the portion of total value added accruing to capital as surplus value and the smaller the portion of value added paid to labor as wages and salaries. A rate of surplus value of 100 percent indicates that value added was divided equally between capital and labor—that is, 50 percent of the total value added in the manufacturing production process and appropriated by capital as surplus value. A rate of 200 percent indicates that two-thirds of value added was thus appropriated.

This procedure is not without problems. To begin with, value added by manufacture is calculated by subtracting the cost of raw materials from the value of final shipments. It is therefore likely to reflect the amount of surplus value realized rather than that produced and may therefore, in certain circumstances, underestimate $s/v$.

Second, it is not possible to tell without a good deal of further empirical and theoretical work whether the assumption that 50 percent of salaries can be considered productive gives an accurate reflection of the combination of productive and unproductive labor in the salaried work force. To the extent that southern states, like North Carolina, are dominated by relatively labor-intensive industries whose salaried work forces are relatively small, relatively undifferentiated, and include a smaller proportion of unproductive occupations, it is possible that the 50 percent assumption overstates their rates of surplus value. This should not affect the broad outlines of the argument, however. To take a concrete example, if 60 percent of salaries in North Carolina are considered productive, the state's rate of surplus value in 1978 is reduced from 178 percent to 168 percent, still higher than the U.S. average of 164 percent and significantly higher than the northeastern average of 151 percent. Even if a more unrealistic figure of 70 percent is used, the North Carolina figure (158 percent) is still higher than the average in the Northeast. In addition, it seems likely that interregional variations in the extent of unproductive labor will narrow to some extent as the domination of North Carolina's traditional industries declines.

Third, the analysis of depreciation costs also presents some difficulties since depreciation data in the *Census of Manufactures* reflect not so much the actual cost of capital depreciated in production, but rather the menu of depreciation allowances made available by the U.S. government through the taxation system. This may again lead to an underestimation of the rate of surplus value. This problem should not affect the utility of these calculations in comparing class relations across states and regions, however, unless it can be shown that capitalists in one region have a greater propensity to take advantage of these opportunities than their counterparts elsewhere.

A further problem arises in estimating the proportion of value added attributable to depreciation. Before 1977 these data are not available. Mandel therefore takes an arbitrary 7 percent for his calculation. Such a figure will not reflect changes in the amount and rate of capital utilization over time.

It is possible to arrive at a better approximation. The National Bureau of Economic Analysis collects data on income originating in the manufacturing sector that excludes, among other things, depreciation costs, and the data are published in the *Survey of Current Business*. In a special study in 1957 the Census Bureau attempted to estimate some of the costs included in value added that were excluded from national income estimates. In that study, depreciation amounted to 4.9 percent of value added and 21.6 percent of the difference between value added and national income originating in manufacture. By taking the difference between these two figures for the years between 1957 and 1976, it is possible to obtain a series of figures for the percentage of value added attributable to depreciation, as follows:

| | | | |
|------|-----|------|-----|
| 1957 | 4.9 | 1967 | 5.5 |
| 1958 | 5.2 | 1968 | 5.5 |
| 1959 | 5.0 | 1969 | 5.8 |
| 1960 | 5.1 | 1970 | 6.0 |
| 1961 | 5.1 | 1971 | 6.0 |
| 1962 | 5.1 | 1972 | 6.2 |
| 1963 | 5.4 | 1973 | 6.5 |
| 1964 | 5.3 | 1974 | 7.4 |
| 1965 | 5.2 | 1975 | 7.2 |
| 1966 | 5.1 | 1976 | 6.9 |

The calculations of rates of surplus value presented in the introduction use these figures for depreciation. For years prior to 1957 an arbitrary 5 percent is used. For 1977 and 1978 the depreciation figures provided by the 1977 *Census of Manufactures* and the *1978–79 Annual Survey of Manufactures* equal 6.6 percent and 6.8 percent of value added, respectively.

In summary, the results of these calculations are not presented as precise measures of $s/v$, and they would not be particularly useful in developing an econometric model. The estimates are being used here, rather, as broad summary measures of state-by-state variations in the social relations of production. The size and persistence of these variations should more than outweigh any inaccuracies resulting from the problems discussed above.

# Notes

## 1. Introduction

1. Calculated from data in U.S. Department of Commerce, Bureau of the Census, *1978–9 Annual Survey of Manufactures* (Washington: U.S. Government Printing Office, 1983), 1–6, table 4.

2. Calculated from data in U.S. Department of Commerce, Bureau of the Census, *Statistical Abstract of the United States, 1982–3* (Washington: USGPO, 1983), 732, tables 10, 11. See also Jim Montgomery, "Deep Poverty Persists in the South Despite New Wealth of Area," *Wall Street Journal* (December 29, 1978), 1, 12; Melinda Beck, "A City's Growing Pains," *Newsweek* (January 14, 1980): 45; Paul Recer, "A Texas City That's Busting Out All Over," *U.S. News and World Report* (November 27, 1978): 47–48; Gurney Breckenfeld, "Business Loves the Sunbelt (And Vice Versa)," *Fortune* (June 1977): 144.

3. See, for example, M. Aglietta, *A Theory of Capitalist Regulation* (London: New Left Books, 1979) and Alain Liepietz, "Towards Global Fordism?," *New Left Review* 132 (March–April 1982): 33–47.

4. Aglietta, *Theory of Capitalist Regulation*, 9; Harold D. Woodman, "Sequel to Slavery: The New History Views the Post-Bellum South," *Journal of Southern History* 43 (November 1977): 534; Goran Therborn, *Science, Class and Society* (London: Verso Books, 1980), ch. 2.

5. George M. Borts and Jerome L. Stein, *Economic Growth in a Free Market* (New York: Columbia University Press, 1964), and "Regional Growth and Maturity in the United States: A Study of Regional Structural Change," in L. Needleman (ed.) *Regional Analysis* (Harmondsworth, Eng.: Penguin Books, 1968); Robert Higgs, *The Transformation of the American Economy, 1865–1914* (New York: Wiley, 1971), 108–14; Richard A. Easterlin, "Regional Income Trends, 1840–1950," in Seymour E. Harris (ed.), *American Economic History* (New York: McGraw-Hill, 1961), 525–47; Jeffrey A. Williamson, "Regional Inequality and the Process of National Development: A Description of the Patterns," *Economic Development and Cultural Change* 13 (July 1965, pt. 2): 3–84.

6. Easterlin, "Regional Income Trends," 528; U.S. Department of Commerce, Bureau of the Census, *Statistical Abstract of the United States, 1984* (Washington: USGPO, 1984), 11, 456.

7. See, e.g., Calvin B. Hoover and B. U. Ratchford, *Economic Resources and Policies of the South* (New York: Macmillan, 1951); Clarence Danhof, "Four Decades of Thought on the South's Economic Problems," in M. L. Greenhut and F. Tate Whitman, *Essays in Southern Economic Development* (Chapel Hill: University of North Carolina Press, 1964), ch. 1; W. H. Nicholls, "Southern Tradition and Regional Economic Progress," *Southern Economic Journal* 26 (January 1960); Thomas Naylor and James Clotfelter, *Strategies for Change in the South* (Chapel Hill: University of North Carolina Press, 1974); James G. Maddox et al., *The Advancing South: Manpower Prospects and Problems* (New York: Twentieth Century Fund, 1967); Joseph J. Spengler, "Demographic and Economic Change in the South, 1940–1960," in Allan P. Sindler, *Change in the Contemporary South* (Durham: Duke University Press, 1963), 26–63; V. O. Key, *Southern Politics in State and Nation* (New York: Vintage Books, 1949).

8. This is the name given to this group of authors by Woodman, "Sequel to Slavery," 544.

9. Jay R. Mandle, *The Roots of Black Poverty: The Southern Plantation Economy after the Civil War* (Durham: Duke University Press, 1978); Jonathan M. Wiener, *Social Origins of the New South: Alabama, 1860–1885* (Baton Rouge: Louisiana State University Press, 1978) and "Class Structure and Economic Development in the American South, 1865–1955," *American Historical Review* 84 (October 1979): 970–92; Dwight B. Billings, Jr., *Planters and the Making of a "New South": Class, Politics and Development in North Carolina, 1865–1900* (Chapel Hill: University of North Carolina Press, 1978). Additional evidence of the postwar persistence and impact of planters can be found in William Cooper, *The Conservative Regime: South Carolina, 1877–1890* (Baltimore: Johns Hopkins University Press, 1968); and James Tice Moore, "Redeemers Reconsidered: Change and Continuity in the Democratic South, 1870–1900," *Journal of Southern History* 44 (August 1978): 357–78. Other analyses of southern development present social relations in the southern states as being specifically "feudal." See, for instance, Stanley Aronowitz, *False Promises: The Shaping of American Working-Class Consciousness* (New York: McGraw-Hill, 1973), 190; Brad Heil, "Sunbelt Migration," in Union for Radical Political Economics (ed.), *U.S. Capitalism in Crisis* (New York: URPE, 1974), 87–102. For a more detailed discussion of a single representative of the "new social history" school, see my review of Wiener's *Social Origins of the New South: Alabama, 1860–1885*, in *Review of Radical Political Economics* 13 (Summer 1981): 63–64.

10. Wiener, *Social Origins*, 71–72; Billings, *Planters*, ch. 5.

11. Mandle, *Roots*, 9–10.

12. Ibid., 34–35, chs. 6, 7; Wiener, *Social Origins*, chs. 3, 6. Billings takes his argument furthest: "behind the skyscraper development of the Carolina Piedmont one hears the gallop of Jeb Stuart's cavalrymen" (*Planters*, 218). The contemporary South provides a wealth of empirical evidence on the survival of the region's "peculiar" production relations. For instance, widespread coercion of migrant farm workers continues. Farm labor crew bosses, who contract with farmers to provide cheap labor during harvest time, are regularly found guilty of withholding wages and charging exorbitant rates for housing and other necessities. Since 1980 ten of twenty-one federal slavery convictions in the United States have occurred in North

Carolina, where an estimated 35,000 migrant farm workers are used at harvest time. In 1982 the Workers' Defense League of New York estimated that ten thousand workers in the eastern United States were held in debt peonage, and the Washington-based Migrant Legal Action put the national figure at one hundred thousand. On July 13, 1983, 119 years after the passage of the thirteenth amendment to the U.S. Constitution, the North Carolina House of Representatives approved legislation making it a felony to hold a worker in involuntary servitude. As a result of opposition from the State Farm Bureau, a clause affixing criminal liability to anyone "knowingly or willfully" employing a crew leader who is holding others in involuntary servitude was deleted (*New York Times*, July 14, 1983). It is not the existence of such phenomena that is at issue, however, but their theoretical implications.

13. See, for instance, Joseph Schumpeter, *Capitalism, Socialism and Democracy* (New York: Harper and Row, 1962), 45–47 and Lucio Colletti, "Marxism as a Sociology," in *From Rousseau to Lenin: Studies in Ideology and Society* (New York: Monthly Review Press, 1972), 14–15.

14. The brief discussion of the Marxian framework presented here deals with only those aspects that seem to be necessary in order to explain the "developmental paradox" in the south. This discussion is based on my reading of, among other things, Karl Marx, *Capital* 1 (Harmondsworth, Eng.: Penguin Books, 1976); Ernest Mandel, *Marxist Economic Theory* (London: Merlin Press, 1974); John Eaton, *Political Economy* (New York: International Publishers, 1966); Michael Evans, *Karl Marx* (London: Allen and Unwin, 1975), 95–105; Geoffrey Kay, *Development and Underdevelopment: A Marxist Analysis* (New York: St. Martin's Press, 1975); John Harrison, *Marxist Economics for Socialists* (London: Pluto Press, 1978).

15. Marx, *Capital* 1, 270–73.

16. Karl Marx, *Capital* 3 (Moscow: Progress Publishers, 1977), 879–81.

17. Marx, *Capital* 1, 274.

18. Ibid., 275.

19. Ibid., 377, 790.

20. Ibid., 747–48.

21. Ibid., 645.

22. Ibid., 899–900.

23. Ibid., 389–411, 533.

24. For an extended discussion of the moments of "formal" and "real" subsumption of labor under capital, see ibid., 1019–38.

25. Ibid., 429–38.

26. Ibid., 533–34, 899; Kay, *Development and Underdevelopment*, 53; Ben Fine, "On the Origins of Capitalist Development," *New Left Review* 109 (May–June 1978): 88–95.

27. Marx, *Capital* 1, 579–80.

28. Charles Bettelheim, "Theoretical Comments," in Arghiri Emmanuel, *Unequal Exchange* (London: New Left Books, 1972) 286, appendix 1.

29. David Harvey, *The Limits to Capital* (Chicago: University of Chicago Press, 1982), 389, regards all locational increases in rates of surplus value as forms of relative surplus value. Geographical restructuring of capital as a means of in-

creasing *s/v* is discussed in a variety of different social contexts in Bennett Harrison, "Regional Restructuring and 'Good Business Climates': The Economic Transformation of New England Since World War II," in Larry Sawers and William Tabb (eds.), *Sunbelt/Snowbelt: Urban Development and Regional Restructuring* (New York: Oxford University Press, 1984), 48–96; Michael Storper and Richard Walker, "The Spatial Division of Labor: Labor and the Relocation of Industries," in Sawers and Tabb, *Sunbelt/Snowbelt*, 19–47; Doreen Massey, "Capital and Locational Change: The U.K. Electrical Engineering and Electronics Industries," *Review of Radical Political Economics* 10 (Fall 1978): 39–54.

30. Bettelheim ("Theoretical Comments," 287) points out that this situation is a common one in third world countries today.

31. Defined as gross book value of depreciable assets in manufacturing industry per manufacturing employee. Calculated from data in U.S. Department of Commerce, Bureau of the Census, *1977 Census of Manufactures* 1, I-103 to I-105 and 3 (Washington: USGPO, 1981).

32. For a discussion of these dimensions of capital relocation, see Barry Bluestone and Bennett Harrison, *The Deindustrialization of America: Plant Closings, Community Abandonment and the Dismantling of Basic Industry* (New York: Basic Books, 1982), 7–8.

33. See, for example, John Shelton Reed, *The Enduring South: Subcultural Persistence in Mass Society* (Lexington, Mass.: D. C. Heath, 1972).

34. Calculated from data in U.S. Department of Commerce, Bureau of the Census, *1977 Census of Manufactures* (Washington: USGPO, 1981), 1–104.

35. *1977 Census of Manufactures* 3, pt. 2, 34-11; U.S. Department of Commerce, Bureau of the Census, *Statistical Abstract of the United States, 1953* (Washington: USGPO, 1954), 804.

36. U.S. Department of Labor, Bureau of Labor Statistics, *Employment and Earnings, United States, 1909–75* (Washington: USGPO, 1976), passim; U.S. Department of Labor, Bureau of Labor Statistics, *Employment and Earnings, States and Areas, 1939–75* (Washington: USGPO, 1976), passim; U.S. Department of Commerce, Bureau of the Census, *Statistical Abstract of the United States, 1982–3* (Washington: USGPO, 1983), 771.

37. Richard A. Easterlin, "State Income Estimates," in Simon Kuznets and Dorothy Thomas, *Population Redistribution and Economic Growth, United States, 1870–1950* 1 (Philadelphia: American Philosophical Society 1957), table Y-1; *Statistical Abstract of the United States, 1984*, 457.

## 2. The Origins of Industrial Capitalism in North Carolina

1. Key, *Southern Politics*, 207, table 19.

2. Ibid., 208; Hugh T. Lefler and Albert R. Newsome, *North Carolina: History of a Southern State* (Chapel Hill: University of North Carolina Press, 1973), 391, 420, 423.

3. Roger W. Shugg, *Origins of Class Struggle in Louisiana* (Baton Rouge: Louisiana State University Press, 1968), ch. 8; Mandle, *Roots*, ch. 4; Wiener, *Social Origins* ch. 1; Roger L. Ransom and Richard H. Sutch, *One Kind of Free-*

*dom: The Economic Consequences of Emancipation* (Cambridge: Cambridge University Press, 1977), 78–80.

4. Adapting data presented in Ransom and Sutch, *One Kind of Freedom*, tables 1.1, A.1, A.4, and A.5, it is possible to construct the following estimates of the exploitation of slave labor in 1859. Rows d. and g. assume that 50 percent of supervisory costs form part of the surplus. Although this estimate takes the form of a calculation of $s/v$ for comparative purposes, it should not be strictly considered as such, since row f. is not based on the alienation of labor power by free wage laborers.

|  | Average per slave, all farms ($) | Average per slave, farms with 51 or more slaves ($) |
|---|---|---|
| a. Output | 127.55 | 147.93 |
| b. Depreciation to capital | 4.53 | 4.52 |
| c. Depreciation to land | 12.83 | 14.71 |
| d. Supervisory costs × 50 percent | 2.50 | 2.50 |
| e. Value added (row a minus rows b and d) | 107.69 | 126.20 |
| f. Slave's consumption | 28.95 | 32.12 |
| g. Supervisory costs × 50 percent | 2.50 | 2.50 |
| h. Variable capital (row f plus row g) | 31.45 | 34.62 |
| i. Surplus value (row e minus row h) | 76.24 | 91.58 |
| j. Rate of surplus value (row i divided by row h, multiplied by 100) | 242% | 265% |

5. Harold D. Woodman, "Post–Civil War Southern Agriculture and the Law," *Agriculture History* 53 (January 1979): 322; Ransom and Sutch, *One Kind of Freedom*, 66–67.

6. Woodman, "Post–Civil War Southern Agriculture," 323–24.

7. Ransom and Sutch, *One Kind of Freedom*, 87–88.

8. Marjorie Mendenhall Applewhite, "Sharecropper and Tenant in the Courts of North Carolina," *North Carolina Historical Review* 31 (1954).

9. Ransom and Sutch (*One Kind of Freedom*, 91) provide an example of such a sharecropping contract from North Carolina in 1886. The authors interpret the notion of share set out in the contract literally, however, and distinguish this from a wage system (95), suggesting that sharecropping "offered the potential of a higher income than could be obtained working for the fixed standard wage." In *Nothing But Freedom* (Baton Rouge: Louisiana State University Press, 1983), 45, Eric Foner also suggests that sharecropping offered "more hope of economic advancement than many other modes of labor organization." Neither work presents compelling evidence that such potential was realized, although they may explain why former slaves preferred sharecropping to other arrangements and why planters acted quickly to redefine its content.

10. Woodman, "Post–Civil War Southern Agriculture," 324–25, especially note 10; Oscar Zeichner, "The Legal Status of the Agricultural Laborer in the South," *Political Science Quarterly* 55 (1940): 418.

11. Woodman, "Post–Civil War Southern Agriculture," 328–29.

12. Ibid., 330.

13. Wiener, *Social Origins*, 106–8. On the abandonment of self-sufficiency by small white farmers and their collapse into tenancy, see Gavin Wright, *The Political Economy of the Cotton South: Households, Markets and Wealth in the 19th Century* (New York: Norton, 1978), 164ff.

14. Woodman, "Post–Civil War Southern Agriculture," 330.

15. Applewhite, "Sharecropper and Tenant," 144–45. For a contemporary description of the impact of the Landlord-Tenant Act on agricultural labor in North Carolina, see George Henry White, "Testimony Before the U.S. Industrial Commission," *Report of the U.S. Industrial Commission* X "Agriculture," (Washington: USGPO, 1901), 416–33.

16. U.S. Bureau of the Census, *Plantation Farming in the United States* (Washington: USGPO, 1916), 13, quoted in Warren C. Whatley, "Labor for the Picking: The New Deal in the South," *Journal of Economic History* 43 (December 1983): 914; Wright, *Political Economy*, 179. Both of these accounts perhaps overemphasize the importance of supervision and discipline as a defining characteristic of wage labor. In reality these are characteristics of the labor process, which is variable, and they are not defining characteristics of the wage relation itself.

17. U.S. Department of the Interior, Bureau of the Census, *Report on Cotton Production in the United States at the Tenth Census, North Carolina* (Washington: USGPO, 1884), 77.

18. For data on raw cotton prices in New York, see Ben F. Lemert, *The Cotton Textile Industry of the Southern Appalachian Piedmont* (Chapel Hill: University of North Carolina Press, 1933), 27.

19. Bureau of the Census, *Report on Cotton Production* (1884), 77.

20. For data on cotton production in the United States and producer states, see Lemert, *Cotton Textile Industry*, 23.

21. Estimates of the market value of cotton produced in North Carolina are calculated from data in Lemert, *Cotton Textile Industry*, 27.

22. U.S. Department of the Interior, Bureau of the Census, *Tenth Census of the United States, 1880* 3, "Report on the Culture and Curing of Tobacco in the United States" (Washington: USGPO, 1884), 158.

23. U.S. Department of the Interior, Bureau of the Census, *Twelfth Census of the United States, 1900* 5, pt. 1 (Washington: USGPO, 1902), cxxxi.

24. William A. Graham, "Testimony before the U.S. Industrial Commission," *Report of the U.S. Industrial Commission*, 434; U.S. Census Office, *Report on Cotton Production, 1884*, 77.

25. The antebellum debate on the southern economy and industrialization is discussed in Broadus Mitchell, *The Rise of the Cotton Mills in the South* (Baltimore: Johns Hopkins University Press, 1921), ch. 1; Carl N. Degler, *The Other South: Southern Dissenters in the Nineteenth Century* (New York: Harper and Row, 1974), chs. 2, 3; Eugene D. Genovese, *The Political Economy of Slavery: Studies in the Economy and Society of the Slave South* (New York: Vintage

Books, 1967), ch. 8; Harriet Herring, "Early Industrial Development in the South," *Annals of the American Academy of Political and Social Science* 153 (January 1931).

26. See Lemert, *Cotton Textile Industry*, 22.

27. Billings, *Planters*, 58.

28. Ibid., 59.

29. Herring, *Southern Industry*, 9.

30. Wright, *Political Economy*, ch. 1.

31. Lefler and Newsome, *North Carolina*, 98–99. The value of textile production at this date was roughly equal to that in the tobacco and lumber industries. The state's leading "industry" in 1860 was the production of turpentine.

32. Both were slaveholding families—the Battles in Edgecombe County in the eastern part of the state and the Fries in Forsyth County in the Piedmont region. The latter met with opposition from within the antislavery Moravian community of Salem in 1831 for "wishing to start a kind of Negro speculation in our settlement." [Adelaide Fries et al., *Forsyth: The History of a County on the March*. (Chapel Hill: University of North Carolina Press, 1976), 105.]

33. Melton A. McLaurin, *Paternalism and Protest* (Westport, Conn.: Greenwood Press, 1971), 4; Lefler and Newsome, *North Carolina*, 399.

34. Richard W. Griffin, "Reconstruction of the North Carolina Textile Industry, 1865–1885," *North Carolina Historical Review* 41 (1964): 34–35.

35. Genovese, *Political Economy of Slavery*, 187.

36. Griffin, "Reconstruction," 46. These historical links between plantation agriculture and textile manufacture make it possible to conceive of North Carolina's ruling class in the early decades after the Civil War as a "planter–industrial" class. The theoretical implications of this conception in the long term are far from clear, however. Billings wants to take the argument farthest, as indicated in the introduction, to argue that "planter values" guided and constrained the process of industrialization. Yet his analysis of planter control of the textile industry extends only until 1884. Of seventy-eight mills operating between 1865 and 1884, 23 percent were owned by men identified as "planters" and 34 percent by "prominent agrarians." In another 11 percent of the cases, mills were associated with men who shared the same family name with prominent farmers, raising the possible rate of planter ownership of textile mills to 68 percent. Therefore, even at this early stage, prior to the major periods of textile capital relocation from New England, between 32 and 43 percent of the mills could not be directly linked with the pre–Civil War planter ruling class. Billings does not make it clear why he thinks that the owners of *these* mills should have been guided by planter values. See Billings, *Planters*, 62–69. For a compilation of data on mill ownership, see Griffin, "Reconstruction," appendix, "North Carolina Cotton Mills Operating 1865–1884."

37. Lefler and Newsome, *North Carolina*, 505; Billings, *Planters*, ch. 4; Griffin, "Reconstruction," appendix, "North Carolina Cotton Mills Operating 1865–1884."

38. On the failure of the "internal improvements" part of the 1876 Compromise, see C. Vann Woodward, *Origins of the New South, 1877–1913* (Baton Rouge: Louisiana State University Press, 1971), ch. 2; also, by the same author, *Reunion and Reaction*, revised edition (Garden City, N.Y.: Anchor Books, 1956).

On the rise of agrarian radicalism in the southern states, see Woodward, *Reunion and Reaction*, 257–67. On the surface, agrarian radicalism does not seem to have been as significant a threat in North Carolina as in other southern states, where under varying labels the movement had significant political success, winning a number of Congressional seats and, in 1879 in Virginia, the state legislature. Their weakness in North Carolina may be related to the persistent strength of Republicanism in the state. In no state election in the 1880s did the Republicans win fewer than thirty-five counties. Lefler and Newsome (*North Carolina*, 528) date the beginning of the Radical threat to 1887, therefore, when the first representatives of the Farmers' Alliance arrived in the state. Goodwyn, on the other hand, suggests that Radicalism was already widespread by this time. [Lawrence Goodwyn, *Democratic Promise: The Populist Moment in America* (New York: Oxford University Press, 1976), 91–93.] Even if Lefler and Newsome are correct, however, there could be no guarantee that Agrarian Radicalism, as a response to agricultural conditions that existed in all southern states, would not spread into North Carolina. For an account of the Readjuster movement in Virginia, see Degler, *The Other South*, ch. 9.

39. Herbert Collins, "The Idea of a Cotton Textile Industry in the South, 1870-1900," *North Carolina Historical Review* 34, no. 3 (1957): 373; Paul M. Gaston, *The New South Creed: A Study in Southern Mythmaking* (New York: Alfred A. Knopf, 1970), 22.

40. Woodward, *Origins of the New South*, 133–35.

41. Collins, "Idea of a Cotton Textile Industry," 370–71.

42. Ibid., 370. For an example of an important role played by machinery manufacturers in Southern textile industrialization, see e.g., George S. Gibb, *The Saco-Lowell Shops: Textile Machinery Building in New England, 1813–1949* (Cambridge, Mass.: Harvard University Press, 1950), 397–99, appendices 10 and 12.

43. Mitchell, *Rise of the Cotton Mills*, 241–42, 247.

44. Robert F. Durden, *The Dukes of Durham, 1865–1929* (Durham: Duke University Press, 1965), ch. 7.

45. Fries, *Forsyth*, 231–33.

46. Collins, "Idea of a Cotton Textile Industry," 383.

47. Mitchell, *Rise of the Cotton Mills*, 235.

48. Ibid., 251–52; Solomon Barkin, "The Regional Significance of the Integration Movement in the Southern Textile Industry," *Southern Economic Journal* 15 (April 1949): 396–97.

49. McLaurin, *Paternalism and Protest*, 53–54; Harry Boyte, "The Textile Industry: Keel of Southern Industrialization," *Radical America* 6 (March–April 1972): 20; Melton A. McLaurin, *The Knights of Labor in the South* (Westport, Conn.: Greenwood Press, 1978), 32–33. The problem of mobilizing and stabilizing a wage labor force is one that is common wherever industrial capital penetrates peripheral agricultural regions. For an analysis of this problem in the colonies, see Marx *Capital*, ch. 33.

50. McLaurin, *Paternalism and Protest*, 4; Tom Terrill, "Eager Hands: Labor for Southern Textiles, 1850–1860," *Journal of Economic History* 36 (1976): 84–99.

51. Gaston, *New South Creed*, especially ch. 1.

52. Mitchell, *Rise of the Cotton Mills*, 127–8, 132, 137; Lefler and Newsome, *North Carolina*, 506–7.

53. W. J. Cash, *The Mind of the South* (New York: Vintage Books, 1969), 182.

54. Mitchell, *Rise of the Cotton Mills*, 161–62.

55. Boyte, "Textile Industry," 17–19.

56. "Our workers down here are not like the people who work in the mills up north. The people we have are just as good Americans as any. The best blood in the country runs in their veins. They are the people who made this country. Good sturdy Anglo-Saxon stock, much better than the rich loafers who spend their time playing billiards and pool. . . . But they are like children, and we have to take care of them." —southern millowner, quoted in Frank Tannenbaum, *Darker Phases of the South* (New York: Negro Universities Press, 1969), 40. Northern capitalists considered their workers to be equally childlike. See Tamara Hareven and Randolph Langenbach, *Amoskeag: Life and Work in an American Factory-City* (New York: Pantheon, 1978), 23.

57. Boyte, "Textile Industry," 14.

58. Mitchell, *Rise of the Cotton Mills*, 95. Elements of the philanthropic theory of textile industrialization and its consequences in terms of social integration remain popular: "Unions were weaker and workers were relatively more satisfied. Although wages were lower, Southerners worked as a family, acquired most of their supplies from company stores and lived in company houses." —Ray F. Marshall, *Labor in the South* (Cambridge, Mass.: Harvard University Press, 1964), 80.

59. Harry Braverman, *Labor and Monopoly Capital: The Degradation of Work in the Twentieth Century* (New York: Monthly Review Press, 1974), 65–67; Norman Ware, *The Industrial Worker, 1840–1860: The Reaction of American Industrial Society to the Advance of the Industrial Revolution* (Chicago: Quadrangle Books, 1964). The provision of housing by southern textile millowners has been interpreted as part of an attempt to reconstruct the distinct paternalism of southern plantation society in the textile industry (e.g., Cash, *Mind of the South*, 205). Clearly, in the cases of both pre- and postwar plantation agriculture and the emerging cotton textile industry, it is the poverty of workers that creates the need for such housing, as well as the need to maintain social control on the part of the owners. Neither the provision of housing by employers, nor its use as a lever for social control is a distinctly southern phenomenon, but rather it is a characteristic response to the problems caused by an unstable rural labor force. Textile mills in New England provided the same facilities in order to attract female labor from the family farms of that region and later to attract and control migrant labor from Quebec and Europe. See Ware, *Industrial Worker*, ch. 5; Hareven and Langenbach, *Amoskeag*, 21–23.

60. Tannenbaum, *Darker Phases*, 64.

61. Jennings J. Rhyne, *Some Cotton Mill Workers and Their Villages* (Chapel Hill: University of North Carolina Press, 1930), 124; Tannenbaum, *Darker Phases*, 42–44.

62. Boyte, "Textile Industry," 54.

63. Tannenbaum, *Darker Phases*, 65.

64. Cathy L. McHugh, "Earnings in the Post-bellum Southern Cotton Textile Industry: A Case Study," *Explorations in Economic History* 21 (1984): 28–39.

65. Rhyne, *Some Cotton Mill Workers*, 65–72.

66. U.S. Bureau of the Census, *Twelfth Census* 8, pt. 2, 666–67.

67. McLaurin, *Paternalism and Protest*, 32.

68. Tannenbaum, *Darker Phases*, 46–47.

69. Ibid., ch. 2; Rhyne, *Some Cotton Mill Workers*, passim; Harriet Herring, *Welfare Work in the Mill Villages* (Chapel Hill: University of North Carolina Press, 1929); Lois MacDonald, *Southern Mill Hills: A Study of Social and Economic Forces in Certain Mill Villages* (New York: Alex Hillman, 1928); Liston Pope, *Millhands and Preachers: A Study of Gastonia* (New Haven: Yale University Press, 1942); Glenn Gilman, *Human Relations in the Industrial Southeast: A Study of the Textile Industry* (Chapel Hill: University of North Carolina Press, 1955).

70. *First Annual Report of the North Carolina Bureau of Labor Statistics* (Raleigh, 1887), 140, quoted in Collins, "Idea of a Cotton Textile Industry," 386.

71. H. R. Fitzgerald, president of Riverside and Dan River Cotton Mills, to W. D. Anderson, Bibb Manufacturing Company, 1928, quoted in Robert Sidney Smith, *Mill on the Dan: A History of the Dan River Mills, 1882–1950* (Durham: Duke University Press, 1960), 242.

72. Boyte, "Textile Industry," 25. According to McHugh, "Earnings," education was *not* an important determinant of wages at the Alamance Mill.

73. Pope, *Millhands and Preachers*, 29.

74. Rhyne, *Some Cotton Mill Workers*, 164; Pope, *Millhands and Preachers* chs. 2–5.

75. Wright, *Political Economy*, 31.

76. Note that in the southern textile industry labor shortage usually meant a reduction in the excess labor supply in mill villages. (McLaurin, *Paternalism and Protest*, 19.)

77. Ibid., 60–65.

78. Durden, *Dukes of Durham*, 145.

79. U.S. Department of the Interior, Bureau of the Census *Report on the Manufactures of the United States at the Tenth Census, 1880* (Washington: USGPO, 1883), 131, 161–62; U.S. Census Office, *Twelfth Census* 8, pt. 2, 350, 666–67. For agricultural wage rates, see the sources cited in nn. 22 and 23 of this chapter.

80. "Machinery, by throwing every member of that family into the labour market, spreads the value of the man's labour-power over his whole family. It thus depreciates it. To purchase the labour-power of a family of four workers may perhaps cost more than it formerly did to purchase the labour-power of the head of the family, but, in return, four days' labour takes the place of one day's, and the price falls in proportion to the excess of the surplus labour of four over the surplus labour of one. In order that the family may live, four people must now provide not only labour for the capitalist, but also surplus labour. Thus we see that machinery, while augmenting the human material that forms capital's most characteristic field of exploitation, at the same time raises the degree of that exploitation. . . . Pre-

viously, the worker sold his own labour-power, which he disposed of as a free agent, formally speaking. Now he sells his wife and child. He has become a slave-dealer" (Marx, *Capital*, 518). On the concept of a "family wage," see McLaurin, *Paternalism and Protest*, 22; U.S. Senate, Committee on Manufactures, Hearings, *Working Conditions of the Textile Industry in North Carolina, South Carolina and Tennessee*, 71st Congress, 1st session (Washington: USGPO, 1929), 27–28.

81. U.S. Department of the Interior, Bureau of the Census *Eleventh Census of the United States, 1890*, 6, pt. 1 (Washington: USGPO, 1892), 538–39; U.S. Bureau of the Census, *Twelfth Census*, 666–67.

82. McLaurin, *Paternalism and Protest*, 21–23.

83. See, for example, Jeffrey G. Williamson, *Late Nineteenth-Century American Development: A General Equilibrium History* (London: Cambridge University Press, 1974), ch. 4 and appendix A.

84. Woodward, *Origins of the New South*, 224.

85. Rhyne, *Some Cotton Mill Workers*, 18, 19.

86. In the earliest New England textile mills, the mill village and the company store formed the basis of two distinct methods of controlling an unstable labor force. In the Waltham system, closely controlled mill villages were used to attract female labor from New England family farms. Wages were reduced by the amount of rent necessary in the mill villages and the cost of educational facilities. In the general context of early Puritan paternalism, the impact of these mill villages appears to have been relatively benevolent. The company store, on the other hand, was the core of the more aggressive, laissez-faire Rhode Island system, which operated by reducing wage levels through inflated store prices. Ware notes that as soon as significant competition emerged between the two areas the relative benevolence of the Waltham system disappeared. (Ware, *Industrial Workers*, ch. 5.)

87. Tannenbaum, *Darker Phases*, 59; William F. Dunne, *Gastonia: Citadel of the Class Struggle in the New South* (New York: Workers' Library Publishers, 1929), 55.

88. Boyte, "Textile Industry," 24.

89. Mitchell, *Rise of the Cotton Mills*, 261–62.

90. Ibid., 265.

91. Smith, *Mill on the Dan*, 29–30.

92. U.S. Department of Commerce, Bureau of the Census, *Fourteenth Census of the United States, 1920*, 9 (Washington: USGPO, 1923) 1120–23.

93. Ibid., 10, 148.

94. Department of Labor and Industries of the Commonwealth of Massachusetts, General L. E. Sweetser, Commissioner, *Report of a Special Investigation into Conditions in the Textile Industry in Massachusetts and the Southern States* (Boston, August 1923), 2. Lower building costs, differences in the age structure of installed machinery, and southern concentration on the production of lower count goods by relatively labor-intensive methods may have also contributed to this difference.

95. U.S. Bureau of the Census, *Fourteenth Census*, 9, 1109.

96. Ibid., 1112.

97. Ibid., 1109.

98. U.S. Department of Commerce, Bureau of the Census, *Thirteenth Census*

*of the United States, 1910,* 3 (Washington: USGPO, 1912), 268; U.S. Department of Commerce, Bureau of the Census, *Statistical Abstract of the United States, 1918* (Washington: USGPO, 1919) 46.

99. U.S. Department of Commerce, Bureau of the Census, *Fifteenth Census of the United States, 1930,* 3, pt. 2 (Washington: USGPO, 1932), 333.

100. Mitchell, *Rise of the Cotton Mills,* 161; George Mitchell, *Textile Unionism in the South* (Chapel Hill: University of North Carolina Press, 1931); Boyte, "Textile Industry," 31–38; Woodward, *Origins of the New South,* 228–34.

101. The historical material in this section is drawn largely from the later chapters of McLaurin, *Paternalism and Protest.*

102. McLaurin, *Paternalism and Protest,* 69–76; the Knights' membership figures are from Ken Lawrence, "Roots of Class Struggle in the South," *Radical America* 9 (1976): 24. For an account of the Southwestern strike, see Jeremy Brecher, *Strike!* (San Francisco: Straight Arrow Books, 1973), ch. 2.

103. McLaurin, *Paternalism and Protest,* ch. 5.

104. Anthony Bimba, *The History of the American Working Class* (Westport, Conn.: Greenwood Press, 1968), ch. 21.

105. Applewhite, *Sharecropper and Tenant,* 144.

106. McLaurin, *Paternalism and Protest,* 19.

107. Ibid., 142.

108. Ibid., 148.

109. Ibid., 154–55.

110. Ibid., 156; Woodward, *Origins of the New South,* 422; Lefler and Newsome (*North Carolina,* 583) report eighty-two union locals in the state in 1900, including sixteen in the textile industry.

111. McLaurin, *Paternalism and Protest,* 156–59.

112. Ibid., 161.

113. Ibid., 168–74 and ch. 7.

114. Ibid., 204–5.

## 3. The Relocation of the Cotton Textile Industry, 1895–1939: The Political Economy of the "Stretch-Out"

1. George B. Tindall, *Emergence of the New South, 1913–1945* (Baton Rouge: Louisiana State University Press, 1967), 467. U.S. Department of Commerce, Bureau of the Census, *Sixteenth Census of the United States, 1940,* "Manufactures, 1939," 2, (Washington: USGPO, 1942), 304.

2. This general discussion of the structure of the textile industry relies on the following: E. B. Alderfer and H. E. Michl, *Economics of American Industry* (New York: McGraw-Hill, second edition, 1950), chs. 21 and 22; and Lowell D. Ashby, *The North Carolina Economy: Its Regional and National Setting with Particular Reference to the Structure of Employment,* Research Paper No. 7 (School of Business Administration, University of North Carolina at Chapel Hill, March, 1961). See also Cecil E. Fraser and Georges F. Doriot, *Analyzing Our Industries* (New York: McGraw-Hill, 1932), ch. 6; Stanley Vance, *American Industries* (Englewood Cliffs, N.J.: Prentice-Hall, 1955), ch. 19; and John G. Glover and W. B. Cornell (eds.), *The Development of American Industries: Their Economic Significance,* third edition (New York: Prentice-Hall, 1951), ch. 7.

3. Alderfer and Michl, *Economics of American Industry*, 12.

4. Chip Hughes, "A New Twist for Textiles," *Southern Exposure* 3 (Winter 1976): 78.

5. Barry E. Truchil, "Capital-Labor Relationships in the United States Textile Industry: The Post–World War II Period" (Ph.D. diss., S.U.N.Y. at Binghamton, 1982) 77–78.

6. The 1967 technical composition of capital figure is from Truchil, "Capital-Labor Relationships," 23. All the other indicators of labor intensity are taken from U.S. Department of Commerce, Bureau of the Census, *1977 Census of Manufactures*, Subject Series, General Summary (Washington: USGPO, 1981), 1-7 to 1-11, 1-55, 1-57.

7. *1977 Census of Manufactures*, 1, 9-18 to 9-21; U.S. Department of Commerce, Bureau of the Census, *Statistical Abstract of the United States, 1982–3* (Washington: USGPO, 1983), 784.

8. Tindall, *Emergence of the New South*, 468.

9. Collins, *Idea of a Cotton Textile Industry*, 378.

10. Woodward, *Origins of the New South*, 305.

11. Alderfer and Michl (*Economics of American Industry*, 354) explain this reluctance in terms of the "conservatizing effect" of the textile industry's slow growth on textile manufacturers. It appears more likely that, because of the social legislation in operation in Massachusetts, for instance, the cost of new machinery could not be justified in terms of the reduction in the cost of labor power that would result from its use. See the discussion of this theoretical point in Marx, *Capital*, 515–17.

12. Richard H. Edmonds, "Cotton Manufacturing Interests of the South," *Transactions of the New England Cotton Manufacturers' Association* 59, 196–97, 199–200, quoted in Collins, *Idea of a Cotton Textile Industry*, 381–82, 388.

13. Woodward, *Origins of the New South*, 307.

14. Collins, *Idea of a Cotton Textile Industry*, 381–82.

15. Woodward, *Origins of the New South*, 306–7; Lefler and Newsome, *North Carolina*, 509. In aggregate terms the northern presence was substantial, although not dominant. In 1922 an effort to test the "colonial economy" thesis with respect to the textile industry revealed that 16.2 percent of southern spindles were owned or controlled by corporations based outside the South but provided no estimate of the extent to which the southern industry included outright relocations, as opposed to branch plant operations, or of how much northern capital was invested in southern owned or controlled operations. (Massachusetts, Department of Labor and Industries, *Report*, 17.)

16. Mimi Conway, *Rise Gonna Rise: A Portrait of Southern Textile Workers* (New York: Anchor Press, 1979), 12–15, 46–47.

17. Alderfer and Michl, *Economics of American Industry*, 357; Irving Bernstein, *The Lean Years: A History of the American Worker, 1920–1933* (Baltimore: Penguin Books, 1966), 3.

18. Bernstein, *The Lean Years*.

19. Louis Galambos, *Competition and Cooperation: The Emergence of a National Trade Association* (Baltimore: Johns Hopkins University Press, 1966), 40; Richard M. Abrams, *Conservatism in a Progressive Era: Massachusetts Politics, 1900–1912* (Cambridge, Mass.: Harvard University Press, 1964), 230–31.

20. Examples of all these themes can be found in U.S. Senate, Committee on Manufactures, *Working Conditions of the Textile Industry*, 39–40; Richard Spillane, "Striking Facts about Southern Cotton Mills," *Manufacturers' Record* 86 (December 11, 1924), 195–96; Sinclair Lewis, *Cheap and Contented Labor: The Picture of a Southern Mill Town in 1929* (New York: United Textile Workers of America, 1929), especially p. 31; Duke Power Company, Industrial Department, *Piedmont Carolinas: Where Wealth Awaits You* (Charlotte, N.C.: 1927), especially pp. 17–19.

21. Abrams, *Conservatism*, 28.

22. U.S. Department of Commerce, Bureau of the Census, *Sixteenth Census of the United States, 1940*, 1, pt. 3 (Washington: USGPO, 1942), 161; U.S. Bureau of the Census, *1942*, 3, "Agriculture," 161.

23. Bernstein, *The Lean Years*, 4; Tindall, *Emergence of the New South*, 111; Boyte, "Textile Industry," 11.

24. See table 2.1 above. For data on the southern states as a whole, see Tindall, *Emergence of the New South*, 125.

25. According to Tindall, *Emergence of the New South*, 95, with the advent of the automobile, "before the end of the 1920s, a pattern of commuting from farm to mill was already established in the Piedmont."

26. U.S. Department of Commerce, Bureau of the Census, *Census of Agriculture, 1935*, "North Carolina" (Washington: USGPO, 1936), 8–9; U.S. Bureau of the Census, *1942*, 3, "Agriculture," 161, 342, 349.

27. See, for example, Tindall, *Emergence of the New South*, ch. 12; Arthur M. Ford, *Political Economics of Rural Poverty in the South* (Cambridge, Mass.: Ballinger, 1973); Donald H. Grubbs, *Cry from the Cotton: The Southern Tenant Farmers' Union and the New Deal* (Chapel Hill: University of North Carolina Press, 1971).

28. H. C. Nixon (ed.), *Southern Workers Outside the Legislative Pale* (New York: American Labor Education Service, 1942), 8.

29. See table 2.1.

30. U.S. Department of Commerce, Bureau of Foreign and Domestic Commerce, *Statistical Abstract of the United States, 1930* (Washington: USGPO, 1931), 8–9; U.S. Bureau of the Census, *Fourteenth Census* 9, 636, 639, 1102, 1120.

31. Tindall, *Emergence of the New South*, 331–36; Lefler and Newsome, *North Carolina*, 584.

32. For a discussion of the decline of the labor movement in the 1920s and the emergence of the "American Plan" and its variations, see Bernstein, *The Lean Years*, chs. 2 and 3.

33. Rhyne, *Some Cotton Mill Workers*, 205–6; Paul Blanshard, "One Hundred Percent Americans on Strike," *Nation* 128 (May 8, 1929): 554–56. Although the jobs or unions alternative has become more complex over time, it remains a powerful element in the ideology of industrialization in North Carolina. See, for example, the discussion of unions, jobs, and the problem of labor market competition in *News and Observer* (Raleigh, N.C., April 17, 1978), 25, 26.

34. Abrams, *Conservatism*, 28–29.

35. Ibid., 226–27.

36. For more detailed accounts of the Lawrence strike and its historical background, see ibid., 228–29; Melvyn Dubofsky, *We Shall Be All: A History of the*

*Industrial Workers of the World* (New York: Quadrangle Books/New York Times, 1969), ch. 10; Richard O. Boyer and Herbert M. Morais, *Labor's Untold Story*, third edition (New York: United Electrical, Radio and Machine Workers of America, 1970), 174–77; Bimba, *History of the American Working Class*, 242–43.

37. Massachusetts, Department of Labor and Industries, *Report*, 3–4; Bimba, *History of the American Working Class*, 297–98.

38. Abrams, *Conservatism*, 11.

39. Ibid., 131–32.

40. Bernstein, *The Lean Years*, 225–34.

41. Massachusetts, Department of Labor and Industries, *Report*, 2. This restriction was relaxed in 1933 in order to allow women to work until ten P.M. The ban on night work for women and children remained, however.

42. Elizabeth H. Davidson, *Child Labor Legislation in the Southern Textile States* (Chapel Hill: University of North Carolina Press, 1939), 104–5 and, generally, ch. 6.

43. Ibid., 12–14.

44. Ibid., 157–58.

45. Ibid., 257–65; Bernstein, *The Lean Years*, 235–37; Tindall, *Emergence of the New South*, 321–22. In 1924 both houses of Congress passed a constitutional amendment authorizing federal child labor legislation. Opposition was led by an organization known as the Sentinels of the Republic, based largely on the National Association of Manufacturers, the textile industry, and the American Farm Bureau Federation. This organization denounced the federal effort as a Communist plot to destroy states' rights and to turn the American child into federal property. The amendment was never ratified by the required number of states.

46. Davidson, *Child Labor Legislation*, 173–76. Census of Manufactures data indicate a large decline in the child labor portion of the cotton goods labor force in North Carolina between 1909 and 1919—from 18.9 percent to 6.0 percent. (U.S. Bureau of the Census, *Thirteenth Census*, 9, 914–15; U.S. Bureau of the Census, *Fourteenth Census*, 9, 1120–21. The latter figure was roughly equal to that in Massachusetts—5.7 percent—that had been stable since 1890. It is quite possible that this reduction reflects the efforts of textile manufacturers to hide their use of child labor rather than an actual reduction to this magnitude. On the other hand, the availability of cheap rural labor after the agricultural collapse of 1920–21 and a North Carolina workman's compensation law in 1929 possibly reduced the advantages and increased the hazards of employing child labor. (Pope, *Millhands and Preachers*, 195ff.) In any event, efforts to investigate the magnitude of the use of child labor in the 1920s were strongly resisted. (Davidson, *Child Labor Legislation*, 273.)

47. Davidson, *Child Labor Legislation*, 177; Marian D. Irish, "The Proletarian South," *Journal of Politics* 2 (August 1940): 243; Addison T. Cutler, "Labor Legislation in the Thirteen Southern States," *Southern Economic Journal* 7 (January 1941): 300–302.

48. Massachusetts, Department of Labor and Industries, *Report*, 2.

49. In 1929 the Senate Committee on Manufactures found that southern workers worked longer shifts at night than during the day. U.S. Senate Committee on Manufactures, *Hearings*, 24. Wright and Shiells consider the expansion of

night work to be a rational response by workers to the prospect of unemployment as the labor supply expanded and by millowners to wage rates that, for a variety of reasons, were not falling proportionately with the expansion of the labor force. See Gavin Wright and Martha Shiells, "Night Work as a Labor Market Phenomenon: Southern Textiles in the Interwar Period," *Explorations in Economic History* 20 (1983): 331–50.

50. Abraham Berglund, George T. Starnes, and Frank T. De Vyver, *Labor in the Industrial South* (Charlottesville: Institute for Research in the Social Sciences, University of Virginia, 1930), 84–85, table 21.

51. Bernstein, *The Lean Years*, 3–4; U.S. Senate, Committee on Manufactures, *Hearings*, 6; Broadus Mitchell and George S. Mitchell, *The Industrial Revolution in the South* (Baltimore: Johns Hopkins University Press, 1930), 15, 165–66; Irving Bernstein, *The Turbulent Years: A History of the American Worker, 1933–41* (Boston: Houghton Mifflin, 1970), 298–300.

52. Frank Stricker, "Affluence for Whom?—Another Look at Prosperity and the Working Classes in the 1920s," *Labor History* 24 (Winter 1983): 15.

53. A similar configuration appears in the more detailed and exhaustive study of the years 1920 and 1922 by the Massachusetts Department of Labor and Industries, *Report*, 6–9.

54. Data on hourly wage rates from Berglund et al., *Labor in the Industrial South*, 74. Data on actual weekly earnings from U.S. Senate, Committee on Manufactures, *Report on the Working Conditions of the Textile Industry in North Carolina, South Carolina and Tennessee*, Senate Report No. 28, 71st Congress, 1st session (1929), part 2, p. 4.

55. National Industrial Conference Board, Research Report No. 22, Special Report No. 8, quoted by Paul Blanshard in U.S. Senate, Committee on Manufactures, *Hearings*, 147–48. Other studies have found small differences between costs of living in the southern and northern states. These differences were not sufficient to compensate for the large regional wage differential. See, for example, Berglund et al., *Labor in the Industrial South*, ch. 9; Lois MacDonald, "The Labor Scene" in Nixon, *Southern Workers*, 12.

56. Textile Workers' Union of America, cio, *Half a Million Forgotten People: The Story of the Cotton Textile Workers* (New York, 1944), 12, 17–18; MacDonald, "Labor Scene."

57. For a discussion of the relationship between corn, pork, and pellagra, see Richard Sutch, "The Care and Feeding of Slaves," in Paul A. David et al., *Reckoning with Slavery: A Critical Study in the Quantitative History of American Negro Slavery* (New York: Oxford University Press, 1976), 270–74. See also Tindall, *Emergence of the New South*, 277–78; D. A. Roe, *A Plague of Corn: The Social History of Pellagra* (Ithaca: Cornell University Press, 1973); Elizabeth W. Etheridge, *The Butterfly Caste: A Social History of Pellagra in the South* (Westport, Conn.: Greenwood Press, 1972).

58. Massachusetts, Department of Labor and Industries, *Report*, 18.

59. In our attempt to demonstrate the practical links between the social relations of production established in North Carolina and the dynamics of labor-intensive capitalist production, we have emphasized the importance of the inter-regional migration of capital. It should be stressed, however, that the social and political conditions we have discussed also allowed local expansion and accumula-

tion to continue. As late as 1931 a survey showed that only 15 percent of southern spindles and 12 percent of southern looms were owned by "northern corporations." In addition, a number of corporate mergers and other types of consolidation involved both northern and southern capital. Where local accumulation was less evident, the proportion of northern ownership increased. In Alabama 36 percent of spindles and 37 percent of looms were northern-owned. In North Carolina's silk mills the proportions were 24 and 46 percent, respectively. (Barkin, "Regional Significance," 398.) Like the earlier study, no effort was made to document either formerly northern corporations that had by relocating become "southern" or the proportion of nonsouthern capital invested in southern-owned or -controlled companies.

An important example of rapid, large-scale, and predominantly local capital accumulation during the 1920s and 1930s is the expansion of Burlington Mills, based on advances in the cheap chemical production of rayon fiber, its immunity from the New Deal's cotton-processing tax, and the increasing availability of investment capital. This early period of growth and consolidation formed the basis for the postwar expansion of the Burlington Industries textile empire. See Bill Finger, "Looms, Loans and Lockouts," *Southern Exposure* 3 (Winter 1976): 54–65.

60. Tindall, *Emergence of the New South*, 76.

61. Barkin, "Regional Significance," 398.

62. On the extent and impact of various early forms of corporate rationalization, see ibid., 398–401.

63. Data and calculations from U.S. Bureau of the Census, *1942*, "Manufactures, *1939*," 3, 748–51. For the cigarette industry the relevant figures are as follows ($000): salaries 1,666.2; wages 13,878.5; value added 117,581.1; productive salaries 833.1; depreciation 5,879.1; surplus value 96,990.4; variable capital 14,711.6; rate of surplus value 659 percent.

64. Marshall, *Labor in the South*, 26–27.

65. Tindall, *Emergence of the New South*, 339; Bernstein, *The Lean Years*, 8.

66. Tindall, *Emergence of the New South*, 340; Lois MacDonald, "Normalcy in the Carolinas," *New Republic* (January 29, 1930), 268–69.

67. Marshall, *Labor in the South*, 102; Tindall, *Emergence of the New South*, 341; Bernstein, *The Lean Years*, 13.

68. See, especially, Bernstein, *The Lean Years*, ch. 1; Tindall, *Emergence of the New South*, 342–53; U.S. Senate, Committee on Manufactures, *Hearings and Report*; Vera B. Weisbord, "Gastonia 1929: Strike at the Loray Mill," *Southern Exposure* 1 (Winter 1974): 185–203; William F. Dunne, *Gastonia, Citadel of Class Struggle in the New South* (New York: Workers' Library Publishers, 1929); Lewis, *Cheap and Contented Labor*; Pope, *Millhands and Preachers*, 207–330; Thomas Tippett, *When Southern Labor Stirs* (New York: Cape and Smith, 1931); Bert Cochran, *Labor and Communism: The Conflict that Shaped the Unions* (Princeton: Princeton University Press, 1977), 34–38. Numerous eyewitness accounts are also available in the pages of the *Nation* and the *New Republic* during the second half of 1929 and early 1930. Most notable are: Benjamin Stolberg, "Madness in Marion," *Nation* 129 (October 23, 1929): 262–64; Paul Blanshard, "Communism in Southern Cotton Mills," *Nation* 128 (April 24, 1929): 500–501; Paul Blanshard, "One Hundred Percent Americans on Strike," *Nation* 128 (May

8, 1929): 554–56; Nell Battle Lewis, "Tar Heel Justice," *Nation* 129 (September 11, 1929): 272–73; Marion Bonner, "Behind the Southern Textile Strikes," *Nation* 129 (October 2, 1929): 351–52; Weimar Jones, "Southern Labor and the Law," *Nation* 131 (July 2, 1930): 14–15; Lois MacDonald, "Normalcy in the Carolinas," *New Republic* 61, no. 791 (January 29, 1930): 268–69; George Fort Milton, "The South Fights the Unions," *New Republic* 59, no. 762 (July 10, 1929).

69. In Elizabethton, an isolated mill community in the foothills of the Blue Ridge Mountains, the strike was a spontaneous one against the modern rayon-producing plants owned by the German Bemberg and Glantzsoff Corporations. Only after the strike had begun did the workers form Local 1630, United Textile Workers of America (UTWA, part of the AFL). In contrast, Gastonia lay at the center of the southern textile producing region. Concentrated heavily in cotton spinning, Gastonia had a well-established labor force of up to 22,000 when the mills were running at full capacity. In Gaston County, there were 112 mills and 1.25 million spindles—roughly a sixth of the total in the state. The workers' target in Gastonia was the Loray mill, part of the tire fabric division of the Manville-Jenckes Corporation of Rhode Island. The strike was preceded by a period of preparation and was conducted by the National Textile Workers' Union, an affiliate of the Communist party's dual trade union federation, the Trade Union Unity League. The Marion Manufacturing Company had been established in 1909 in Marion, an isolated community in western North Carolina. In 1929 its President was a southerner, a native of Baltimore. The AFL-affiliated UTWA was nominally in charge at Marion but opposed the strike and sent little practical help apart from union organizers. (Bernstein, *The Lean Years*, 14–15, 20–22, 29–30; Dunne, *Gastonia*, 17–19; Stolberg, "Madness in Marion," 462.)

70. Bernstein, *The Lean Years*, 40; Blanshard, "One Hundred Percent Americans on Strike"; Samuel Yellen, *American Labor Struggles* (New York: S. A. Russell, 1936), 301.

71. Ethelbert Stewart, U.S. Commissioner of Labor Statistics, Speech to the Labor College of Philadelphia, April 27, 1929, quoted in Dunne, *Gastonia*, 20.

72. See note 37, above. Bernstein (*The Lean Years*, 4) quotes a story that was popular in the South at the time: "A man went to the plant and asked for a job. The boss said 'All right. But before we give you a job I will give you a test.' The boss gave him a handbrush and said: 'You throw that handbrush as far as you can.' The fellow had been a baseball player, and flung the brush down to the other side of the weave shop. The boss said: 'All right. The job is yours. You run all these looms.' "

73. Tom Terrill and Jerrold Hirsch (eds.), *Such As Us: Southern Voices of the Thirties* (New York: Norton, 1979), 179.

74. Statement of Miss Margaret Bowen, Secretary, Local 1630, UTWA, Elizabethton, in U.S. Senate, Committee on Manufactures, *Hearings*, 77–78.

75. Millworker, Elizabethton, Tennessee, quoted in Bonner, "Behind the Textile Strikes," 351.

76. U.S. Senate, Committee on Manufactures, *Hearings*, 78.

77. Bernstein, *The Lean Years*, 20.

78. Ibid., 29.

79. Lewis, *Cheap and Contented Labor*, 18–19.

80. Ibid., 19–20.

81. Bernstein, *The Lean Years*, 22.

82. Ibid.

83. The following material on institutional and other forms of officially sanctioned violence is drawn from Bernstein, *The Lean Years*, ch. 1.

84. Heywood Broun, "It Seems to Heywood Broun," *Nation* 129 (September 25, 1929): 19.

85. Pope, *Millhands and Preachers*, especially chs. 7 and 8.

86. Jones, "Southern Labor," 16.

87. Bernstein, *The Lean Years*, 32–33.

88. The revolt was not completely without beneficial effects for the workers. Mills in Gaston County reduced hours to fifty-five per week without pay cuts. At Marion hours were shortened by six per week, wages were increased by 5 percent, and welfare programs were liberalized. None of these changes significantly reduced the competitive advantage enjoyed by the mills and, in view of the operation of the stretch-out, probably did not significantly improve the lot of the millworkers. In addition, the Cotton Textile Institute voted to abolish night work for women and minors under eighteen—a promise only partially fulfilled, as we have seen, in 1937. (Bernstein, *The Lean Years*, 40; Pope, *Millhands and Preachers*, ch. 14.)

89. Marshall, *Labor in the South*, ch. 8; Bernstein, *The Lean Years*, 34; testimony of William Green, AFL President, in U.S. Senate, Committee on Manufactures, *Hearings*, 17; William Green, "Labor's Message to the South," address made to the Conference to Inaugurate the Southern Organizing Campaign, Charlotte, N.C., January 6, 1930 (Washington: American Federation of Labor, 1930), passim.

90. Bernstein, *The Lean Years*, 36–40.

91. The following brief account of the 1934 strike is taken from Bernstein, *The Turbulent Years*, 298–315; Brecher, *Strike!*, 166–77; Margaret Marshall, "Textiles: An NRA Strike," *Nation* 139 (September 19, 1934): 326–28; Hamilton Basso, "Gastonia: Before the Battle," *New Republic* 80, no. 1033 (September 19, 1934): 148–49; Jonathan Mitchell, "Here Comes Gorman," *New Republic* 80, no. 1035 (October 3, 1934), 203–5; Mary W. Hillyer, "The Textile Workers Go Back," *Nation* 139 (October 10, 1934): 414.

92. Tindall, *Emergence of the New South*, 437; Galambos, *Competition and Cooperation*, ch. 7.

93. For an account of the 1937 CIO organizing campaign, see Bernstein, *The Turbulent Years*, 616–23; Tindall, *Emergence of the New South*, 517–21; Nicholas Reed, "CIO Invades North Carolina," *The Carolina Magazine* 66 (May 1937): 3–7.

94. Len de Caux, *Labor Radical* (Boston: Beacon Press, 1970), 288.

95. Irish, "The Proletarian South," 246–47.

## 4. Capital, Exploitation, and the State in North Carolina: Theoretical Considerations

1. Milton Friedman, *Capitalism and Freedom* (Chicago: University of Chicago Press, 1962).

2. The area in and around Spartanburg, South Carolina, was Friedman's specific focus.

3. Karl Marx, "Critique of Hegel's Doctrine of the State," in Quinton Hoare (ed.), *Karl Marx: Early Writings* (New York: Vintage Books, 1975), 57–198.

4. V. O. Key, Jr., *Southern Politics in State and Nation* (New York: Vintage Books, 1949). The "racial" theory of the southern state by no means originates with Key. For instance, Paul Lewinson said: "It is impossible to trace white political issues and cleavages without reference to the Negro as the common enemy, the red herring across all political trails." [Lewinson, *Race, Class and Party: A History of Negro Suffrage and White Politics in the South* (London: Oxford University Press, 1932), 5.] It was Key, however, who was responsible for most systematically investigating the implications of race for virtually all aspects of southern politics. Recent analyses of southern politics have continued to follow Key's emphasis. They are now directed to documenting and explaining the South's movement away from the forms of political behavior and organization described by Key as a result of legislative and judicial action with respect to racial discrimination, the effects of differential migration patterns, and other factors. See, for example, Donald R. Matthews and James W. Prothro, *Negroes and the New Southern Politics* (New York: Harcourt, Brace and World, 1966); William C. Havard, *The Changing Politics of the South* (Baton Rouge: Louisiana State University Press, 1972); Jack Bass and Walter DeVries, *The Transformation of Southern Politics: Social Change and Political Consequences since 1945* (New York: Basic Books, 1976); Numan V. Bartley and Hugh D. Graham, *Southern Politics and the Second Reconstruction* (Baltimore: Johns Hopkins University Press, 1975); Carol Ann Cassel, "A Longitudinal Analysis of Political Change in the American South" (Ph.D. diss., Florida State University, 1975).

5. Key, *Southern Politics*, 7; Lewinson, *Race, Class and Party*, 3.

6. Key, *Southern Politics*, 66.

7. Key in fact referred to the southern political system as a "no-party" system because of the extent of factionalization within the Democratic party: "the Democratic Party in most states of the South is merely a holding company for a congeries of transient, squabbling factions, most of which fail by far to meet the standards of permanence, cohesiveness and responsibility that characterize the political party." (Key, *Southern Politics*, 16.)

8. Ibid., ch. 14.

9. Ibid., 310.

10. Ibid., 4. For a similar view, see W. J. Cash, *The Mind of the South* (New York: Vintage Books, 1969), especially 131–32.

11. Key, *Southern Politics*, 205–6.

12. Ibid., 211.

13. Ibid., 208.

14. "If there is a single grand issue, it is that of public expenditure" (ibid., 307).

15. For a more systematic development of this point, see Dennison Moore, "The Origins and Development of Racial Ideology in Trinidad" (Ph.D. diss., Queen's University, 1980), especially ch. 5; Oliver C. Cox, *Caste, Class and Race* (New York: Monthly Review Press, 1970), especially ch. 16.

16. This functionalist approach is best exemplified by the work of the late Nicos Poulantzas. It is an emphasis, however, that can be found in the work of many other Marxist writers on the State. For instance, although Ralph Miliband

disagrees with Poulantzas on why the State acts on behalf of capital and is less prone to use systemic reasoning, his work also incorporates an element of functionalism. And from a different point of origin again, a number of participants in the German "State derivation debate" propose an essentially functionalist solution to the problem of the relationship between the State and capitalist competition. See Nicos Poulantzas, *Political Power and Social Classes* (London: New Left Books, 1973); Ralph Miliband, *Marxism and Politics* (London: Oxford University Press, 1977), ch. 4; Wolfgang Muller and Christel Neususs, "The Welfare State Illusion and the Contradiction between Wage-labour and Capital," Elmer Altvater, "Some Problems of State Interventions," and Bernhard Blanke et al., "On the Current Discussion on the Analysis of Form and Function of the Bourgeois State," chapters 2, 3, and 6 of John Holloway and Sol Picciotto, *State and Capital: A Marxist Debate* (London: Edward Arnold, 1978). The best discussions of some or all of these writers can be found in John Holloway and Sol Picciotto, "Towards a Materialist Theory of the State," in Holloway and Picciotto, *State and Capital*, 1–31; Bob Jessop, "Recent Theories of the Capitalist State," *Cambridge Journal of Economics* 1 (December 1977), and Simon Clarke, "Marxism, Sociology and Poulantzas' Theory of the State," *Capital and Class*, no. 2 (1977).

17. F. Engels to Conrad Schmidt, October 27, 1890, in K. Marx and F. Engels, *Selected Correspondence* (Moscow: Foreign Languages Publishing House, 1953), 503.

18. This is a relatively common theme in the study of the American State, although it is not usually put in these terms. See, for example, Samuel P. Huntington, *Political Order in Changing Societies* (New Haven: Yale University Press, 1968), ch. 2.

19. Andrew Gamble, "Critical Political Economy," in R. J. Barry-Jones (ed.), *Perspectives on Political Economy* (London: Frances Pinter, 1983), 84.

20. Karl Marx, *Capital*, vol. 3 (Moscow: Progress Publishers, 1977), 791.

21. Ibid., 791–92.

22. Bob Jessop, "Accumulation Strategies, State Forms and Hegemonic Projects," *Kapitalistate* 10/11 (1983): 89–111.

23. Marx, *Capital*, 899.

24. Ibid., 899–900.

25. See, for example, James Weinstein, *The Corporate Ideal in the Liberal State, 1900–1918* (Boston: Beacon Press, 1968); Gabriel Kolko, *The Triumph of Conservatism: A Reinterpretation of American History, 1900–1916* (Chicago: Quadrangle Books, 1967). For a general overview of the emergence of the American corporate State at the federal level, see Edward S. Greenberg, *Understanding Modern Government: The Rise and Decline of the American Political Economy* (New York: Wiley, 1979), especially chs. 3 and 4.

## 5. Capital, Exploitation, and the State in North Carolina: From the Civil War to the New Deal and Beyond

1. Lefler and Newsome, *North Carolina*, 323.

2. Ibid., 490.

3. Ibid.; W. E. B. Du Bois, *Black Reconstruction in America, 1860–1880* (New York: Atheneum, 1970), 655–57; J. Morgan Kousser, "Progressivism—

For Middle Class Whites Only: North Carolina Education, 1880–1910," *Journal of Southern History* 66 (May 1980): 173.

4. Du Bois, *Black Reconstruction*, 531.

5. Ibid.; Lefler and Newsome, *North Carolina*, 493–94.

6. Du Bois, *Black Reconstruction*, 531–32; for the South as a whole, this argument is presented by T. Harry Williams, *Romance and Realism in Southern Politics* (Baton Rouge: Louisiana State University Press, 1966), 17–29. See also Lewinson, *Race, Class and Party*, 52; Degler, *The Other South*, 216.

7. Lefler and Newsome, *North Carolina*, 492–98; Lewinson, *Race, Class and Party*, 54.

8. Kousser, "Progressivism," 173; Lefler and Newsome, *North Carolina*, 534–35.

9. Lefler and Newsome, *North Carolina*, 498–99; Woodward, *Origins of the New South*, 54.

10. The conservatives adopted the name "Democratic party" in time for the 1876 election for Governor.

11. Lefler and Newsome, *North Carolina*, 541–42. According to Woodward (*Origins of the New South*, 87), North Carolina's debt adjustment was the most drastic in the whole South.

12. Woodward, *Origins of the New South*, 58–66; Richard Sylla, "The Economics of State and Local Government Sources and Uses of Funds in North Carolina, 1800–1977" (paper presented at the National Bureau of Economic Research (NBER) Conference on Research in Income and Wealth, Williamsburg, Va., March 1984), 27–28; Eric Foner, *Nothing But Freedom*, 70–71.

13. Helen G. Edmonds, *The Negro and Fusion Politics in North Carolina, 1894–1901* (Chapel Hill: University of North Carolina Press, 1951), 10.

14. Ibid., 10–11; Lefler and Newsome, *North Carolina*, 542.

15. Lefler and Newsome, *North Carolina*, 542.

16. Key, *Southern Politics*, 7; Lewinson, *Race, Class and Party*, 58–60; Lefler and Newsome, *North Carolina*, 501–2.

17. J. Morgan Kousser, *The Shaping of Southern Politics: Suffrage Restriction and the Establishment of the One-Party South, 1880–1910* (New Haven: Yale University Press, 1974), 183; Degler, *The Other South*, 265; Lefler and Newsome, *North Carolina*, 543–44.

18. Robert C. McMath, Jr., *Populist Vanguard: A History of the Southern Farmers' Alliance* (New York: Norton, 1977), 39.

19. Ibid., ch. 4, pp. 43, 44, 66, 125; Goodwyn, *Democratic Promise*, ch. 5.

20. Michael Schwartz, *Radical Protest and Social Structure: The Southern Farmers' Alliance and Cotton Tenancy, 1880–1890* (New York: Academic Press, 1976), 102–3, ch. 16; Billings, *Planters*, ch. 8.

21. Ibid., 183–87; David Montgomery, "On Goodwyn's Populists," *Marxist Perspectives* 1 (Spring 1978): 171–72; Harold D. Woodman, "Post-bellum Social Change and its Effects on Marketing the South's Cotton Crop," *Agricultural History* 56 (1982): especially 228–30.

22. McMath, *Populist Vanguard*, ch. 8; Goodwyn, *Democratic Promise*, chs. 8, 9, 11; Woodward, *Origins of the New South*, ch. 9; Degler, *The Other South*, 330.

23. Kousser, *Shaping of Southern Politics*, 183; Lefler and Newsome, *North Carolina*, 548.

24. Kousser, *Shaping of Southern Politics*, 184.

25. The following account of the Fusion reforms is taken from Lefler and Newsome, *North Carolina*, 550–54; Kousser, *Shaping of Southern Politics*, 186–87; Kousser, "Progressivism," 177, 179; Edmonds, *Negro and Fusion Politics*, 34–57, 153; Oliver H. Orr, *Charles Brantley Aycock* (Chapel Hill: University of North Carolina Press, 1961), 103–6; Sylla, "Economics of State and Local Government," 27–28.

26. Billings, *Planters*, 177.

27. Ibid., 177–78; Lefler and Newsome, *North Carolina*, 552–53.

28. Edmonds, *Negro and Fusion Politics*, 138. For a more detailed account of the campaign to overthrow the Fusion government, see Edmonds, *Negro and Fusion Politics*, passim.

29. Ibid., 139; Billings, *Planters*, 201; Joseph L. Morrison, *Governor O. Max Gardner: A Power in North Carolina and New Deal Washington* (Chapel Hill: University of North Carolina Press, 1971), 10.

30. *Charlotte Observer* (NC), November 17, 1898, quoted in Edmonds, *Negro and Fusion Politics*, 151. See also Lefler and Newsome, *North Carolina*, 558–59.

31. Quoted in Edmonds, *Negro and Fusion Politics*, 153.

32. *Charlotte Observer* (NC), November 19, 1898, quoted in ibid., 153.

33. Ibid., 149.

34. Lefler and Newsome, *North Carolina*, 559.

35. Ibid., 559–60. Only white grandfathers counted, of course: "when I first took hold o' registerin' voters, a right smart o' niggers come to register at first, claimin' they could meet the requirements. Some wrote the Constitution, I reckon, as good as a lot o' white men, but I'd find somethin' unsatisfactory, maybe an *i* not dotted or a *t* not crossed, enough for me to disqualify 'em. The law said "satisfactory to the registrar." A few could get by the grandfather clause, for they was some free niggers before the Civil War, but they couldn't get by an undotted *i* or an uncrossed *t*." (Roger T. Stevenson, J.P., former Redshirt, Seaboard, North Carolina, 1939, quoted in Tom Terrill and Jerrold Hirsch (eds.), *Such As Us: Southern Voices of the Thirties* (New York: Norton, 1978), 262–63.

36. Kousser, *Shaping of Southern Politics*, 50, 55, 191; Edmonds, *Negro and Fusion Politics*, ch. 12.

37. Kousser, *Shaping of Southern Politics*, 192–93.

38. Ibid., 194, 249; Edmonds, *Negro and Fusion Politics*, 209.

39. McMath, *Populist Vanguard*, 100.

40. A Mississippian, Chicago *Inter-Ocean*, no. 4, 1890, quoted in John L. Love, *The Disenfranchisement of the Negro* (Washington, 1899), and excerpted in Herbert Aptheker (ed.), *A Documentary History of the Negro People in the United States* (New York: Citadel Press, 1969), 763.

41. See, for example, C. Vann Woodward, *The Strange Career of Jim Crow*, third revised edition (New York: Oxford University Press, 1974).

42. William H. Chafe, *Civilities and Civil Rights: Greensboro, North Carolina, and the Black Struggle for Freedom* (New York: Oxford University Press,

1980), 18–19. For the southern states generally, see Tindall, *Emergence of the New South*, 161–62. Apart from the socially necessary intercourse between white capital and black labor, one of the few acceptable forms of interracial intercourse was sexual intercourse. When a law was proposed in the state legislature to prohibit this practice, it was fought successfully by every leading Democrat in the eastern part of the state. (Edmonds, *Negro and Fusion Politics*, 187.)

According to standard economic analysis, excluding blacks from employment implies an artificial reduction in the supply of labor and requires that employers pay higher wages. If correct this view would also imply, *ceteris paribus*, that the rate of surplus value would be reduced, and that the long-term political interests of employers would conflict, therefore, with their political interests. An alternative logic, suggested by Albert Szymanski and Michael Reich, seems more plausible in the context of North Carolina, however. This is that economic discrimination against blacks seriously weakens the ability of workers generally to achieve better conditions, worsens the economic position of both black and white workers, and results in higher levels of income and educational inequality among whites. From this perspective the political and economic interests of North Carolina's capitalists may not have been in conflict, and the extension of racial segregation in the North Carolina economy after 1900 may have served to increase the rate of exploitation rather than to reduce it. See, for example, Albert Szymanski, "Race Discrimination and White Gains," *American Sociological Review* 41 (June 1976): 403–13; Michael Reich, "The Economics of Racism," in Richard C. Edwards et al. (eds.), *The Capitalist System*, second edition (Englewood Cliffs, N.J.: Prentice-Hall, 1978), 381–88; Michael Reich, *Racial Inequality* (Princeton: Princeton University Press, 1981).

43. Lefler and Newsome, *North Carolina*, 563.

44. Kousser, *Shaping of Southern Politics*, 24, 72; Key, *Southern Politics*, 215–18.

45. Kousser, *Shaping of Southern Politics*, 250; Woodward, *Origins of the New South*, 330–31.

46. Kousser, *Shaping of Southern Politics*, 71, 226, 241.

47. Key, *Southern Politics*, 504–5. By the end of World War II, at least, some blacks were voting. In 1946 and 1947 two independent studies estimated that 75,000 blacks were registered to vote in North Carolina. At the time, this figure represented roughly fifteen percent of the adult black population (ibid., 522–23n).

48. *Statistical Abstract*, 1978, tables 834, 840, 841.

49. E. E. Schattschneider, *The Semi-Sovereign People* (Hinsdale, Ill.: Dryden Press, 1975), 78.

50. Walter Dean Burnham, "Party Systems and the Political Process," in William Nisbet Chambers and Walter Dean Burnham, *The American Party Systems*, second edition (New York: Oxford University Press, 1975), 301.

51. Key, *Southern Politics*, 505.

52. Calculated from data in U.S. Department of Commerce, Bureau of the Census, *Historical Statistics of the United States, Colonial Times to 1970*, 2 (Washington: USGPO, 1975), 1072; U.S. Department of Commerce, Bureau of the Census, *Statistical Abstract*, 1978, 523.

53. Data on voting age population are from U.S. Bureau of the Census, *1943*,

2, pt. 5, 296–301. 1940 voting data are from University of North Carolina at Chapel Hill, Political Studies Program, *North Carolina Votes* (Chapel Hill: University of North Carolina Press, 1962). See also Key, *Southern Politics*, 318–23.

54. Tannenbaum, *Darker Phases*, 59.

55. Rhyne, *Some Cotton Mill Workers*, 177.

56. Calculated from data in U.S. Bureau of the Census, *1943*, 2, pt. 5, 296–301, 322–34; UNC Political Studies Program, *Votes*.

57. Key (*Southern Politics*, 205–10) and Lefler and Newsome (*North Carolina*, 562) suggest that such an exception can be explained by North Carolina's commitment to a "progressive" social policy.

58. Billings, *Planters*, 202–12; Edmonds, *Negro and Fusion Politics*, 205; Hugh C. Bailey, *Liberalism in the New South: Southern Social Reformers and the Progressive Movement* (Coral Gables, Fla.: University of Miami Press, 1969), chs. 4, 5; Joseph F. Steelman, "The Progressive Era in North Carolina, 1884–1917" (Ph.D. diss., University of North Carolina at Chapel Hill, 1955). For concrete examples of this definition of education, see R. D. W. Connor and Clarence Poe, (eds.), *The Life and Speeches of Charles Brantley Aycock* (New York: Doubleday, Page, 1912), especially 132, 248–51, 318. See also C. E. Vawter, "The Need of Industrial and Technical Education in the South," *Southern Workman* (February 1901). For general discussions of the relationships between class formation, capital accumulation, and education, see Samuel Bowles and Herbert Gintis, *Schooling in Capitalist America: Educational Reform and the Contradictions of Economic Life* (New York: Basic Books, 1976), especially ch. 6; Joel Spring, *Education and the Rise of the Corporate State* (Boston: Beacon Press, 1972).

59. Sylla, *Economics of State and Local Government*, 28; Kousser, "Progressivism," 179, 181.

60. Lefler and Newsome, *North Carolina*, 604–5; Paul Betters et al., *State Centralization in North Carolina* (Washington: Brookings Institution, 1932), 41–42, 122–25.

61. The following discussion of educational control and finance relies on the following: Betters, *State Centralization*, 30–46; Tindall, *Emergence of the New South*, 225–26; Lefler and Newsome, *North Carolina*, 604–5; Puryear, *Democratic Party*, ch. 3.

62. During the 1920s proposals for reform originated in the executive branch of the state government. After 1900, although the influence of industrial capital within the predominantly rural Democratic political machine increased, the number of counties that were dominated by industrial capital remained a minority. Consequently, the state legislature continued to be dominated by the interests of agricultural capital. The political power of industrial capital was therefore most evident in the statewide elections for governor, where its financial power could be used most effectively in a context of generally low popular participation. The three governors elected during the 1920s—Cameron Morrison, 1921–25, Angus McLean, 1925–29, and O. Max Gardner, 1929–33—all had extensive links with industrial capital, and all played important roles in efforts to expand the activities of the State on behalf of this capital.

Morrison was a corporate lawyer in Charlotte, North Carolina, between 1905 and 1920, a millionaire, and a large stockholder in the Duke Power Company.

McLean was president of the Bank of Lumberton, the Robeson Development Company, and the McLean Trust Company, and vice president of the Lumberton Cotton Mills and the Jennings Cotton Mills. Gardner, founder of the aggressively procapitalist "Shelby Dynasty" that ruled North Carolina between 1929 and the late 1940s, was perhaps the most important of the three. His career and economic interests reflected almost perfectly the combination of agricultural and industrial interests and cultural and political values represented within the evolving Democratic State. As acting governor in 1919, and as governor in 1929, Gardner was responsible for the use of troops in the strikes at Charlotte, Gastonia, and Marion. The legal partnership of Gardner and Clyde Hoey (Gardner's brother-in-law and governor from 1937 to 1941) acted as counsel and lobbyists for textile, tobacco, and power companies in their struggles against regulation. Gardner's personal fortune was created in agriculture, where he made money by rebuilding abandoned farms using tenant labor, diversified production, and the use of the most modern methods of cultivation. In 1925 he founded the multimillion dollar Cleveland Cotton Mills and produced rayon goods. He also held shares in the R. J. Reynolds Tobacco Company, and profited from the interwar boom in cigarettes. He had close connections with the Wachovia Bank and Trust Company of Winston-Salem, was a director of the First National Bank and of the Dover, Dilling, and Belmont Mills, and was President of the Cleveland Springs Corporation, the Cleveland County Chamber of Commerce, and the Cleveland Board of Agriculture. [*National Cyclopedia of American Biography* 49 (New York: James T. White and Co., 1966), 36; Puryear, *Democratic Party*, 137; *Who Was Who in America* 1, 1897–1942 (Chicago: A. N. Marquis Co., 1943), 819; Hope M. Brogden, "The Electoral Bases of Representation in North Carolina, 1916–1972" (Ph.D. diss., University of North Carolina at Chapel Hill, 1976); Morrison, *Governor*, 15–55.]

63. Lefler and Newsome, *North Carolina*, 587–88, 600, 603; Betters, *State Centralization*, 62–64.

64. Lefler and Newsome, *North Carolina*, 606; Betters, *State Centralization*, 125–27.

65. Lefler and Newsome, *North Carolina*, 607–8.

66. Betters, *State Centralization*, 72–79; Morrison, *Governor*, 84–86; Paul W. Wager, "Effects of Centralization in NC," *University of North Carolina Newsletter* 23 (November 3, 1937): 1; C. H. Donovan, "The Readjustment of State and Local Fiscal Relations in North Carolina, 1929–1938" (Ph.D. diss., University of North Carolina at Chapel Hill, 1940), 5. The use of convict gang labor for highway construction and maintenance was discontinued in July 1973. In 1937 the North Carolina state legislature passed "progressive" legislation allowing misdemeanor offenders to work on regular jobs outside the prison system, provided that they returned each night and for weekends to their cells. In this way the state prison system provided cheap labor for nonunion employers and supplemented county jail and state prison budgets. In addition, in 1973 the state had eleven prison industries that employed approximately one thousand prisoners and that were established so as not to provide competition for local industry. In 1973 profits amounted to over $1.5 million. North Carolina's prison population of over 14,000 in 1973 was the largest in the United States as a proportion of the state's population. For every 100,000 North Carolinians, 183 were incarcerated in the state

prison system. For black males the rate was 1,040 per 100,000. [Michael Myerson *Nothing Could Be Finer* (New York: International Publishers, 1978), 173–75.]

67. Betters, *State Centralization*, ch. 4; Morrison, *Governor*, 88; Wager, "Effects of Centralization"; Albert Coates, compiler, *Commentaries on Proposals in 1933 and 1935 for the Revision of the Constitution of North Carolina* (Chapel Hill: Institute of Government, University of North Carolina, 1958), 37–38, 43.

68. Lefler and Newsome, *North Carolina*, 603–4. These earlier changes had included the establishment of a Department of Conservation and Development whose task it was to attract capital. These efforts, however, did not reach major proportions until the late 1930s. In 1937 a $250,000 advertising campaign was conducted by the department in national newspapers to publicize the state's economic advantages. By the end of the following year 33,000 enquiries from outside the state had been received and between fifteen million dollars and eighteen million dollars in new capital investments had resulted. (*News and Observer*, Raleigh, N.C., December 26, 1937 and December 11, 1938.)

69. Tindall, *Emergence of the New South*, 232; Betters, *State Centralization*, 159, 161–74.

70. Betters, *State Centralization*, 53–54.

71. Ibid., 56–57.

72. Ibid., 121.

73. Puryear, *Democratic Party*, 74–75.

74. Ibid., 86–87; Betters, *State Centralization*, 138–43; Morrison, *Governor*, 89–91, Tindall, *Emergence of the New South*, 368.

75. Betters, *State Centralization*, 121.

76. Lefler and Newsome, *North Carolina*, 611; Wager, "Effects of Centralization."

77. Betters, *State Centralization*, 144–45.

78. A. W. McAllister, "A Tax Program for North Carolina," *University of North Carolina Extension Bulletin* 12 (November 1932): 75–80.

79. Lefler and Newsome, *North Carolina*, 612.

80. Ibid.

81. Puryear, *Democratic Party*, 115.

82. Lefler and Newsome, *North Carolina*, 613.

83. Wager, "Effects of Centralization."

84. Calculated from data presented in T. N. Grice, "State Revenues and Expenditures," *University of North Carolina Newsletter* 22 (1936): 1.

85. James A. Wilde, "The Tax Structure in North Carolina," in Thad L. Beyle and Merle Black, *Politics and Policy in North Carolina* (New York: MSS Information Corporation, 1975), ch. 16.

86. Ibid. See also S. Kenneth Howard, "Taxes: North Carolina and the Nation: A Comparison of State and Local Taxes in North Carolina with National Patterns," *Popular Government* 33 (October 1966): 1–4. For a justification of the 1961 decision to reimpose the "food tax," see Terry Sanford, *But What About the People?* (New York: Harper and Row, 1966), ch. 2. For comparisons of tax systems within the South, see Eva Galambos, *State and Local Taxes in the South, 1973* (Atlanta: Southern Regional Council, 1974).

87. See Robert J. Newman, *Growth in the American South: Changing Re-*

*gional Employment and Wage Patterns in the 1900s and 1970s* (New York: New York University Press, 1984), ch. 5; Barry Bluestone and Bennett Harrison, *The Deindustrialization of America: Plant Closings, Community Abandonment and the Dismantling of Basic Industry* (New York: Basic Books, 1982), 180, and, generally, ch. 6.

88. See, for example, Puryear, *Democratic Party*, ch. 9.

89. Lefler and Newsome, *North Carolina*, 563.

90. Ibid., 572.

91. Tindall, *Emergence of the New South*, 3.

92. Ibid., 10–16.

93. Ibid., 6, 16–17.

94. Weinstein, *Corporate Ideal*, 200.

95. Tindall, *Emergence of the New South*, 389–90.

96. Marian D. Irish, "The Southern One-Party System and National Politics," *Journal of Politics* 4 (February 1942): 82–84.

97. Key, *Southern Politics*, chs. 16 and 17. For later analyses of southern congressional solidarity and the issues on which it was most apparent, see W. Wayne Shannon, "Revolt in Washington: The South in Congress," in William C. Havard (ed.), *The Changing Politics of the South* (Baton Rouge: Louisiana State University Press, 1972); John F. Manley, "The Conservative Coalition in Congress," in Robert L. Peabody and Nelson W. Polsby (eds.), *New Perspectives on the House of Representatives*, third edition (Chicago: Rand McNally, 1977), 97–117.

This solidarity occurred despite variations in the social background and direct material interests of southern congressmen. For data on these variations, see James T. Patterson, *Congressional Conservatism and the New Deal: The Growth of the Conservative Coalition in Congress, 1933–1939* (Lexington: University of Kentucky Press, 1967), 18–27, 29–31, 42–45, 64–66.

All of these analyses share the limitation that they fail to discuss theoretically either the importance of the issues on which southerners were agreed or the legislation itself and the process of political struggle through which it emerged.

98. Available accounts of the role of southerners in the New Deal point to 1935 or 1936 as watershed years between a period of acquiescence in the New Deal and a period of increasing opposition. (See Tindall, *Emergence of the New South*, 618; Patterson, *Congressional Conservatism*, passim.) What we are interested in here is not necessarily the extent of southern acquiescence or opposition, however, but the impact of southern congressional power on the content of New Deal legislation in both periods.

99. This account of work relief and social security is based on Frances Fox Piven and Richard Cloward, *Regulating the Poor: The Functions of Public Welfare* (New York: Vintage Books, 1971), 95, 111–141; Tindall, *Emergence of the New South*, ch. 14; Donald S. Howard, *The WPA and Federal Relief Policy* (New York: Russell Sage Foundation, 1943), 160; Thomas S. Morgan, "A Folly . . . Manifest to Everyone: The Movement to Enact Unemployment Insurance Legislation in North Carolina, 1935–6," *North Carolina Historical Review* 52 (July 1975); E. J. Eberling, "The Southern Worker and Unemployment Compensation," in Nixon (ed.), *Southern Workers*, 19–22.

100. Fox Piven and Cloward, *Regulating the Poor*, 126.

101. California, Connecticut, Illinois, Massachusetts, Michigan, New Jersey, New York, Ohio, Pennsylvania, and Rhode Island.

102. For discussions of later trends in public assistance, AFDC, and other welfare programs in North Carolina, see S. H. Hobbs, Jr., "Public Assistance in North Carolina," *University of North Carolina Newsletter* 36 (February 15, 1950); Clif ton M. Craig, "Public Welfare Trends in North Carolina," *University of North Carolina Newsletter* 53 (December 1968). In 1949, according to Hobbs's data, average payments in North Carolina for old age assistance, aid to dependent children, and general assistance were $21.65, $41.78, and $14.50, respectively, compared with averages for the United States as a whole of $44.46, $73.15, and $48.66, respectively.

103. The priority given to public welfare in the North Carolina General Assembly was summed up effectively by a professional lobbyist at the height of the "welfare explosion" in 1967: "I've got the easiest job over there. I'm trying to get a welfare bill killed." (*News and Observer*, Raleigh, N.C., July 12, 1967.)

104. U.S. Department of Commerce, Bureau of the Census, *Statistical Abstract of the United States, 1978* (Washington: USGPO, 1978), 359.

105. Ibid., 352–53.

106. U.S. Department of Commerce, Bureau of the Census, *1977 Census of Manufactures*, Subject Series, General Summary (Washington, USGPO, 1981), 1-99.

107. Ibid., 1-15 to 1-27, 1-99.

108. For discussions of the relationship between welfare policy and the relocation of capital, see, for example, Robert L. Weinstein and Robert E. Firestine, *Regional Growth and Decline in the United States* (New York: Praeger, 1978); Bluestone and Harrison, *Deindustrialization of America*, ch. 6; Brad Heil, "Sunbelt Migration," in Union for Radical Political Economics, *U.S. Capitalism in Crisis* (New York: URPE, 1978). The above coefficients are taken from P. Wood, "The Social Wage and Regional Capitalist Development in the United States" (Unpublished manuscript, 1984).

109. This discussion is based on Patterson, *Congressional Conservatism*, 18–31, 149–50, 242–56; Tindall, *Emergence of the New South*, chs. 13, 15; Marian D. Irish, "The Proletarian South," *Journal of Politics* 2 (August 1940): 252–53; Orme W. Phelps, "The Legislative Background of the Fair Labor Standards Act," *Journal of Business of the University of Chicago* 12 (April 1939): 1–71; M. H. Ross, "The Operation of the Wage and Hour Law in North Carolina and the South," *North Carolina Law Review* 30 (1952): 248–74; Elizabeth Brandeis, "Organized Labor and Protective Labor Legislation," in Milton Derber and Edwin Young (eds.), *Labor and the New Deal* (Madison: University of Wisconsin Press, 1957), 217–30.

110. For an account of the consequences of this omission, see ch. 3.

111. *Schechter* v. *United States*, 195 U.S. 495 (1935).

112. Quoted in Irish, "Proletarian South," 252.

113. Ross, "Operation," 270.

114. This section is based on Tindall, *Emergence of the New South*, ch. 12; Arthur M. Ford, *The Political Economics of Rural Poverty in the South* (Cambridge, Mass.: Ballinger, 1973), ch. 3; Sidney Baldwin, *Poverty and Politics: The*

*Rise and Decline of the Farm Security Administration* (Chapel Hill: University of North Carolina Press, 1967); Grant McConnell, *The Decline of Agrarian Democracy* (Berkeley: University of California Press, 1953); Gordon W. Blackwell, "The Displaced Tenant Farm Family in North Carolina," *Social Forces* 13 (1934–35): 65–73; H. C. Nixon, "Agricultural Disadvantages," in Nixon (ed.), *Southern Workers*, 8–10; Donald H. Grubbs, *Cry from the Cotton: The Southern Tenant Farmers' Union and the New Deal* (Chapel Hill: University of North Carolina Press, 1971); Warren C. Whatley, "Labor for the Picking: The New Deal in the South," *Journal of Economic History* 43 (December 1983): 905–29; Douglas C. Abrams, "North Carolina and the New Deal, 1932–1940" (Ph.D. diss., University of Maryland, 1981), ch. 4.

115. Quoted in Tindall, *Emergence of the New South*, 400.

116. *United States v. Butler*, 297 U.S. 1 (1936).

117. Blackwell, "Displaced Tenant," 69.

118. McConnell, *Decline of Agrarian Democracy*, 93.

119. Ibid., 89.

120. These counterproposals are quoted in full in ibid., 99.

121. This discussion of labor relations legislation is based on Harry A. Millis and E. C. Brown, *From the Wagner Act to Taft-Hartley: A Study of National Labor Policy and Labor Relations* (Chicago: University of Chicago Press, 1950), especially chs. 8–10, part 3; Richard C. Wilcock, "Industrial Management's Policies toward Unionism," in Derber and Young, *Labor and New Deal*, 275–315; T. W. Fleming, "The Significance of the Wagner Act," in Derber and Young, *Labor and New Deal*, 121–55; Solomon Barkin, *The Decline of the Labor Movement: And What Can be Done About It* (Santa Barbara: Center for the Study of Democratic Institutions, 1961), 20–23; Akosua Barthwell, "Trade Unionism in North Carolina: The Strike Against Reynolds Tobacco, 1947," Occasional Paper no. 21 (New York: American Institute for Marxist Studies, 1977); Lois MacDonald, "The Labor Scene," in Nixon (ed.), *Southern Workers*, 11–18; Robert K. Millard, "The Work of the National Labor Relations Board in North Carolina under the Taft-Hartley Act" (Unpublished thesis, University of North Carolina at Chapel Hill, 1952); M. H. Ross, "Labor Law: Employer Refusals to Bargain Collectively in the Southern Textile Industry," *North Carolina Law Review* 29 (1950–51): 81–89.

122. *National Labor Relations Board v. Jones and Laughlin Steel Corporation*, 301 U.S. 1 (1937).

123. Representative Graham A. Barden went on to become a major figure (as chairman of the House Committee on Education and Labor and an important leader of the southern Democratic congressional bloc) in some of the major congressional struggles in the 1950s in the areas of education, racial integration, and social reform generally. For accounts of some of these struggles and of the part played by Barden, see, for example, Richard F. Fenno, "The House of Representatives and Federal Aid to Education," in Robert L. Peabody and Nelson W. Polsby (eds.), *New Perspectives on the House of Representatives*, first edition (Chicago: Rand McNally, 1963); Alan K. McAdams, *Power and Politics in Labor Legislation* (New York: Columbia University Press, 1964).

124. For a brief account of the historical background of the right-to-work

movement, see Daniel H. Pollitt, "Union Security in America," in Richard L. Rowan (ed.), *Readings in Labor Economics and Labor Relations*, third edition (Homewood, Ill.: Richard D. Irwin, 1976), 281–88. For an account of more recent events, see Seth Kupferberg, "The Right-to-Work Fad," *New Republic* 178 (January 1978): 22.

125. AFL-CIO, "The Truth about Right-to-Work Laws" (Washington, 1977): 18–20. Louisiana had passed a right-to-work law in the aftermath of the sugarcane strike of 1953. This was repealed two years later and replaced with a law applying only to agricultural workers.

126. *AFL-CIO News* (Washington, D.C., November 11, 1978), 1–2.

127. Calculated from data in U.S. Department of Commerce, Bureau of the Census, *Statistical Abstract of the United States, 1982–3* (Washington: USGPO, 1983), 10.

128. Ibid., 409.

129. Calculated from data on man-hours and wages in U.S. Department of Commerce, Bureau of the Census, *1977 Census of Manufactures*, Subject Series, General Summary (Washington: USGPO, 1981), 1-15 to 1-27.

130. Pope, *Millhands and Preachers*, 191–94. For an alternative view that sees the sale of mill houses as a step in the process of southern moral and social integration into the national mainstream, see Harriet Herring, *Passing of the Mill Village: Revolution in a Southern Institution* (Chapel Hill: University of North Carolina Press, 1949).

131. Comparative wage rates for the period are set out in table 3.3 above.

132. Pope, *Millhands and Preachers*, 194.

## 6. State Economic Development Policy and the Pattern of Postwar Industrialization

1. Rupert B. Vance, *Human Geography of the South: A Study in Regional Resources and Human Adequacy* (Chapel Hill: University of North Carolina Press, 1935), 474; Howard W. Odum, *Southern Regions of the United States* (Chapel Hill: University of North Carolina Press, 1936), 219; Harriet Herring, *Southern Industry and Regional Development* (Chapel Hill: University of North Carolina Press, 1940), chs. 1, 2.

2. Vance, *Human Geography*, 485–89.

3. For example, Odum, *Southern Regions*, ch. 19.

4. Herring, *Southern Industry*, p. 35.

5. Ibid., 3.

6. North Carolina State Planning Board, *Report, 1935–7* (Raleigh, 1937), 3–5.

7. Tindall, *Emergence of the New South*, 586–87; Albert Lepawsky, *State Planning and Economic Development in the South* (Washington: Committee of the South, National Planning Association, 1949), 26; Naylor and Clotfelter, *Strategies for Change*, 54; Robert S. Rankin, *The Government and Administration of North Carolina* (New York: Thomas Y. Crowell, 1955), 325; Lawrence Durisch, "Southern Regional Planning and Development," in Avery Leiserson (ed.), *The American South in the 1960s* (New York: Praeger, 1964), 41–59.

8. John Van Sickle, *Planning for the South: An Enquiry into the Economics of Regionalism* (Nashville: Vanderbilt University Press, 1943), especially chs. 1, 4.

9. Luther Hodges, former textile executive, later secretary of commerce under President Kennedy and governor of North Carolina from 1954 to 1960, involved economist Harriet Herring and the University of North Carolina's Institute for Research in Social Science in commissions set up to study the problem of the state's low per capita income and the state's revenue structure and incorporated a number of their proposals into his industry-hunting campaigns. [Guy B. Johnson and Guion Griffis Johnson, *Research in Service to Society: The First Fifty Years of the Institute for Research in Social Science at the University of North Carolina* (Chapel Hill: University of North Carolina Press, 1980), 215, 223.]

10. James W. Patton, (ed.), *Addresses and Papers of Governor Luther Hartwell Hodges*, Volumes 1 and 2 (Raleigh: North Carolina State Department of Archives and History, 1960) 473–74 (Volume 1), 230 (Volume 2).

11. See the descriptions of the functions of the divisions of Commerce and Industry, and Community Planning, in the Department of Conservation and Development, in William C. Bell, *Directory of Services to Industry Offered by North Carolina State Agencies* (unpublished manuscript, Raleigh, N.C., 1963).

12. Patton, *Governor Hodges*, vol. 3, p. 92. It is worthwhile noting that these two motives should not necessarily be considered as alternatives. For instance, policies to attract new capital from other states may also promote capital accumulation by banks and power companies within the state.

13. Ibid., 191; Luther H. Hodges, *Businessman in the Statehouse* (Chapel Hill: University of North Carolina Press, 1962), ch. 3.

14. Memory F. Mitchell, *Messages, Addresses and Public Papers of Daniel Killian Moore, Governor of North Carolina, 1965–9* (Raleigh: State Department of Archives and History, 1971), 205–9.

15. Ibid., 205.

16. *News and Observer* (Raleigh, N.C., January 22, 1978), 4.

17. The following account of the role of the State in the Henderson strike is taken from Michael Myerson, *Nothing Could Be Finer* (New York: International Publishers, 1978), 60–63; F. Ray Marshall, *Labor in the South* (Cambridge, Mass.: Harvard University Press, 1967), 274–76; Patton, *Governor Hodges*, vol. 3, 280–82, 561–72; Hodges, *Businessman*, ch. 10; Memory F. Mitchell (ed.), *Messages, Addresses, and Public Papers of Terry Sanford, Governor of North Carolina, 1961–5* (Raleigh: State Department of Archives and History, 1966), 552, 638.

18. Myerson, *Nothing Could Be Finer*, 63.

19. Barbara Koeppel, "Something Could Be Finer Than to be in Carolina," *The Progressive* 40 (June 1976): 21–22.

20. The Research Triangle Park, a state-funded attempt to attract business and government research organizations to North Carolina, is frequently cited as an example of the State's commitment to the creation of a high-wage economy. In broad outline, however, the origins and development of this facility confirm exactly the opposite—the State's commitment to high rates of exploitation and low wages. Situated in a tract of "empty pineland" between Raleigh, Durham, and Chapel Hill, the park was conceived in large part as a means to expand the state's relatively small middle class by providing jobs for graduates from the state's

three major universities (University of North Carolina, Duke, and North Carolina State) and by attracting research workers and scientists from elsewhere. As a result, it was intended to increase the state's per capita income levels without affecting productive relations generally. After a long period of indebtedness and apparent failure, two factors transformed the park into a success without in any way compromising its original functions. In the first place, the appointment of ex-governor Hodges as secretary of commerce in the Kennedy administration opened the door to federal patronage, beginning in 1965 with the establishment of a National Environmental Health Sciences Center. Second, the "pure research" rule was relaxed, and a portion of the park was devoted to "research application" or research-oriented production. The major consequence of this latter change seems to have stimulated the interest of corporations producing and researching synthetic fibers for the textile and apparel industries. Hodges, *Businessman,* ch. 9; W. B. Hamilton, "The Research Triangle of North Carolina: A Study in Leadership for the Common Weal," *South Atlantic Quarterly* 65 (Spring 1966); "Research Triangle Growth Potential Gains," *News and Observer* (Raleigh, N.C., February 11, 1973), 3; Richard F. Lonsdale, *North Carolina Report* (Charlotte: Research and Planning Department, First Union National Bank of North Carolina, 1972), 63–64.

21. U.S. Department of Commerce, Bureau of the Census, *Statistical Abstract of the United States, 1978* (Washington: USGPO, 1978), 688; C. Horace Hamilton, *What's Happening to North Carolina Farms and Farmers?* (Raleigh: Agricultural Experimentation Station, North Carolina State College, 1958), 7, 10.

22. U.S. Department of Commerce, Bureau of the Census, *Statistical Abstract of the United States, 1961* (Washington: USGPO, 1961), 616–17.

23. Hamilton, "Research Triangle," 15–16; George L. Simpson, "The North Carolina Situation," *University of North Carolina Newsletter* 45 (June 1960).

24. U.S. Department of Commerce, Bureau of the Census, *1950 Census of Agriculture*, General Report, 2 (Washington: USGPO, 1953), 186. The phenomenon of part-time farming is discussed in Hamilton, "Research Triangle," 28–30; Gordon W. Blackwell et al., *Part-Time Farming in North Carolina* (Chapel Hill: Institute for Research in Social Science, University of North Carolina at Chapel Hill, 1954); Alton C. Thompson, "The Geography of Part-Time Farming in North Carolina," *University of North Carolina Newsletter* 50 (December 1965); Francis E. McVay, "The Impact of Industrialization Upon Agriculture in Two North Carolina Piedmont Counties" (Ph.D. diss., University of North Carolina at Chapel Hill, 1946).

25. *Statistical Abstract, 1978,* 688.

26. *Statistical Abstract, 1982–83,* 652, 655; U.S. Department of Commerce, Bureau of the Census, *Census of Population, 1970,* 1, pt. 35 (Washington: USGPO, 1973), 223. Because the census definition of what constitutes a "farm" became more restrictive for the 1974 and 1978 censuses, these figures may not be strictly comparable. The Bureau of the Census estimates that 3.4 percent of farms were not included in the 1978 census. Since these farms were characteristically very small, producing less than one thousand dollars per year in sales, it is possible that the 1978 figure overstates the decline in farm population and understates the size of the pool of surplus labor power available for industrial work.

27. See, for example, "Modern Science Leads Industrial Development" and

"Labor Ready, Willing and Able," *New York Times* (November 17, 1957), "Supplement on North Carolina," 5, 9; Hodges, *Businessman*, 60, 312; "Address to Ohio Valley Industrialists and Businessmen," in Mitchell, *Papers of Terry Sanford*, 130–35.

28. Patton, *Governor Hodges*, vol. 1, 187–88.

29. North Carolina Department of Administration, *The Statewide Development Policy* (Raleigh: North Carolina Department of Administration, March 1972), 21. Competitive market theorists, like government officials, see these efforts to encourage decentralization as theoretically justified attempts to increase regional equality within the state and discourage migration, rather than strategies to maximize surplus value and profitability. See, for example, Williamson, "Regional Inequality," 18, note 33.

30. Bell, *Directory of Services*; Rankin, *Government of North Carolina*, 330–31; Hodges, *Businessman*, ch. 2; Thomas B. Broughton, "New Divisions Gird for Economic Development," *News and Observer* (Raleigh, N.C., February 5, 1978); "Supplement on the NC Economic Outlook for 1978," 8; *News and Observer* (Raleigh, N.C., February 6, 1978), 7.

31. Thomas B. Broughton, "1978 was a banner year in many ways in economic development of NC," *News and Observer* (Raleigh, N.C., February 11, 1979), "Supplement on the NC Economic Outlook for 1979," 12.

32. Patton, *Governor Hodges*, vol. 1, 232–33; Bell, *Directory of Services*; Committee to Study Financing for Industrial Development, *Report to the Governor of North Carolina* (Raleigh, 1962), 12; Hodges, *Businessman*, 36–42.

33. Patton, *Governor Hodges*, vol. 3, 92.

34. David E. Bartlett, "Local Development Corporations as a Factor in Industrial Location" (M.A. thesis, University of North Carolina at Chapel Hill, 1970), 47–48; Joseph E. Ferrell, (ed.), *County Government in North Carolina*, revised edition (Chapel Hill: Institute of Government, University of North Carolina at Chapel Hill, 1975), 388–400; *News and Observer* (Raleigh, N.C., April 17, 1978), 25.

35. Robert E. Agger et al., *The Rulers and the Ruled: Political Power and Impotence in American Communities* (New York: Wiley, 1964), 210.

36. *News and Observer* (Raleigh, N.C., September 13, 1969), 3.

37. "North Carolina Economic Profile," *Southern Exposure* 4 (Spring/Summer 1976): 191.

38. Paul Luebke et al., "Selective Recruitment in North Carolina," *Working Papers for a New Society* 6 (March–April 1979): 17–20; Steve Berg, "Written Policy Against Unions Unique Here," *News and Observer* (Raleigh, N.C., November 17, 1975), 1, 2. In an interview in 1980 Steve Kelly, a director of economic development of the Raleigh Chamber of Commerce, was quoted as saying, "We aren't interested in companies that will break with our tradition of nonunionization." [Bruce A. Jacobs, "Growth for the Sunbelt's Smaller Cities," *Industry Week* (February 4, 1980): 48.]

39. *North Carolina Anvil* (Durham, N.C., July 28, 1977), 4; *Wall Street Journal* (February 10, 1978), 1, 18; Luebke, "Selective Recruitment."

40. *Wall Street Journal* (February 10, 1978), 1.

41. Ibid.; for a description of the efforts of the Greenville, South Carolina, Chamber of Commerce to "fit" new capital into local conditions, see Cliff Sloan

and Bob Hall, "It's Good to be at Home in Greenville—But It's Better if You Hate Unions," *Southern Exposure* 7 (Spring 1979): 82–93.

42. *Wall Street Journal* (February 10, 1978), 18; *News and Observer* (Raleigh, N.C., April 5, 1978), 5; Luebke, "Selective Recruitment."

43. *Wall Street Journal* (February 10, 1978), 18.

44. See, for example, *News and Observer* (Raleigh, N.C., April 17, 1978), 25, 36.

45. Ibid., 36. Having publicly criticized the Roxboro Economic Development Commission and local capital for turning down the Brockway plant, Governor Hunt immediately made peace with North Carolina's major industries with a new law to repeal the state's manufacturers' inventory tax. See Luebke, "Selective Recruiting," 18.

46. Edward M. Humberger, "The Politics of Regional Human Services: A Non-Metropolitan Region in North Carolina," (Ph.D. diss., University of North Carolina at Chapel Hill, 1975), 263.

47. *News and Observer* (Raleigh, N.C., April 17, 1978), 36; *Wall Street Journal* (February 10, 1978), 18.

48. Tom Vass, "Exaggerated Claims found in Gov. Hunt's Bid for Microelectronics Center," *North Carolina Anvil* (July 3, 1981), 1, 9; Stephen Peters, "Another View of Hunt's Microelectronics Plan," *North Carolina Anvil* (August 28, 1981), 5. For a general discussion of contemporary conditions in the semiconductor industry, see Guy de Jonquieres and Louise Vehoe, "The high flyers of Silicon Valley come down to earth," *Globe and Mail* (Toronto, November 23, 1981), 38. This contradiction is not confined to economic development policy. See the discussion of the attempt to enact an air pollution control law in 1967 in James C. Cobb, *The Selling of the South: The Southern Crusade for Industrial Development, 1936–1980* (Baton Rouge: Louisiana State University Press, 1982), 230–31.

49. In March 1975 North Carolina's official unemployment rate reached 11.7 percent. Most of the unemployed were in the textile, apparel, hosiery, and furniture industries, where approximately 30 percent were either partially or wholly unemployed and were filing claims for unemployment insurance benefits. ["North Carolina Economic Profile," *Southern Exposure* 4 (Spring/Summer 1976): 190.]

50. Ibid.

51. The following brief account is drawn from Bill Finger, "Textile Men: Looms, Loans and Lockouts," *Southern Exposure* 3 (Winter 1976): 54–65; Milton Moskowitz et al. (eds.), *Everybody's Business: An Almanac* (San Francisco: Harper and Row, 1980), 133–35; "North Carolina Economic Profile," *Southern Exposure* 4 (Spring/Summer 1976): 190; John W. Kennedy, "A History of the Textile Workers' Union of America CIO" (Ph.D. diss., University of North Carolina at Chapel Hill, 1950), 18.

52. In his memoirs John Kenneth Galbraith describes the ties between southern textile mills and southern Democratic congressmen and senators in the 1940s as "bordering on incest." [John K. Galbraith, *A Life in Our Times* (Boston: Houghton Mifflin, 1981), 137.]

53. U.S. Department of Labor, Bureau of Labor Statistics, *Employment and Earnings, States and Areas, 1939–1975* (Washington: USGPO, 1977), 555.

54. This account of the growth of J. P. Stevens is taken from Moskowitz, *Everybody's Business*, 138–41; Mimi Conway, *Rise Gonna Rise* (New York: Dou-

bleday Anchor, 1979), 16–20; Barkin, "Regional Significance," 395–416; "The Bolt in Cotton Textiles," *Fortune* 36 (July 1947): 61–67, 178; Jim Overton et al., "Men at the Top: The Story of J. P. Stevens," *Southern Exposure* 6 (Spring 1978): 52–63.

55. Stevens has continued to benefit from military orders. Robert Stevens became Eisenhower's secretary of the army during the 1950s. During the Vietnam War A. W. Anthony, a Stevens vice president, served as chairman of the Military Fabrics Committee of the American Textile Manufacturers' Institute. Between 1966 and 1970 Stevens's sales to the government were valued at just under $205 million. (Moskowitz, *Everybody's Business*, 139; Overton, "Men at the Top," 61.)

56. For a description of the process of concentration, see Barkin, "Regional Significance."

57. Kennedy, "Textile Workers' Union," 14.

58. E. B. Alderfer and H. E. Michl, *Economics of American Industry*, second edition (New York: McGraw-Hill, 1950), 382.

59. Barkin, "Regional Significance," 404.

60. Ibid., 406–8.

61. U.S. Department of Commerce, Bureau of the Census, *1977 Census of Manufactures*, 1 (Washington: USGPO, 1981), 9-19 to 9-20.

62. Kennedy, "Textile Workers' Union," 29, 34.

63. Paul Kelly, "Huge Post-War Growth of NC Textiles: Many New Plants," *North Carolina Employment Security Commission Quarterly* (Summer–Fall 1952): 90–92.

64. North American Congress on Latin America (NACLA), "Capital's Flight: The Apparel Industry Moves South," *Latin America and Empire Report* 11 (March 1977): 10.

65. *1977 Census of Manufactures*, 1-59.

66. NACLA, "Capital's Flight," 7.

67. Elaine Gale Wrong, *The Negro in the Apparel Industry* (Philadelphia: University of Pennsylvania Press, 1974), 35, 83.

68. U.S. Department of Commerce, Bureau of the Census, *1978–9 Annual Survey of Manufactures* (Washington: USGPO, 1983), part 6.

69. NACLA, "Capital's Flight," 13.

70. William E. Fulmer, *The Negro in the Furniture Industry* (Philadelphia: University of Pennsylvania Press, 1973), 100; *1977 Census of Manufactures*, 3, pt. 2, 34-13.

71. *1977 Census of Manufactures*, 1, 1-60.

72. Fulmer, *Negro in Furniture Industry*, 7.

73. Ibid., 102.

74. The *1978–79 Annual Survey of Manufactures*, pt. 6.

75. "North Carolina Economic Profile," *Southern Exposure*, 190.

76. *1977 Census of Manufactures*, 3, pt. 2, 34-14; William H. Quay, *The Negro in the Chemical Industry* (Philadelphia: University of Pennsylvania Press, 1969), 12.

77. Theodore V. Purcell and Daniel P. Mulvey, *The Negro in the Electrical Manufacturing Industry* (Philadelphia: University of Pennsylvania Press, 1971), 77.

78. *1978–79 Annual Survey of Manufactures* 1-5, 6-190 to 6-192.

79. For a discussion of these patterns as they affected the racial composition of employment in a number of areas, see, for example, Herbert Northrup, *The Negro in the Automobile Industry* and *The Negro in the Rubber Tire Industry* (Philadelphia: University of Pennsylvania Press, 1969); Purcell and Mulvey, *Electrical Manufacturing Industry*, 40–46.

80. Thomas B. Broughton, "Industrial Growth Sets New NC Record," *News and Observer* (Raleigh, N.C., February 10, 1974), 3.

81. *Statistical Abstract*, *1978*, 12, 20–22.

82. The 1953 figure is from Ray Marshall, "The Development of Organized Labor," *Monthly Labor Review* 91 (March 1968): 67.

83. The 1964 and 1973 figures are taken from *Statistical Abstract*, *1978*, 430. The 1980 figure is from *Statistical Abstract*, *1982–83*, 409.

84. "North Carolina Economic Profile," *Southern Exposure*, 190.

85. H. William Constangy, *North Carolina Employer-Employee Handbook* (Norcross, Ga.: The Harrison Co., 1976), 53.

86. U.S. Department of Labor, Bureau of Labor Statistics, *News Release* (Atlanta: Southeastern Regional Office, September 6, 1971), 3.

87. F. Ray Marshall, *Labor in the South* (Cambridge, Mass.: Harvard University Press, 1967), 271–78. The liquidation of the Deering-Milliken plant at Darlington, South Carolina, initiated a long legal dispute on the legality of liquidation as a response to unionization. Deering-Milliken's guilt was established in January 1969. Litigation on the subject of backpay took until December 14, 1980, when 553 former employees or their heirs (about one-third of the original workers were by this time dead) voted to accept a five million dollar backpay deal. The record of the NLRB's pay settlement trial, which lasted from May 1975 to October 1979, reached thirty-seven thousand pages. [*AFL-CIO News* (December 20, 1980): 1, 3.]

88. Ibid., 278.

89. Bill Finger and Mike Krivosh, "Stevens v. Justice," *Southern Exposure* 4 (Spring/Summer 1976): 39. Because of the virtually exclusive focus on Stevens, the other major textile corporations remain almost untouched by labor organizations. For instance, only four of Burlington's ninety-eight U.S. mills in 1980 were unionized, and all had been unionized prior to their acquisition by Burlington. (Moskowitz, *Everybody's Business*, 134.)

90. The following brief account of these obstacles is taken from more extensive discussions in Finger and Krivosh, "Stevens v. Justice," 38–44; J. Gary diNunno, "J. P. Stevens: Anatomy of an Outlaw," *American Federationist* 83 (April 1976): 1–8; Ed McConville, "The Southern Textile War," in Mark Green and Robert Massie Jr., (eds.), *The Big Business Reader: Essays on Corporate America* (New York: Pilgrim Press, 1980), 59–71; *News and Observer* (Raleigh, N.C., April 3, 1978), 1, 6; "Textile Union Hails Victory at Stevens," *North Carolina Anvil* (Durham, N.C., October 12, 1979), 4.

91. Finger and Krivosh, "Stevens v. Justice," 41.

92. For more extensive discussions of the rapidly growing "union busting" industry in North Carolina, the South, and the United States generally, see Tony Dunbar and Bob Hall, "Union-Busters: Who, Where, When, How and Why?,"

*Southern Exposure* 8 (Summer 1980): 27–48; Robert Georgine, "From Brass Knuckles to Briefcases: The Modern Art of Union-Busting," in Green and Massie, (eds.), *Big Business Reader*, 89–104.

93. *AFL-CIO News* (Washington, D.C., March 31, 1979), 3.

94. *North Carolina Anvil* (Durham, N.C., March 31, 1979), 2; *AFL-CIO News* (September 16, 1978), 1, 2. Other corporations drawn into the conflict were Goldman Sachs and Company, The Seaman's Bank for Savings, and Metropolitan Life Insurance Company.

95. *AFL-CIO News* (October 25, 1980), 1, 3; *North Carolina Anvil* (October 24, 1980), 1, 9; *New York Times* (October 20, 1980), A-1, A-16 and (October 21), A-16; *Wall Street Journal* (October 20, 1980), 1, 17, 22; "Stevens Victory," *Southern Exposure* 8 (Winter 1980).

96. Tony Dunbar, "Interview with George Hood," *Southern Exposure* 8 (Summer 1980): 48.

97. Calculated from data in *1978–79 Annual Survey of Manufactures*, 1-6.

98. Between 1947 and 1963 the tendency begun in the textile industry in the interwar period for workers in North Carolina to work fewer hours than their counterparts elsewhere disappeared. In 1947 the average production worker in North Carolina worked 52.6 hours less than his or her U.S. counterpart (about one hour less per week). By 1972 the average North Carolina production worker worked 31.3 hours more than his or her U.S. counterpart. In 1977 the North Carolina advantage was 8.1 hours or about one full day in the year. [Calculated from data on man-hours and wages in U.S. Department of Commerce, Bureau of the Census, *1947 Census of Manufactures*, 3 (Washington: USGPO, 1950), 452; U.S. Department of Commerce, Bureau of the Census, *1972 Census of Manufactures*, 1 (Washington: USGPO, 1975), 47, 52; *1977 Census of Manufactures*, 1-15 and 3, pt. 2, 34-11.]

99. Reese Cleghorn, "The Mill: A Giant Step for the Southern Negro," *New York Times Magazine* (November 9, 1969): 35; Richard L. Rowan, "The Negro in the Textile Industry," in Herbert R. Northrup et al., *Negro Employment in Southern Industry* (Philadelphia: University of Pennsylvania Press, 1970), 135–36, Wrong, *Apparel Industry*, 88; Fulmer, *Negro in Furniture Industry*, 67.

100. George H. Esser, *The Development of Manpower Programs in Rural Areas* (Washington: Brookings Institution, 1965), 4–6; Paul R. Johnson et al., "An evaluation of the Labor Mobility Demonstration Project of the North Carolina Fund" (Research Paper, Department of Economics, North Carolina State University, 1967); Dwayne E. Walls, *The Chickenbone Special* (New York: Harcourt Brace Jovanovich, 1971), 160–66.

101. *News and Observer* (Raleigh, N.C., April 4, 1969) quoted in Robert M. Fearn, "Labor Markets, Incentives and Occupational Education" (Research Monograph No. 3, Center for Occupational Education, North Carolina State University, 1969), 47.

102. Cleghorn, "The Mill," 144.

103. Rowan, "Textile Industry," 160.

104. Cleghorn, "The Mill."

105. Conway, *Rise Gonna Rise*, 119.

106. Ibid., 108–13; DiNunno, "J. P. Stevens," 2; Cleghorn, "The Mill," 144.

107. Conway, *Rise Gonna Rise*, 119.

108. See, for example, Cleghorn, "The Mill," 142; Harry Boyte, "The Textile Industry: Keel of Southern Industrialization," *Radical America* 6 (March–April 1972): 40–41; Dale Newman, "Work and Community Life in a Southern Textile Town," *Labor History* 19 (Spring 1978): 222–23.

109. Cleghorn, "The Mill," 145.

110. Conway, *Rise Gonna Rise*, passim.

111. See Walls, *Chickenbone Special*, 53–58; John Siceloff, "Tobacco in Transition," *Southern Exposure* 3 (Winter 1976): 46–52; Robert Dalton, "Changes in the Structure of the Flue-Cured Tobacco Farm: A Compilation of Available Data Sources," in William R. Finger (ed.), *The Tobacco Industry in Transition* (Lexington, Mass.: D. C. Heath, 1981), 65, 72; J. Barlow Herget, "Industrial Growth: An Alternative for North Carolina's Tobacco Farmers," in Finger, *Tobacco Industry*, 104.

112. Walls, *Chickenbone Special*, 164.

113. Scott Wright and Martha Clark, "The South Moves South," *Southern Exposure* 7 (Spring 1979): 101–6.

114. Burlington Industries, *Annual Report 1977* (Greensboro, N.C., 1977). Similarly, by 1971 J. P. Stevens had plants in Canada, Belgium, France, Mexico, Australia, and Japan (J. P. Stevens Co., Inc., *Annual Report 1971*, New York, 1971).

115. Burlington, *Annual Report*; U.S. Bureau of Labor Statistics, *1977*, 549.

116. For Burlington Industries, net income fell from $106.5 million in 1974 to $36.6 million in 1975. For Stevens the figures were $39.4 million and $19.9 million, respectively. (Burlington, *Annual Report*, 27; J. P. Stevens, *Annual Report*, 1.)

117. Burlington, *Annual Report*, 26.

118. J. P. Stevens Co., Inc., *Annual Reports, 1975* and *1977* (New York, 1975 and 1977), p. 1 in both cases.

119. Burlington, *Annual Report*, 26–27.

120. Moskowitz, *Everybody's Business*, 133.

121. Joseph Pelzman, "The Textile Industry," *Annals of the American Academy of Political and Social Sciences* (March 1982): 92–100.

122. *News and Observer* (Raleigh, N.C., February 5, 1978), 8–iv.

123. World Bank, *World Tables 1976* (Baltimore: Johns Hopkins University Press, 1976).

124. Burlington Industries, *1977 Annual Report*.

125. Moskowitz, *Everybody's Business*, 135.

126. Bureau of Labor Statistics, *Employment and Earnings, States and Areas, 1939–1975*, 549; Employment Security Commission of North Carolina, *State Labor Summary* (October 1982): 7.

127. On the interregional demographic shifts of the 1970s and the social characteristics of migrants, see Niles Hansen, "Does the South Have a Stake in Northern Urban Poverty?," *Southern Economic Journal* 45 (April 1979): 1220–23.

128. The contraction of the American textile industry is also providing a num-

ber of spinoffs for its Central American counterparts, adding a new twist to the "rise of the sunbelt." See "Carolinian Finds a Textile Job in Guatemala," *New York Times* (April 14, 1985), 25.

## 7. Conclusion: Prospects for the Future

1. Peter A. Lupsha and William J. Siembieda, "The Poverty of Public Services in the Land of Plenty: An Analysis and Interpretation," in David Perry and Alfred Watkins (eds.), *The Rise of the Sunbelt Cities* (Beverly Hills: Sage, 1977), 169–90.

2. David A. Shannon (ed.), *Southern Business: The Decades Ahead* (Indianapolis: Bobbs-Merrill, 1981), passim.

3. Marx, *Capital*, 389–411.

4. Bennett Harrison and Barry Bluestone, "The Incidence and Regulation of Plant Closings," in Sawers and Tabb, *Sunbelt / Snowbelt*, 368–402.

5. *New York Times* (August 21, 1983), 32. On 20 August 1983 the Pittsburgh law was declared invalid by the Allegheny County Common Pleas Court.

6. Harrison and Bluestone, "Plant Closings," 389–92.

7. Ibid., 392–94. The "free market" justification for capital's opposition can be found in Richard B. McKenzie, *Restrictions on Business Mobility: A Study in Political Rhetoric and Economic Reality* (Washington: American Enterprise Institute, 1979).

8. These impediments continue to be reinforced by contemporary events such as the Greensboro Massacre of November 1979. For descriptions of the combination of public and private organizations arrayed against dissenting opinion and action in this case, see Michael Parenti and Carolyn Kazdin, "The Untold Story of the Greensboro Massacre," *Monthly Review* (November 1981): 42–50; Institute for Southern Studies, "The Third of November," *Southern Exposure* 9 (Fall 1981): 55–67.

9. John Gaventa, *Power and Powerlessness: Quiescence and Rebellion in an Appalachian Valley* (Urbana: University of Illinois Press, 1980).

10. Bennett M. Judkins, "Occupational Health and the Developing Class Consciousness of Southern Textile Workers: The Case of the Brown Lung Association," *The Maryland Historian* 13 (1982): 55–71.

11. CBLA organizer, quoted in Judkins, "Occupational Health," 59.

12. Goran Therborn, *The Ideology of Power and the Power of Ideology* (London: Verso/New Left Books, 1980), 98.

13. Ibid., 98, 120.

14. Judkins, "Occupational Health," 59.

15. Ibid., 58.

16. Mimi Conway, "Cotton Dust Kills," *Southern Exposure* 6 (Summer 1978): 29–39; Chip Hughes, "Tobacco vs. Textiles: Brown Lung's Day in Court," *North Carolina Anvil* (March 27, 1981), 5. In 1977 Burlington Industries tried to convince OSHA that its workers were victims of bronchitis. (*North Carolina Anvil*, June 15, 1979, 2.) The July 10, 1969, issue of the *Textile Reporter* dismissed byssinosis as "a thing thought up by venal doctors who attended last year's International Labor Organization (ILO) meetings in Africa where inferior races are bound to be afflicted by new diseases more superior [*sic*] people defeated years ago." (Quoted in Conway, *Rise Gonna Rise*, 21–22.)

17. Judkins, "Occupational Health," 59, 62.

18. Provided they could survive long enough to collect. See "Death often ends claims of brown-lung sufferers," *News and Observer* (February 26, 1978), 17-1.

19. Judkins, "Occupational Health," 60–61.

20. Ibid., 60.

21. For instance, "unreasonable and unnecessary standards will threaten the livelihood of workers," Jerry Roberts, secretary-treasurer of the North Carolina Textile Manufacturers' Association, quoted in the *North Carolina Anvil* (March 24, 1977), 4.

22. Judkins, "Occupational Health," 65.

23. The vast majority of victims still receive benefits at the expense of the general taxpayer through the social security disability and retirement programs, however, rather than through the worker's compensation system. (*North Carolina Anvil*, March 27, 1981, 4.)

24. Judkins, "Occupational Health," 63–64, 67–68; *North Carolina Anvil* (March 31, 1978), 1, 11.

25. Recent attitude survey results may strengthen this conclusion. See, for example, Joseph A. McDonald and Donald A. Clelland, "Textile Workers and Union Sentiment," *Social Forces* 63 (1984): 502–18.

# Bibliography

## Government Documents

Commonwealth of Massachusetts, Department of Labor and Industries. *Report of a Special Investigation into Conditions in the Textile Industry in Massachusetts and the Southern States.* Boston, 1923.

North Carolina, Committee to Study Financing for Industrial Development. *Report to the Governor of North Carolina.* Raleigh, 1962.

North Carolina Department of Administration. *The Statewide Development Policy.* Raleigh, 1972.

North Carolina Employment Security Commission. *State Labor Summary, October, 1982.* Raleigh, 1982.

North Carolina State Planning Board. *Report, 1935–7.* Raleigh, 1937.

U.S. Department of Commerce, Bureau of the Census. *Thirteenth Census of the United States, 1910.* Washington: U.S. Government Printing Office, 1912.

———. *Statistical Abstract of the United States, 1918.* Washington: USGPO, 1919.

———. *Fourteenth Census of the United States, 1920.* Washington: USGPO, 1922.

———. *Biennial Census of Manufactures, 1921.* Washington: USGPO, 1924.

———. *Biennial Census of Manufactures, 1927.* Washington: USGPO, 1930.

———. *Fifteenth Census of the United States, 1930.* Washington: USGPO, 1932.

———. *Biennial Census of Manufactures, 1931.* Washington: USGPO, 1935.

———. *Biennial Census of Manufactures, 1933.* Washington: USGPO, 1936.

———. *Census of Agriculture, 1935.* Washington: USGPO, 1936.

———. *Biennial Census of Manufactures, 1937.* Washington: USGPO, 1940.

———. *Sixteenth Census of the United States, 1940.* Washington: USGPO, 1943.

———. *Census of Manufactures, 1947.* Washington: USGPO, 1949.

———. *Census of Agriculture, 1950.* Washington: USGPO, 1953.

———. *Statistical Abstract of the United States, 1953.* Washington: USGPO, 1954.

———. *Census of Agriculture, 1954.* Washington: USGPO, 1956.

———. *Census of Manufactures, 1954.* Washington: USGPO, 1957.

———. *Census of Population, 1960.* Washington: USGPO, 1963.

———. *Statistical Abstract of the United States, 1961.* Washington: USGPO, 1961.

————. *Census of Agriculture, 1964.* Washington: USGPO, 1967.

————. *Census of Agriculture, 1969.* Washington: USGPO, 1972.

————. *Census of Population, 1970.* Washington: USGPO, 1973.

————. *Census of Manufactures, 1972.* Washington: USGPO, 1976.

————. *Annual Survey of Manufactures, 1975.* Washington: USGPO, 1977.

————. *Annual Survey of Manufactures, 1976.* Washington: USGPO, 1978.

————. *Census of Manufactures, 1977.* Washington: USGPO, 1981.

————. *Statistical Abstract of the United States, 1978.* Washington: USGPO, 1979.

————. *Annual Survey of Manufactures, 1978–9.* Washington: USGPO, 1983.

————. *Statistical Abstract of the United States, 1982–3.* Washington: USGPO, 1983.

U.S. Department of Commerce, Bureau of Foreign and Domestic Commerce. *Statistical Abstract of the United States, 1930.* Washington: USGPO, 1931.

————. *Statistical Abstract of the United States, 1931.* Washington: USGPO, 1931.

U.S. Department of the Interior, Census Office. *Manufactures of the United States in 1860.* Washington: USGPO, 1865.

————. *Ninth Census of the United States, 1870.* Washington: USGPO, 1872.

————. *Report on the Manufactures of the United States at the Tenth Census, 1880.* Washington: USGPO, 1883.

————. *Tenth Census of the United States, 1880.* Washington: USGPO, 1884.

————. *Report on Cotton Production in the United States at the Tenth Census.* Washington: USGPO, 1884.

————. *Eleventh Census of the United States, 1890.* Washington: USGPO, 1892.

————. *Twelfth Census of the United States, 1900.* Washington: USGPO, 1902.

U.S. Department of Labor, Bureau of Labor Statistics. *Employment and Earnings, States and Areas, 1939–1975.* Washington: USGPO, 1977.

————. *Employment and Earnings, United States, 1909–1975.* Washington: USGPO, 1976.

————. *News Release, September 6, 1971.* Atlanta, 1971.

U.S. Industrial Commission. *Report of the U.S. Industrial Commission.* Washington: USGPO, 1901.

U.S. National Emergency Council. *Report on the Economic Conditions of the South.* 1938. Reprint. New York: De Capo Press, 1972.

U.S. Senate, Committee on Manufactures. *Hearings on the Working Conditions of the Textile Industry in North Carolina, South Carolina and Tennessee.* 71st Cong., 1st sess., 1929.

————. *Report on the Working Conditions of the Textile Industry in North Carolina, South Carolina and Tennessee.* Senate Report 28, 71st Cong., 1st sess., 1929.

## Books

Abbott, Carl. *The New Urban America: Growth and Politics in Sunbelt Cities.* Chapel Hill: University of North Carolina Press, 1981.

Abrams, R. M. *Conservatism in a Progressive Era: Massachusetts Politics, 1900–1912.* Cambridge, Mass.: Harvard University Press, 1964.

Agger, Robert E., et al. *The Rulers and the Ruled: Political Power and Impotence in American Communities*. New York: Wiley, 1964.

Aglietta, Michel. *A Theory of Capitalist Regulation: The U.S. Experience*. London: New Left Books, 1979.

Alderfer, E. B., and H. E. Michl. *Economics of American Industry*. 2d ed. New York: McGraw-Hill, 1950.

American Federation of Labor-Congress of Industrial Organizations (AFL-CIO). *The Truth about Right-to-Work Laws*. Washington: AFL-CIO, 1977.

Amin, Samir. *Accumulation on a World Scale*. New York: Monthly Review Press, 1974.

———. *Uneven Development*. New York: Monthly Review Press, 1976.

Aptheker, Herbert, ed. *A Documentary History of the Negro People in the United States*. New York: Citadel Press, 1969.

Aronowitz, Stanley. *False Promises: The Shaping of American Working-Class Consciousness*. New York: McGraw-Hill, 1973.

Ashby, Lowell D. *The North Carolina Economy: Its Regional and National Setting with Particular Reference to the Structure of Employment*. Chapel Hill: School of Business Administration, University of North Carolina, 1961.

Bailey, Hugh C. *Liberalism in the New South: Southern Social Reformers and the Progressive Movement*. Coral Gables: University of Miami Press, 1969.

Baldwin, Sidney. *Poverty and Politics: The Rise and Decline of the Farm Security Administration*. Chapel Hill: University of North Carolina Press, 1967.

Baran, Paul A. *The Political Economy of Growth*. 1957. Reprint. Harmondsworth, Middlesex: Penguin Books, 1973.

———, and P. M. Sweezy. *Monopoly Capital*. New York: Monthly Review Press, 1966.

Barkin, Solomon. *The Decline of the Labor Movement: And What Can Be Done About It*. Santa Barbara: Center for the Study of Democratic Institutions, 1961.

Barnet, Richard J., and Ronald E. Muller. *Global Reach*. New York: Simon and Schuster, 1974.

Barry-Jones, R. J., ed. *Prospectives on Political Economy*. London: Frances Pinter, 1983.

Bartley, Numan V., and Hugh D. Graham. *Southern Politics and the Second Reconstruction*. Baltimore: Johns Hopkins University Press, 1975.

Bass, Jack, and Walter DeVries. *The Transformation of Southern Politics: Social Change and Political Consequences since 1945*. New York: Basic Books, 1976.

Bell, William C. *Directory of Services to Industry Offered by North Carolina State Agencies*. Raleigh: n.p., 1963.

Berglund, Abraham, George T. Starnes, and Frank T. de Vyver. *Labor in the Industrial South: A Survey of Wages and Living Conditions in Three Major Industries of the Industrial South*. Charlottesville: Institute for Research in the Social Sciences, University of Virginia, 1930.

Bernstein, Irving. *The Lean Years: A History of the American Worker, 1920–1933*. Baltimore: Penguin Books, 1966.

———. *The Turbulent Years: A History of the American Worker, 1933–41*. Boston: Houghton Mifflin, 1970.

Best, Michael H., and W. E. Connolly. *The Politicised Economy*. Lexington, Mass.: D. C. Heath, 1972.

Betters, Paul, et al. *State Centralization in North Carolina*. Washington: Brookings Institution, 1932.

Beyle, Thad, and Merle Black. *Politics and Policy in North Carolina*. New York: MSS Information Corporation, 1975.

Billings, Dwight B., Jr. *Planters and the Making of a "New South": Class, Politics and Development in North Carolina, 1865–1900*. Chapel Hill: University of North Carolina Press, 1978.

Bimba, Anthony. *The History of the American Working Class*. 1927. Reprint. Westport, Conn.: Greenwood Press, 1968.

Blackburn, Robin. *Ideology in Social Science*. London: Fontana, 1973.

Blackwell, Gordon W., et al. *Part-time Farming in North Carolina*. Chapel Hill: Institute for Research in Social Science, University of North Carolina, 1954.

Blauner, Robert. *Alienation and Freedom*. Chicago: University of Chicago Press, 1964.

Bleaney, Michael F. *Underconsumption Theories*. New York: International Publishers, 1976.

Bluestone, Barry, and Bennett Harrison. *The Deindustrialization of America*. New York: Basic Books, 1982.

Bolton, Roger E. *Defense Purchases and Regional Growth*. Washington: Brookings Institution, 1966.

Borts, G. H., and J. L. Stein. *Economic Growth in a Free Market*. New York: Columbia University Press, 1964.

Bowles, Samuel, and Herbert Gintis. *Schooling in Capitalist America: Educational Reform and the Contradictions of Economic Life*. New York: Basic Books, 1976.

Boyer, Robert O., and H. M. Morais. *Labor's Untold Story*. 3d ed. New York: United Electrical, Radio and Machine Workers of America, 1970.

Braverman, Harry. *Labor and Monopoly Capital: The Degradation of Work in the Twentieth Century*. New York: Monthly Review Press, 1974.

Brecher, Jeremy. *Strike!* San Francisco: Straight Arrow Books, 1972.

Buck, Paul H. *The Road to Reunion, 1865–1900*. Boston: Little, Brown, 1937.

Burlington Industries. *Annual Report 1977*. Greensboro, North Carolina, 1977.

Cash, W. J. *The Mind of the South*. 1941. Reprint. New York: Vintage Books, 1969.

Chafe, William H. *Civilities and Civil Rights: Greensboro, North Carolina, and the Black Struggle for Freedom*. New York: Oxford University Press, 1980.

Coates, Albert, comp. *Commentaries on Proposals in 1933 and 1935 for the Revision of the Constitution of North Carolina*. Chapel Hill: Institute of Government, University of North Carolina, 1958.

Cobb, James C. *The Selling of the South: The Southern Crusade for Industrial Development*. Baton Rouge: Louisiana State University Press, 1982.

Cochran, Bert. *Labor and Communism: The Conflict that Shaped the Unions*. Princeton: Princeton University Press, 1977.

Cockcroft, J. D., et al. *Dependence and Underdevelopment*. Garden City, N.Y.: Doubleday Anchor, 1972.

Colletti, Lucio. *From Rousseau to Lenin: Studies in Ideology and Society*. New York: Monthly Review Press, 1972.

Connor, R. D. W., and Clarence Poe, eds. *The Life and Speeches of Charles*

*Brantley Aycock*. New York: Doubleday, Page, 1912.

Constangy, William H. *North Carolina Employer-Employee Handbook*. Norcross, Ga.: The Harrison Co., 1976.

Conway, Mimi. *Rise Gonna Rise: A Portrait of Southern Textile Workers*. New York: Anchor Press, 1979.

Cooper, William. *The Conservative Regime: South Carolina, 1877–1890*. Baltimore: Johns Hopkins University Press, 1968.

Cox, Oliver C. *Caste, Class and Race*. New York: Monthly Review Press, 1970.

Dabney, Virginius. *Liberalism in the South*. Chapel Hill: University of North Carolina Press, 1932.

Daniel, Pete. *The Shadow of Slavery: Peonage in the South, 1901–1969*. London: Oxford University Press, 1973.

David, Paul A., et al. *Reckoning with Slavery: A Critical Study in the Quantitative History of American Negro Slavery*. New York: Oxford University Press, 1976.

Davidson, Elizabeth H. *Child Labor Legislation in the Southern Textile States*. Chapel Hill: University of North Carolina Press, 1939.

De Caux, Len. *Labor Radical*. Boston: Beacon Press, 1970.

Degler, Carl N. *The Other South: Southern Dissenters in the Nineteenth Century*. New York: Harper and Row, 1974.

de Kadt, Emmanuel. *Sociology and Development*. London: Tavistock, 1974.

Derber, Milton, and Edwin Young, eds. *Labor and the New Deal*. Madison: University of Wisconsin Press, 1957.

Dubofsky, Melvyn. *We Shall Be All: A History of the Industrial Workers of the World*. New York: Quadrangle Books/New York Times, 1969.

DuBois, W. E. B. *Black Reconstruction in America, 1860–1880*. 1935. Reprint. New York: Atheneum, 1970.

Duke Power Company, Industrial Department. *Piedmont Carolinas: Where Wealth Awaits You*. Charlotte, 1927.

Dunne, William F. *Gastonia: Citadel of Class Struggle in the New South*. New York: Workers' Library Publishers, 1929.

Durden, Robert F. *The Dukes of Durham, 1865–1929*. Durham: Duke University Press, 1965.

Eaton, John. *Political Economy*. New York: International Publishers, 1966.

Edmonds, Helen G. *The Negro and Fusion Politics in North Carolina, 1894–1901*. Chapel Hill: University of North Carolina Press, 1951.

Edwards, Richard C., et al. *The Capitalist System*. 2d ed. Englewood Cliffs, N.J.: Prentice-Hall, 1978.

Egerton, John. *The Americanization of Dixie: The Southernization of America*. New York: Harper's Magazine Press, 1974.

Emmanuel, Arghiri. *Unequal Exchange*. London: New Left Books, 1972.

Engels, Frederick. *The Origins of the Family, Private Property and the State*. New York: International Publishers, 1973.

Esser, George H. *The Development of Manpower Programs in Rural Areas*. Washington: Brookings Institution, 1965.

Etheridge, Elizabeth W. *The Butterfly Caste: A Social History of Pellagra in the South*. Westport, Conn.: Greenwood Press, 1972.

Evans, Michael. *Karl Marx*. London: Allen and Unwin, 1975.

Federal Writers' Project, Works Progress Administration. *These Are Our Lives*. 1939. Reprint. New York: Norton, 1975.

Fernbach, David. *Karl Marx: The Revolutions of 1848*. Harmondsworth, Middlesex: Penguin Books, 1973.

Ferrell, Joseph E., ed. *County Government in North Carolina*. Revised edition. Chapel Hill: Institute of Government, University of North Carolina, 1975.

Finger, William R., ed. *The Tobacco Industry in Transition*. Lexington, Mass.: D. C. Heath, 1981.

Fleer, Jack D. *North Carolina Politics: An Introduction*. Chapel Hill: University of North Carolina Press, 1968.

Foner, Eric. *Nothing But Freedom: Emancipation and Its Legacy*. Baton Rouge: Louisiana State University Press, 1983.

Flynt, J. Wayne. *Dixie's Forgotten People: The South's Poor Whites*. Bloomington: Indiana University Press, 1979.

Ford, Arthur M. *Political Economics of Rural Poverty in the South*. Cambridge, Mass.: Ballinger, 1973.

Frank, Andre G. *Capitalism and Underdevelopment in Latin America*. New York: Monthly Review Press, 1969.

Fraser, C. E., and G. F. Doriot. *Analyzing Our Industries*. New York: McGraw-Hill, 1932.

Friedman, Milton. *Capitalism and Freedom*. Chicago: University of Chicago Press, 1962.

Fries, Adelaide, et al. *Forsyth: The History of a County on the March*. 1949. Revised. Chapel Hill: University of North Carolina Press, 1976.

Fuchs, Victor R. *Changes in the Location of Manufacturing in the United States since 1929*. New Haven: Yale University Press, 1962.

Fulmer, William E. *The Negro in the Furniture Industry*. Philadelphia: University of Pennsylvania Press, 1973.

Galambos, Eva. *State and Local Taxes in the South*. Atlanta: Southern Regional Council, 1974.

Galambos, Louis. *Competition and Cooperation: The Emergence of a National Trade Association*. Baltimore: Johns Hopkins University Press, 1966.

Galbraith, John K. *A Life in Our Times*. Boston: Houghton Mifflin, 1981.

Gastil, Raymond D. *Cultural Regions of the United States*. Seattle: University of Washington Press, 1975.

Gaston, Paul M. *The New South Creed: A Study in Southern Mythmaking*. New York: Knopf, 1970.

Gaventa, John. *Power and Powerlessness: Quiescence and Rebellion in an Appalachian Valley*. Urbana: University of Illinois Press, 1980.

Genovese, Eugene. *The Political Economy of Slavery*. New York: Vintage Books, 1967.

Georgakas, Dan, and Marvin Surkin. *Detroit: I Do Mind Dying*. New York: St. Martin's Press, 1975.

Gibb, George S. *The Saco-Lowell Shops: Textile Machinery-Building in New England, 1813–1949*. Cambridge, Mass.: Harvard University Press, 1950.

Gillman, Joseph M. *The Falling Rate of Profit*. London: Denis Dobson, 1957.

Gilman, Glenn. *Human Relations in the Industrial Southeast: A Study of the Textile Industry.* Chapel Hill: University of North Carolina Press, 1955.

Glover, J. G., and W. B. Cornell, eds. *The Development of American Industries: Their Economic Significance.* 3d ed. New York: Prentice-Hall, 1951.

Goodman, Robert. *The Last Entrepreneurs: America's Regional Wars for Jobs and Dollars.* Boston: South End Press, 1979.

Goodwyn, Lawrence. *Democratic Promise: The Populist Moment in America.* New York: Oxford University Press, 1976.

Green, Mark, and Robert Massie, Jr., eds. *The Big Business Reader: Essays on Corporate America.* New York: Pilgrim Press, 1980.

Greenberg, Edward S. *Understanding Modern Government: The Rise and Decline of the American Political Economy.* New York: Wiley, 1979.

Greenhut, Melvin L., and F. T. Whitman. *Essays in Southern Economic Development.* Chapel Hill: University of North Carolina Press, 1964.

Grubbs, Donald H. *Cry from the Cotton: The Southern Tenant Farmers' Union and the New Deal.* Chapel Hill: University of North Carolina Press, 1971.

Hamilton, C. Horace. *What's Happening to North Carolina Farms and Farmers?* Raleigh: Agricultural Experimentation Station, North Carolina State College, 1958.

Hareven, Tamara, and Randolph Langenbach. *Amoskeag: Life and Work in an American Factory-City.* New York: Pantheon, 1978.

Harris, Seymour E., ed. *American Economic History.* New York: McGraw-Hill, 1961.

Havard, William. *The Changing Politics of the South.* Baton Rouge: Louisiana State University Press, 1972.

Heer, Clarence. *Income and Wages in the South.* Chapel Hill: University of North Carolina Press, 1930.

Herring, Harriet. *Passing of the Mill Village: Revolution in a Southern Institution.* Chapel Hill: University of North Carolina Press, 1949.

――――. *Southern Industry and Regional Development.* Chapel Hill: University of North Carolina Press, 1940.

――――. *Welfare Work in the Mill Villages.* Chapel Hill: University of North Carolina Press, 1929.

Higgs, Robert. *The Transformation of the American Economy, 1865–1914.* New York: Wiley, 1971.

Hoare, Quintin, ed. *Karl Marx: Early Writings.* New York: Vintage Books, 1975.

Hobbs, S. H., Jr. *North Carolina: An Economic and Social Profile.* Chapel Hill: University of North Carolina Press, 1958.

Hodges, Luther H. *Businessman in the Statehouse.* Chapel Hill: University of North Carolina Press, 1962.

Hoffman, Joan. *Racial Discrimination and Economic Development.* Lexington, Mass.: D. C. Heath, 1975.

Holland, Stuart. *Capital versus the Regions.* London: Macmillan, 1976.

――――. *The Regional Problem.* London: Macmillan, 1976.

Holloway, John, and Sol Picciotto. *State and Capital: A Marxist Debate.* London: Edward Arnold, 1978.

Hoover, Calvin B., and B. U. Ratchford. *Economic Resources and Policies of the South.* New York: Macmillan, 1951.

Howard, Donald S. *The W.P.A. and Federal Relief Policy*. New York: Russell Sage Foundation, 1943.

Huntington, Samuel P. *Political Order in Changing Societies*. New Haven: Yale University Press, 1968.

Jensen, Merrill, ed. *Regionalism in America*. Madison: University of Wisconsin Press, 1951.

Johnson, Guy B., and Guion G. Johnson. *Research in Service to Society*. Chapel Hill: University of North Carolina Press, 1980.

Kay, Geoffrey. *Development and Underdevelopment: A Marxist Analysis*. New York: St. Martin's Press, 1975.

Key, V. O. *Southern Politics in State and Nation*. New York: Vintage, 1949.

Killian, Lewis M. *White Southerners*. New York: Random House, 1970.

Killingsworth, C. C. *State Labor Relations Acts: A Study of Public Policy*. Chicago: University of Chicago Press, 1948.

Kolko, Gabriel. *The Triumph of Conservatism: A Reinterpretation of American History, 1900–1916*. Chicago: Quadrangle Books, 1967.

Kousser, J. Morgan. *The Shaping of Southern Politics: Suffrage Restriction and the Establishment of the One-Party South, 1880–1910*. New Haven: Yale University Press, 1974.

Lefler, Hugh T. *A Guide to the Study and Reading of North Carolina History*. 3d ed. Chapel Hill: University of North Carolina Press, 1969.

——————, and Albert R. Newsome. *North Carolina: History of a Southern State*. Chapel Hill: University of North Carolina Press, 1973.

Leiserson, Avery, ed. *The American South in the 1960s*. New York: Praeger, 1964.

Lemert, Ben F. *The Cotton Textile Industry of the Southern Appalachian Piedmont*. Chapel Hill: University of North Carolina Press, 1933.

Lepawsky, Albert. *State Planning and Economic Development in the South*. Washington: Committee of the South, National Planning Association, 1949.

Lewinson, Paul. *Race, Class and Party: A History of Negro Suffrage and White Politics in the South*. London: Oxford University Press, 1932.

Lewis, Sinclair. *Cheap and Contented Labor: The Picture of a Southern Mill Town in 1929*. New York: United Textile Workers of America, 1929.

Liner, E. Blaine, and Lawrence K. Lynch, eds. *The Economics of Southern Growth*. Durham: Southern Growth Policies Board, 1977.

Lonsdale, Richard F. *North Carolina Report*. Charlotte: Research and Planning Department, First Union National Bank of North Carolina, 1972.

McAdams, Alan K. *Power and Politics in Labor Legislation*. New York: Columbia University Press, 1964.

McConnell, Grant. *The Decline of Agrarian Democracy*. Berkeley: University of California Press, 1953.

MacDonald, Lois. *Southern Mill Hills: A Study of Social and Economic Forces in Certain Mill Villages*. New York: Alex Hillman, 1928.

McKenzie, Richard B. *Restrictions on Business Mobility: A Study in Political Rhetoric and Economic Reality*. Washington: American Enterprise Institute, 1979.

McKinney, John C., ed. *The South in Continuity and Change*. Durham: Duke University Press, 1965.

McLaughlin, Glenn E., and Stefan Robock. *Why Industry Moves South*. Washington: Committee of the South, National Planning Association, 1949.

McLaurin, Melton A. *Paternalism and Protest*. Westport, Conn.: Greenwood Press, 1971.

――――. *The Knights of Labor in the South*. Westport, Conn.: Greenwood Press, 1978.

McMath, Robert C. *Populist Vanguard: A History of the Southern Farmers' Alliance*. New York: Norton, 1977.

Maddox, J. G., et al. *The Advancing South: Manpower Prospects and Problems*. New York: Twentieth Century Fund, 1967.

Mandel, Ernest. *Late Capitalism*. London: New Left Books, 1976.

――――. *Marxist Economic Theory*. London: Merlin Press, 1974.

Mandle, Jay R. *The Roots of Black Poverty: The Southern Plantation Economy after the Civil War*. Durham: Duke University Press, 1978.

Marshall, Ray. *Labor in the South*. Cambridge, Mass.: Harvard University Press, 1964.

Marx, Karl. *Capital*, vol. 1. Harmondsworth, Middlesex: Penguin Books, 1976.

――――. *Capital*, vol. 3. Moscow: Progress Publishers, 1977.

――――, and Friedrich Engels. *Selected Correspondence*. Moscow: Foreign Languages Publishing House, 1953.

Matthews, Donald R., and James W. Prothro. *Negroes and the New Southern Politics*. New York: Harcourt, Brace and World, 1966.

Miliband, Ralph. *Marxism and Politics*. London: Oxford University Press, 1977.

Millis, H. A., and E. C. Brown. *From the Wagner Act to Taft-Hartley*. Chicago: University of Chicago Press, 1950.

Mitchell, Broadus. *The Rise of the Cotton Mills in the South*. Baltimore: Johns Hopkins University Press, 1921.

――――, and George S. Mitchell. *The Industrial Revolution in the South*. Baltimore: Johns Hopkins University Press, 1930.

Mitchell, George S. *Textile Unionism in the South*. Chapel Hill: University of North Carolina Press, 1931.

Mitchell, Memory F., ed. *Messages, Addresses and Public Papers of Daniel Killian Moore, Governor of North Carolina, 1965–9*. Raleigh: State Department of Archives and History, 1971.

――――, ed. *Messages, Addresses and Public Papers of Terry Sanford, Governor of North Carolina, 1961–5*. Raleigh: State Department of Archives and History, 1966.

Moore, Barrington, Jr. *Social Origins of Dictatorship and Democracy*. Boston: Beacon Press, 1967.

Morrison, Joseph L. *Governor O. Max Gardner: A Power in North Carolina and New Deal Washington*. Chapel Hill: University of North Carolina Press, 1971.

Moskowitz, Milton, et al., eds. *Everybody's Business: An Almanac*. San Francisco: Harper and Row, 1980.

Myerson, Michael. *Nothing Could Be Finer*. New York: International Publishers, 1978.

*National Cyclopedia of American Biography*, vol. 49. New York: James T. White, 1966.

Naylor, Thomas, and James Clotfelter. *Strategies for Change in the South*. Chapel Hill: University of North Carolina Press, 1975.

Needleman, Leslie, ed. *Regional Analysis*. Harmondsworth, Middlesex: Penguin Books, 1968.

Newman, Robert J. *Growth in the American South*. New York: New York University Press, 1984.

Nixon, H. C., ed. *Southern Workers Outside the Legislative Pale*. New York: American Labor Education Service, Inc., 1942.

Northrup, Herbert. *The Negro in the Automobile Industry*. Philadelphia: University of Pennsylvania Press, 1969.

——— et al. *Negro Employment in Southern Industry*. Philadelphia: University of Pennsylvania Press, 1970.

———. *The Negro in the Rubber Tire Industry*. Philadelphia: University of Pennsylvania Press, 1969.

Odum, Howard W. *Southern Regions of the United States*. Chapel Hill: University of North Carolina Press, 1936.

Orr, Oliver H. *Charles Brantley Aycock*. Chapel Hill: University of North Carolina Press, 1961.

Oxaal, Ivor, et al. *Beyond the Sociology of Development*. London: Routledge and Kegan Paul, 1975.

Patterson, James T. *Congressional Conservatism and the New Deal: The Growth of the Conservative Coalition in Congress, 1933–1939*. Lexington: University of Kentucky Press, 1967.

Patton, James W., ed. *Addresses and Papers of Governor Luther Hartwell Hodges*, 3 volumes. Raleigh: North Carolina, State Department of Archives and History, 1960.

Peabody, Robert L., and Nelson W. Polsby, eds. *New Perspectives on the House of Representatives*. Chicago: Rand McNally, 1963.

———. *New Perspectives on the House of Representatives*. 3d ed. Chicago: Rand McNally, 1977.

Perloff, H. S., et al. *Regions, Resources, and Economic Growth*. Lincoln: University of Nebraska Press, 1960.

Perry, David C., and Alfred J. Watkins. *The Rise of the Sunbelt Cities*. Beverly Hills: Sage, 1977.

Piven, Frances Fox, and Richard Cloward. *Regulating the Poor: The Functions of Public Welfare*. New York: Vintage Books, 1971.

Political Studies Program, University of North Carolina at Chapel Hill. *North Carolina Votes*. Chapel Hill: University of North Carolina Press, 1962.

Pope, Liston. *Millhands and Preachers: A Study of Gastonia*. New Haven: Yale University Press, 1942.

Poulantzas, Nicos. *Political Power and Social Classes*. London: New Left Books, 1973.

———. *State, Power, Socialism*. London: New Left Books, 1978.

Purcell, Theodore V., and Daniel P. Mulvey. *The Negro in the Electrical Manufacturing Industry*. Philadelphia: University of Pennsylvania Press, 1971.

Puryear, Elmer. *Democratic Party Dissension in North Carolina, 1928–1936*. Chapel Hill: University of North Carolina Press, 1962.

Quay, William H. *The Negro in the Chemical Industry*. Philadelphia: University of Pennsylvania Press, 1971.

Radice, Hugo. *International Firms and Modern Imperialism*. Harmondsworth,

Middlesex: Penguin Books, 1975.

Rankin, Robert S. *The Government and Administration of North Carolina.* New York: Thomas Y. Crowell Co., 1955.

Ransom, Roger L., and Richard H. Sutch. *One Kind of Freedom: The Economic Consequences of Emancipation.* Cambridge: Cambridge University Press, 1977.

Reed, John S. *The Enduring South: Subcultural Persistence in Mass Society.* Lexington, Mass.: D. C. Heath, 1972.

Reich, Michael. *Racial Inequality.* Princeton: Princeton University Press, 1981.

Rhyne, Jennings J. *Some Cotton Mill Workers and Their Villages.* Chapel Hill: University of North Carolina Press, 1930.

Richardson, Harry W. *Regional Growth Theory.* London: Macmillan, 1973.

Roe, D. A. *A Plague of Corn: The Social History of Pellagra.* Ithaca: Cornell University Press, 1973.

Roland, Charles P. *The Improbable Era.* Lexington: University Press of Kentucky, 1975.

Rosengarten, Theodore. *All God's Dangers: The Life of Nate Shaw.* New York: Knopf, 1974.

Rowan, Richard L., ed. *Readings in Labor Economics and Labor Relations.* 3d ed. Homewood, Ill.: Richard D. Irwin, 1976.

Sale, Kirkpatrick. *Power Shift: The Rise of the Southern Rim and Its Challenge to the Eastern Establishment.* New York: Random House, 1975.

Sanford, Terry. *But What About the People?* New York: Harper and Row, 1966.

Sawers, Larry, and William K. Tabb, eds. *Sunbelt / Snowbelt: Urban Development and Regional Restructuring.* New York: Oxford University Press, 1984.

Schumpeter, Joseph. *Capitalism, Socialism and Democracy.* New York: Harper and Row, 1962.

Schwartz, Michael. *Radical Protest and Social Structure: The Southern Farmers' Alliance and Cotton Tenancy, 1880–1890.* New York: Academic Press, 1976.

Shannon, David A., ed. *Southern Business: The Decades Ahead.* Indianapolis: Bobbs-Merrill, 1981.

Sharkansky, Ira. *Regionalism in American Politics.* Indianapolis: Bobbs-Merrill, 1970.

Shugg, Roger W. *Origins of Class Struggle in Louisiana.* 1939. Revised. Baton Rouge: Louisiana State University Press, 1968.

Sindler, Allen P., ed. *Change in the Contemporary South.* Durham: Duke University Press, 1963.

Smith, Robert S. *Mill on the Dan.* Durham: Duke University Press, 1960.

Spring, Joel. *Education and the Rise of the Corporate State.* Boston: Beacon Press, 1972.

Sternlieb, George, and J. W. Hughes. *Post-Industrial America: Metropolitan Decline and Inter-Regional Job Shifts.* New Brunswick: Center for Urban Policy Research, Rutgers University, 1975.

J. P. Stevens Co., Inc. *Annual Reports, 1971, 1975, and 1977.* New York: n.p., 1971, 1975, 1977.

Sweezy, Paul M. *The Theory of Capitalist Development.* 1942. Reprint. New York: Monthly Review Press, 1970.

Tannenbaum, Frank. *Darker Phases of the South.* 1924. Revised. New York: Negro Universities Press, 1969.

Terrill, Tom, and Jerrold Hirsch, eds. *Such as Us: Southern Voices of the Thirties.* New York: Norton, 1978.

Textile Workers' Union of America, CIO. *Half a Million Forgotten People: The Story of the Cotton Textile Workers.* New York: CIO, 1944.

Therborn, Goran. *The Ideology of Power and the Power of Ideology.* London: Verso/New Left Books, 1980.

———. *Science, Class and Society.* London: Verso, 1980.

Tindall, George B. *Emergence of the New South, 1913–1945.* Baton Rouge: Louisiana State University Press, 1967.

Tippett, Thomas. *When Southern Labor Stirs.* New York: Cape and Smith, 1931.

Union for Radical Political Economics. *U.S. Capitalism in Crisis.* New York: URPE, 1974.

Vance, Rupert. *Human Geography of the South.* Chapel Hill: University of North Carolina Press, 1935.

Vance, Stanley. *American Industries.* Englewood Cliffs, N.J.: Prentice-Hall, 1955.

Van Sickle, John. *Planning for the South: An Enquiry into the Economics of Regionalism.* Nashville: Vanderbilt University Press, 1943.

Wallerstein, Immanuel. *The Modern World System.* New York: Academic Press, 1974.

Walls, Dwayne E. *The Chickenbone Special.* New York: Harcourt Brace Jovanovich, 1971.

Ware, Norman. *The Industrial Workers, 1840–1860: The Reaction of American Industrial Society to the Advance of the Industrial Revolution.* 1924. Reprint. Chicago: Quadrangle Books, 1964.

Weare, Walter B. *Black Business in the New South: A Social History of the North Carolina Mutual Life Insurance Company.* Urbana: University of Illinois Press, 1973.

Weinstein, B. L., and R. E. Firestine. *Regional Growth and Decline in the United States: The Rise of the Sunbelt and the Decline of the Northeast.* New York: Praeger, 1978.

Weinstein, James. *The Corporate Ideal in the Liberal State, 1900–1918.* Boston: Beacon Press, 1968.

*Who Was Who in America,* vol. 1, 1896–1942. Chicago: A. N. Marquis, 1943.

Wiener, J. M. *Social Origins of the New South: Alabama, 1860–1885.* Baton Rouge: Louisiana State University Press, 1978.

Wilber, C. K., ed. *The Political Economy of Development and Underdevelopment.* New York: Random House, 1973.

Williams, T. Harry. *Romance and Realism in Southern Politics.* Baton Rouge: Louisiana State University Press, 1966.

Williamson, Jeffrey G. *Late-Nineteenth Century American Development.* London: Cambridge University Press, 1974.

Woodward, C. Vann. *Origins of the New South, 1877–1913.* 1951. Reprint. Baton Rouge: Louisiana State University Press, 1971.

———. *Reunion and Reaction.* Revised ed. Garden City, N.Y.: Anchor Books, 1956.

———. *The Burden of Southern History.* New York: Mentor Books, 1968.

———. *The Strange Career of Jim Crow.* 3d rev. ed. New York: Oxford University Press, 1974.

World Bank. *World Tables 1976*. Baltimore: Johns Hopkins University Press, 1976.

Wright, Gavin. *The Political Economy of the Cotton South: Households, Markets and Wealth in the 19th Century*. New York: Norton, 1978.

Wrong, Elaine G. *The Negro in the Apparel Industry*. Philadelphia: University of Pennsylvania Press, 1974.

Yellen, Samuel. *American Labor Struggles*. New York: S. A. Russell, 1936.

## Articles

Applewhite, Marjorie M. "Sharecropper and Tenant in the Courts of North Carolina." *North Carolina Historical Review* 31 (1954).

Barkin, Solomon. "The Regional Significance of the Integration Movement in the Southern Textile Industry." *Southern Economic Journal* 15 (April 1949).

Barthwell, Akosua. "Trade Unionism in North Carolina: The Strike Against Reynolds Tobacco, 1947." Occasional Paper No. 21, American Institute for Marxist Studies, New York, 1977.

Basso, Hamilton. "Gastonia: Before the Battle." *New Republic* 80, no. 1033 (September 19, 1934).

Blackwell, Gordon W. "The Displaced Tenant Farm Family in North Carolina." *Social Forces* 13 (1934–35).

Blanshard, Paul. "One Hundred Percent Americans on Strike." *Nation* 128 (May 8, 1929).

Bonner, Marion. "Behind the Southern Textile Strikes." *Nation* 129 (October 2, 1929).

Boyte, Harry. "The Textile Industry: Keel of Southern Industrialization." *Radical America* 6 (March–April 1972).

Broun, Heywood. "It Seems to Heywood Broun." *Nation* 129 (September 25, 1929).

Ciscel, David, and Tom Collins. "The Memphis Runaway Blues." *Southern Exposure* 4 (Spring/Summer 1976): 143–49.

Clarke, Simon. "Marxism, Sociology and Poulantzas' Theory of the State." *Capital and Class*, No. 2 (1977).

Cleghorn, Reese. "The Mill: A Giant Step for the Southern Negro." *New York Times Magazine* (November 9, 1969).

Collins, Herbert. "The Idea of a Cotton Textile Industry in the South, 1870–1900." *North Carolina Historical Review* 34 (1957).

Conway, Mimi. "Cotton Dust Kills." *Southern Exposure* 6 (Summer 1978): 29–39.

Craig, Clifton M. "Public Welfare Trends in North Carolina." *University of North Carolina Newsletter* 53 (December 1968).

Cutler, Addison T. "Labor Legislation in the Thirteen Southern States." *Southern Economic Journal* 7 (January 1941).

DiNunno, J. Gary. "J. P. Stevens: Anatomy of an Outlaw." *American Federationist* 83 (April 1976).

Dunbar, Tony. "Interview with George Hood." *Southern Exposure* 8 (Summer 1980).

————, and Bob Hall. "Union-Busters: Who, Where, When, How and Why?" *Southern Exposure* 8 (Summer 1980).

Fearn, Robert M. "Labor Markets, Incentives and Occupational Education." Research Monograph No. 3, Center for Occupational Education, North Carolina State University, Raleigh, 1969.

Finger, Bill. "Looms, Loans and Lockouts." *Southern Exposure* 3 (Winter 1976).

———, and Mike Krivosh. "Stevens v. Justice." *Southern Exposure* 4 (Spring/Summer 1976).

Grice, T. N. "State Revenues and Expenditures." *University of North Carolina Newsletter* 22 (February 26, 1936).

Griffin, R. W. "Reconstruction of the North Carolina Textile Industry, 1865–1885." *North Carolina Historical Review* 41 (1964).

Hamilton, W. B. "The Research Triangle of North Carolina: A Study in Leadership for the Common Weal." *South Atlantic Quarterly* 65 (Spring 1966).

Hansen, Niles. "Does the South Have a Stake in Northern Urban Poverty?" *Southern Economic Journal* 45 (April 1979).

Herring, Harriet. "Early Industrial Development in the South." *Annals of the American Academy of Political and Social Science* 153 (January 1931).

Hillyer, Mary W. "The Textile Workers Go Back." *Nation* 139 (October 10, 1934).

Hobbs, S. H., Jr. "Public Assistance in North Carolina." *University of North Carolina Newsletter* 36 (February 15, 1950).

Howard, Kenneth S. "Taxes: North Carolina and the Nation." *Popular Government* 33 (October 1966).

Hughes, Chip. "Tobacco v. Textiles: Brown Lung's Day in Court." *North Carolina Anvil* (June 15, 1979): 2.

———. "A New Twist for Textiles." *Southern Exposure* 3 (Winter 1976).

Institute for Southern Studies. "The Third of November." *Southern Exposure* 9 (Fall 1981): 55–67.

———. "North Carolina Economic Profile." *Southern Exposure* 4 (Spring/Summer 1976).

Irish, Marion D. "The Proletarian South." *Journal of Politics* 2 (August 1940).

———. "The Southern One-Party System and National Politics." *Journal of Politics* 4 (February 1942).

Jessop, Bob. "Accumulation Strategies, State Forms and Hegemonic Projects." *Kapitalistate* 10/11 (1983).

———. "Recent Theories of the Capitalist State." *Cambridge Journal of Economics* 1 (December 1977).

Johnson, Paul R., et al. "An Evaluation of the Labor Mobility Demonstration Project of the North Carolina Fund." Research Paper, Department of Economics, North Carolina State University, Raleigh, 1967.

Jones, Weimar. "Southern Labor and the Law." *Nation* 131 (July 2, 1930).

Judkins, Bennet M. "Occupational Health and the Developing Class Consciousness of Southern Textile Workers: The Case of the Brown Lung Association." *The Maryland Historian* 13 (1982): 55–71.

Kelly, Paul. "Huge Post-War Growth of N.C. Textiles: Many New Plants." *North Carolina Employment Security Commission Quarterly* (Summer–Fall, 1952).

Kendrick, B. B. "The Colonial Status of the South." *Journal of Southern History* 8 (1942).

Koeppel, Barbara. "Something Could Be Finer than to be in Carolina." *The Progressive* 40 (June 1976).

Kousser, J. Morgan. "Progressivism—For Middle Class Whites Only: North Carolina Education, 1880–1910." *Journal of Southern History* 66 (May 1980).

Kupferberg, Seth. "The Right-to-Work Fad." *New Republic* 178 (January 1978): 22.

Lawrence, Ken. "Roots of Class Struggle in the South." *Radical America* 9 (1976).

Lewis, Nell Battle. "Tar Heel Justice." *Nation* 129 (September 11, 1929).

Liepietz, Alain. "Towards Global Fordism?" *New Left Review* 132 (March–April 1982): 33–47.

Luebke, Paul, et al. "Selective Recruitment in North Carolina." *Working Papers for a New Society* 6 (March–April 1979): 17–20.

McAlister, A. W. "A Tax Program for North Carolina." *University of North Carolina Extension Bulletin* 12 (November 1932).

McDonald, Joseph A. "Textiles: The Political Economy of a Peripheral Industry." *Humanity and Society* 5 (June 1981): 100–19.

McDonald, Joseph A., and Donald A. Clelland. "Textile Workers and Union Sentiment." *Social Forces* 63 (1984).

MacDonald, Lois. "Normalcy in the Carolinas." *New Republic* 61, no. 791 (January 29, 1930).

McHugh, Cathy L. "Earnings in the Post-bellum Southern Cotton Textile Industry: A Case Study." *Explorations in Economic History* 21 (1984): 28–39.

Malizia, Emil. "Earnings, Profits and Productivity in North Carolina." Institute for Urban Studies and Community Service, University of North Carolina, 1976.

Marshall, Margaret. "Textiles: An NRA Strike." *Nation* 139 (September 19, 1934).

Marshall, Ray. "The Development of Organized Labor." *Monthly Labor Review* 91 (March 1968).

Milton, George F. "The South Fights the Unions." *New Republic* 59, no. 762 (July 10, 1928).

Mitchell, Jonathan. "Here Comes Gorman." *New Republic* 80, no. 1035 (October 3, 1934).

Montgomery, David. "On Goodwyn's Populists." *Marxist Perspectives* (Spring 1978).

Moore, James T. "Redeemers Reconsidered: Change and Continuity in the Democratic South, 1870–1900." *Journal of Southern History* 44 (August 1978).

Morgan, Thomas S. "A Folly . . . Manifest to Everyone: The Movement to Enact Unemployment Insurance Legislation in North Carolina, 1935–6." *North Carolina Historical Review* 52 (July 1975).

Newman, Dale. "Work and Community Life in a Southern Textile Town." *Labor History* 19 (Spring 1978).

Nicholls, W. H. "Southern Tradition and Regional Economic Progress." *Southern Economic Journal* 26 (January 1960).

North American Congress on Latin America. "Capital's Flight: The Apparel Industry Moves South." *Latin America and Empire Report* 11 (March 1977).

Overton, Jim et al. "Men at the Top: The Story of J. P. Stevens." *Southern Exposure* 6 (Spring 1978).

Parenti, Michael, and Carolyn Kazdin. "The Untold Story of the Greensboro Massacre." *Monthly Review* (November 1981): 42–50.

Peet, Richard. "Class Struggle, The Relocation of Employment, and Economic Crisis." *Science and Society* 48 (Spring 1984): 38–51.

————. "Relations of Production and the Relocation of United States Manufacturing Industry Since 1960." *Economic Geography* 59 (April 1983).

Pelzman, Joseph. "The Textile Industry." *Annals of the American Academy of Political and Social Sciences* (March 1982): 92–100.

Persky, Joe. "Regional Colonialism and the Southern Economy." *Review of Radical Political Economics* 4 (Fall 1972).

Phelps, Orme W. "The Legislative Background of the Fair Labor Standards Act." *Journal of Business of the University of Chicago* 12 (April 1939).

Reed, Nicholas. "CIO Invades North Carolina." *The Carolina Magazine* 66 (May 1937).

Ross, M. H. "Labor Law: Employer Refusals to Bargain Collectively in the Southern Textile Industry." *North Carolina Law Review* 29 (1950–51).

————. "The Operation of the Wage and Hour Law in North Carolina and the South." *North Carolina Law Review* 30 (1952).

Shannon, Jasper B. "Presidential Politics in the South." *Journal of Politics* 1 (May and August 1939).

Siceloff, John. "Tobacco in Transition." *Southern Exposure* 3 (Winter 1976).

Simpson, George L. "The North Carolina Situation." *University of North Carolina Newsletter* 45 (June 1960).

Sloan, Cliff, and Bob Hall. "It's Good to Be at Home in Greenville—But It's Better if You Hate Unions." *Southern Exposure* 7 (Spring 1979).

Spillane, Richard. "Striking Facts about Southern Cotton Mills." *Manufacturers' Record* 86 (December 11, 1924).

Stillman, Don. "Runaways: A Call to Action." *Southern Exposure* 4 (Spring/Summer 1976): 50–59.

Stolberg, Benjamin. "Madness in Marion." *Nation* 129 (October 23, 1929).

Stricker, Frank. "Affluence for Whom?—Another Look at Prosperity and the Working Classes in the 1920s." *Labor History* 24 (Winter 1983): 5–33.

Szymanski, Albert. "Race Discrimination and White Gains." *American Sociological Review* 41 (June 1976).

Terrill, Tom. "Eager Hands: Labor for Southern Textiles, 1850–1860." *Journal of Economic History* 36 (1976).

Thompson, Alton C. "The Geography of Part-time Farming in North Carolina." *University of North Carolina Newsletter* 50 (December 1965).

Vawter, C. E. "The Needs of Industrial and Technical Education in the South." *Southern Workman* (February 1901).

Wager, Paul W. "Effects of Centralization in North Carolina." *University of North Carolina Newsletter* 23 (November 3, 1937).

Weeks, John. "The Sphere of Production and the Analysis of Crisis in Capitalism." *Science and Society* 41 (Fall 1977).

Weisbord, Vera B. "Gastonia 1929: Strike at the Loray Mill." *Southern Exposure* 1 (Winter 1974).

Whatley, Warren C. "Labor for the Picking: The New Deal in the South." *Journal of Economic History* 43 (December 1983): 905–29.

Wiener, Jonathan M. "Class Structure and Economic Development in the American South, 1865–1955." *American Historical Review* 84 (October 1979).

Wilde, James A. "The Tax Structure in North Carolina," in Thad L. Beyle and Merle Black, eds. *Politics and Policy in North Carolina*. New York: MSS Information Corporation, 1975. Ch. 16.

Williamson, Jeffrey G. "Regional Inequality and the Process of National Development: A Description of the Patterns." *Economic Development and Cultural Change* 13 (July 1965): pt. 2, 3–84.

Woodman, Harold D. "Post-bellum Social Change and Its Effects on Marketing the South's Cotton Crop." *Agricultural History* 56 (1982): 215–30.

――――. "Post–Civil War Southern Agriculture and the Law." *Agricultural History* 53 (January 1979).

――――. "Sequel to Slavery: The New History Views the Post-Bellum South." *Journal of Southern History* 43 (November 1977).

Wright, Gavin. "Cheap Labor and Southern Textiles, 1880–1930." *Quarterly Journal of Economics* 96 (November 1981): 605–29.

――――, and Martha Shiells. "Night-Work as a Labor Market Phenomenon: Southern Textiles in the Interwar Period." *Explorations in Economic History* 20 (1983): 331–50.

Wright, Scott, and Martha Clark. "The South Moves South." *Southern Exposure* 7 (Spring 1979).

Zeichner, Oscar. "The Legal Status of the Agricultural Laborer in the South." *Political Science Quarterly* 55 (1940).

## Theses and Manuscripts

Abrams, Douglas C. "North Carolina and the New Deal, 1932–1940." Ph.D. diss., University of Maryland, 1981.

Bartlett, David E. "Local Development Corporations as a Factor in Industrial Location." M.A. thesis, University of North Carolina at Chapel Hill, 1970.

Brogden, Hope M. "The Electoral Bases of Representation in North Carolina, 1916–1972." Ph.D. diss., University of North Carolina at Chapel Hill, 1976.

Cassel, Carol Ann. "A Longitudinal Analysis of Political Change in the American South." Ph.D. diss., Florida State University, 1975.

Donovan, C. H. "The Readjustment of State and Local Fiscal Relations in North Carolina, 1929–1938." Ph.D. diss., University of North Carolina at Chapel Hill, 1940.

Humberger, Edward M. "The Politics of Regional Human Services: A Non-Metropolitan Region in North Carolina." Ph.D. diss., University of North Carolina at Chapel Hill, 1975.

Kennedy, John W. "A History of the Textile Workers' Union of America, CIO." Ph.D. diss., University of North Carolina at Chapel Hill, 1950.

McVay, Francis E. "The Impact of Industrialization upon Agriculture in Two North Carolina Piedmont Counties." Ph.D. diss., University of North Carolina at Chapel Hill, 1946.

Millard, Robert K. "The Work of the National Labor Relations Board in North Carolina under the Taft-Hartley Act." M.S. thesis, University of North Carolina at Chapel Hill, 1952.

Moore, Dennison. "The Origins and Development of Racial Ideology in Trinidad." Ph.D. diss., Queen's University, 1980.

Steelman, Joseph F. "The Progressive Era in North Carolina, 1884–1917." Ph.D. diss., University of North Carolina at Chapel Hill, 1955.

Sylla, Richard. "The Economics of State and Local Government Sources and Uses of Funds in North Carolina, 1800–1977." Paper presented at the National Bureau of Economic Research (NBER) Conference on Research in Income and Wealth, Williamsburg, Virginia, 1984.

Truchil, Barry E. "Capital-Labor Relationships in the United States Textile Industry: The Post–World War II Period." Ph.D. diss., State University of New York at Binghamton, 1982.

## Newspapers and Periodicals

*AFL-CIO News*, Washington, D.C.

*Business Week*, New York.

*Fortune*, New York.

*Globe and Mail*, Toronto.

*Industry Week*, New York.

*New York Times*, New York.

*News and Observer*, Raleigh, North Carolina.

*Newsweek*, New York.

*North Carolina Anvil*, Durham, North Carolina.

*U.S. News and World Report*, New York.

*Wall Street Journal*, New York.

# Index

Phillip J. Wood is an assistant professor of political science at St. Francis Xavier University in Nova Scotia.